Jack O'Connell
Seattle
20 novembre 1982

Folklore by the Fireside

Folklore
by the Fireside

Text and Context of the Tuscan *Veglia*

by Alessandro Falassi

Foreword by Roger D. Abrahams

University of Texas Press, Austin

The publication of this book was assisted by a grant
from the Andrew W. Mellon Foundation.

Library of Congress Cataloging in Publication Data

Falassi, Alessandro.
    Folklore by the fireside.

    "Appendix of Italian texts."
    Bibliography: p.
    Includes index.
    1. Folk-lore—Italy—Tuscany. 2. Tuscany—
Social life and customs. I. Title. II. Title: Veglia.
GR117.T8F34   390'.0945'5   79-11903
ISBN 0-292-72430-6

For my father, Giovanni,
a good judge of people and things and therefore a free man;
to the *veglie* of the two of us in Castellina

Contents

Foreword

Given the training and the research methods drawn upon here by Alessandro Falassi in this remarkable monograph, it is tempting to see this study in terms of the best of the Old World joining with the best of the New. Trained in the sociological tradition in Italy, Falassi came to the United States to do further work in folklore with Alan Dundes at the University of California at Berkeley. There he built upon his already profound interest in systems of significance and meaning, that disciplinary place where sociology of knowledge, phenomenology, semiotics, and ethnography come together.

Ironically, the American experience resulted in a return to roots as well, for the Tuscan countryside occasion described here comes from the region of his birthplace. A member of an old Tuscan family (his people have been there seven hundred years), he still calls Castellina in Chianti home, as well as Siena, about ten miles away. His earlier study, *La Terra in Piazza* (with Alan Dundes), addressed the urban traditions of Siena. Here he looks back toward his country heritage, with its very different occasions of performance and celebration. While Sienese life revolves around the Palio, the Tuscan countryman centered his creative energies on the *veglia* described here. The *veglia* is a focused gathering in which Falassi participated often during his growing years. His description is couched in a personal and nostalgic past tense, even though the practice is not totally moribund.

The best of the old and new meet in other ways as well. Folklore scholarship has maintained its integrity as a discipline by a simultaneous interest in the folk and their lore, in traditions as they are maintained in the lives of people who entertain and instruct, who play and celebrate with each other, especially those who live in communities still based on a simple pastoral or agricultural economy. In the main, this has meant that folklorists have pursued their materials in what used to be called an antiquarian spirit, now renamed cultural or social history. The items of tradition as maintained in performances and other play forms, or in ritual, festival, and ceremonial events, are collected and studied as if they have a meaning of their own apart from the immediate occasion for their enactment. That is, because they have an ontological status of their own achieved because of their traditional usage, they are susceptible to being studied by how they achieve this kind of status, this integrity. Consequently, folklore of the Old School was primarily a matter of collection and analysis in terms of regional distinctiveness and, in the case of extralocal items, by dissemination—and distribution—patterns. This book continues to operate within that scholarly tradition, that outgrowth of romantic nationalism that sought the validification of the spirit of the people through their collective expressions tied to past beliefs and practices.

For some time, however, this romantic and antiquarian approach has been under attack by those more hard-minded rationalists, the ethnographers who are more concerned with the description and elaboration of sociocultural systems as they are to be observed. In such a synchronic, present-oriented view, tradition has little place except as a cultural construct, a fiction of the people being studied. More important to such revisionist-folklorists is the placement of lore within living contexts, attending to the ways in which lore was employed as part of the negotiations carried on by those seeking status or rebelling *carnival style* against such negotiations. In place of the analysis and distribution of texts, this breed of folklorists looks to the constraints and conventions of expressive situations as the way into an understanding of the traditional process. Thus, items exist only in so far as they are given embodiment within specific (if recurrent) contexts.

Thus, performance- or enactment-centered folklorists look at items primarily in terms of (1) their "deep structure," that is, the *idea* of the genre from which the item is to be understood through interpretation; (2) their uses by individuals and groups within the community as a way of establishing status (as, say, a performer of

note, a wise man, or whatever) or of creating some sense of group-
ness, by establishing some sense of sharing of interests, values, a
universe of discourse (including local references and stereotypical
renderings of outsiders); and (3) the structure of context, in which
elements of time, place, and occasion of enactment are brought to
bear in the analysis of significant actions and events.

Through this last method (derived ultimately from the Malinow-
skian "situation of context") it has become known that certain times
and places are endowed with significance by a community. But this
has seldom been actually demonstrated in the folklore literature. To
be sure, there is no little anecdotal commentary on, say, the importance of *palaver houses* for men in Africa, native American, and Mel-
anesian and Polynesian groups. But very few actual studies of the
goings on at special times in these places are to be discovered. Similarly, we know that the coffeehouse, the rum shop, the saloon, and
the pub have a similar importance in the social and cultural ecology
of European and Euro-American communities; but again we have
few actual ethnographies of such play-behavior or ceremonies
therein. Thus, we know very little about the situation of creativity
and community comment in such public places of gathering, to say
nothing of the more private occasions in which men and women,
old and young, are brought together in any symbolic landscape to
interact, play, perform, ceremonialize, and make fun. Is this because folklorists have not taken the time to sit and observe in such
places long enough to be able to write the rules for these occasions?

Whatever the answer, the greatest virtue of Falassi's work is that
we have here a carefully observed and documented study of the cultural ecology of a series of events through representative texts and
through an elaborate but commonsensical description of the symbology of place, the intensification and stylization of everyday behaviors as the structures of family and community are put into expressive activities.

The *veglia* described here is an expressive organization of community diversity, contrasts, and contentions. It is an occasion for
talk, indeed for the entire range of social actions; but as so often
happens when so many familiars are brought together, the *veglia*
constantly threatens to break into performance. Literally a *vigil* or
wake held in the kitchen of a peasant house, what is presented here
is a series of rule-regulated types of fun making which presents the

very kind of material and the discussion of the organization of expressive behavior that the performance-centered folklorist has cried out for but not often carried out. Falassi demonstrates that, by attending to such patterned details, we can not only understand but also vicariously enter into the folklife of this set of peasant communities. In focused engagements like this, the people of a community bring out their most significant expressive treasures, ones which overtly state and characterize both the ideals and the practices of the community. Moreover, with folkloric enactments, the materials are so heavily redundant and so reflexive and self-analyzed that in the deepest sense the lore bespeaks the group. There is never any question about the representative character of such lore as reported; for every example picked as characteristic of the repertoire ten others must be left out not only for lack of space but also because they repeat the point, the basic organization, and the themes of the items given. To be sure, the folklorist chooses the fullest or most easily grasped items to make a point; but this material is, though often of rare beauty, nevertheless of such a conventional nature that its representative character cannot be questioned.

So we are in Professor Falassi's debt for bringing to bear hard-core ethnographic observation of an important expressive event and using it as a means of understanding a fascinating system of life. He set a model for all of us to follow in the fullness and integrity of this pursuit.

Roger D. Abrahams

Acknowledgments

This study is indeed "more in debt than the hare is" (*ha piu debiti della lepre*). The preparation for the field work was made possible by an Italian-American Fellowship from the University of California at Berkeley. In that phase, I received decisive help from Arnolfo Ferruolo and Ruggero Stefanini, both Tuscan, who shared their personal and scholarly knowledge of Tuscan Culture. Seymour Chatman and Richard Hutson contributed their rhetoric and literary expertise; Alan Dundes, *Magister atque Amicus*, followed this study from beginning to end. It is to their merit that I went to the field with clear guidelines and at the same time with openness to my materials.

Field work was carried out mainly in 1973–74, thanks to a fellowship from the American Council of Learned Societies, in a number of villages and farms of the provinces of Florence, Siena, Arezzo, Livorno, Pisa, and Grosseto. While in the field, I profited greatly from long and illuminating discussions with Paolo Fabbri and Glauco Carloni. After a first draft of the study was completed, a research fellowship from Italy's Ministero della Pubblica Istruzione made possible the conclusive field work in the areas of Lucca, Pistoia, and Massa Carrara, as well as the final revision of the research into the present form, while I was affiliated with the University of Urbino.

"*Traduttore, traditore*" sounds the proverb. The way from Tuscan folklore to this book in English has been a long one. First, Gail Kligman at Berkeley, then the manuscript readers Gianpaolo Biasin and Roger Renwick and finally Roger Abrahams, equally generous as a scholar and as a friend, helped me going through grammatical, syntactic, logical, and rhetorical aspects of my arguments that in English would not make the same sense as they did in Italian. Salvatore Cintorino and Jolanda Mazzuoli provided the musical transcriptions, Frances Terry transformed all this into a typescript, and Barbara Burnham and Barbara Spielman at the Press made it become the book it is now. But the greatest debt which the study and myself have contracted is the one with those who are usually termed "informants." Each one of them has been *lo mio maestro a 'l mio autore*, my master and my author: friend, guide, scientific consultant, colleague, teacher, listener, host, companion in my work and in my journey through these traditions of my Culture. Their number is above two hundred, their ages vary between three and ninety-three years, their occupations and roles in life are equally varied, yet their kindness has been one and the same. Those that follow have favored me with their time and their humanity in a special way, and I thank them very deeply while mentioning them very simply. They are Ferdinando Anichini, schoolteacher; Palma Anichini, housewife; Biranti Azzurini, peasant; Eugenio Bargagli, folk poet; Mirella Bargagli, folk singer; Goffredo Bartalini, middleman; Dino Bindi, baker; Francesco Bernabei, clarinet player; Ida Braconi, peasant; Caterina Bueno, folklorist and folk singer; Gino Ceccarini, folk poet; Ezio Canocchi, shopkeeper; Enzo Carli, priest; Fabrizio Cioni, student; Sestilio Cioni, peasant; Sidonia Fanetti, housewife; Giacco Ferruzzi, peasant; Carlo Fondelli, quadrille director; Antonio Gramigni, shoemaker and folk poet; Teresa Masini, shepherdess; Rodolfo Mezzedimi, cart maker; Ilva Milanesi, housewife; Rosa Minucci, my old nanny; Palmira Mori, peasant; Dodi Moscati, folk singer; Mauro Neri, country politician; Franco Pancolini, woodcarver; Amato Patacchini, peasant; Virgilio Pieralli, shopkeeper and middleman; Alfredo Pogni, woodworker; Antonio Salcini, peasant; Camillo Soderi, barber; Pierluigi Stiaccini, cook; Francesca and Giovanna Taddei, preschool children; Ilda Vettori, housewife; Nada Vettori, housewife; Amilcare Vettori, mailman.

I must also thank all members of my own Tuscan family for having always shown me how important tradition is to learn new ways of continuity and of change. This study has also been a precious occasion to discover and think over my own roots; in doing so I have already been rewarded generously. And now I leave the stories of all these people with you, hoping, as did Boccaccio, that "you will be at peace, and remember me if having read them will bring some benefit to some of you." *Vale.*

Alessandro Falassi

Introduction

Situated in central Italy, Tuscany is a region that has maintained over the centuries definite geographic and cultural boundaries. In its great historical period, the fourteen hundreds, Tuscany witnessed the birth of the Italian Renaissance in its cities and, in its countryside, the final assessment of an agrarian economic system based on sharecropping. The ownership of the land was typically of the town bourgeoisie; the size of the estates was relatively small, consisting usually of a few, sometimes even one or two, *poderi*, or farms, which had mixed cultures and animals. Each farm was inhabited by a patriarchal family of peasants that provided the labor, tended the animals, and in return shared the profits from the farm economy approximately on a fifty-fifty base. From *mezzo* [half] came *mezzeria* or *mezzadria* [going halves]. The system has lasted to our days, giving rural Tuscany a cultural stability that has not been substantially threatened by an industrial revolution as in the north or by greatly polarized social tensions and economic disparities as in the south of Italy.

In this microcosm, the *podere* remained the basic economic unit: the large farmhouse was the dwelling unit; the family, the social unit. In a world where cities were perceived as distant and different places, and the larger concepts of national and political life became real only to result in military service, bureaucracy, and taxes, the only form of social life that maintained consistent reality and deep importance was family life. Its main social event—except for the larger gatherings that took place sporadically in the villages—was the *veglia*, the ritualized evening gathering of family and friends by the fireplace. The importance of the *veglia* in the life of the folk is symbolized by its location in front of the fire, the central focus of the house just as the house was the center of the farm, and confirmed by the fact that at the *veglia* practically all genres of Tuscan folklore were performed regularly.

In the folk perception, a *veglia* consisted of several parts placed in sequence: the first part was the storytelling of such popular märchen as "Princess and the Frog," "Cinderella," and "Little Red Riding Hood." Next followed a time for riddles, catches, lullabies, and folk prayers as children went to bed. Afterward came courtship through folk song, often sung in dialogue form by young people. Finally, there was the part devoted to narratives and folk songs about married couples, which served to emphasize further the expected behavioral norms for both sexes. Each period of the *veglia* was felt as preeminently pertinent to a specific age group of the family, for which each genre was performed in the main.

At the end of the *veglia* season, during Carnival, the dances replaced the *veglie* held at the fireplace but maintained the same name, had the same socializing function, and transmitted the same social meanings. The family values of the *veglia* contrasted with the ones of the anti-*veglia* held at the tavern. There, card games, blasphemy, and political, obscene, and misogynous songs demonstrated male hostility toward traditional courtship and family patterns as well as toward political and religious ones. The articulation of antifamily and antisociety norms was both a very vocal statement of protest and a tacit acknowledgment of the strength of the prevailing social system. As in the dance the *veglia* had its summary, at the tavern it had its contrary.

The *veglia* was a crucial socializing and stabilizing force in traditional and even modern Tuscany. Young children were taught through folklore how to behave, and adolescents were shown through folktales, folk songs, and dance the conventional path to adulthood, courtship, and marriage. The parallelism of Tuscan narrative structures to the rites of passage is demonstrated in detail by these texts. The consistency of Tuscan worldview with respect to family values is manifested repeatedly in the different folklore genres. Although the impact of mass media and the breakup of *mez-*

zadria have tended to weaken the *veglia* tradition, the values communicated by the *veglia* and its folklore, nonetheless, will continue to dominate the conduct of rural Tuscan life for many years to come.

As does any folklorist who is fond of his materials, I had the curse of being selective in the choice of my texts. I opted for the most widespread ones as well as for those that exemplify the most common performative and contextual elements. The development of the book follows that of the *veglia*. In my discussion, I tried to follow consistently both textual and contextual analysis, the former tending toward a structural reading, the latter toward a strategic-interactional one, because through the enactments of the *veglia* both performative and family roles were negotiated.

Each text had a defined performative context, which in turn was placed in the larger context of the Culture as a whole. I maintained all three as references for my discussion, not only because the folk at the *veglia* did the same, but mainly because neglecting any one of them would have been an oversimplification of both the complexity and the aesthetic value of my materials.

1
The World by the Fireplace

"*. . . lietamente il ricevette e seco al fuoco famigliarmente il fé sedere . . .*"

["*. . .* cheerfully she welcomed him and she made him sit familiarly with her, by the fire . . ."]

      Giovanni Boccaccio, *Decameron*, the Second Day, Novella 2

"*. . . io producerei le istorie in mezzo, e quelle tutte piene mostrerei d'antichi uomini e valorosi . . .*"

["*. . .* I would produce the stories in the middle, and I would show them all to be full of ancient and worthy men . . ."]

      Ibid., the Fourth Day, Introduction

It is not strange that in folk communities like those of the Tuscan landscape, the fireplace hearth maintained its place in the life of the country folk. The modern conveniences of central heating and pre-packaged foods, even a consistent flow of wage moneys, are a set of relatively recent phenomena. Only the last decade has seen the dissolving of the old ways, the sternly patriarchal ways, that singular bundle of cultural oppositions in which the father of the house ruled through the force of tradition but had little actually to do with the running of the house. The family and the fire were *mother's*, and it was she who nurtured and protected the spark by which life could be lived, measured, and regulated.

That the fire should also be central to the major social and cultural event of these folk emerges naturally, organically. In a very real sense, the larger the gathering, the greater need for the heat and light of the fire and the more important the social arrangement with regard to who must keep it going at what tempo and who will be placed nearest to it. One way into the *veglia*, originally the in-gathering of family and friends arising from a death, is to look closely at how the fire cast its lights and shadows over a gathering, a room, and, most important, an occasion.

La veglia: the word and the custom that surrounds it have an old-fashioned ring to Tuscans today. Yet these fireside evenings and their homespun performances are not so far removed from contemporary people's experience, for it is only in the last decade or so that the occasion has lost its vitality. Even now it is practiced in many places in this central Italian *regione*, but with ever decreasing frequency, making its departure with the agricultural system of "going halves" (*mezzadria*) and the strongly paternalistic family system. Roughly translatable as "wake," the term *veglia* maintains the resonances of the Latin etymon, *vigilia*,[1] both meaning "space and time to be awake."[2] The term has come to mean many social occasions. More current meanings of *veglia* and *vegliare* are, for instance, "social behavior pertinent to the time of being awake," "groups who attend the vigil," "to be awake when one should be asleep,"[3] "dance at an all-night ball,"[4] "passing the evening visiting other houses and families," "working in groups in the winter evening," "to watch at the bedside of a sick person or a dead person," or "praying in adoration to the divinity or to the holy Sepulchre"[5] covered with candles, flowers, and plants brought by the parishioners. Despite these various usages, all the meanings of the term implicitly contain a "social" attribute and "socializing" qualifications. Building upon this common characteristic, throughout this discussion *veglia* will mean an evening gathering with a ceremonial character and a social and socializing function.

In the Tuscan countryside, the *veglia* has for centuries constituted the main occasion for meeting and the place of social reality for the members of the patriarchal families and their friends and acquaintances. The *veglia* united all the members of the patriarchal rural Tuscan family: the head of one family,[6] the housewife,[7] the sons with their wives, the young men of the age "to take a wife," the girls of marriageable age, the adolescents, and the little children, including those who could hardly stand up. There were also the tenants who worked as laborers or odd-jobbers.[8] At times the neighbors came to help with certain "jobs," such as peeling chestnuts and shucking corn, during the occasion. The neighbors would soon receive a return visit. Other participants at the *veglia* could be relatives "of the same blood" or those acquired through marriage; young men came to meet young girls, to learn to know them, or to carry on the small talk of lovers between engagement and marriage, *fare l'amore in casa*. The patriarchs came to talk about their interests: animals, prizes, agricultural work. Sometime there might have been a *cozzone*, the go-between attempting to arrange a marriage,[9] or a *treccone*, a financial matchmaker or barterer to sell or buy animals, oil, wine, and foodstuffs.[10] Or someone might have been invited to play a small organ, to tell tales, or to sing poetry. Normally, the *veglia* would bring together ten to twenty family members, friends, or acquaintances. To go to the *veglia*, one had to be a member of the family, invited, well known, or at least in the company of someone familiar to the others. It was not a casual, drop-in occasion or an open house but a much more private kind of get-together. "Come tonight to my *veglia*" was a formal invitation and an act of friendliness, simple but essential—to join the daily and most intimate ritual of the family and to share in the most significant and spontaneous pastimes of autumn and winter evenings.

The time of the *veglia* was traditionally during the period of the year between the fall and winter sowing of the crops and Lent, even if the meeting occasion and the common rituals were extended to cover the complete cycle of the year and all four seasons. The *veglia* took place "at dark," after supper, usually on Thursday, Saturday, and Sunday evenings, and lasted for about three hours or more, corresponding in duration to the Roman *vigilia* that lasted for the fourth part of the night. However, these time limits were quite flexible. The *veglia* could also take place in the afternoon or in the early morning hours. The old Ancilla, informant of Temistocle Gradi, greeted him like this one morning in October about 1850: "Look who I see! What are you looking for in this part at such early hours? . . . It is a poor person's house, but you will see that the good heart is not missing. Oh, come and sit down; you will stay a little at the *veglia* and you will have breakfast." [11]

Often guests stayed till after midnight. The duration of the *veglia* was determined in the last analysis by the eloquence of the narrators and the singers, the mood of the company, the importance of the guests, and the work to be done the next day. A very well known proverb says: "At night a lion, in the morning a fool" ["*La sera leoni, la mattina coglioni*"] [12] exhorting the people to go to bed early.

All the members of the family came back from the fields at evening, "almost at dark," a little before sundown—the men with their hoes on their shoulders guiding the oxen, the women from the fields, the children with the animals from pasture. Before supper plenty remained to be done on the threshing floor and near the home. About that time they used to go to get fresh vegetables for the evening meal. They cut grass for the rabbits, [13] branches for the animals, [14] a small bundle to start the fire, [15] and the kindling that would keep it going; they fed and cleaned the animals in the barn, the ones in the threshing area, and those in the chicken coop. They

A *cozzone* getting ready for his daily run in 1885 (courtesy of Lucia Rossi-Ferrini).

tied the dog and secured the stalls, the sties, and the chicken coop.

And so everyone had to be home at dusk and not at a determined hour, because the day of twenty-four hours with each hour of sixty minutes that assumed a real significance in a technological culture had no such function in a rural one. The watch was a family jewel and not something in common use. ("My watch? It has just now gone down beyond the hill," Teresa told me one evening jokingly.) The farmers did not work by the hour but by the job or by the day. They ate at noon, when the nearest church bells rang. They finished work when twenty-three o'clock was rung by the church bells one hour before sundown. The sundown was marked by the sound of the twenty-fourth hour, or "Avemaria," the real end of the day: "At the 'Avemaria,' at home, or on the way home" ["*All' Avemmaria o a casa o per la vía*"].[16] The bell then rang the *or di notte* to indicate that the passage between two temporal and significant entities, day and night, had occurred.[17] The relativity of the hours was confirmed by the fact that each church rang the bells at different times ("Listen tonight how late San Gusmé rang the night hour!"). At dark, after the night hour, all the members of the family had to be home.

"It became dark on his way" signified with a note of disapproval that "he wasted time," "he did not arrive in time." "Worse than going out at night" is another metaphorical expression in which to be out after sundown was used as a negative term of comparison. Going out at night did not suit the women, in particular: "From the night hour to the morning bells, go out only the prostitutes" ["*Dal tramonto alla campana, va di fuori la puttana*"] [18] was a proverb in rhyme of Florentine origin often used in the countryside to cut short the request of young maidens who wished to "go for a short walk" or to go out for any reason or pretext. Other proverbs reminded one that it was a real danger to go out at night: "Who goes out at night looks for a beating" ["*Chi va di notte cerca le botte*"] or, simply, "who goes out at night looks for death" ["*Chi va di notte cerca la morte*"]. [19] Besides this folklore which gave prescriptions for practical living or rules to follow, there were popular beliefs about night birds and the spirit of darkness. To "go out at night like the cats" or "go out at night like night bats" [20] compared the night wanderers to equivocal animals belonging to the god of darkness, to the Enemy. "At night dogs go out, wolves and toads"— these animals also have diabolical connotations like the fox, the hare, and the owl. In sum, the "good" animals were locked up or tied, the "bad" animals went out at dark. In the same way the "bad persons" went out at night, while the "good persons" stayed at home with their families at the *veglia*.

The family was reunited only at dark for supper. In the morning each one left at a different hour, working either separately or in small groups. They usually ate breakfast, lunch, and an afternoon snack wherever they were, in the fields or in the woods, without returning home. Supper, instead, gathered all the family members together at the same time and place. The dinner's ritual, even if it wasn't strictly codified, nevertheless constituted the rite of passage between diurnal time, spent individually and devoted to work, and nighttime, social and devoted to the *veglia* within the family.

On returning from the fields, the family members informed the head of the family about the work done during the day and, with him, programmed their work for the next day: the children were

A family portrait of 1890: four generations working in the fields with the Tuscan oxen (courtesy of Lucia Rossi-Ferrini).

told which slope, field, or part of the woods to bring the sheep or the pigs to; the men, where to plow, hoe, or harrow; the women, where to cut the firewood or pick fruit. For everything concerning the family, the head of the family planned and checked the work day by day besides taking part in it as a guide. In addition, he acted as an intermediary between his family, which he represented solidly, and the other families, the steward, or the master when, as in the majority of cases, the farm was conducted in a sharecropping system. When it came time to square accounts, the head of the family was the one to go "to the writing desk."[21]

While the men were talking of work, of business, of animals, about unimportant matters, or about the day's events, the housemother, helped by the young housewives, the young maidens, and the little girls who learned by helping, reactivated the fire in the fireplace and prepared supper. It is significant that all the Tuscan verbs referring to this process (i.e., *rammontare, rinfocolare, rimpolpare*, etc.) have the iterative (ri). In fact, the task of the little girls was not to light the fire but to increase it in volume again, because it never really ceased to burn in the fireplace during the cold season of the year.

The fire that extinguished by itself or that did not relight was a bad omen: hence, the expression *focolare spento* [lit., fireplace out]. It metaphorically signified a family hit by disgrace and dissolution. When the women remained at home without fire, they relied upon an ancient custom to get fire from a neighbor who had some, namely, "to set fire to a rag," that is, with a rag soaked in oil. From this custom were derived such proverbial phrases as "I would not find who could set fire to the rag" ["*non troverei chi mi desse fuoco a cencio*"] (in other words, I cannot find anyone to give me the least bit of help); "do not give fire with the rag" ["*non dare del fuoco col cencio*"] (i.e., to refuse to do even a symbolic favor which does not require effort); and "who ever called it benefit to give fire to the rag?" ["*chi chiamò mai beneficio dar fuoco al cencio?*"].[22]

The fire as it appears in these examples seems to constitute a significant exception in a world that has among its most basic principles the conception of a limited good, that is, the idea that everything exists in a limited quantity; therefore, all we can obtain at someone else's expense. Contrarily, the fire seems to exist symbolically in an unlimited quantity as do all metaphysical substances; to give it does not bring merit, to receive it doesn't bring obligations. "Do not thank for the fire" ["*Del fuoco non si ringrazia*"], often remarked the old people, refusing my thanks after lighting my pipe or half-smoked Tuscan cigar in the corner of the fireplace.[23] The housemother, the custodian of the house, was the guardian of the fire, which all the other family members tended only sporadically. More than once I found myself observing some housewife who at first looked disapprovingly at someone's vain efforts to light the fire or to reanimate it, and then commented, "Who wants to see good-for-nothing people puts them to light the fire" ["*Chi vuol vedere gente da poco, li metta ad accendere il fuoco*"].[24] The fireplace supplied trials by fire, simple though they were.

It was the mother of the house who stooped in front of the andirons to blow on the fire to communicate by contagious magic[25] her soul, the vital breath that popular belief considered to be exactly fire.[26] She was the one "to make it start," putting sticks and branches gathered in the woods over the burning coals. Over these, she put wood from the heap, cut in pieces about a half meter each, and over these, pieces of tree trunks split in four with the ax and then left to dry inside the fireplace, in a gap carved in the hearth between the floor level and the fireplace floor. It was always the mother who with the tongs purged the fire of smoking and stinking pieces. (To "take with the tongs" signified to handle vexatious or troublesome and potentially dangerous items or people.) It was always she who regulated the fire's intensity, adding or removing pieces with the poker or the tongs, according to necessity.

Besides the tongs and the poker, the housewife handled the straw fire fan and the shovel with which she sometimes signaled the end of the *veglia* by beating it with some impatience on the floor or which she jokingly threatened to use like a cudgel if the conversation passed the limits of decency: "Let us talk politely, big mouth; if not I will give you the shovel on your back." With the shovel, the house-mother prepared the "hand warmers" that were filled with coals covered with cinders.[27] The old women, especially, carried these with them to warm themselves and rested them on the table, in their lap, on the ground, and at times under their large dome-shaped skirts. In the same way, the mother of the house also pre-pared the *caldanelle*, or *cecie*,[28] to be hung at the center of the bed warmer (also called "priests" or "little arches"). The other women "put the fire to bed," arranging the bed warmers, one per person, under the covers.

At night mother was the last one to go to bed, after having cov-ered the coals with cinders, but taking care not to choke them be-cause the fire had to "brood" under the ashes. In the morning when she got up "with the rooster" before daylight to make some barley coffee for the men, and milk and coffee for the boys, before they left for the fields, she again found the fire under the ashes where "it had slept" like the family had rested in their rooms. Then she divided the ashes from the coals, leaving the necessary part in the fireplace and throwing the rest into the chicken feed and into the pile of manure. The best part of the ashes was used with the lye to whiten and clean spots from the laundry.[29]

Some of the coals were used in the charcoal burner[30] and the trivet. The former was a quadrangular hole built in the fireplace, with a grate in the upper part so that the ashes could fall under and be removed. Over this the pots were heated. The latter was a metal triangular grill, supported by three feet and put over a bed of burning coals near the andirons. Over this the food was roasted. In a pan with a long handle held directly on the fire, the house-mother fried food, using leaf lard or boiling olive oil, while the roast was secured to the andirons and turned by hand or by a clock-type roasting spit.

The fire needed for cooking was different than the "weak" one that kept the copper cauldron which hung by a chain on the fireplace hook grumbling all day. The culinary and gastronomical fire that daily transformed the raw into cooked edibles, thereby constituting the passage between Nature and Culture, had to be continuous and stable, like the one of the *veglia*. A "straw fire" that did not last or a "fire of green wood" that burned badly was not desirable; in fact, "to load oneself with green wood" resulted in "a lot of smoke and little roast." All the preceding expressions also have a metaphorical meaning. Any explosion of enthusiasm without justification, predictably transient, can be termed "fire of straw." "Fire of green wood" can be a business drive without preparation, while loading oneself with it may refer to getting involved in the wrong investments. Smoke and roast as opposites commonly signify negative appearances and positive substance.[31]

There were different kinds of fire in the fireplace, depending on what had to be cooked. Therefore, one spoke of fire as "fresh" if it was just reactivated, "low" or "slow" if the heat was uniform and low, "temperate" if it was a little higher. A more vivacious fire was "happy" or "brisk"; that for frying was "alive" and "high," that is, intense and suitable for frying food with the proper rapidity.

The housemother chose the proper combustibles as well because the taste and the smell of the table company were often sophisticated enough to distinguish even the wood used in the cooking of what was on their plates.[32] Each type of fire had a different strength. The one of coals, for example, was known to have more strength than that of the charcoal in light sticks, which was in turn stronger than that of wood.[33] At the top of the fire hierarchy was the roasting fire, which as a rule had to be of oak or ilex oak and burn without smoke or high flame; if the flame rose, the housemother extinguished it immediately with a handful of salt, as though to exorcise it. "It is not a fire to cook a roast" ["*Non è fuoco da cuocerci arrosto*"], in its common usage, refers to things not adequate to fulfill important or delicate tasks. The housemother knew by experience and kept in mind that "a good fire helps the cook" ["*buon fuoco aiuta il cuoco*"] and "who knows how to make a fire, can make a home" ["*chi sa far fuoco, sa far casa*"].[34]

In conclusion, the fireplace, before the advent of both wood and electrical stoves, provided the specific type of fire for the soup, the stew ("boiled meat"), fried dishes, the spit roast, and the grilled meat.[35] All of the various ways of transforming natural products and ingredients into edible dishes, "cookery," artificial and therefore cultural, happened inside the fireplace.

Before serving at the table, the housemother performed the last act of the preparatory ritual: she sliced the bread, dressed the vegetables or the salad, and tasted the foods—one by one.[36] As she had previously chosen and methodically proportioned the ingredients before putting them on the fire, so she verified their correct transformation into edibles before taking them off the fire and serving them. Tasting itself required a series of ritualistic gestures: usually the housemother turned toward the table, lifted a small quantity of food with the wooden spoon or with the ladle, and brought it to her mouth with a certain explicit gravity. Only when she said, "It is done," "It is ready," or "It is cooked," did the table companions sit at the long kitchen table that was placed in front of the opening of the fireplace parallel to the chimney wall.

The head of the family sat at the head of the table, as a rule with the housemother at his left. The eldest son sat at his right with his wife next to him, followed by the second son, and continuing like this for all the males, each with his woman near him and with the small children "in arms" in her lap. Farther down from the head of the family were other young unmarried children, the boys and babies capable of eating by themselves; on the other side of the table, the girls sat with the housemother.

The menu of Tuscan cuisine is generally relatively simple, especially that of the rustic cuisine based almost exclusively on what the farm produced during the different seasons of the year.[37] The farmers went shopping only once a week in the village or even more seldom at the local fair.

In a diet arising from poverty, the search for quality became more important than in a situation based on quantity, variety, and consumption like that of a technological gastronomy. In fact, due to the generally modest quantity of food and to the limited variety of dishes, the role of the cook was particularly important in the family.

There was also a precise consciousness of the primary necessity to nourish oneself. Before being a familiar gastronomical rite, supper was a feeding operation that permitted, above all, a biological survival. Peasants had to eat to live; to live to eat could only be permitted to the rich. "Who eats too much has a stomach ache and who does not eat cannot work" ["*Chi mangia troppo la pancia li dòle, e chi non mangia lavorar non pòle*"].[38] For the same reason, "it is better to get up from the table still hungry" ["*E' meglio alzarsi da tavola colla fame*"].[39] Equally precise in the folk mentality and, therefore, in the folklore was the awareness of the straight relation between the foods ingested and the physiological substances into which they were transformed. There are several Tuscan proverbs on this matter, such as, "one meat makes another, and the wine makes good strength" ["*Una carne fa l'altra, e il vino fa la forza*"],[40] and the one in rhyme,

> The meat makes meat,
> the bread sustains,
> wine makes good blood,
> fish makes blisters,
> and grass makes shit.[41]

Bread, especially in the poorer meals, was of capital importance. The table companions could usually even distinguish the ingredients used in making the bread: "This is Frassineto, Roma, and Mentana."[42] Such finesse, on the contrary, regularly escaped more sophisticated or "disgusted" palates like that of Crawford, who wrote, "I must in truth confess that it would require me to be tolerably far advanced in the process of starvation, before I should feel the least inclination to repeat the experiment I made on the black bread which constitutes the Tuscan peasant's staple of food."[43] The bread pap "is good for everything, even for headaches, and makes you good looking."

A special place in the menu was held by the soup, especially the noodle soup that in the poorest house frequently constituted the entire meal: "The noodle soup is the oats of man" ["*La minestra è la biada dell'omo*"].[44] This proverb gives it a special priority, and at times *cucina* [cooking], in the folk speech, meant "soup or noodle soup."[45]

The cook had to make do with very little; that is, she had to cook economically, being careful not to have leftovers. The table companions were not supposed to leave leftovers. "Hunger is the best dish,"[46] and usually everyone finished willingly everything that the housewife had put on the plates. At times a child might throw a tantrum, crying, "I do not like it" or "I cannot eat it." In this case a very quick solution was taken—"Down, down, anyway it's dark in the body!"—or, with the help of a couple of slaps, the child might end up "warm, warm, and to bed," that is, spanked. In case such scenes were repeated, the same plate, half emptied, was given to the child at the next meal, and so on until it was finished. The child was threatened, "Watch out, later I will not tell you the fairytale," or that he or she would be carried away by some sinister character ("Look out, I will give you to the man in black!). In other cases the elders reverted to proverbial expressions: "Either you eat the noodle soup or you jump from the window" ["*O mangiar questa minestra, o saltar dalla finestra*"].[47] "Oh, you will feel the bite of the wolf!" meaning the bite of hunger. Or even, "If some other children could have it!" to remind the child that the food existed in limited quantity and that for every child that ate there were others who were hungry. By the same token the mother of the house often served herself last, after having assured herself that all the others had food on their plates. Even the famous and often derided formula of courtesy, "Take, take, a little more, anyway we throw it to the pigs" or "We give it to the cats!" is connected to the logic of the scarcity, signifying "You do not take more because you believe to take it from our mouths, but we have all been served sufficiently. This food that remains is exactly for you; if you take it, it will not deprive anyone."

The mother of the house, in addition to preparing the food, divided and distributed what was available in limited quantities and also controlled the wine that she poured out to the men, usually three times during the meal—"To eat good or bad, you have to drink three times"[48]—and watered the wine for the children. The poorer families often drank "thin wine" made with ascorbic-acid water and grape stalks left from the wine making, or even *cercone*,[49] which was made with the grapestalks left over from the thin wine, then dissolved another time in water. The only one who was permitted to remark on the food (after having established the menu) was the head of the family. It was he who evaluated the quality

of the food and could permit himself to comment, "It has no taste"
or "It's too salty," while as a rule he intervened to quiet anyone
who made negative comments on the supper: "You should talk only
when the chickens piss," that is, "never." At times, the head of the
family took the occasion of a badly cooked dish to vent his bad humor on the housemother or to reaffirm his supremacy over her in
front of all the assembled family.

In spite of this inconvenience, the status of the cook was crucial
for the life of the family, and the Tuscan housewife was careful
to maintain her role.[50] To learn how to cook took many years of
practice and careful observation. Written recipes were nonexistent
in the country kitchen, and women learned by remembering the
ingredients in their proper order and how they should be transformed; everything was done "by eye" and the woman of the
house, even had she wanted to, could not easily divulge her secrets.
Her position was safeguarded by the nature of learning and the
functioning of her working role. To preserve it she often taught
her culinary skills to the girls who were to be married and moving
out of the house; they would not become unpleasant competitors
as could her daughters-in-law. I have recorded numerous examples
of cooking conversations, such as this one:

CARLA LAPI: Chop the herbs.
ALESSANDRO FALASSI: What herbs should I use?
CARLA: But, those that you find . . . put all of them. And then you
    slice a little pepper thin, thin . . .
AF: How much pepper should I put?
CARLA: Depending on how you want to cook it . . . just enough.
AF: And how much would it be per person?
CARLA: Well, the right quantity. You can see by eye . . . a little . . .
    then salt.
AF: Do I salt right away?
CARLA: No, first you put two garlic cloves. You salt when it starts to
    fry. . . . Then when it starts to color you take it out . . .
AF: What color?
CARLA: Golden . . . the right color, in a word, . . . you will see it . . .

The housewife avoided showing what was boiling in the pan, and
the expression came to signify in general "what is prepared secretly." When she started supper, the domestic animals, normally ad-

mitted with familiarity, were resolutely thrown out from the fireplace, the dog grabbed by the collar, the cat by the neck—"When
the cat stays near the fire it makes even the cook thin" ["*Quando
la gatta sta sul fòco la fa magra anche il còco*"].[51] Even the intruders
who came to pry or to give advice around the fire were regularly
dismissed, at times with the proverb "Too many cooks spoil the
cooking!"[52] That also indicates, in the metaphor, that the supervision of one is preferable. To this the intruder could reply, "Eh,
don't be afraid; no one will take the ladle from your hand!"—that
is, "Nobody disputes your authority."[53] The ladle is mentioned
in this case because in the symbolism of the kitchen it signifies
control and command: "Who has the ladle in his hand makes the
soup his way" ["*Chi ha il mestolo in mano, fa la minestra a modo suo*"].[54]
Equally, "to pour the soup" signifies "to distribute in one's own
way," "to give according to one's own interest," "to get rid of something according to one's benefit"; that is, "You see how she poured
the soup well!"

Even if the Tuscan housewife did not manage the major part of
the family finances as did women in other regions, nonetheless
sources of profit from small earnings that accrued from her activity
or from that of the other women of the family were many; they
sold eggs, milk, chickens, pigeons; then mushrooms, asparagus,
onions, fruit; at times they sold products of embroidery or knitting
made during the *veglia* or in spare time, or straw or braided baskets.
Occasionally, hidden from her husband and especially from the
master, the housewife might scrounge a few kilos of olives, a flask
of oil or of wine to sell to farm buyers who were going around in
the countryside. To these little earnings, refer such playful songs as:

> Blessed madonna of the chestnut tree!
> Make me the grace that my husband becomes blind!
> So he will not be able to see my profit!
> Blessed madonna of the chestnut tree![55]

More than an economical power, the housemother exercised a moral
one within the family. The prestige and the importance of the housemother appeared clearly to a foreign resident in the Tuscan countryside of more than a half century ago: "It is impossible to exaggerate
the position of the Italian mother—*la madre*—who, however little

she may share the outside interest of her husband and sons, exerts an extraordinary influence over them all. Indeed, one may say that she wields a power of life and death." [56]

At the end of the meal, the men stayed at the table to smoke their pipes, puff on a hard Tuscan cigar, or roll a cigarette. The women, helped by the young girls, washed dishes at the sink. If there was something to ask the head of the family, such as permission to go to a dance, to the feast of the village patron saint, or to the fair or if someone was in need of a pair of new shoes or a dress, this was the most opportune moment to receive a positive answer, because he would then be in a better mood: "body full, rejoiced soul" ["*corpo pieno, anima consolata*"]. [57]

Afterward, everyone moved toward the fireplace, where they brought the benches if they had been used at the table during supper. The chairs were placed in a semicircle in front of the fire, which again required the care of the housemother because "as long as the peasant has supper, the fire suffers." ["*Quando il villan fa cena, il fuoco stenta*"]. [58] This was one of the moments in which the housemother made the fire "blaze," [59] which besides reviving the fire served "to amuse the boys." Tigri, among others, noted that the flame exercised a natural attraction for children. [60] The housemother could throw an armful of dry straw on the fire to surprise them with a high flame, sudden and dazzling, or throw on some branches of juniper that cracked, sending around a myriad of sparks ("we make some crash for these boys"). At times the old woman came close to the high flames and facing the children said, smiling, "Look, I capture the fire!" Then, passing her hand rapidly on the other side of the andirons between the flames, she pretended to catch them one by one and put them in her lap. These ritual gestures, always accompanied by phrases directed at the children ("Be careful, don't burn yourselves," "Watch out, do not come too close," "Stay back"), aimed to establish positions of differentiated propinquity in relation to the fire, and their performance signified and dramatized the power of the old woman over the fire as well as the legitimacy of her control over it. The children learned to go near the fire to be warm, but also to stay far enough away not to get burned. They were taught to maintain a position "of respect" toward the fire, and similarly they had to maintain a position of respect toward the family authority. While they learned to respect the fire, they also learned to respect the elders who controlled it. The old woman made the fire rise suddenly or explode in sparks and she, and only she, could go close to the fire without danger; she knew how to tame it and "put it again" in her lap; thus, she had complete control over it.[61] After the large flame flared up, they put a log on the andirons that would burn for the entire *veglia*. Meanwhile, the *vegliatori*, the participants, had all arrived. Some had traveled quite a way on foot to come to the house, taking short cuts and little paths in the woods and farm fields.

The Tuscan farmhouse was almost invariably in the center of the farm and the cultivated land.[62] The boundaries between one farm and another were delimited with precision. Stones called *confini*, used as markers to note the boundaries, were placed at the corners of the land. Part of the border line could run along a road or a gully. The rest was marked by walls, creeks, ditches, edges of blackberry bushes or brambles, hawthorns, or rows of cypress, poplars, or elms. In some zones they planted alternating rows of elm, oak, and cypress. Everywhere, particular attention was devoted to determining space exactly, to subdivide it, to organize it, to contrast it, above all, with that of the others. Land surveying, while providing the means to acquire possession, was moreover a means of empirical and analytical knowledge. The precise confines and the absence of intermediate space between two adjacent farms eliminated a "no-man's-land" and also the conceptual possibility of conceiving of an unlimited growth of one's own land; one could only conceive of a limited growth at the expense of others. It is significant that in what has been defined as "the world of approximation"[63] the external borders were always exactly defined, so that the indeterminate and the unknown were denied.

The elders were repositories of experience and knowledge and likewise knew the boundaries better than the owner. With them as a guide, one toured the borders; that is, one knew the dimensions and the limits of the space in which one could and had to move, not only physically. "One cannot go beyond the farm" is a proverb that warns against venturing beyond the familiar dimensions, relying on a very significant metaphor: the farm was the extension and the measure of the world.

The farm, for the land register, was divided into *bosco* [woods] and *coltivato* [fields or lands]. Even in the proverbial expression

The countryside converged toward the house, the "center of the world" (photo by Mario Salvi, Siena).

"He lost woods and lands" (i.e., "He lost everything"), the terms constituted the two complementary components of the totality. The woods were always more distant from the house and were materially the uncultivated space and symbolically the "other" space. In "élite" literature, as in folklore, the word was chosen to localize the point of contact or of passage, if not the topical space of the "otherworld." Of this symbolic aspect, the savage woods of the *Comedy* are the most illustrious example although not the only one.[64] In the glade in the middle of the woods "dance the witches"; out from the woods came the demonic wolf:

> Came out the wolf from the woods
> with the black, black muzzle
> and brought away the nicest little goat
> that the young shepherdess had . . .[65]

The *dossi* grazing lands with their nature-made design and a field with its man-made texture (photos by Mario Salvi, Siena).

In the forest lived the savage man, that is, the Latin *silvanus*, in the version of Tuscan folklore. He was believed to be harmful to the children to the point that, during childbirth, men, usually in threes, kept a vigil so that he would not steal the child.[66]

The woods is one of the places in which the devil appears and comes to take the souls destined to damnation.[67] Here, however, the divinity also shows itself,[68] to confirm its omnipotence and omnipresence, as in the story of the Crucifix of Spaltenna. In the woods the "unwelcome" newborn were abandoned by the servants of the perfidious mother of the king.[69] Also in the woods, the cruel stepmother and stepsister left the heroine tied to an oak tree after having blinded her.[70]

Macchiaioli,[71] "children of the bush," was the term for foundlings in Florentine dialect. "Bushes" here signified "out" of the cultural and familiar society; the children of no one were metaphorically the children of the woods who were supposedly found in the bushes. For the same reason the shy man, who escaped the company of other men, was called *selvatico*, "man of the woods."[72] Even the modern Italians maintain the expressions "give oneself to the bushes" and "hide in the woods" to disappear, to hide, to enter into another dimension, to render oneself concealed, spacially and socially. The same connotation, more symbolic than literal, is reflected in admonitions in daily conversations, such as "Are you passing by Ferrale? Be careful not to enter in the thick woods; in those fretful woods, one could get lost, and not come out."

The woods, the space of wild and potentially hostile nature, was perceived as pertinent, being visible; as present, being inside the confines of the farm; and as incumbent, being ready to "eat" the fields as soon as one let them go. The abandoned farms again became forests, that is, returned to a state of Nature that was considered to be their original state. Between the woods and the cultivated, there were often fields and borders of fields that had been let go yet in which one could still recognize the terraces, the walls, the rows of grape vines, and the olives now growing wild, no longer part of the realm of the cultivated, just as the wild men were excluded from that domain. The dialogue between man and Nature has lasted for centuries in Tuscany, with the same love and hate, the same deep sense of ambivalence, a sense which emerged in the abrasive but affectionate dialogue songs of the *veglia*.

From generation to generation the farmer has wrested strips of land from Nature, from the forests. Other spaces between the woods and the cultivated were the steep or firm ground, fields of "hard" ground kept for grass or hay and used for pasturing. Nearer to the houses began the terraced fields, held by dry walls, seeded with wheat in the middle, and separated by rows of grape vines and olive trees scattered here and there. The best part of the farm was the olive groves and vineyards. The olive trees could be planted as woods or planted in regular rows, and they could also be planted in zones not well located, because olive trees thrive in the cold. The proverb "It isn't land for vineyards" ["*Non è terren da porci vigna*"],[73] meaning not good for successful development, uses the vineyard as a metaphor for the best.

To reach the house in which the *veglia* was held, the travelers went on the good journey to Culture, walking over, in the middle or in sight of, the significant elements of the passage, between Nature and Culture: from the bushes, the forest, the thick woods, to the thin woods to the row of oaks all along the road to the stock of the strawpile to the oak tree in the threshing area (the latter, being a sign relating the woods to the inhabited space, stated the presence of Nature but at the same time established man's claim to control it); from the gulley to the fountain for the animals to the little fountain of the vegetable garden to the well under the house; from the slopes to the fields with scattered rows of vines to the thick rows of the vines; from the olive groves planted "like woods" to the fields with the olive trees here and there to the ones along the vines to the olive groves with trees planted in orderly rows that let themselves be read horizontally or vertically by whomever walked along the borders of the olive grove; from the fruit trees isolated to the fruit orchard; from the bottom and along the line of the dry walls until the summary walls of the little stable and the barn, then to the more precise walls of the house built "according to the rules of art"; from the woods to the little path of the country road to the large road to the unpaved threshing area to the paved one, to the one with brick floor, to the sandstone carved stairway, to the kitchen paved with brick cooked twice and placed in fishbone design. The *vegliatori* moved along lines of convergence between areas of major density, from the thick woods to the thickly cultivated.[74] "Thick" and "scattered" are terms commonly used in

Near the farmhouse, the big tree surrounded by a dry wall marks the border between Nature and Culture (photo by Paul Hoffman, San Francisco).

opposition also in judging the ecological equilibrium between men and Nature. "We are too thick" one occasionally comments to justify the fact that the earth does not produce enough for all.[75] As a rule the woods were pertinent to man. Boys were sent into the thick woods with animals only for hate or punishment in real life as in the fairy tales. When they started to go into the fields with the older ones, they felt advanced to a higher status. The barren fields and the cultivatable ones were meaningful spaces, traversable by both men and women. The house, on the contrary, was the space identified with women. The proverb, "My house, my woman" made an explicit equivalence of the two. The farm in its totality was perceived as an independent entity by visitors and inhabitants alike. Duff-Gordon wrote, "Each farm was like a town within itself."[76] So said Lilla to Longo Kiniser: "A farm in the middle in a nice place! Where no one arrives because there is no road: only a path for the oxen."[77]

The farmhouse represented the center of the farm and the cultivated land; the kitchen, where the *veglia* was held, represented the architectural and significant space of the same house.[78] Underneath, on the ground floor, were the stalls and the sheds for the different animals and farm produce, all the products of the domestication of the natural. On the second floor were the dove or pigeon coop, shelves, holes for the swifts. On the main floor between them were located "the rooms," the living spaces for the family. The stairs,[79] always outside, bypassed the ground floor almost so fully that it would be overlooked. They led directly to the landing of the first floor where the door opened into the large kitchen, the central and by far the largest room, from which one gained access to the bedrooms and other rooms. Corridors were nonexistent and to go from one room to the other, one usually had to pass through the kitchen.

Besides representing the center of the horizontal floor on which it was situated, the kitchen was also in a central position with respect to verticality: it was, in fact, the only room to be in direct communication with the "under" (through the stairway) and with the "upper" (through the chimney cowl in which were walled pegs that allowed access to the top). The kitchen, central point of the house, also became the metaphor of it.[80] "I am home!" replied someone at times, signifying "I am in the kitchen," while from the other rooms, they replied time after time, "I am in my room," "I am on the flooring," "in the pigeon coop," "in the passage," and so forth.

Within the home-kitchen there was another "home": that of the fire.[81] The fireplace of the Tuscan kitchens was constructed along a main wall or between two of them; that is, the fireplace and the house coincided in part, but in part they differed. The fireplace was always elevated from the kitchen floor to confirm its autonomous structure. Its shape was like "a house"; among its elements was a roof, and inside that a "cowl," or tube, through which the smoke rose externally. Like every other house it had a doorstep, an architrave, corners, a floor, and also a little window that could open into the kitchen or to the exterior, in which case it had a double morphological function: being, at the same time, the window of the house and that of the fireplace.

The fireplace was, as we saw, the place of preparation and the center of distribution of food and heat. In addition to these two primary attributes was a third: light. Oil for the lamps, lanterns, candles, and wicks were stored inside the fireplace. There the pea-

The staircase was a bridge between the earth and the kitchen (photo by Mario Salvi, Siena).

sants lit by hand the lamps that were to be hung on the beams or on a support that was placed on the table during the *veglia*. The support had a foot and a rod with holes at different heights in which they placed the spigot to which "the light" would be secured; the more persons to be illuminated, the higher went the spigot. However, the principal light for the *veglia* was that provided by the flame in the fireplace. After they fixed the fire for the *veglia*, the light of the flame progressively took its proper place in the room. This night light was of a different type than the technological type that "pierced the eyes,"[82] that which started suddenly at the touch of a switch and had a continuous intensity. The light of the *veglia* corresponded to its duration. "La durée qui dure en coulant et la durée qui dure en brulant viennant ici harmoniser leurs images," Bachelard observed.[83] Just as musical time is a special category of time and for that reason is metaphorical, regardless of what happens there,[84] so the time of the *veglia* "was worth the candle" and had a special duration because it was day in the night (*giorno* also means "light" in the Tuscan usage), constructed by man and a sign of the day within its opposite. The light of the flame was also an expression of verticality,[85] bypassing the existential plan that it unstably illuminated. All this made it a catalyst of images and companions of dreams, shifter between the planes of the real and the symbolic. The fireplace and the fire provide that place where ultimate if inconstant illumination takes place, where experience and the symbolic rendering of life come together perfectly. The real and the symbolic reflect each other as long as the flame endures. While the flame of the candle or of the little light was an operator of eminently individualistic images, the flame of the fireplace, social light, was an operator of an imagery appropriate to the group and shared by its members.

The light of the *veglia* did not deny darkness like the electric light that lasted "always," but instead created the unstable and temporary compromise of light and dark[86] that redefined all the objects and the familiar persons. This light snatched a limited and precarious duration from the night and, to be maintained, it required attentive and frequent care and not the sporadic and definitive gesture of turning on a switch.

In the center of the fireplace was the "fireplace stone"; it was a fireproof slab over which the fire burned. Even this had its specific symbolic meaning: the tradition said that the umbilical cord of the newborn boys was to be put under it; in this way, the babies would not fall, would grow up to be good, and, above all, would never leave the house.[87] This usage showed clearly that the stone of the fireplace was an important element for the values of the patriarchal Tuscan family. Above it, the fire burned "perennially"; under it, they laid a votive offering to obtain the grace of union and family continuity—all this qualified it as a functional equivalent of the altar in the family context. Moreover, the fire of the fireplace, like that of the religious ritual, represented an element of purification through the separation of the substance: the smoke had to rise to the top, *ad astra*, through the chimney. If it stayed low, or if it was forced back by the wind, it brought bad luck and became one of the elements that chased man from the house. The cinders, product of transformation more than discarded material, returned back to the animal and vegetable world. Because they came from the fire, they remained a fecundative element: "The cinders are the honor of the fire" ["*La cenere è l'onor del fòco*"].[88] The fire that burned on the slab of the fireplace remained as a pure element and continually purified itself.

The main substance of the fire of the *veglia*, the log which came from the part of the tree next to the roots, contributed to the religious dimension of the occasion. The log that burned between the andirons and was conserved for the next *veglia* was to the ritual of the end of the day what the Christmas log was to that of the end of the year.[89] *Ceppo* [log] also meant "group of houses" or "family";[90] a pregnant woman was sometimes called "*ceppa inceppita*," that is, a log ready to sprout a branch; the log was a symbol of the marriage from Roman times, and the woman symbolized the tree of life. *Ramo* [branch] meant "member, part of the family,"[91] and *ramaglia* [bad branches] or *ramo di galera* [branch of prison] in the common language meant "bad part of the family." The double equivalence man/tree–tree/man is common in folklore.[92] In this way the fire of the *veglia* consumed, refined, and separated into their components elements the polysemy of which included the significance of the family and its parts. In the fireplace, therefore, the significance and the symbolic components of the family and its members were consumed and renewed perenially. The fire of the *veglia* could with reason be regarded as the "Domestic Phoenix."[93]

But to this symbolic plan others were superimposed. Fire in native as well as psychoanalytic imagery represents the principle of male sexuality; the combustion represents and imitates both the sexual and the generative act; the sparks, the male seeds.[94] In this respect the fire of the fireplace represented the primogenial act of foundation of the patriarchal family and that of its renovating continuity. *Fuoco* means not only fire but also family.[95] Until very recently the civil and religious censuses were conducted "by fire" or "by lighted fire." The "hearth money," a tax that was paid for lighted fire (or for every patriarchal family), constituted the equivalent and the precursor of the more recent "family tax."[96] "Divide the fire" means "separating the family"; "keep the fire going" means "to have a stable residence."[97] One can see that there is a convergent bundle of significations. The fire (= generator act of the family = family), nourished by the log (= family = groups of houses that = groups of families), burns in the center of the fireplace (= family) in the center of the kitchen (= house that = family), which is the center of the living space of the family in the center of the house (= family), which is, in turn, the center of convergence of the special and symbolic coordinates of the rural Tuscan world. That the fire is a central explanatory element shows clearly one of the preferred games of Tuscan children: "water and fire."[98] A boy is made to leave the room while the other children hide an object. The child who "went out" returns and starts to look for the hidden object that he may or may not have seen before. While he is looking around the room, the other children guide him, giving him some indication like "water! high water! some water! little water! very little water!" the more he gets away from the object; and, on the contrary, as he gets nearer to the object the other children scream: "small fire! little fire! larger fire! fire! large fire!" (The English cognate form "you're hot, you're cold," may refer to the same positioning with relation to the fire.) The object looked for, and the solution of the game, is indicated by the fire that resides in the center of the space arbitrarily delimited by the game. The search for the hidden object and for the solution of the game is the search for life or the life-giving force itself, and the development of the game is a journey toward a center, like that of the *vegliatori* toward the fireplace.

The fireplace was the center of the house. It was the center of convergence of the significant space and, at the same time, the center of irradiation (or "fireside") of heat, light, and food. It was the center of the transformation of Nature into Culture,[99] but a culture that is always poised at the edge of the natural, precarious topos of the simultaneous presence of male (the fire, the spark) and female (the kettle, the chimney, the chain) sexual symbols; therefore, it was the symbol of the generative act of life and of the family.

As a subject of opposite and incompatible qualities (convergence, divergence, permanence) and yet not subject to the contradiction relative to them, the fire was the explanatory principle and primary signifier of both magical transformation and the metaphysics of the family.[100] It is logical that just in the house of the fire the dramatized and ritualized transmission of family values and of a worldview pertinent to them took place. To this center of centers, to the fireplace, the *vegliatori* came to assist in the *veglia* and perform it.

The old woman placed herself in the center, inside the fireplace, at the fireside, that is, in direct contact with the fire, which together with herself became an evocator and operator of images, mediator of the past and present, now and once upon a time, real truth and imagined truth, good and bad. Through the reverie in the ambiguous light and dark, the narrator and her familiar public once again found, by renewing it, a primary and most human cultural function of mankind: storytelling.

2

Fairy Tales for the Young and the Old
"Oh, Listen to Me, Now. Once upon
a Time . . ."

"S'io non erro, io mi ricordo avere molte volte udito dire che . . ."

["If I am not mistaken, I remember having heard many times that
. . ."]

Boccaccio, *Decameron*, the First Day, Novella 3

*". . . quando c'invecchiamo . . . ci cacciano in cucina a dir delle favole
con la gatta . . ."*

[". . . when we grow old . . . they put us in the kitchen to tell stories
with the cat . . ."]

Ibid., the Fifth Day, Novella 10

Storytelling, the first genre of folklore performed at the *veglia*, was also the most complex.[1] As the *veglia* progressed with the evening, less and less negotiation and confrontation of roles and values would take place, both within the stories themselves and in their performative context: after the children went to bed, fewer role relationships needed to be negotiated, exemplified, and embodied in the performances.[2]

These storytelling events are fascinating because what is being recounted in the stories themselves is precisely a reflection of many of the problems faced by both performers and listeners. Thus we can see in each storytelling event at least three main levels of significant movement, unevenly mixed but always present. The first is the developmental thread of the narrative, which parallels the ideal ritual pattern of growing up, courting, and marrying; the second is the surface resemblance between tales and actual occurrences within the community—sometimes even members of the audience; and the third is the patterned interaction between the storyteller and the members of the audience, in which the power role of teller may be negotiated for or passed around during the evening.[3]

The old storytellers would never begin on their own initiative. They would not want to err, as did the blindman of Peretola, "who needed a coin to begin, and ten to stop." Even though everyone knew they would finally concede, and happily, they still looked for a lot of coaxing first. It seemed to be part of the performance itself, not just a happy prelude but a way of establishing the proper mood and the right way to frame the scene.

The children had been murmuring since dinner was over, "Come on, grandma, tell us a story," and they kept it up while the table was being cleared and as the dishes were being washed. The old woman procrastinated, and in so doing caused the expectation to grow. She scoffed and joked, being careful, however, not to imply a flat refusal. She made them understand from the tone of her voice and from her replies that she would give in, perhaps; actually, she wanted to be begged, so as to obtain from all who stayed awake an explicit and formal invitation and an implicit commitment to pay attention and to keep silent. "No, now there is work to be done . . ." "But, sweetie, I am dead tired . . ." "Who can remember stories! Ah, if I could only remember them!"

In the meantime she sat down near the fire, holding the hand warmer in her lap, moving the coals around inside the terra-cotta bowl to get the most warmth. "By now you know them all anyway. I've told them to you a thousand times." "Fairy tales—do you think I've a quarry of fairy tales?" And in the meantime she called to her favorite grandson, "Come sit here on the bench next to me," and she would pet the cat or the dog, who were allowed to come near the fireplace for the occasion. The animals rubbed themselves on her long skirts.

By this time even the conversation of the adults often contained indirect references to the fairy tale world, a story, a legend: they named characters or titles; some complained in loud voices of forgetting the name of this or that story; some remembered, on hearing a title mentioned, that they had already heard the story at a previous *veglia* some time before. The storyteller continued to act stubborn, still scoffing and teasing, until she decided she had played with the audience enough or until someone in the brigade, one of the more important members, "officially" insisted that she begin. Almost never have I heard storytellers start out with the story most requested. No one, they explained to me, wants to be prompted and least of all do they want to be given an order "by four little brats." Furthermore, the storyteller loses prestige if she seems to know the same stories that everyone else knows, while it is better to demonstrate that she knows rare and ancient stories known only to a few. In this way the audience was to be firmly convinced that it was a kindness of the old woman to narrate her stories to the group; it was not the audience that was doing her a favor by agreeing to sit and listen to her.

Some storytellers used verbal formulas to indicate that they were about to begin their narration. These are often hedges to excuse ahead of time any mistakes or awkward phrasing. Nada, for ex-

Getting ready for the *veglia* by the fireplace, the center of the centers (photo by Mario Salvi, Siena).

ample, excused herself over and over again (but making it understood that she was just being polite), saying that her memory was not what it used to be and that she was not sure of being able to "spin" her tales well. After having made me declare repeatedly that I did not already know her stories and after I assured her that

I was indeed interested, she changed her tone and said, with determination: "Well, there are so many tales to tell. Many people know many of them; several people know several of them.[4] But there are a few people who know only a few of them, and this evening I want to tell one of those that I bet no one knows: the tale of Marinella. Does anyone know it?" When we replied negatively, she said, "When I first heard this story, you weren't even born yet!" Then she turned to me: "Let me tell you how old this story is. I learned it when I lived in Doccia, from my grandmother, and she had heard it from her grandparents. So figure it out for yourself; it's more than two hundred years old." At times someone replied to the same question saying, "Of course we know it!" or "I know it!" or "Everybody knows that one!" And then the old woman would become cross and reply, "Well then, you tell it, if you're so smart!" or else: "And I'm going to tell it anyway. If you don't like it, the door is there; you can leave if you want, and let the fresh air in!"—permitted grumpiness, just a part of the opening ceremony illustrating how the dynamic of the family pervades these tellings. Everybody begged her again and began to reprimand the person who was spoiling the fun, until peace was once more restored. Other storytellers had their own special way of presenting their stories. Like "Grandpa Pule," who around 1920 was invited to houses in the Chianti area to tell fairy tales to the children and was compensated with some cigars, a few coins, or half a fiasco of wine. Before beginning his stories he would recite this couplet as an introduction: "Grandpa Pule, also known as 'lampante,' Mr. Bright [because he liked his wine crystal clear], who for two cigar butts will tell you lots of stories."

And so, finally, the actual story began. The storyteller looked around at her audience; she indicated to a latecomer or to someone in the kitchen to be quiet;[5] and, staring at the fire for a moment, then at her listeners but more often looking into the fire, thereby suggesting to her audience that they concentrate on the flame, she would begin to narrate: "Oh, listen to me now, children. Once upon a time . . ."[6]

After having gone through all the phases of the ceremony—dinner, guests, cleaning up the kitchen, transforming the dinner into family theater, the fire in the fireplace, the requests, the refusals, more requests, the agreements—the storyteller, Nada Vettori (it was an October evening in 1973 at Castellina) began to tell some tales.[7] The first was that of Marinella.

Oh, listen to me, now. Once upon a time there was a woman who had two daughters: one had only one eye and the other had three. At this time one of the mother's sisters died, leaving her with a little girl, but this one was a perfect little girl with two eyes just like all little girls, and her name was Marinella. Marinella went to live with her aunt and cousins.

When Marinella's aunt realized that Marinella was much prettier than her own little girls and that everyone stopped to look at her, she began to hate Marinella. So she purchased a little goat, and everyday, to get Marinella out of the house, her aunt made her take the goat out to pasture in the forest; in other words, Marinella's aunt didn't like her very much. She would give Marinella a bit of stale bread to eat and leave her . . . with this goat every morning and every evening. Marinella in the beginning obeyed, but then she got tired.

One day when she was more depressed than ever, she cried a lot. Then . . . a fairy . . . a fairy appeared to her. She saw a lady, a beautiful lady who spoke to her, "Why are you crying, Marinella?" "Oh, can't you see. I'm always here in the forest all alone, with a crust of stale bread and with my little goat," she said. "But I would like to be like the others, like my cousins," she said. "I would like to stay at home a little and then, and then I am also hungry." "Don't be upset," said the fairy. "Listen and I will tell you what to do. When you are hungry, whisper in the ear of your little goat and say to it: 'little goat, little goat, set a little table.' You'll see," she said, "that you will no longer be hungry."

At first Marinella did not believe the fairy. When the fairy had gone away, however, she said, "I want to try it." In fact, she tried, and a sumptuous table appeared with every good thing to eat. Marinella was happy, and from that moment on she was glad to take the little goat out to pasture.

When her aunt discovered that Marinella had gotten back her lovely color, that she was as beautiful as before after having withered a bit, she realized that something was happening. So she sent one of her daughters with Marinella, the one with only one eye, telling her to watch carefully what went on. "Yes, yes," said the daughter. The two girls remained together all day long until the one-eyed daughter fell asleep, and while she slept Marinella went to the little goat to get her table set and her

Nada Vettori, storyteller, putting her grandchildren to bed after a story-telling session (photo by Mario Salvi, Siena).

cousin didn't see a thing. That evening the mother asked her daughter what she had seen. "Nothing," she replied, "absolutely nothing." And she said she didn't want to go back.

As time passed, they saw that Marinella became more and more beautiful. But if she only eats a crust of bread, how can she be so lovely and full of energy? So this time the woman sent her other daughter; she sent the daughter with three eyes and she, too, ended up falling asleep, but she kept one eye open. And so she saw the table already set appear to Marinella.

That evening she related the episode to her mother, who then took the little goat and killed it. Marinella returned to the forest to cry and to invoke the help of the fairy. The fairy appeared and asked Marinella what was wrong. "What's wrong?" replied Marinella. "They've killed my little goat and now I can't even come here anymore . . . I don't even have the satisfaction of coming here with my goat anymore." The fairy replied: "Listen, go home and ask for the heart of the goat. You'll see, they'll give it to you. Then bury it in the garden." Marinella did as she was told. She returned home, she asked for the goat's heart, and she buried it in the garden. Then she went to bed.

The next morning her aunt and her cousins saw this tree. From the heart of the goat a tree had grown, a pomegranate tree. All the pomegranates were gold and the leaves were silver [Taking her eyes from the fire, the storyteller turned to me, laughing, "How nice if this would actually happen!"] So they tried to climb, but no way, they could not climb it. Then it was the hunting season; after a while came by the prince. He told the aunt, "O woman," he says, "whose tree is that, that pomegranate there." "It is mine," she said. "Would you give me a little branch as a present." "Yes, yes, of course." She tried to climb it, the first one [the daughter with one eye]. Nothing. The other with the three eyes, nothing. The . . . mother, nothing. The prince could not climb it himself. So nobody could climb this branch. Marinella came out and said, "The tr . . . the pomegranate is mine, because it was born from the heart of my little goat." She says, "I give it to you . . ." She climbed and picked a nice branch of pomegranates and gave it to the prince. The prince saw Marinella and fell in love right away because she was so beautiful. He took the . . . the pomegranate, he took Marinella, hopped on his horse, and they went to the castle. And there he married her. They lived happily ever after. There.[8]

Reading the text according to Propp's functions,[9] as well as from Marinella's viewpoint[10] and at the level of the actual telling, we can clearly detect a sequence of functions. These can usefully be regarded as "moves" of a "game" between aunt and cousins on one side and the fairy and Marinella on the other.[11] These are the significant narrative movements of the tale and certainly provide one of the major ways in which the story is remembered by the teller and followed and appreciated by the hearers.

The family drama before the storytelling simply underscores the family *message* of this tale. It is in-structured in such a way that constant resonances arise between the situation and the attitudes of the family and friends listening in and the drama as it is unfolded. It is useful then, reflecting as it does the patriarchal family romance of the past, to look at some of the ways of getting at such structuring, both as developed by folklorists like Propp and as how the storytellers discuss it. The social importance of these and similar tales is one point upon which narrators and folklorists most generally agree. This is stated in a proverbial rhyme universally known in Tuscany and in other parts of Italy: "The story is not good if it does not have its moral" ["*La novella non è bella se non c' è la giuntarella*"]. [12]

If we accept the explanations of the narrators, according to whom fairy tales were for adults and children alike (since it was necessary to teach children how to get along in the world, while at the same time amusing them, one had to use the metaphor, that is, "say one thing in place of another"), we can carry out a reading of the text in an interpretative key, conducted on the level of the force of family institutions and marital traditions. Marinella's aunt sends her out of the house as soon as she discovers that Marinella is uncomfortable competition for her own two daughters in search for a husband. So she sends Marinella away into the forest—far from any cultural contacts, into a nonsocial situation—hoping to make her inaccessible and reducing her to ugliness through planned malnutrition.

The fairy—Marinella's helper—and the goat represent "good" maternal figures who give advice (the fairy is a beautiful lady; "She was a fully grown woman, not an old lady," the storyteller explained to me) and provide nourishment. The goat, like the cow, is the *mater lactans* in Tuscan folk imagination. And so, contrary to the plan of the wicked aunt, Marinella becomes ever more beautiful. Her aunt sends spies to obtain information; then on the basis of this information she kills one of her competitors—the goat. The fairy reappears and shows Marinella how to procure a precious tree, the gold-and-silver pomegranate, probably the imaginary equivalent of a dowry. A traditional compliment says that the woman's hands "paiono un giardin di melagrani" ["they seem a garden of pomegranate trees"]. Furthermore, girls in love used to have and tend personally a small tree that was called *amorino* [little love], or tree of good wishes. [13] And traditional folksongs often refer to "the house of my love in a nice plain / before her door in a garden / there is a pomegranate tree." [14] In fact, the shape of the pomegranate is similar to a little coin bank, a *salvadanaio*, and the Tuscan nuptial hopechest is a coffer containing a small treasure. The pomegranate tree in the fairy tale cannot be touched by anyone but Marinella ("the pomegranate is mine, because it was born from the heart of my little goat"), and it originates from the heart of the goat,

My oldest informants, Grandma Zoe (age 91) and Caterina (age 93), discussing a folktale's moral (photo by Paul Hoffman, San Francisco).

a maternal symbol and provider of the metaphoric dowry. Then the prince is introduced; his attributes are "son," "bachelor," and "hunter." Hunting is often used in Tuscan dialect folklore as a metaphor for courting: "The man does the hunting, but the woman does the fishing" ["*L'uomo è cacciatore, ma la donna è pescatrice*"] is a proverb used in this sense. [15] When someone wishes to marry advantageously, it is commonly said that he is a dowry hunter. A bachelor who wears his hunting outfit and is seen wandering around the vicinity of a girl's home with the excuse that he is hunting is sometimes asked maliciously, "Oh, are you out hunting birds?" ("Birds" or "game" are commonly used to indicate feminine sexual organs: an old woman in a rest home in Radda once confessed to me, laughing, that her "game" was hurting.) The prince then asks for the dowry of pomegranates. Neither the cousins, nor the aunt, nor the prince himself are able to climb the tree; that is, they are unable to take direct possession of it. Marinella herself breaks off the branch and hands it to him, a pledge of love and a promise. In fact, a traditional compliment goes "Di bellezze voi siete una rama" ["You are a branch of beauties"] and is addressed to young women in song or speech.[16] The prince takes Marinella (and her dowry of pomegranates) home with him and marries her. The game between the fairy and the aunt ends with the story: the fairy marries off Marinella; the aunt remains at home with her two daughters.

The begging and insistence of the audience were not repeated after every fairy tale that was told. After the first tale of that evening, which was listened to by all in rapt silence, it was enough for one girl to say, "Come on, Nada, tell us another," and the storyteller immediately began once more and in good humor, after having moved the log with the poker, sending a handful of sparks up the chimney.

Oh, listen to me, children. The princess and the frog. Let's begin. Once upon a time there was a king who had seven daughters, all of whom were beautiful, but the youngest one was the most beautiful of all. The girls spent all day in the garden playing with a golden ball. One day it happened that [when they were] playing near a small lake the golden ball rolled into the water. The youngest daughter began to cry, "My ball, my ball." She was afraid to go into the water to get the ball. A frog came to the surface of the water and said to her: "Why are you crying, lovely daughter of the king? Lovely youngest daughter of the king, what have you to cry about?" "Oh," she said, "what have I to cry about—my ball fell into the lake and I cannot go in to get it." The frog said, "I'll go get it for you, but on one condition: that you take me to your home, that you let me eat with you, and that you take me to bed with you." At first the little girl said yes to him, to get her ball back. Then when the frog came up out of the water with the ball in his mouth and placed it on the grass, the little girl took it and ran with it toward her house. And the frog ran after her: "Beautiful youngest daughter of the king, wait for me, wait for me." But she couldn't even hear him anymore. And she kept going.

When she got home everyone sat down at the table. After a while, a servant came in and said, "There's a frog at the door, asking for the beautiful youngest daughter of the king." Her father, who had already guessed that a spell had been cast or something, told the servant, "Open the door and let him in." The servant did so, and the frog came jumping in behind him saying: "Put me next to you and give me something to eat in your plate." This made the girl shiver with disgust, but the king instead wanted his daughter to feed the frog. After he had eaten, the frog said to her, "Take me to your bedroom." Well, you can imagine, she was scared, he was so disgusting.

When she got to her bedroom she grabbed him and threw him out the window. Then she went to bed. But she couldn't sleep. She began to have bad dreams. After a time she heard a knock on the door. She got up and asked who it was. The voice said: "It's me, the frog. You threw me out the window and now I have a broken leg. Take me in and help me." The girl felt sorry for the frog and so she picked him up and put him on her bed and saw that he was bleeding. "I'll call a doctor," she said. "A doctor? No," said the frog, "you must take care of me. Put a bandage around my leg." So she took his little leg into her hands, this time without fear, and she bandaged it. She bound the leg and put the frog on the pillow next to her to sleep. She fell asleep and had many beautiful dreams. The morning when she woke up, in the armchair she found a handsome prince . . . a . . . a handsome young man, that is. And she told him: "What about you?! Who brought you here?" "I? See there, there is the skin of the frog. I had . . . I was bewitched, enchanted. A fairy who wanted to marry me. I did not want her, and she said that I would . . . I would have become a man again when a princess would take me to bed with her. Now this has happened," he said, "and I am here to marry you if you want me." And she liked this young man, so she took him to the king and so they were married and lived happily thereafter, them too. [17]

This fairy tale too ends in marriage: the loss of the magic object makes it necessary, in trying to get it back, to nourish and take the frog to bed because he has the golden ball. The girl has to overcome her aversion to the frog, a phallic symbol repulsive at first but rewarding at last.[18] A similar process happened in the sexual maturation of the young women to whom the story was familiar. The princess tries twice to shirk her duty but to no avail; her own father makes her keep her promise because he had "already guessed" that a spell had been cast (and perhaps he thought it would be a good marriage for his daughter). In folktales, families always know the youngsters' plans, as they should, according to the social norms, in real life. In the case of the frog, if we analyze the story from his point of view, we see clearly that we are dealing with a metaphoric "journey to culture." We can read the story in retrospect to understand more fully, as these Tuscans would, what family dynamic is being played out in this world of fantasy. The prince (that is, the "son") refuses to marry the fairy, his idealized mother.[19] This fairy, according to the storyteller, was "blonde and dressed in light turquoise, young but no longer a girl," as was clear in our subsequent conversation. Refusing an incestuous or self-consuming relationship. the prince-son is transformed into a temporary form within animal-nature from which he is saved by a princess (girl) who agrees to "take him to bed with her." Sleeping with a princess is a metaphoric rite of passage between two metaphoric states of being, an act which is total in its sense of family-cum-cultural commitment. Dramatically, it is a frog, that most repulsive of ambiguous creatures (neither animal nor fish, neither land- nor water-dwelling), into which he is transformed and out of which he re-emerges. The frog (it is interesting to note that in Tuscany "froggie," "little frog," or "frog" are affectionate nicknames occasionally used when referring to children) becomes a man when the princess takes him to bed with her, turning him into a member of the cultural world in every respect and enabling him to marry, which the prince immediately attends to. In other words, the sequence of the fairy tale seems analogous to that of coming into the cultural world from a more innocent state:

Tale	Refusal to marry the fairy	State of being a frog in the lake	Sleeping with the princess	Transformation into a prince again	Marriage
Culture	Retreat from incest	State of latency, pre-socialized	Sexual contact with a girl	Transformation into a man	Marriage

Adolescents pass from the stage of latency after having accomplished an act of virility. Men, according to tacit unwritten tradition of Tuscan culture, had to arrive at the altar with some sexual experience, which represented a kind of rite of passage from one stage to another. This pattern of maturation through magical transformations is common in many tales from this region—as it is in many other traditions. The differences, of course, reside in the way in which the process of growing up through a rejection of the offer of incest and becoming a member of a new family unit is articulated. A further story that illustrates many of these same patterns of development is the fairy tale of Donkey Skin, which is also very common in Tuscan folklore and lends itself to a parallel reading. Here is a version from 1976 originating in Casentino, where Sidonia Fanetti heard it at least a half century before.

I will now tell it to you. Once upon a time there was a king. And . . . his wife had died and had left him a ring. And she said to him, "You will remarry the person, the woman, who can wear this ring." And he tried, he had tried everywhere, and this ring didn't fit anyone.

One day his daughter went into her mother's bedroom and saw the ring lying on the bedside table, and she put it on. She then went to her father and said, "Look, father, how nice it looks on me . . . mother's ring." Her father said, "I have to marry you, because I promised your mother." "But father, you must be joking," said the girl. "Marry your daughter?" "But I promised and I must keep my promise."

So the girl went to her godmother, who was a fairy, and said: "Godmother, I tried on my mother's ring, and my father told me that he wanted to marry me. What should I do?" "Listen," said the godmother, "you must ask him for a new dress." "What kind of dress should I ask for?" "You must ask him for a dress covered with little silver bells and with fish, with every kind of fish that exists in the sea."

She went to her father and naturally did what she had been told. Her father knew people here and there who travel a lot, and after some time had passed, a merchant returned from a long journey and brought her the dress. She ran desperately back to her godmother. "Godmother, he brought me the dress." "Ask him for another one." "How should it be?" "With the moon and with the stars." "Listen, father, I want a dress with the moon and the stars." "All right." And he sent his merchants everywhere to look for such a dress . . . and . . . after some time had passed the merchants brought back this dress too. The girl was more desperate than ever. "What can I do? Godmother, what can I do? My father found the dress." "You ask him for a dress with the sun, a sun that shines just as the sun really shines." "Listen, father, I want a dress with the sun on it but a sun that shines just as the sun really shines." And her father found it.

"And now, godmother, now that he has found all three of them, what should I ask for?" "Ask him for the skin of a donkey." "Oh, what a strange request. What in the world will you do with it?" "Never mind, give me the skin of a donkey." Once she had got it . . . "Godmother, I have the skin of a donkey too." "Listen, tonight you pack your suitcase, put this donkey skin on so that no one will recognize you, and leave." During the night the girl put on the donkey skin, picked up her suitcase in which she had packed her beautiful three dresses and other things, and left. When she got to the door she came upon the guards . . . "Oh, what kind of animal is this?" "Oh, I'm just a poor little thing, let me pass . . ." "Yes, yes, yes, go, go." And out she went.

And she walked, and walked, and walked, and walked until sunrise when she found herself outside her father's kingdom in the kingdom of another king. And she, poor thing, did not know what to do. She overheard some women talking along the street: "Did you hear that the king's guard in charge of the geese died? He is looking for a replacement . . ." The girl said, "I will apply for the job." And she went to the king, to the palace of the king. The palace guard said, "What do you want?" "I heard that the guard in charge of the geese is dead." "But," the guard said, "the geese will be frightened if they see such a . . . such a . . . I don't know, you're certainly not a human being, nor are you beast. I don't know what you are. But anyway, let's ask the king." "Yes, yes," said the king, "do what you like. Do what you like, just as long as there is a guard for those little animals." The girl entered a room: "This is your room. This is the coop where all the geese are and in the morning you must feed them and then you must take them outside; you do this and that for them," and he gave her all the instructions. "Yes, yes," she said. The next morning she thought she was alone in the room and she took off the donkey skin and she put on one of her dresses. The geese, when they saw her . . . And she goes to take care of the geese. The geese begin to chant:

Honk, Honk, Honk
What a lovely guard is she
Perfect for the son of the king she'd be.

The servants of the royal house and the neighbors whose windows were nearby said, "Listen to those geese; they've never been so noisy before, just listen to them . . ."

> *Honk, Honk, Honk*
> *What a lovely guard is she*
> *Perfect for the son of the king she'd be.*

They said, "Let's go take a look at this guard in charge of the geese." So they went to look at her. They knocked on the door, and she opened it, but she had already put her donkey skin back on. The next morning the same thing happened; she put on another dress and went to care for the geese. And the geese naturally repeated the same rhyme. The cook said, "Your majesty, do the geese always have to make so much noise?" The king's son said, "I'll hide." And in fact the king's son hid himself in the girl's room and saw that once she had taken off the donkey skin she was a lovely girl, elegant, well mannered; in short, she was pretty, she had everything!

After four days had passed, the king's son said he wasn't feeling well. "I want some porridge made by Donkey Skin." And so they go and tell this to the girl called Donkey Skin. She replied, "But I don't know how to make porridge . . ." "Never mind, just make it and bring it to the king's son." "I'll bring it to him." The girl made the porridge and brought it to the kitchen. "Now you must bring it to him." "I must bring it to him!" "Yes. The king has given orders, the king's son has given orders, and therefore you must bring him the porridge." "But I'm not able to, I can't, I don't know how . . ." "You must bring him the porridge." "All right, I'll bring him the porridge." And so, she brought him the porridge. After she had given it to him, the king's son said to the servant, "You may leave now." "You must remain here." "You stay there. Close the door." And he closed the door. "Take off the donkey skin." "Oh, no, I can't take it off." "Take off that donkey skin because otherwise, well, just look, I don't know what I'll do to you. Take off that donkey skin because I want you to." The girl, whether she wanted to or not, removed the donkey skin. And she was left wearing . . . a dress with the sun on it.

The king's son was astonished. "Tell me, why did you disguise yourself like this? And why . . . where do you come from . . . who are you?" "I am the daughter of the king whose kingdom is next to yours." "Then

why all this masquerading?" "Because my father wanted to marry me.
Since my mother had left him a ring and had said to him, 'Whoever can
wear this ring you will marry,' and since the ring fit me, my father wanted
to marry me, and I . . . it seemed . . . it seemed absurd to me." "All
right," he said, "then you will be my bride. However, we will also invite
your father, because he must give his consent to the marriage; he must
be happy too."

A big dinner was planned, and all the neighboring kings were invited,
all the princes, and all the most important people, the very best of society.
And this king came too. Donkey Skin said, "I'll prepare a course." And
she made a meat course without . . . salt. When the people began to eat
the meat, they said, "This course was prepared by the princess, the future
wife of the king's son." "It's good," said her father, the king. "However,
it needs salt; it has no taste." She stood up and said to him, "It has no
taste, just as the man who wants to marry his own daughter has no taste."
And so they recognized each other, he gave his consent to the marriage,
and there was a grand feast . . . They reigned happily ever after, with
no more problems. [20]

The development of the story of Donkey Skin is significantly
parallel to the preceding story, with a reversal of the sexes, of course.
Here we have a girl who refuses the incestuous proposal of her
father and runs away from home (the kingdom) wearing a donkey's
skin (in other versions we find the cork of a tree or the wrinkled
skin of an old woman, functional equivalents that make the girl
unapproachable and sexually "unappetizing" like the frog). Significantly, under the donkey skin is a symbol of enduring and radiating
vitality: the perpetual light of the sun. As we will see more fully
explored in the tale of Cinderella, an ugly covering can be symbolically equated with the apparently dead fire. But like a good fire
within the fireplace within the home, the cool cinders are used to
bank over the glowing embers—the sun in this story, a star on the
forehead in the first version of Cinderella. In disguise the girl goes
to work and passes the test of taking care of the geese (in other
versions she takes care of the house or she goes to three dances
wearing the three gifts from her father, winning the heart of the
prince). The Donkey Skin in our story takes a suitcase with her,
a symbol perhaps of the hopechest. The prince, after the qualify-

ing test of the geese is successfully passed, puts her to a second test: the porridge is not objectively necessary because the sickness is not real; the porridge becomes a symbolic gift. After Donkey Skin presents him with the porridge, she is recognized as a woman and receives a marriage proposal. Parallel to the real life of Tuscan girls, the narrative sequence is developed for the king's daughter in correspondence with the structure of a rite of passage:

Donkey Skin	Refusal of incest	Intermediate phase, "neither human being nor beast," indeterminate ugliness	Success in the qualifying tests	Recognition	Marriage with the prince
Real life	Refusal of incest	Latency phase	Learning feminine abilities	Recognition of status of womanhood	Marriage

The allusion to incest makes this narrative the object of what has been defined as "a singular censorship." Donkey Skin is, in fact, one of the most famous stories in Italy, but it is also one that is not liked very much.[21] The allusion to incest is substituted in other stories, which are just as well known but which are more popular, by the refusal of the girl to marry a magician (paternal figure), who in revenge turns the girl into a frog.

The motif of the girl who must pass tests after which she is "rewarded" with marriage is, in fact, among the most common in Tuscan folk narratives. Often the heroine is obliged by her stepmother to pass tests; other times she must do it in the disguise of a frog. In fact, abandoned girls often ended up being servants in the city, like the *innocentine* in Florence.[22] These girls were, in real life, in a marginal state just as Donkey Skin is in the tale. The tests can be summarized in a few categories: cooking, spinning or weaving, housekeeping, taking care of animals, bringing up or taking care of puppies and kittens, making oneself beautiful.[23] These are, of course, the same tests required of a girl in real life before finding a husband. Many housekeepers, like Palmira's mother, continually repeated, "I won't give my daughter to any man until she knows how to dress him." All women in fact knew how to weave and spin; many also learned how to sew and embroider. Little girls learned very early how to take care of the house. I've watched many little girls as they stood on chairs to reach the sink to help their mothers or grandmothers wash the dishes, "just like a nice little lady" in accordance with tradition, and the little girls were praised and encouraged by their relatives as they performed these tasks. One little girl, named Franchina, five years old, explained her chores to me in a traditional poem she had learned in kindergarten:

> Little delicate hands!
> So many things they can do!
> They know how to wash and iron!
> They like to caress mother!

The puppies and kittens in the stories seem to be the equivalent of children in real life. A well-known proverb in Tuscany, of bourgeois origin, reads as follows:

> Puppies, kittens, peasants' children;
> They are cute when they are little ones.[24]

This proverb clearly equates the three terms. Furthermore, I was able to find a recurring "Freudian slip" in the narratives of my storytellers, who often in telling the story of "the palace of cats" said "children" and then corrected themselves, saying "kittens." All this seems to indicate that bringing up kittens and puppies in fairy tales constitutes a simple substitution for bringing up children in real life.[25]

In this way the heroine of the stories became or returned to being a woman ready to marry the prince by demonstrating that she knew how to take care of the house, to spin and weave, to make herself beautiful. Only then she became "ready for marriage" with her "prince on a white horse" (as a fiancé was often jokingly referred to).

A woman's world in 1905: sewing was a traditional woman's chore, and little girls were taught early in life how to embroider (courtesy of the Falassi family).

The next story elaborates upon the escape from incest into the marriage pattern, portraying it on a larger social screen. In this tale, the sexual advance is again made by a more powerful older person, though a magician-transformer rather than a father or stepmother. The dimension of superordination and subordination within the household is projected then somewhat beyond the nuclear family and onto the larger community—much as it used to be in this region under the *padrone* system.

"Tell me your story now that I've told you mine" is the way Nada finished the last tale. "We'll tell ours another time," one of the old people replied, laughing. "Come on, tell another one to the children." "Things always happen in threes." A woman named S., about forty years old, who had come to listen with her two children, asked them, "Do you want to hear the one about Rolando and Brunilde?" When the children replied yes, S. said: "The one about Rolando and Brunilde, Nada! Tell them that one!" Nada removed her eyes from the fire and looked first at her, then at me, winking at me with a half smile of understanding. "Do you know the story?" she asked. "No, I really don't think I do," I replied. "Well, then, I will tell it to you."

A mother and her daughter lived in a village. The daughter was happy because she was engaged to a boy who lived in the same village, a wood-cutter, and they were to be married within a few weeks. So she passed all her time helping her mother a little, working in the fields a little, gathering wood a little; and then in her free time she sat at the window and sang . . . as she spun. She spun and she sang, waiting for her fiancé to return from the forest.

One day, a magician passed through town, and he heard singing; she had a pretty voice. He turned around and saw this girl at the window. Seeing her and falling in love with her was one and the same for the magician. And so he sent . . . he sent someone to ask if she would marry him; this prin . . . this girl said, "No, because I am already engaged to be married. I have a fiancé and I am very fond of him," she replied, "and in a few weeks we are getting married," she said, "so I don't need a magician or these riches," because he had told her that he would make her a rich lady because she was poor.

Then the magician, who had become indignant at her refusal, sent an eagle to kidnap the girl, who was called Brunilde, and it carried her to his castle where he showed her all his riches, all his castles, all his gold, all his money, but she didn't care about any of it. She said, "I will marry Rolando and I want Rolando." The magician then told her, "If you don't marry me then you will never leave this castle." And in fact he locked her up . . . he locked her in a room near his bedroom. Since the magician slept very soundly during the night and snored, for fear that someone would steal her he had an effigy made of himself as big as he was and then he had bells put on it, a thousand tiny bells, so that if anyone bumped into this effigy he would wake up.

Now, her mother and Rolando were worried because the girl didn't come home, and her fiancé wanted to go and kill the magician. But her mother said, "No, wait, let's wait a little." She said, "If not, he could hurt you, too; let's wait a bit." And they tried one night to get into the garden, but there was . . . the magician had had a wall built that surrounded the garden and it was so tall that it was impossible to enter. And the girl's mother sat all day and cried. Finally, one day when she was in the forest she came upon a fairy in the form of an old lady who said to her, "Tell me, why are you crying so?" And the girl's mother told the old woman about her Brunilde and how she had been carried off. "Listen," she said, "listen, I don't have much power in this case because the magician is much more powerful than I. I can't do anything," she said. "However, I can help you," and she told her that he had closed the girl in a room and that he had had an effigy made of himself. So she said, "You can't go there because if one of those bells should ring, he'll wake up." She said: "Listen to what you should do. This is the season when the cotton falls from the trees. You should go everyday and fill a bag with cotton. In the evening when Rolando comes home from the forest, you have him take the cotton to the castle and I'll help you crawl through a hole." She said: "I get the bag into the garden and you'll get inside the palace . . . into the castle. In the castle you must stuff a few bells each night with cotton. Until you have stuffed them all, so that they will not ring anymore, then we'll see what we can do." And, in fact, this poor woman said: "Of course, I'll do it. It will take time but I'll do it gladly."

So they talked to the young man; during the day the mother gathered the cotton while he went to work, and in the evening they took the bag of cotton to the castle, and the mother stuffed the bells. Until one night the bells had finally all been stuffed. She went back to the old woman in the forest and told her that the last bell had been stuffed that same evening. Then the old woman said, "Take Rolando with you." And so the young man was made to enter through the same door that was used to stuff the bells, and the old woman gave him a sword and told him that when they were near enough he should cut off the left ear of the magician. All the power of the magician lies in his left ear, she said . . . In fact they entered the castle and went to get the girl. And the young man went to cut off the magician's ear. After he cut off the ear, the left ear where all his power lay, the entire castle crumbled, everything crumbled. The young couple took all the gold, the silver, and everything that belonged to the magician. They became rich, they got married, and they lived happily ever after. [26]

The next day, while we were talking about fairy tales in private, Nada explained to me why she had winked when S. had requested the story about Rolando and Brunilde. "You see, S. likes the story

because she recognizes herself in it. The story seems her own."
In fact, S., before getting married, had lived with her widowed
mother and was engaged to a charcoal man. The owner of G.'s
estate, who gave work to everyone in the village, including the
two women and the charcoal man, had S. come to work in his
house, "and he made her sleep at the end of the corridor and would
hardly ever let her go out; with the excuse that she might be tempted
to steal, he had her watched by the head housekeeper. In the meantime, he made verbal advances, some passes . . . you know; he
would say, 'I have a necklace with large beads . . . ' or 'when will
you come to Florence with me and have some fun?' Sometimes
he even tried to put his hands on her. But she would have none
of it. On the other hand, she could not leave his house since all
three of them were fed by him. She even had to meet her fiancé
secretly, you know. The head housekeeper was sympathetic to her;
she was almost related to her on her mother's side." In the end,
the engaged couple planned everything in secret; they even found
a house to live in. When they had also obtained the necessary docu-
ments from the church to get married, they went to Mr. V. and
told him only then that S. was about to "leave his service." At first
Mr. V. did not want her to go because "he said she was needed
in his house." But in the end B., the charcoal man-fiancé, had quite
an argument with him. In fact it ended up that all three stopped
working for Mr. V. and now the man works in Poggibonsi "and
they all live in town and her mother, A., lives with them, too."

If we read the story from S.'s perspective, the analogies with her
real life story are remarkable, as is shown in the following outline:

Fiction	Characters: girl, mother, fiancé	Magician has Brunilde kidnapped	Brunilde is locked up and guarded by mannequin	Mother and fiancé are helpless
Real life	Characters: girl, mother, fiancé	Mr. V. sends for S.	S. is locked up and guarded by housekeeper	Mother and fiancé are helpless

Fiction	The magician makes advances	Brunilde refuses	The old woman helps	They formulate a plot		
Real life	Mr. V. makes advances	S. refuses	The housekeeper helps	They prepare the wedding		
Fiction	They enter the castle	Fight between Rolando and the magician	Rolando wins	They marry	Couple gains fortune	Magician dies
Real life	They go to the villa of Mr. V.	Fight between charcoal man and Mr. V.	Charcoal man wins	Wedding	Couple loses fortune	Mr. V. dies

Only the endings of Brunilde's story and S.'s real life story are dramatically different. The fairy tale provides a final bonus to the young couple at the expense of the magician, while in real life things ended differently. In fact, the three characters of the story lost their jobs and their homes. This is just one more reason for the particular pleasure experienced by S. Besides identifying with and recognizing herself in the story, seeing that after all even her existence was in some way a "fairy tale," she also received some satisfaction from feeling compensated. The story also provided the fulfillment of a desire which the laws of real life deny. "It is always better than nothing," ended Nada shrugging her shoulders. "In any case, it wasn't a happy ending for Mr. V., either, who died lonely as a dog, and he couldn't even take any of his money with him." So the parallel was completed by the narrator. "They're stories, but sometimes they come true. Am I right? Oh, have another drop of *vin santo* [dry sherry]!"[27]

Nada's stories, every time I was at the *veglia* at her place, were heard in religious silence by adults and children alike. Nevertheless, this was only one of the many possible reactions of the listeners. In other storytelling sessions, for example, several people would begin to interrupt,[28] correcting the narrator and then telling the story in competition with the storyteller to see who could tell the best stories or the least known ones, or the best version (each person was convinced that his or hers was the only true version, of which the other versions were only variations, incorrect or badly told), citing authorities and names of very old, competent, and well-known storytellers to support their versions.

Sessions more similar to this latter extreme, often punctuated by squabbles or agitated chatter, were rather common in the Cioni house, where I was invited often for the *veglia*, in Lecchi in Chianti during the autumn and winter of 1973–74.

Old women were not the only people who told stories, even though normally they were the experts. For example, at Cioni's *veglia* more or less everbody knew how to tell a story: Annina, Sestilio, the grandparents, even the children, among whom was Fabrizio, seven years old, a very outspoken, candid, witty, and excellent storyteller. Giacco, Biranti, and others also came often, along with friends of the grandparents and parents who brought their children, among whom was Rosanna, one of Fabrizio's classmates.

Between stories we drank new wine,[29] we talked about specific meanings of the stories, we unwound and commented on the moral of each story, and we talked about current happenings. In that season the topics of conversation were the new wine and the olive crop, but also the war in the Middle East and the oil crisis, the foreigners who were buying farmhouses in Chianti and the industrialists who were buying the wine cellars and pretending to be vinegrowers and winemakers. "Just think, they want to make wine like orangeade, artificially." The old men and women talked about people and things of the past and they showed us how much the world had changed. "Let us tell you about the world that we knew! Bread cost one penny!" The young and the old discussed the news of the day, each treating the other as a peer. The children asked questions and meddled freely at times, halting momentarily only when they heard gruff tones or an affectionate voice say: "Keep quiet! You always want to go ahead of everybody else!"

Sometimes in the early part of the evening the adults would go

Fabrizio posing for "the American book" with proud grandparents, Annina and Sestilio Cioni (photo by Mario Salvi, Siena).

on talking about other things for a long time, and the children would begin to protest; often they would whine from sleepiness and they would ask to hear stories that had been promised to them that afternoon: "You told me today that if I did my homework you would tell me that story!" And so once more they began to tell stories.

On that November evening stories about King Faisal, Henry Kissinger, and Princess Anne of Great Britain, "who got married with horses and carriage," alternated with those about Cinderella, Capo di Becco, and Little Red Riding Hood.

The fact that Cinderella is one of the two or three most common tales encountered in the *veglia* is obviously significant, given the deep morphological structure of the stories discussed above. Here, too, one encounters on the narrative level a retreat to an "ugly" ambivalent persona, one not accorded full human status in order to bypass the blocking figure (in this case, the stepmother), leading, of course, to the discovery through the shoe trick and thus to marriage. The deep structural pattern holds, then, while the surface renderings are pleasantly (if conventionally) diverse.

It is useful to proceed in the investigation in this manner because there is ample testimony from observation that this pattern has a sense of the real with the Tuscan storyteller. On one of many such occasions three versions of the story were told by three different people, one the kind of old woman that commonly tells such fireside stories, one an old man, and, finally, the grandchild of the woman who in fact was the hostess for the occasion. What was both significant and amusing in this narrative situation was that the child was able, through adept maneuvering, to tell the story more clearly and successfully than his grandmother.

That evening, an animated discussion began on the variations of Cinderella: some called it the story of Lina, some knew it as Cinderella, others as the Cenderacchiola; Gino repeated: "No! No! It's the one about the count!"

GRANDFATHER SESTILIO CIONI: *Gino knows it, too.*

GINO ANICHINI (friend of grandfather): *No, I heard it was being told to my little girl.*

GRANDMOTHER ANNINA: *There was a woman who had two children, no . . .*

GINO: *Three!*

GRANDMOTHER: *Two! Not three!*

GINO: *Three! She had two daughters of her own and another one. Whom they kept as . . . They made her into a cinder girl; she sat near the ashes and tended the ashes . . .*

GRANDMOTHER: *Yes, in short, one of them always remained behind to take care of the ashes and the others went dancing. You're right. So there were three. Well, two or three.*

ALESSANDRO FALASSI: *But two of them were hers?*

GRANDMOTHER: *One was not hers and two were hers. So this poor little Cinderella . . . One of them was called . . .*

FABRIZIO CIONI (the seven-year-old): *No, listen, I'll tell it!*

GRANDMOTHER: *Well, then you tell it.*

FABRIZIO: *There is . . . there was a man and wife. They got married and they already had two little girls. One day his wife died. So he was left all alone. And he had these two little girls.*

GRANDFATHER: *Not so loud!*

FABRIZIO: *One day he went to look for a . . . for a . . . for another woman. And he found one. But this woman . . .*

GRANDFATHER: *Don't yell!*

FABRIZIO: *No . . . yes, yes, yes, she had . . .*

GRANDMOTHER: *Keep quiet, you're getting everything all mixed up.*

FABRIZIO: *I'm all confused.*

GRANDMOTHER: *Shut up now, this is how it goes!*

FABRIZIO: *The man had one daughter and the other woman had two. The stepsisters!*

GRANDMOTHER: *I'll tell it this way, because there are one hundred ways of telling it. I'll tell it as I remember it. And then . . .*

AF: *That's right, you tell it as you know it, [to Fabrizio] and then we'll hear the way you know it.*

GRANDMOTHER: *Yes. I know it this way. There once was a woman and a man and they had two daughters. One always took care of the ashes and the other always went dancing. So . . .*

GINO: *No, that's a different one!*

GRANDMOTHER: *In the evening she got all dressed up. You can see that it's another one.*

AF: *Let's hear yours!*

GRANDMOTHER: *And she said, "Well, are you going to the dance tonight?" "No, no," she replied. "I'm not going to the dance because I like to tend the ashes . . ." "Oh, come on to the dance, you'll see how much fun it is." "Hmm. No, no, I'm not coming." So one day her mother said to her, "Listen, you have to come to the dance, because if you don't, I'm not going to take your sister either." But she still refused. At this point, let's see, how does it go . . .*

FABRIZIO: *Well, it isn't the one that I was thinking of . . .*

GRANDMOTHER: *Yes, yes, this is how it goes. All right now, all right. So in the evening she had this little bird called Verzicolò, and after the others had gone she said:*

Verzicolò, little bird,
Make me more beautiful
Than has ever been heard.

The little bird turned her into a beautiful woman and then she entered the ballroom to dance. But as suddenly as she arrived, just as suddenly she disappeared at midnight. Every evening they saw this beautiful girl enter the ballroom but at a certain moment she would disappear. A young man said, "Oh, dammit, you'll see; some evening I'm going to get her."

One evening after the dancing and dancing and dancing, this Cinderella lost a shoe. Oh, dear! The next morning her sister said to her: "So you didn't come to the dance! But at midnight a beautiful girl came . . . if you would only have seen her . . . " "Oh, what do I care," she said. "I take care of the ashes . . ." "Oh, come on, always here taking care of the ashes . . ." So this night then she came home missing a shoe, and she said, "Oh, what should I do, what shall I do, what shall I do." Then she said, ". . . ah, this young man had the shoe in his pocket; you'll see, she'll come back." So that evening she ran out after the other had gone to the dance; she started out once more. She started out, however, this time without one shoe. She didn't have the shoe and the little bird was unable to provide her with another one; it did not help her:

> *Verzicolò, little bird,*
> *Make me more beautiful*
> *Than has ever been heard.*

Well, to make it short . . . this young man put the shoe by the door saying, "I want to see who you are." When she entered and . . . turned around and saw the shoe at the door, she put it on and danced all night long. He said, 'Now, when you leave, I'll follow you," this young man said to her. So then while they were dancing her mother recognized her. She stopped her, saying, "Well, look at you, you must be my daughter." So when it was time to leave she said to the other sister, call her: "Lina!" She said. "Call her, you'll see that that is Lina." So when they left they both left together.

When they arrived home her mother said to her, "You came to the dance without saying anything! Ah, but you'll see," she said. She said to her other daughter: "I'll show her. You know what we'll make her do tomorrow morning? Tomorrow morning we'll send her to where the kittens live. You'll see that the kittens will scratch her. Tomorrow morning you know what we'll make? We'll make polenta *[corn bread]." So her mother said to Cinderella, "You go and get the sieve where the kittens live." She replied, "No, I won't go." "What do you mean, you won't go; you will go!" Then she said, "Well, if she won't go then you go." She told the ugly daughter: "Listen to me. When you climb the stairs ask if you might have the sieve to make polenta. And go slowly because the stairs are made of glass." And she said nothing to the beautiful daughter. But the beautiful daughter was also intelligent. One day she sent the ugly daughter to get the sieve. And she carefully explained to her how to go about getting it.*

GINO: *Cinderella!*

GRANDMOTHER: *No, her sister, the other one. She got to the door and knocked. She said, "My mother sent me to get the sieve to make polenta." "Yes, but be careful, the stairs are made of glass." And she stomped so hard she broke every step. And they gave her the sieve.*

When she got back home she said, "Mamma, I brought you the sieve." "Were you careful?" She answered, "I broke all the steps, and the kittens scratched me all over." "Poor thing," said her mother. "Now tomorrow morning I'll send Cinderella." She was well mannered and said to her, "Go to where the kittens live and take the sieve back." And so she went slowly, slowly with much care, and didn't break a single step asking permission of the kittens and the kittens didn't touch her. She gave back the sieve and returned home. Her mother saw that nothing happened to her; how is that possible? "Tomorrow morning you go back to the kittens again." "No, I will not go back there." She said to the ugly daughter: "You've got to go back. And along the road when the rooster crows turn around, and when the ass sings don't turn around." So the ugly daughter took her leave. The rooster crowed and she did not turn around. The ass sung and she turned around, and she grew a long tail. So the next evening . . . the next evening she sent Cinderella saying, "When the rooster crows, don't turn around, when the ass sings, turn around." But, instead, when the ass sang she did not turn around. When the rooster crowed she turned around. And a star appeared in the middle of her forehead. So one of them ended up with a star and the other with a tail. But it was beautiful. But this must be only a part of the story.

In fact, Annina's tale was a mixture of motifs taken from two different tale types: Cinderella and Beauty and the Beast.[30]

Some observations on obedience and the relationship between the mother and her daughters should be made. The stepmother asks Cinderella to go to the dance and to go get the sieve. In both cases Cinderella refuses and disobeys, "she does as she likes." On the other hand, her stepmother gives Cinderella orders that are destined to do her harm. By doing just the opposite or not following the orders at all, Cinderella avoids getting scratched, she marries, and she receives a star on her forehead. In fact, a folk song still sung says "Quando ti vedo quella stella in fronte/voglio piu bene a te che a mamma mia" ["When I see that star in your forehead/I love you more than my mother"]—further folk evidence of the equation between mature femininity, enduring light, and the fire on the hearth. The mother gives good advice instead to the daughter she prefers, who disobeys and does just the opposite and ends up badly: she gets scratched, she doesn't marry, and an ass tail grows in the middle of her forehead. [31]

In this and in numerous other examples of Tuscan folklore, two aspects of motherhood are presented: the mother who always gives good advice but only to the daughter she prefers, and the mother who gives bad advice to the daughter she does not like. A daughter, then, must obey the orders of her own good mother (lacking the mother, then she had to obey the fairy) and do the opposite of what stepmothers or bad mothers say.

The version of the loss of the shoe is interesting, being a loss which is not made up for even with the help of the magic powers of the little bird (he "was unable to provide her with another one"). The shoe can be hypothesized as a virginity symbol, a feminine virtue which once lost cannot be replaced but remains in the hands of the man responsible for the loss. In the story the shoe remains with the prince. In everyday conversation, when referring to a girl who seems particularly adapted to a certain young man, one says, "She is just the right shoe for his foot" ["*è la scarpa pel su' piede*"]. At the same time the proverb warns that "two feet cannot fit into the same shoe" ["*due piedi in una scarpa non ci stanno*"], that is, a woman cannot have two lovers. Another folk expression is "If you want my shoe you must wear a sock" ["*se vuoi la mi' scarpa mettiti il calzino*"], demanding the man to use a contraceptive during sexual intercourse. An old woman is often referred to as "an old slipper" or a "worn-out shoe." Also, losing one or both shoes during a dance as well as taking them off voluntarily were acts that a woman did if she got caught up in the rhythm of a dance and the excitement it caused, and the act was considered excessive and improper:

"She even took off her shoes!" meant "She has really let herself go." In the story Cinderella loses her shoe during a dance, the erotic meaning of which is common in the symbolism of folklore: one of the famous examples of dishonest womanhood is that of the woman who was made to dance by the devil until she dropped dead. Duff-Gordon relates that, at a country dance at the turn of the century, a girl lost her shoes and her partner kneeled and put her shoes back on, while the audience laughed, having interpreted the incident as a parallel of the Cinderella tale.[32] The future husband putting the shoes on the bride was one of the most widespread customs related to the engagement ritual in Tuscany.[33]

Annina, responding to a question asked by the children, explained that "afterward the young man married her," even if the ending had been omitted in the story. The young man in fact had danced all evening with Lina-Cinderella, committing her and himself in the eyes of everyone present. Just as in stories, so it was in reality at dances in Tuscany: the woman who danced with only one man indicated that she belonged exclusively to him. The young man in the story, after having put her to the test, married her and did his duty as would every other well-intentioned young man in reality, as witnessed by Annina and her stories. The central narrative structure appears to be the following:

The girl has the virtue object that is magic and irreplacable	She loses it, passing it on to a young man	The young man puts her to the test	She passes the test
He gives the magic object back to her		They marry	

Events in real life, according to traditional custom, as expressed in the rite of passage, take place along parallel lines:

The girl is a virgin and respected	She goes with a young man	She loses her respectability, compromising herself	Her respectability is in his hands	He puts her to the test

She passes the test	She is "respected" again as a fiancée	He marries her

Annina admitted that her story was perhaps "not exact." And Gino replied immediately, "But you had almost begun the one about . . ." Then she asked him, "But how does yours go?" And he replied, "I've always heard my Nunzia tell it this way." And after a pause he cleared his throat and began:

GINO: *The one about the count goes like this. Once there was a woman who had three daughters. She was fond of two of them and could not stand the other one. The third girl always sat near the cinders. One evening the two daughters decided to go to the ball. They told the third daughter they were going to the ball and that she had to stay home and tend the cinders. "I don't care, I don't care if I stay home," she replied. "I don't care, not at all!" So the others went to the ball, and as soon as they arrived at the ball, the fairy appeared to the third sister and turned her into a beautiful woman with beautiful clothes and every-thing. As they entered the ballroom no one recognized them. Dressed in that way not one knew who she was.*

AF: *Do you mean the fairy?*

GINO: *No, the fairy was with her. The one who was with her was the fairy.*

FABRIZIO: *The fairy was with her.*

GINO: *So they entered the ballroom and began to dance. "However," said the fairy, "when you dance with someone who asks who you are . . . 'I don't know' you have to say, 'I don't know!' At midnight on the dot . . ."*

FABRIZIO: *You have to go home. Leave immediately, eh! Uh, huh!*

ROSANNA BERNINI (age 6): *Uh, huh.*

GINO: *You leave, eh! Me too. Get into the coach and leave. Eh. So she arrived at the ball. There was a count who grabbed this lovely girl and danced with her. "Miss," he said, "tell me, how old are you?" She replied, "I don't know." "Well, where are you from?" "I don't know." [The children laugh.]*

GRANDMOTHER: *He wasn't able to get anything out of her.*

GINO: *At midnight she was dancing with the count, with this young man.*

All of a sudden she disappeared. Boh. *They did not see a thing.*

FABRIZIO: *Hah, hah.*

GINO: *This is strange. And she left. And returned home. The other two returned from the dance. They came back from the ball. Cinderella was already back tending the ashes. She was at home again. They said to her: "If only you could have seen the girl who danced with a young man . . . she was dressed so well . . . she was beautiful! But really beautiful! I've never seen anything like this."*

FABRIZIO: *Her sisters! It's that one, it's that one!*

GINO: *Yes, yes! Well! What do I care . . . what do I care. The next evening the same old thing. The next evening the same thing all over again. They go again to the ball. "You come along, too," they said, "so you can see that girl too, that beautiful girl, she's really something. Oh, come, come, come." "No, no, no. I'll not come. I'll stay here; I want to stay here." And so she stayed home . . . And after the sisters had gone, when they'd already arrived at the ball . . .*

FABRIZIO: *The fairy appeared again! The fairy came back. She dressed her up!*

ROSANNA: *Good! Good! And she went to the ball!*

GINO: *And . . . she began to dance again with the count. Virgin Mary! She was, she was, she was an eyeful for the count. And so during the evening . . . the usual words. "Miss, where are you from, you didn't want to tell me." "I don't know!" [Laughter.]*

GRANDMOTHER: *God screwed, then!*

GINO: *"I don't know!" And everytime he asked her something she replied, "I don't know." [children's laughter.] At midnight the same thing happened again.*

FABRIZIO: *On the road . . .*

ROSANNA: *. . . the road.*

GINO: *Along the road when she was climbing into the coach, she lost a shoe.*

ROSANNA: *The shoe . . .*

GINO: *And this count ran and found this shoe. No—Yes! He found this shoe and asked all the women who were at the ball if any of them had lost a shoe. One replied, "Not I"; another said, "No"; another said, "No." "Try it on and see who it fits. It doesn't fit anyone."*

ROSANNA: *No one!*

FABRIZIO: *Yes, yes, it's that one, it's that one!*

GRANDMOTHER: *The one you know, eh!*

ROSANNA: *It's that one [story]!*

GINO: *Eh . . . and so there . . . So then what did he do. He went . . . he went down . . . to that family, the one that knew something about the mystery of who the shoe would fit and who it wouldn't fit. He went down there saying, "But you, housewife, housemother," however he called her, "you have three daughters." She said: "Yes! I have three. Two are here but the other is always tending the ashes; she's there." "Try on this shoe, he said to the two daughters. "Does it fit?" "No." To the other daughter he said, "Oh, try it on." "No." "I'd be pleased if the daughter who takes care of the ashes would try it on too," said the count.*

FABRIZIO: *Just in case she would fulfill his eye! He put the shoe on her, and it fit.*

GINO: *It fit her, he said whoever the shoe fit . . .*

FABRIZIO: *Will be my wife!*

ROSANNA: *I'll marry her, I'll marry her!*

GINO: *And in fact he married her, she became the wife of a count and . . .*

FABRIZIO: *Rich.*

GRANDMOTHER: *And they married and had fun,*
 And of this to me they gave none.
 They gave me a tiny doughnut.
 In that little hole I put it,
 And now it's all gone.

[Laughter]

AF: *Listen here, didn't that fairy dance?*

GINO: *No, no, she disappeared.*

GRANDMOTHER: *Eh, the fairy disappeared.*

GINO: *She disappeared. She reappeared at midnight.*

ROSANNA: *Yes.*

FABRIZIO: *To take her back home.*

GINO: *To take her away. The . . . the fairy accompanied her.*

The basic structure characterized in the fragment of the preceding narrative is present in this story too. In addition, we can observe the presence of the fairy as the maternal figure (pertinent to Cinderella) who, besides making her into a beautiful woman, accompanies her to the dance and waits for her at the exit, but without participating in the ball, just like Tuscan mothers. Following the fairy's advice —not speaking to strangers, coming away at the right time—the heroine ends up marrying a man with a title, "and rich," as Fabrizio added to ensure the happy ending. "There are also counts without money," he explained to me later, laughing. The fairy finds a husband for Cinderella, the evil mother ends up like the mother in the story of one little eye and three little eyes, with her two old maids at home. It is interesting to note that the count goes to the family that "already knew" something and asks formal permission to put the daughters to the test. The mother suggests he try the shoe on the two daughters she wants to marry off. The count is allowed to test Cinderella only after her sisters have failed. In reality a similar order of preference existed for girls in a patriarchal Tuscan family. So it is that the characters in the story are obliged by the storyteller to follow the social rules of real life courtship.

It was at the end of the version proposed by Gino that Fabrizio— at seven years one of the youngest storytellers I have ever listened to—got the attention of the audience after having repeated over and over, "Can I tell it my way, can I tell it my way?" Finally his grandfather, recognized by his guests as host in charge of the storytelling session, gave his consent. The boy began from the beginning and narrated his version of Cinderella, which previously he had left hanging because he couldn't remember it.

FABRIZIO: *Once upon a time there was a man and a woman who got married. The woman . . . they had one daughter. Cinderella. It's almost the same one as he told. It's almost the same. They had one daughter, this man and this woman. The woman died. So he was left alone with his little girl. What did he do? He took another wife. And this one had two daughters. Those two stepsisters that he mentioned.*

GINO: *So there were three.*

FABRIZIO: *There were three. They come to three. And this . . . his wife was fond of her two girls, and her husband was fond of his own girl. However, he . . . the two of them were two and the others were three. What could he do? He went to work, and the others made his little girl clean the ashes out of the fireplace because they didn't like her.*

The others went out dancing. One day something happened, like you said. The fairy appeared. She made Cinderella beautiful. She called for a coach and sent her to the dance. Yes. And she sent her to the dance. Then . . . however, the fairy said, "At midnight on the dot you must come home because if not next time I won't make you beautiful and I won't let you go to the dance." When it was midnight "ding, dong!" The girl, when she heard the clock strike midnight, she ran! Waiting for her . . . waiting for her was the coachman with the carriage. She climbed in and away they went. And she went back among the cinders.

That night when . . . in the morning when she saw her stepsisters, they said to her: "Virgin Mary, there was a beautiful woman at the dance," like Gino said . . . "I would like to know who she was." [His grandmother laughs.] "Well," said Cinderella, "it certainly wasn't me. Because you always leave me here in the midst of all these ashes." And . . . "Well, then, you come this evening," said her stepsisters. "No, no, I want to stay here in the cinders with my little cat; it's fun, I play with it, I pet it, I cry . . . " and so on. The following evening, after they had left, the fairy reappeared; she made Cinderella beautiful once more and away she went. Virgin Mary!

GINO: *It's very similar, eh!*

FABRIZIO: *And she kept on dancing with this . . . no like you said in your story, it wasn't a count. It was a . . . king, the son of a king.*

GRANDMOTHER: *A king!*

AF: *The son of a king?*

FABRIZIO: *The son of a king. And so she said to him . . . and so he says: "Virgin Mary, but that girl there is a real beauty! I must see why it is that she disappears like that at midnight." And so he puts glue on the stairs. So naturally that evening when midnight came she left the dance, and naturally when she got to the last step where he had put the glue her shoe got stuck. And away she went. She didn't even stop to pick it up. She climbed into the coach and away she went. And she did the same as before. In the evening . . . the next evening the prince didn't see anyone. "Virgin Mary! Oh, what has she done?" And he found this shoe, the night she ran home. And he said, "Oh, whose shoe is this?" He tried it on everyone but it fit no one [he hits his fist on the table]. So then he sent . . . what's his name, he sent these . . .*

GRANDMOTHER: *The coachmen?*

FABRIZIO: *Not the coachmen. These . . . what did they call those men who went around with megaphones making public announcements . . .*

AF: *The town crier?*

FABRIZIO: *Town criers! He sent town criers around. And so they also went to this family and said: "There's a shoe . . . last evening it was lost! It was lost while she was dancing—whose is it, whose is it?" Everyone came to the door. And the town crier said to the mother, "It couldn't be yours, could it?" She tried it on; it didn't fit. She said to him: "I have two daughters. I can let them try it on. I have three. However, I'm not very fond of one of them. You can try it on them." "Yes, yes," he said . . . said the king's son. "However, I must marry whoever this shoe fits. Even if she's ugly I have to marry her." And so all three tried the shoe on, but it didn't fit.*

GRANDFATHER: *Eh, eh, eh!*

FABRIZIO: *Said the mother: "I also have this other daughter, another girl who is more pea-brained . . . as we say in Italian, she's always sitting in the cinders . . . she's all . . . she's all covered with ashes . . .*

GRANDMOTHER: *Yes, yes, but . . . all this bungling, wait till you hear what comes next. Go on, go on!*

GRANDFATHER: *Shut up!*

FABRIZIO: *She's all covered with soot. And you keep quiet! She's all covered with soot. She's all dirty. And so . . . [to his grandmother] you get me all mixed up!*

GINO: *Go on, go on!*

FABRIZIO: *And so he said, "Yes, yes, let's try it on her, too." When she tried the shoe on, it fit. "Eh," said the prince, "so then this is the shoe that fits . . . that fits that girl who came. Oh, how did someone who's so dirty . . . someone who's so dirty get so beautiful?" [He hits his fist on the table.] The prince sat with his mouth open and said, "I'll marry her." And so they left in the town crier's coach and . . . and went to the castle. And the king's son said to the king, "Father I have found my bride." Then the king said, "Well, when will the wedding take place?" "On such and such a day," he said . . . he said. And on such and such a day they got married. And the stepsisters all . . . all . . . all . . . not all . . .*

GINO: *Dirty?*

GRANDMOTHER: *Scared!*

FABRIZIO: *They were . . . not scared. They were . . . [he says excitedly] they wanted to be more beautiful than she was and so they put on some*

make-up, but they put on so much . . . they seemed to be wearing masks!
[Everyone laughs.] 34

FABRIZIO: *[He continues in an excited tone.] And so then they were so ugly.*
They got married . . . [slowly, in a lower tone] and . . . they went to
the king and lived in the castle happily ever after. 35

GRANDMOTHER: *My goodness, that boy! [She smiles, satisfied.]*

That's how Fabrizio got to "tell it his way." As the transcription
shows, his first attempt was interrupted as soon as the occasion
presented itself—at his first mistake—by his grandmother, who
was then his rival for the attention of the audience. The boy had
to resign himself and return to the rank of listener to prepare his
comeback. He immediately changed seats and went to sit near his
grandfather. He then began to make comments when the other
storytellers paused—thereby participating in the narration himself
—repeating that he knew and recognized the story being told. He
subsequently obtained our invitation to tell a story, with the formal
consent of the head of the house. He then told his story, replying
brusquely to his grandmother's interruptions, supported in this by
his grandfather and by Gino, who was happy for having been able
to tell his story and in particular because it had been well received
by us.

The three versions of the story had also brought about a unan-
imous stipulation: Fabrizio had begun by saying that his Cinderella was "the same, almost the same" as Gino's, who commented
halfway through the story ("it's similar"), even though both had
changed it in their own way. Annina's version, instead, was refused: "That's not it." Therefore, "who knew it straight," "who
told it correctly," "who knew it all" was established for the story
as well as in the other discussions of the *veglia*, while disapproval
was expressed by "What story are you telling?" "I never heard
it told like this," "You always want to tell stories your way!" The
basic narrative order of the stories had to be recognizable and accepted, an order that demanded a certain number of actors to guar-
antee the right degree of redundancy, and, with it, the appropriate
underscoring of the social *message* or *point*. Only by establishing
this order firmly could one embellish the stories with individual
details presented by the narrative inspiration and ideological bag-

gage of the storyteller. Fabrizio introduced the town criers who called the women with megaphones—perhaps using as models the dry cleaners or the haberdashers or the itinerant salesmen who came to his village every week, in old automobiles, and with croaking megaphones called all the women to their windows, calling them "ladies" like the criers in the story.

The version of Cinderella told by Fabrizio was liked very much by all, including Annina; her pride as grandmother subordinated her being upstaged by one younger than herself. So that evening she joined with us as we begged Fabrizio to tell us another story. After a sip of wine, which he drank ostentatiously, almost as if to show us that he considered himself on the same level as the adult storytellers inasmuch as like them he, too, had the right to "take a pause and have a drink," Fabrizio began again with a labored voice:

FABRIZIO: *Once upon a time there was a little house in the middle of the forest. A little girl lived there; her name was Little Red Riding Hood. One day her mother said to her, "Little Red Riding Hood." "What?" replied Little Red Riding Hood. "Will you go to see little grandmother? She's not feeling well. Bring her these pancakes and these apples . . ." "Yes," Little Red Riding Hood replied. [Here he imitated the maternal voice:] "But be careful because there is a wolf out on the road and he'll eat you!" "Yes, yes, mother, I won't stop anywhere." And she left with this basket and went to her grandmother's. Along the road she saw a meadow of little flowers and she stopped to pick them to take to her grandmother. All of a sudden out of the shadows came the wolf. "O Little Red Riding Hood . . . Little Red Riding Hood . . . good day, Little Red Riding Hood," said the wolf and . . . "How are you?" he asked her. "I'm fine! My grandmother is ill and so I have to go all the way up there in the hills to, how do you say . . . to take her these pancakes and apples." "Ah," said the wolf. "Shall we have a race?" "Yes!" "You take the short road and I'll take the long one." Instead the wolf took the short road because he wanted to eat the grandmother, and Little Red Riding Hood took the long one because she didn't want . . . because she wanted to get there later. And so away they went! They gave the signal and away they went. The wolf, zoom, zoom, in two steps, he got up the hillside. He knocked—knock, knock. "Who is there?" "It's Little Red Riding Hood! . . ." "Come in, come in my little girl, pull the string . . ." Naturally, the wolf pulled the string and entered and ate the grandmother. And she . . . I mean he climbed into bed. Ten minutes later Little Red Riding Hood arrived. Knock, knock. "Who's there?" said the wolf in a tiny voice.*

GRANDFATHER: *A feminine-like voice.*

FABRIZIO: *"It's your . . . it's your granddaughter," she replied, "Little Red Riding Hood." "Pull the string and come in." Naturally, she pulled the string and entered. And she went . . . and she sat down. Said Little Red Riding Hood: "Oh, what big eyes you have! How come, grandma, your eyes are so big?" "To see you better, my little one!" "Oh, what big ears you have, grandma! What have you done?" "To hear you better!" "Oh, grandma, what a big mouth you have!" "The better to eat you with!" Boom! He ate him . . . her and the basket. Mmmm. And he got into bed because he'd eaten so much his belly was full. Then a what do you call it arrived . . . a man came . . . what are they called?!*

GRANDMOTHER: *A woodcutter!*

FABRIZIO: *A wood . . . there was . . . no! A hunter who was out hunting birds up there in the what do you call it?*

GRANDMOTHER: *Rooks!*

FABRIZIO: *Hunting rooks! Up there in the mountains. And so . . . everytime he passed . . . he would stop and . . . and . . . knock at the door. He passed by and knocked at the door but no one answered. "Good heavens," he said, "maybe she's ill, maybe Little Red Riding Hood's grandmother is ill. I'll knock again." But nothing happened. Then he said, "I'll go in anyway." And he opened the door and saw this wolf. The hunter had a gun . . . bang, bang, and he killed the wolf. Then he cut . . . he cut the wolf's belly open and out came Little Red Riding Hood and her grandmother. And that's the end of the story.* [36]

In carrying out the task assigned to her by her mother, Little Red Riding Hood ends up in the jaws of the wolf, after having disobeyed her mother's orders to keep going without stopping. On the other hand, the infringement has a good side (that of gathering flowers for her grandmother). In addition, Fabrizio explained to me, "If her mother knew there was a wolf in the forest, she shouldn't have let Little Red Riding Hood go!" The mother is presented in a negative light. The series of lapses is interesting, the wolf is "her" and eats "him." That is, in the subconscious mind of Fabrizio, a female wolf eats "him," Little Red Riding Hood, masculine, putting him back into her belly. It's the hunter who frees "him" and "his" grandmother, and the hunter always stopped in at the grandmother's house just as Fabrizio's own father, who was also a hunter, would stop by to see his mother-in-law during his hunting trips. Fabrizio's mother also said to him occasionally, with the intention of showing him affection, "I love you so much that I would put you back into my belly."

These indications show clearly how the identification of children with the characters in stories could include characters of the opposite sex retracing, as in this case, the relationship of the child with both parents at a determined point of his psychological development. Such identification naturally depended on the individual history and personality of the tiny listeners. The adults could identify with the characters during the dramatization of crucial conflicts and complexes not completely or perfectly resolved in their psychological development. For the little girls, the young girls, and the women, there were the stories of girls who became beautiful and had dowries and ended up marrying the prince after having passed tests and tribulations and having defeated their jealous sisters, odious stepmothers, and incestuous fathers. Often the stories compensated the younger children for the disadvantages their role brought them in real life. Instead of marriage, some stories used as a happy ending the reunion with an image of the maternal symbol, as in the story of the shepherdess who remains with her little cow.[37]

As for the little boys, there were stories like the one about Buchettino (AT 327), in which the tiny hero got rid of the ogress by pushing her into the cauldron, and then of the ogre by inducing him to stick a piece of scalding iron up his rear end—a kind of phallic execution which the hero, and the little boys who could identify with him, weren't "able" to provide for or to imagine directly because they were still of prepuberty age.

Even the hidden dreams of the Tuscan Oedipus were able to come true through metaphors in some of the stories: here is an example from Giucco, a very popular tale, in a version which I heard from a man, P., about fifty years old, who lives in Vagliagli with his widowed mother to whom he is extremely attached:[38]

P.: *Then he said, "Look, we climb up to the top of that tree." "And who's going to get me up there,"* replied his mother. *"Who is going to help me climb all the way up there?"* *"Oh, I'll get you up there,"* he said. *He took his mother and carried her to the top of the tree up there, way on top. Then he came back down, grabbed the door, and went back up. And there they remained. After some time had passed, all of a sudden the assassins came. They said they had robbed a farmhouse. They had robbed some farmhouses.*

VEGLIATORI: *Oh, yes, yes, yes, yes.*

P.: *Keep quiet. And so they sat down right underneath the tree where the mother and her son were. There were three assassins and they began to divide the money. "This is for you, and this is for me, this is for you, and this is for me." The boy said to his mother, "Oh, mamma, if you only knew how badly I have to pee."*

VEGLIATORE: *And make poo poo.*

P.: *"But don't, they'll kill us," she said. "Listen, I can't hold it any longer. I've got to let it go." "It must be getting near daytime," they said. "The dew's falling, the dew is falling." After having peed, he said, "I've got to make poo poo, I can't hold it." He began to . . . to make poo poo and down it fell. "The honey is falling, the honey is falling." And they didn't move. "Now I'll make you move."*

VEGLIATORE: *He let the door fall down!*

P.: *"Oh, mamma, this door is awfully heavy for me," he said [laughter]. What do you think, he let that door go and it fell down, boom, boom, on top of the thieves! "It's the devil!" They left the money; they left the candle lit down there beneath the tree and away they went. The woman and her son climbed down the tree and grabbed the money. They had a small box and they put the money in it and took it away. "And now where shall we go?" she said . . . and . . . and . . . "Up . . . ," said the mamma. "Now we go home," he said. "We go home, we'll pick up and leave, we'll take a taxi. We'll pick up and go to Florence; we'll buy a car and drive around the world. You see how you make money! It's nothing like what you had put in the pot," said her son to her. "You see how you make money? This is how you make money. And you didn't want me to throw the door down and pee." [Laughter, everyone laughs.]*

In this story, too, one can hypothesize some references to the individual history of the narrator. When his father died, his two brothers decided to sell their small farm, which constituted the family's patrimony, and then they emigrated. The narrator complained, accusing his brothers of having cheated him, of having made an unequal division. In the story the assassins had robbed a farmhouse. Even though in the story there are three thieves, the money is divided into two parts ("This is for you, and this is for me, this is for you, and this is for me"), just as the narrator maintains his brothers had done in reality. In the story the hero, with whom the narrator perhaps identifies, clearly defeats the assassins (here we can recall the proverb, *"fratelli coltelli cugini assassini parenti tormenti"* ["brothers are knives, cousins assassins, relatives torments"]). They end up with, as in the folk saying, "damage, misfortune, and the door on top of them." He gets the money, the house, and the mother. He leaves with her for Florence, the exotic in his imagination—and from there with his own car he'll "drive around the world." The story satisfies the unrealized desires of the narrator, including probably the Oedipus complex that is not completely resolved in real life.

But the storytelling time, as in the stories themselves, was quickly passing by. To reawaken the children (and not only the children) from the conscious fantasies or from their more obscure subconscious ones, grandfather and mother called in brusque and peremptory tones, "Children, it's time for bed!" And so the first part of the *veglia* was over.

Seven to bed,
Seven under the bed;
In seven to bed we go
And in seven at home we remain.
Children, go to bed.[39]

To bed, to bed, said old Mark,
and those without a bed, go under someone's bed.
To bed, to bed, said the butterfly,
and those without a bed, go to sleep in the stables.[40]

3
Bedtime and Children's Folklore
"The Angel by the Bedside"

". . . l'angiolo la benedisse e levolla in pié, e fecele segno che a letto s'andasse; il che ella, volonterosa d'ubidire, fece prestamente, e l'agnolo appresso con la sua divota si coricò."

[". . . the angel blessed her and made her stand up, and signaled her to go to bed; which she, willing to obey, did quickly, and the angel then with his devoted one laid down."]

Boccaccio, *Decameron*, the Fourth Day, Novella 2

"Fantasima, fantasima che di notte vai, a coda ritta ci venisti, a coda ritta te n'andrai; va nell'orto a pié del pesco grosso, troverai unto bisunto e cento cacherelli della gallina mia; pon bocca al fiasco e vatti via, e non fare male a me né a Gianni mio . . ."

["Ghost, ghost who goes at night, you came with your tail turned up, and you will leave with your tail turned up; go into the garden at the foot of the big peach tree; you will find greasy grease and one hundred turds of my chicken; put your lips on the flask and go away, and do not harm me nor my Gianni . . ."]

Ibid., the Seventh Day, Novella 1

Folklore performed by adults for the "benefit" of children and folklore that children perform for each other present themselves as two different, sometimes opposite, bodies of lore. In such a strongly supervised social event as the *veglia*, there was no room for the latter, which consequently, while performed among the peer group of children, had a remarkable connotation of protest, like the folklore that Tuscan women performed in the absence of men. The "official" folklore for children taught them, in a remarkably straightforward and coherent way, the fundamentals of language, social structure, and social behavior.

The first question a child would ask, at the *veglia* or somewhere else, was *"Mamma, che è?"* ["Mother, what is it?"]. Folklore answered by showing the individuality of terms by stating the differences between things in the long formulaic rhymes. The second question would be *"Perché?"* ["Why?"]. And folklore answered by showing long chains of recited causal and contractual obligations that held together the world confronting the child. The third question would be *"Che vuol dire?"* ["What does it mean?"]. Puns and riddles with their performative context illustrated polysemy and metaphor.

In Tuscany—as elsewhere, as Sanches and Kirshenblatt-Gimblett have aptly shown[1]—the folklore of children (whether performed for them or by them) was instrumental in the acquisition of adult verbal art and of an increasing degree of syntactic competence.[2] With these, children would be able to conjoin, disjoin, and circulate through the different plans of the language they had to master and through the "forest of symbols" of the culture they had to discover.

For the children, the moment of abandoning the *veglia* to go to bed always came too soon and it was almost always accepted unwillingly; they did not like the idea of going to bed while the others stayed up making mysterious "grown-up" conversation and telling stories to each other, stories which were judged not good for them; in addition, the children had the sensation of feeling excluded from the group, and sometimes the fear of darkness kept them up.

The children's resistance depended on their individual character and fatigue and on the degree of permissiveness of the family. But almost always, after having mumbled a little bit, they had to resign themselves to accomplishing the final ceremony of the day: saying good-night to all the members of the family, beginning with the grandfather, the grandmother, and so on, making a general tour of the room and a hierarchical one of the family. The children exchanged a greeting with each person, often an embrace and a kiss. Then they left for their bedrooms *in collo*, that is, in the arms of their mothers. The more grown-up children went by themselves and these were the ones less easy to convince. In these cases the children could be convinced with good manners as well as bad ones, as for instance with the story of Petuzzo, a tale very common all over Tuscany: to the child who did not want to obey one would say: "Don't you want to go to bed? You just wait . . . You'll do as Petuzzo did." Then someone or the child himself would ask who Petuzzo was and the grandmother would begin the story:

Once upon a time there was a child who never wanted to obey. One day his father fell sick. And his mother told him, "Petuzzo, go to the orchard to get some cabbage because your father is sick."

"No, not me. I do not want to go!"

"Then I'll tell the stick to beat you. Stick, beat Petuzzo because he does not want to go to the orchard to get the cabbage because his father is sick."

"No, not me. I do not want to beat Petuzzo!"

"Then I'll tell the fire to burn you. Fire, burn the stick, because the stick does not want to beat Petuzzo, because Petuzzo does not want to go to the orchard to get the cabbage because his father is sick."

"No, not me. I do not want to burn the stick!"

"Then I'll tell the water to put you out. Water, put the fire out because he does not want to burn the stick, because the stick does not want to beat Petuzzo, because Petuzzo does not want to go to the orchard to get the cabbage because his father is sick."

"No, not me. I do not want to put the fire out!"

"Then I'll tell the ox to drink you! Ox, drink the water, because the water does not want to put the fire out, because the fire does not want to burn the stick, because the stick does not want to beat Petuzzo, because Petuzzo does not want to go to the orchard to get the cabbage because his father is sick."

"No, not me. I do not want to drink the water!"

"Then I'll tell the rope to fasten you! Rope, fasten the ox, because the ox does not want to drink the water, because the water does not want to put the fire out, because the fire does not want to burn the stick, because the stick does not want to beat Petuzzo, because Petuzzo does not want to go to the orchard to get the cabbage because his father is sick."

"No, not me. I do not want to fasten the ox!"

"Then I'll tell the mouse to gnaw you! Mouse, gnaw the rope, because the rope does not want to fasten the ox, because the ox does not want to drink the water, because the water does not want to put the fire out, because the fire does not want to burn the stick, because the stick does not want to beat Petuzzo, because Petuzzo does not want to go to the orchard to get the cabbage because his father is sick."

"No, not me. I do not want to gnaw the rope!"

"Then I'll tell the cat to eat you! Cat, eat the mouse, because the mouse does not want to gnaw the rope, because the rope does not want to fasten the ox, because the ox does not want to drink the water, because the water does not want to put the fire out, because the fire does not want to burn the stick, because the stick does not want to beat Petuzzo, because Petuzzo does not want to go to the orchard to get the cabbage because his father is sick."

Said the cat, "I'll eat the mouse, I'll eat the mouse!"
Said the mouse, "I'll gnaw the rope, I'll gnaw the rope!"
Said the rope, "I'll fasten the ox, I'll fasten the ox!"
Said the ox, "I'll drink the water, I'll drink the water!"
Said the water, "I'll put the fire out, I'll put the fire out!"
Said the fire, "I'll burn the stick, I'll burn the stick!"
Said the stick, "I'll beat Petuzzo, I'll beat Petuzzo!"
Said Petuzzo, "I'll go to the orchard, I'll go to the orchard!" [3]

"So you see that you too shall go," concluded the old woman. The story of Petuzzo was also told to children in other circumstances, as for instance "to amuse them," or it had to be learned by heart "to exercise the memory," as Giannini annotated at the end of his collection.[4]

In reality, more than exercising memory, the story of Petuzzo taught children, with characteristic insistent redundancy, the logic of contractual obligations. The narrative structure of the story is articulated according to a sequence of contractual obligations linked together.[5] The mother proposes to Petuzzo the first obligation, which is the primary one: to obey. This one takes the form of a service (to get the cabbage) that is motivated (the father is sick). Petuzzo refuses to fulfill the obligation, and the mother asks the stick for a second obligation, subordinate to the first one, justifying it by the nonfulfillment of the first obligation ("Then I'll tell the stick to beat you"). The stick refuses; the mother asks for a third obligation, subordinate to the first two and justified by the nonfulfillment of the second obligation and so on. Each nonfulfillment provokes the proposal of a new contract, till the fulfillment of the last one provokes a chain reaction of fulfilled contracts. At the end even the first and primary one is fulfilled: Petuzzo must obey and go to the orchard. To be noted (in the original text) is the use of suffixes maintaining a coherent metaphoric dimension of the terms: Petuzzo, *ortuzzo* [little orchard] (or in other versions the *tettuzzo* [little roof]), and the cabbage [*cavoluzzo*] are a triad of standardized terms reduced by rhymes to a childlike dimension.

Listening, repeating, and learning, the children could perceive that the world of their obligations was finite, organized, full, and complete. The nonfulfillment of any obligation created another, bound to the first one. The process can be prolonged and the refusals multiplied, but the logic-causal-contractual chain is omnipresent: there is no refusal which does not provoke another one; as soon as one of the contracts is maintained, the "total causality" provokes the fulfillment of all. So Petuzzo and the other children came to realize the consistency of the logic system of obligations immanent to their culture and the impossibility of escaping it by refusing the first obligation or multiplying the refusals. As soon as the cat ate the mouse, Petuzzo was forced to obey; once one subject in the cultural universe maintains its obligation, sooner or later everyone must follow. In Culture everything is held together.

Other formulaic rhymes do not deal with the conflictual situation but simply present a chain of requests and services performed. Such long rhymes were usually recited at the end of the child's day, after he or she had left the *veglia*, and were especially well liked by the younger children, who enjoyed, as do children from many other cultures,[6] playing with sound for its own sake, with words rather than meaning, with repetition and homophony. And, in fact, most of these texts are considered "nonsense," recited monotonously, structured in verses chained with a *ripresa* (a word at the end of a verse repeated at the beginning of the following one), and rhyming according to the scheme AA, BB, CC, etc., as in this rhyme, among the most common in all Tuscany, in which verses are alternatively tied by rhyme and repetition:

Cecco, Bicecco	Cecco, Bicecco
infilato in uno stecco	stuck into a stick
lo stecco si rompe	the stick breaks
Cecco va sul ponte	Cecco goes on the bridge
il ponte si rovina	the bridge collapses
Cecco va in farina	Cecco goes into flour
la farina si staccia	the flour is sifted
e Cecco si sculaccia	and Cecco is spanked

Later on in life, and after many *veglie*, the grown-up children would learn to appreciate, and often to perform, long series of octaves with a more complex system of rhymes and with a *ripresa* that would link two octaves instead of two verses by repeating concepts instead of single words.[7] Thus, Tuscan folklore was graduated from simple to more complex forms, progressively opened to the increasing competence of the group members. At the bottom of the scale, with Petuzzo, there was usually Mena Ciuffetta:

I went through a narrow street,
I ran into Mena Ciuffetta;
She asked me for the slice [of bread],
The slice I went to get it at the bread-bin;
The bread-bin asked me for the flour,
The flour I went to get it at the miller's;
The miller asked me for the wheat,
The wheat I got it in the field;
The field asked me for the fertilizer,

The fertilizer I got it from the ox;
The ox asked me for the hay,
The hay I went to get it from the lawn;
The lawn asked me for the sickle,
The sickle I went to get it at the blacksmith's;
The blacksmith asked me for the grease,
The grease I went to get it from the pig;
The pig asked me for the acorns,
The acorns I went to get them at the oak;
The oak asked me for the wind,
The wind I brought to the oak.
The oak gave me the acorns,
The acorns I brought to the pig,
The pig gave me the grease,
The grease I brought to the blacksmith,
The blacksmith gave me the sickle,
The sickle I brought to the lawn,
The lawn gave me the hay,
The hay I brought to the ox,
The ox gave me the fertilizer,
The fertilizer I brought to the field,
The field gave me the wheat,
The wheat I brought to the miller,
The miller gave me the flour,
The flour I brought to the bread-bin,
The bread-bin gave me the slice,
The slice I brought to Mena Ciuffetta.[8]

It is noteworthy that the protagonists of these stories are obedient without reward: Petuzzo brings the cabbage to his father; the protagonist of the other story brings the slice to Mena Ciuffetta after having performed eight other services. This shows that obedience was a moral imperative, an act to be performed per se, a concept above and beyond the system of exchanges that was the operational basis of social life in traditional Tuscany. Of course, disobedience was sometimes possible, but other children's rhymes exemplified in metaphor what bad consequences would fall upon disobedient children:

Three chicks walking around
run into the fox,

who was taking a stroll
glancing upon his newspaper.
"Good evening, lil' gentlemen!
and what are you up to?"
"Since mother went out,
we came out of the coop."
"Bravo! really, well done!
I want to shake your hand."
And all of a sudden he came close
and glu-glu- he ate them "live."[9]

Three chicks walking around . . .

My little informants, Francesca, age 4, and Giovanna, age 3, who recited this text for me, provided me with some explanations, energetically suggested by their mother: they were going to walk near her, "*per mano*," holding her hand, and not run away or across the street; more generally, they were going "to obey mother." Yet Francesca added some dissonant remarks to this induced profession of good purposes: "Anyway, the baby Jesus will protect me and guard me and heal me," thus prudently keeping the door open for some more independent behavior. The fact that this world is based on an obedience that has the sole reward of the absence of negative events does not seem too attractive to most Tuscan children I have studied. On the contrary, they have often recited to me with great gusto other folklore texts that express a dissociative attitude toward group norms. These were recited by children at play during the day, when they did not have such strict and omnipresent supervision by adults as in the *veglia*.

Such rhymes are aimed at such sacred figures as the Befana, the Epiphany, which an "official" text greets this way:

The Befana comes at night,
with her shoes all broken,
with her dress Roman style.
Hooray for the Befana!

My youngest informant, Giovanna, age 3 (photo by Paul Hoffman, San Francisco).

The children's countertext says instead:

> The Befana, smooth and sly,
> comes over and pisses
> and she pisses on her skirt.
> Ugly, dirty is the Befana![10]

More commonly, though, such contesting rhymes are related to toilet training. A counting-out rhyme goes

> Under the bridge of Baracca
> there is a child who is taking a shit.
> His shit is hard, hard, hard,
> and the doctor measures it.

He measures it up to thirty-three,
And-you-are-it! [11]

Once upon a time there was a little boy named
Cecco Rivolta who turned his trousers inside out.
He shat in his pants.
His mother yelled at him, and he, just
for spite, shat again in them. [12]

Cecco's rebellion is in any case reduced to spite, an episode of powerless anger which concerns more the possibility of the single violation than the problem of authority and obedience. Here, as elsewhere, folklore shows an ambivalence of content which proves itself to be a representative and meaningful system of basic cultural conflicts, more than a normative monolith that exclusively transmits leading cultural rules. [13]

Revenge against the rules connected with hygienic habits, which probably goes back to an underlying desire of revolt against those who produced such rules (culture) and imposed them (authority), is expressed in another rhyme coming from the area around Pisa:

Maria Teresa peed in the church;
the Priest scolded her,
and for spite she shat there again. [14]

In the versions of these jokes and rhymes recited by the adults, however, the conclusion, without exception, can be traced back to obedience or to punishment given for violation. Here is the ending of another Cecco in a version recited by an adult:

Poor Cecco, poor Cecco,
he has shat, he has peed in bed.
His mother has scolded him;
poor Cecco he fell sick,
he fell so sick so bad,
that poor Cecco has died. [15]

The fairy tales prevailing in the first part of the *veglia* were not the only folk texts for children. Sometimes between one tale and another there were pauses, so the male and female storytellers could rest, while a glass of wine, of sweet wine, was drunk or the roasted chestnuts were eaten. *Ditalini* were made for the children: that is, copper thimbles filled with chestnut flour were put in a row in the fire to heat; then later, when the chestnut flour was cooked to the right point, it was removed from the thimbles and put on the table. Sometimes refreshments were served in the interval between the first and second parts of the *veglia*. While for the children it meant the end of the evening, for the adults it was just a pause. During this time, children were posed riddles, often the same ones asked later on in the evening. The riddle in its essence seems to be a ritual question demanding a fixed answer, but in practice the answer is never deducible from the definition-question. Either one knew the answers or one did not. The riddle was applied to acquired knowledge and to memory, not the capability of articulating individual intelligence and the ability of discovering an answer not known before the question. One was not asked to know how to reason, but rather to learn how to remember.[16]

Only occasionally a meaning (A) in the riddle question corresponded to a meaning (A) in the riddle answer as in this example, which is simply hard to calculate:

Seven old ladies were going to Rome.
Seven bags had each one of them.
In each bag were seven nests.
In each nest were seven birds.
Figure out how many birds?
          [2,401][17]

Almost always, the meaning (A) in the question corresponded to a meaning (B) in the answer, which is plausible only because meanings A and B have some remote semantic relationship.[18] Comparative studies have indicated that riddles are especially found in cultures that emphasize role learning from authority figures, who usually perform direct oral interrogation,[19] exercising a rhetoric and arbitrary power based on prior access to arcane knowledge or more simply as in Tuscany, a larger cultural competence and a higher social or family status.

These riddles were directed to the children collectively by grandparents, parents, or other adults. The grandparents presented the

Grandpa and his audience of grandchildren before a *veglia* in 1913 (courtesy of the Falassi family).

riddles to those who were two generations younger than themselves, the adults to the children. The riddles generally directed to the whole group of people present at the *veglia* could also be addressed to a single person. Among the riddles I collected, many refer to familiar physical objects or natural phenomena:

I have a thing with many rings but is never a bride.
            [bell] [20]

At an ugly window
there's an ugly woman
with a loose tooth
and she calls all the people.
            [bell]

During the day they look at each other;
at night they kiss each other.
            [halves of doors]

Under the bed I've got a little white man who stands with a hand on
   his hip.
            [chamber pot]

The mother becomes skinny to the bone;
the son dances and grows bigger.
            [wood and fire]

Going down it laughs; coming up it weeps.
            [jug]

Guess this one: who has the belly in the back?
            [casserole and its top]

What is it that has an eye in its tail?
            [frying pan] [21]

One hundred sisters are sitting.
To each other they give to drink.
            [roof tiles]

I have a little tilled field; nor oxen nor plough has passed over it.
            [roof] [22]

I have a sheet that's all patched up; nor yarn nor needle have touched
   it.
            [cloudy sky] [23]

The more you take out, the more it grows.
            [hole] [24]

It is born with horns, lives without them, and dies with them.
[moon]

What is that thing that when working drags around its little bowels?
[needle and thread]

Green lawns, red rooms, black friars.
Who guesses it gets three forms.
[watermelon]

One cannot find it raw and one cannot eat it cooked.
[ashes] [25]

One eats it cooked, and one cannot find it raw.
[buttermilk curd]

It eats through the body and shits through the kidneys.
[planer]

Ruggeri is in the bedroom, sighing and weeping.
Be silent Ruggeri, for I cut you willingly.
[roast in the oven] [26]

All day long it is at the window and in the evening it goes away.
[button] [27]

You are a riddlemaker and you believe yourself to be one. Find me an
old woman who is one month old.
[moon] [28]

I've got a beautiful, beautiful hall
all walled in red velvet,
with all white armchairs made of bone,
and in the middle a woman dances.
[mouth, teeth, tongue]

Either seven or eight under an overcoat.
[orange] [29]

Filled pot up to the brim with four eyes and forty fingers.
[pregnant woman] [30]

Among various categories and different levels of reality, through the means of metaphors and symbolism of riddles, a circulation of meanings and definitions was realized. Pot meant woman, eye meant hole, body stood for wood, kidney for openings, tail for handle, sheet for sky, field for roof. The objects meant persons; organs of the human body were parts of objects; she who laughs and weeps is a jug; the person at the window is the button in the buttonhole; the sky is the mended sheet of the microcosm of those who asked or answered riddles.

Another peculiarity of riddles which shows such circulation among levels of meaning is one which embarrassed the collectors, especially in the last century. Giannini wrote, "Most of the riddles, Tuscan and non-Tuscan, while having an honest meaning, are rather obscene in form; therefore, I had to limit myself to a few."[31] More specifically, one could affirm that many lend themselves to double sexual meanings or seem to indicate an obscene answer, sexual or otherwise, while the correct answer is ostentatiously innocent, as in the following examples:

Blackie remains hanging; reddie sticks it in his ass.
       [cauldron and fire][32]

I have it and it's a beautiful one.
I have it under my skirt.
If somebody touches it, I'll throw it in his mouth.
       [pocket][33]

Madeleine lays down.
Clumsy is hanging around.
Rosie underneath
goes into Clumsy's ass.
       [chain, cauldron, and fire][34]

Hairy outside, hairy inside.
Raise your leg and stick it in.
       [woolen sock][35]

Go on a trail;
find a little black man.

Put his pants down;
eat him in a couple of mouthfuls.
[black fig] [36]

I'm back from Milan
with a thing in my hand.
If I find my love
I'll stick it into her hairy thing.
[comb] [37]

You stick it in hard,
you take it out soft.
[spaghetti] [38]

The Pope has it, but he doesn't use it.
The miss doesn't have it, but she wants it.
The lady has it and uses it whenever she wants.
The widow had it, but she lost it.
What is it?
[family name] [39]

Have you got something bony
to give to my hairy one [the ass],
something cooked between bricks [bread],
four berries from the backside [eggs],
the juice of band legs [wine; vines],
and a bit of the white of thighs? [milk, of animals] [40]

A nun is on a tree;
comes the wind and raises her tunic.
What nice things one can see on a nun!
[vine with leaves and grapes] [41]

Some riddles, starting from an openly obscene definition, arrived
at an answer ostentatiously clean:

Pot belly sticking out,
bird hanging out;
those who don't guess it
are real nuts.
[chain and cauldron] [42]

A little old man, in a little old field,
pulls down his trousers and shows his penis.
                [corncob]⁴³

I've got a penis one-arm long,
a testicle lighter than a pound.
Do you want it when I don't want it?
                [one-arm balance]⁴⁴

Little rockie who rocked, between his legs he protected it; so get it, go
    get the little knife to cut the piece that's hanging!
                [sprout of the vine]⁴⁵

The mother portrayed by Tuscan writer Fucini over one century
ago obeys the same logic. At the boring question, "O mommy,
what is the meaning of 'fornicate'?" the mother answers, "It's making the bread in the furnace," and as the child repeated, "What
did you say?" she replied, "It's putting it into the furnace."⁴⁶ Some
riddles come down from many centuries ago, like the following
ones:

Big and thick I would like it,
in flesh and blood I would put it.
The archbishop is so fond of it
that he holds it in his hand all night along.
                [ring]⁴⁷

I take it out small, I want it big,
the more it grows, the less I regret it.
                [spindle of yarn]⁴⁸

Other riddles present a similar but reversed construction: a clean
definition requires a dirty answer:

Before doing it one cannot have it,
and after doing it one cannot enjoy it.
                [shit]⁴⁹

It is born in between two mountains.
It lives without skin.
It dies singing.
                [fart]⁵⁰

It is born, it dies, one does not see it, but one smells it.
          [fart][51]

In this kind of text, to which all the children listened and which
they learned to decipher correctly, sometimes helped by a slap
("What are you laughing at!"), we find the reversibility and the
ambiguous circulation between the symbolic levels of the innocent
and the obscene, of the clean and the dirty. Consequently, the dirty
and the obscene became levels which were only a part of the general system of the symbols of semantics and of communication, not
a unique underlying level, privileged or excluded from the general
lexicon of signs, which showed itself coextended to Culture itself.
At the same time the performative aspect of "playing riddles" allowed one to speak and not to speak, to pronounce dirty or obscene
words, to propose tendential and malicious definitions—sometimes
emphasized by a look, a wink, a sign, or a half-smile—so that he
or she who proposed the riddle would not be stigmatized by the
group.[52] In their turn, those to whom the riddles were posed could
answer the sign given, or the smile of understanding, and then
give the innocent reply. Occasionally, there was someone who refused to play the game, ostentatiously breaking its rules. One evening Teresa asked us: "What is it that a woman has and that a
man has not?[53] Who knows the answer?" ["*Qual' è quella cosa che
la donna ce l'ha e l'uomo no?*"] The answer was the "kerchief" worn
by Tuscan women on their heads. Somebody giggled, but before the
right answer came, big Arturo bawled from the doorway: "It is your
goddamn pussy, women!" And he ran downstairs laughing scorn-
fully, as the indignant women called after him: "Big-mouth," "Foul-
mouth," "Ignorant," "Uh," and the men laughed.[54]

Besides being expressive vehicles that permitted emotional out-
bursts and didactic-cognitive statements which explained, taught,
and reminded of how to speak metaphorically, riddles and riddling also constituted a form of verbal strategy.[55] It was implicit that
whoever asked the ritual questions always had a privileged role in
comparison with those who were asked. In addition, many riddles
constituted real verbal traps through which the persons who recited the riddle proceeded to "capture *in verbis*" the person asked.
A typical strategy in this sense consisted in reciting a series of riddles to someone who did not know the solutions, concentrating on

one single person who became progressively embarrassed in front of everyone because he or she didn't know the answers. In addition to riddles which remained without answers, others were proposed, such as the following:

Green it is and green it remains.
It doesn't lose leaves, for it hasn't any.

[*Verde è e verde sta.
Non perde la foglia perchè non ce l'ha.*]

If the chosen victim answered, "The juniper," the person who asked corrected, "No, the cypress." If instead the victim answered, "The cypress," he or she was corrected, "No, the juniper." So the person who was asked was in the position of having given only a few answers, but wrong ones. When the person proposing the riddles decided the victim had been brought to the boiling point, he or she asked:

Solve the riddle,
who lays eggs in the basket?

[*Indovina indovinello
chi fa l'uovo nel corbello?*][56]

And as soon as the victim hurried to reply, "The hen," satisfied to have finally given a correct answer, the other added an insult in rhyme: "and shit in the mouth of who solves it, then." If the answer was "the frog," then the rhyming comeback was "that you may lose an eye"; if the answer was "the auger," then "that you may be debowled" was added; for "the bell," "shit in the mouth of whoever it calls"; for "the sword," "up the ass of . . . [name of person who answers] that it remained there."[57] The "trap," or catch, was also sometimes inserted in a tale. In Signor Donato's tale,[58] all the characters remained attached to each other; mouse, cat, maidservant, mistress, and Signor Donato. Each of them defecates into the mouth of the person or animal closest to him or her along the chain. "And Mr. Donato?" someone asked. "In the mouth of who asked to hear this story" concluded the storyteller in rhyme. In another tale, the storyteller asked the audience for help, pretending to forget a word, and when somebody suggested *vernaccia*, the storyteller promptly answered in rhyme: "And a prick up your ass, much good may it do you."

An example of the riddling used as verbal strategy to boost the "ego" of the narrator and destroy the listener was given to me by Fabio, a boy of eight, with whom I talked while I warmed myself in the corner by the fireside, one evening in December 1973:

FABIO: *How did you come here?*

ALESSANDRO FALASSI: *By motorcycle.*

FABIO: *I have one with a sidecar [referring to his father's motorcycle]; mine is bigger . . . ; can we play the game called "a cargo-boat has arrived loaded with . . . ?"*

AF: *O.K.!*

FABIO: *A cargo-boat has arrived loaded with W . . .*

AF: *Wine!*

FABIO: *No, window glass. A cargo-boat has arrived loaded with S . . .*

AF: *Stones!*

FABIO: *No, smokes. A cargo-boat has arrived loaded with T . . .*

AF: *Tiles!*

FABIO: *Yes. [He continues to make me make mistakes with turnips, wood, straw, books, sweaters.]*

FABIO: *A cargo-boat has arrived loaded with S . . .*

AF: *Smokes.*

FABIO: *No, salt!*

AF: *But before it was smokes . . .*

FABIO: *Eh, there may be some tricks . . .*

In this way Fabio established contact with me, a complete stranger —who was intruding and getting attention from his family—keeping me at the desired distance and in a subordinate position. His intentions were at once revealed at the opening of the dialogue with the comparison of the motorcycles. He asked me the question already knowing the answer, for he had seen me arrive from the window. After the series of riddles of which he accepted only one answer (perhaps to encourage me), he confessed that he used tricks without being able to explain to me later to what end this strategy was directed. "That's the way you do it" was the explanation after the performance. And successful it was in making me uncomfortable, to such a point that, before realizing it, I was counterattacking and even using metafolklore:

AF: *Now it's my turn. What is pink, attached to the ceiling, and makes a noise like "cri-cri"?*
FABIO: *A cricket?*
AF: *A cricket is not pink.*
FABIO: *An onion?*
AF: *An onion does not make any noise.*
FABIO: *What is it?*
AF: *An eel!*
FABIO: *Pink?*
AF: *I painted it.*
FABIO: *[He looks at me suspiciously.] Hanging from the ceiling?*
AF: *I attached it to the ceiling!*
FABIO: *But how can it make a noise?*
AF: *It would have been too easy otherwise.*
FABIO: *But that's not fair! [He looks at me annoyed.]*

This "anti-riddle," which is also traditional, emphasizes through paradox and joking the impossibility of giving "objectively" satisfactory answers to riddles.[59] The inadequacy of the formulation and the refusal of plausible answers, rejected arbitrarily by the person who presents the riddle, demonstrate the superiority of his role. Whether one answered or not, one always ended up at the mercy of whoever proposed the riddle, asked the question, and requested through the answer the support of and the submission to a cultural catechism and a structure of roles. Who recited the riddles would always affirm implicitly, "Here I am the one who asks the questions." One learned which terms were metaphors of others; those who decided which terms were correct in the metaphorical discourse were the same ones to whom the participants in the event (in this case those present at the *veglia*) assigned, ascribed, or granted the role of examining judge.

In the end the children were taken or accompanied to bed by the mother, who, seated on the bed or on a chair near it, helped the children to undress and to put on their pajamas or nightshirts, took the bed warmer out of the bed (there was always the fear that the children, doing it by themselves, would scatter the ashes or burn the bed), and then tucked in the covers and sang lullabies.[60]

The stereotype of the maternal figure has passed down to us the image of the mother bent over the cradle, in the sweet act of love. In fact the texts of the lullabies that the children then listened to showed motherly love as the prevailing element:

> Go to sleep, my little chicken-thighs!
> Your mother has made a skirt for you.
> She sewed it up all around.
> Go to sleep my little chicken-thighs!
> Go to sleep! If you sleep,
>   may your bed be made of violets,
> The mattress of soft down,
>   the pillow of peacock feathers,
> And the sheets of cloth from Holland.
> Close your eyes, and go to sleep![61]

Go to sleep, my little chicken-thighs . . .

The following lullaby offers the reassurance of unconditional and lasting motherly love and affection under any circumstances:

> And if the rooster should not crow,
> And if the bell should not sound,
> And if the day should not arrive,
> I'll still rock you round and round.
> Go to sleep, my love![62]

In the next lullabies the mother mentions other scenes of motherhood familiar to the child to make him or her fall asleep in a stable, well-balanced, and tranquil world:

May beautiful dreams come around you,
those which show Paradise to children.
The Angels of Heaven are your brothers.
You see them, your smile says it.

 Sleep, sleep, go nighty-night
 little treasure of your mother.
 The river runs, goes splish-splash,
 and the child is already asleep.

Flowers sleep, the birdie is asleep,
 butterflies are asleep, all is quiet around.
You sleep in your little white bed
and dream of your mommy's great love.

Star, tiny star,
The night is drawing near,
The flame is flickering,
The cow is in the stable,
The cow and the calf,
The sheep and the lamb,
The hen and the chickens,
Each has its own children,
Each has its own mother,
And they are all asleep.[63]

Star, tiny star . . .

But motherly love is not a one-string theme in the texts of Tuscan
lullabies. It is not rare to find allusions to the mother who is tired,
often having just finished a very hard day's work divided between
the fields and the house, as in the following lullaby:

Go to sleep, and sleep with God!
You go to sleep, so that I will too.
Close your eyes and go to sleep!

The baby is beautiful, and she belongs to her mother,
To her mother and her father too.
This baby was born at a good hour,
Born at a good hour, and may the hour be good,
The hour at which you were born, my love![64]

Another lullaby is more explicit in reassuring the children about a
noise that might have upset them:

It was the wind;
It blew down the pole.
Little child, go to sleep;
Your mother wants to sleep.[65]

In these last two texts, we see also another motif: the exhaustion
of the mother with a hard day behind and a hard day ahead of
herself. To tell the truth, the moment of birth was not always blessed
as is shown in these lullabies which show that maternal lore was
not the only motif in this folklore.

Nighty-night, nighty-night,
I was better off when you weren't here.[66]

Nighty-night, nighty-night,
Last year this child wasn't here;
And if he wasn't here this year either,
We would have gained some.[67]

I got married to get out of trouble
and now I got in much more trouble.
I got married to be on my own
and now instead of two there are three of us.[68]

This kind of lullaby sometimes constituted a vehicle sanctioned by
the tradition to express (and therefore to exorcise) antithetic and
potentially destructive feelings in respect to the group itself without
having openly and in first person to take antagonistic or heretical

positions in respect to motherhood. Lullabies were not only sung
in the intimacy of mother and child; sometimes they were sung in
the kitchen where the cradle was brought, and sometimes during
the afternoon gatherings when the audience was exclusively made
up of women. Lullabies could also be sung to babies who were
being cared for by an unwilling baby-sitter. In all these situations
antagonistic tendencies occasionally overwhelmed the maternal instinct and the repertoires of lullabies reflected these feelings:

Ninna . . . oh! Ninna . . . oh!
To whom shall I give this little girl!
I will give her to her aunt
And she will throw her away;
She will throw her into the square,
Where a beast has escaped from his lair.
Ninna . . . oh! Ninna . . . oh!

Go to sleep, may you die in your sleep,
That the priest come to take you to keep.
Ninna . . . oh! Ninna . . . oh!
To whom shall I give this little girl?
I'll give her to her mother.
A lullaby she will sing her.
To the boogeyman I'll give her.
For a whole day he will keep her . . .
Ninna . . . oh! Ninna . . . oh![69]

Ninna . . . oh! Ninna . . . oh! . . .

Evil characters are evoked in these texts: the boogeyman, "that
beast," priests. In other versions are found Sgaramagnao Blue-

beard, Marziale the assassin,[70] the little brass man, the grave diggers, the devil, the cat Marmione, the fairy Morgana, Father Capanna, the ogre, Penna, the bad black dog, the white dog, and so on. These are often the same "monsters" to whom, interrupting the storytelling, the narrator threatened sometimes to give away children who did not obey or who got into mischief.[71] Conjuring up monsters was common in both lullabies and stories, and many people have come to judge this as harmful. One century ago, Giuseppe Giusti, attentive collector of Tuscan proverbs and folklore, once wrote ironically, recalling his childhood, "Among the thousand things for which I am grateful to my father is the fact that he always took care that the maids did not amuse me with the usual fairy tales of frightening stories which call upon courage, as if we had courage to spare!"[72] This evocative characteristic of lullabies, as Cocchiara observed,[73] seems to be related to their religious-magic nature. It is possible that originally lullabies were magic formulas for casting spells away and putting curses on others, from which modern lullabies may have taken certain characteristics; for example, baby's name is never mentioned, evil creatures are invoked in order to exorcise them, and sleep is invoked from far away. "The Pisans are coming" or "the Pisans are at the door" is commonly said in Tuscany, meaning "sleep has come."[74]

However, it seems that this gallery of monsters is not meant primarily to terrorize children in order to obligate them to be good. To mention (thereby to conjure up) monsters gave form to the children's generic anxieties, transforming them into specific fears. The children, in this way, passed from the stage of not knowing what to be afraid of to that of fearing a specific creature to whom they might then transfer the conscious or subconscious fears they nourished for real persons. The fear of a specific being could easily be overcome by the presence of a reassuring, protective, and affectionate mother. Thus, if the process was carried out correctly, fears and anxieties were dispelled and the pacifying, soporific function of the lullaby was accomplished.[75] Here is a lullaby which demonstrates this process:

Nanna, oh, Nanna, oh,
To whom shall I give this baby away?

I'll give him to the boogeyman
Who will keep him for a day.
Nanna, oh, Nanna, oh,
To whom shall I give this baby away?
I'll give him to the Epiphany
Who will keep him for a week.
Nanna, oh, Nanna, oh,
To whom shall I give this baby away?
I'll give him to good Jesus
Who will keep him for a year or more.
Nanna, oh, Nanna, oh,
To whom shall I give this baby away?
To his mother I'll give him.
A lullaby she will sing him.[76]

In this way "good Jesus" balances out the boogeyman, as the mother balances out the Epiphany, which is sometimes represented as a fearful old woman by Tuscan children. The antagonistic feelings sometimes expressed in lullabies were not limited, however, only to the mother-child relationship. In the following well-known lullaby the wife-husband relationship is represented instead:

Ninna, nanna, mother is unhappy!
Daddy has fun, and mummy has none.
Daddy goes to the inn,
Mummy stays in trouble all the time;
Daddy eats stockfish,
Mummy suffers a whole lot;
Daddy eats cooked vegetables,
Mummy worries night and day;
Daddy eats the delicacies,
Mummy eats the leftovers.[77]

In other texts, if we adopt the psychoanalytic view, one could read an exhortation to the child so that he could grow up and neutralize the figure of the father-rival. Even if "that bad man" can easily be identified with any threatening male figure, the woman from Colle Valdelsa who dictated the following song to me was regularly beaten up by her husband, and it is probable that "the bad man" in her case was, in fact, her husband:

Go to sleep, my little baby
So that your arms grow big and strong,
So that you can tie up that bad man,
Go to sleep, my little baby.[78]

Monsters, however, were evoked with a grain of salt. In other texts
or in the same one, positive beings, such as protectors, saviors,
and other helpful figures, were also mentioned. In the lexical repertoire of figures familiar to Tuscan children, these protective geniuses
were the divinities of the Catholic religion and popular devotions:
the Holy Spirit, the Madonna, Mary, the Virgin Mary, Jesus, the
Christ Child, God the Father.

Sweet sleep come down from the sky and come,
Come on horseback, don't come on foot;
Come on horseback, on a white horse,
Where the Holy Spirit rides.
Come on horseback, on a fine little horse,
Where the Christ Child rides.
Go to sleep, sleep sweetly!
Mummy sings to you, and you, little child, sleep![79]

Go to sleep, go to sleep!
The Child belongs to his mother,
To his mother and to his grandmother,
To Jesus and to the Madonna,
To the mother and to the aunt,
To Jesus and to Mary.[80]

Go away, ugly black dog!
I don't want to give you my baby;
I want to give him to God in heaven.
Go away, ugly black dog!
Go away, ugly white dog!
I don't want to give you my baby;
I want to give him to the Holy Spirit.
Go away, ugly white dog![81]

Go to sleep, to sleep, to sleep!
To whom shall I give my baby to keep?

If I give him to the Epiphany
She will keep him for a week;
If I give him to the black ox
He will keep him for a whole year.
Go to sleep, to sleep, to sleep,
Put the baby to sleep!
Let him sleep in his cradle
With Jesus and the Madonna.[82]

Go to sleep, seven and two,
The baby has aches and pains.
The aches and pains will go away
And Jesus will help him.[83]

Comparing positive and negative beings we find that evil beings are abductors; they carry children away and keep them in captivity. The good ghosts bring the protection of guardian security and the gift of the good, restorative sleep. In this way the children's journey to their nightly rest took place under the guidance of a protecting mother with the help of benevolent deities and in spite of the threatening presence of frightening evil figures, just as in a traditional narrative with a child as protagonist, magic helpers, and opponents. The lullaby and prayer are closely related, and confirming this is the fact that often children were taught or made to repeat the "devotions" just at the time of lullabies, which, as the children grew up, they gradually substituted before falling asleep. For many generations of children, including my own post–Second World War generation, *veglie* ended with the laborious recital, phrase by phrase, of the Our Father, Hail Mary, Gloria, Apostles' Creed, and Salve Regina.[84]

Besides official Catholic prayers, there were also unofficial folk prayers which in their own way laid the foundations of the future devotion of the children:

Little pretty, pretty angel
with that curly hair,
with those eyes full of love,
My good Jesus I'll give you my heart,
I give it and I donate it,
My good Jesus forgive me.[85]

Raising my eyes to Heaven
I fell in love with Jesus,
I tried to climb up there.
He said, "Don't come;
Go to confession first
If you want to save your soul."
When I was confessed
I was called by a voice:
"Come, come, sinner,
day or night, any time!"[86]

The prayer learning was not without some rebellion, such as the time I heard a little girl begin to cry in anger, boredom, and despair, as she was made to repeat prayers imposed on her by an inflexible mother:

Ave Maria . . .
Ave Maria no!
Gratia plena . . .
Gratia plena no!
Dominus tecum . . .
Minustecu no!

and so on, refusing to pray and garbling the prayer with sobs. However, the prayer was recited and learned notwithstanding her constant refusal, rightly ignored by her "logical" mother, because "omnis negatio est determinatio": even the negative form constitutes an enunciation and nothing can be done on the level of the syntax of values—in this case, to refuse is to affirm and refusal does nothing to change the existence and the truth of the enunciate.

Essentially, the motherly role in the performative-communicative process of the evening lullabies was one of mediation. The mother evoked, enumerated, and qualified supernatural good and evil beings, concluding with the assignment of the children to the beneficent and protective deities, one of which, and in addition the only one physically present, was the mother herself. In this way the child belonged "to his mother" who then attributed him ("I'll give him") to the good beings, closing at the same time the performative aspect of the song and the ideological and theological system of the texts themselves. Just as in all the textual enunciations that were based upon dyadic logic, these lullabies articulated a system of oppositions inside which some choices were made.

Such a minimal dyadic base, the basis of the logic system of the culture of Catholic matrix, was rigorously enunciated in some lullabies like the following:

> Nanna yesterday, Nanna yesterday,
> And baskets are not hampers
> And hampers are not baskets
> And life is not death
> And death is not life
> And the song is already over.
> Nanna, oh, Nanna, oh,
> And the baby fell asleep.[87]

In this text one finds a series of propositions which distinguish pairs of terms according to the rules of logic: *A* is different from *B*; *B* is different from *A*. Lullabies like this deal with the theoretical basis of culture, exemplifying the concept of logical difference between two terms. The argumentative operations were in fact possible only on the inside of a cultural paradigm of terms, which were from the beginning distinctly separate one from the other; only then the syntax would have furnished the possibilities of relationship and articulation allowed and approved by the culture.

A longer series of opposites constructed in the same way comes from a nursery rhyme well known today and dating back at least to Renaissance times:

> One, two, and three!
> The pope is not a king,
> The king is not a pope.
> The snail is not a cochlea,
> The cochlea is not a snail.
> The spin is not a top,
> A top is not a spin.
> A Christian is not a Jew,
> A Jew is not a Christian.
> Millet bread is not wheat bread,
> Wheat bread is not millet bread.

A butterfly is not a cricket,
A cricket is not a butterfly.
A bed is not a stable,
A stable is not a bed.
Sugar is not candy,
Candy is not sugar.
Fat is not lard,
Lard is not fat.[88]

During the course of their *veglia*, Tuscan children were exposed to a series of folk genres which presented to them various ways of the workings of their culture and, in addition, a rather extended lexical repertoire of its values. All of this occurred in a dramatized form. Through the texts the children began to learn differences and oppositions, equivalences and metaphors, connections, disjunctions, and mediations. The narratives allowed them to invest all their emotions in specific and crucial situations and at the same time introduce them to the inescapable and omnipresent cultural logic of obligations and of roles inside of which they would have run the cycle of their whole existence.

The children had fun at the *veglia*; they were taught good behavior and learned "how to live," "how to stay in the world." With good reason Renaissance humanist Pontano wrote in the ninth lullaby of the lullabies he dedicated to his son:

Naenia Luciolum verbaque ficta iuvant.
[Lullabies and fantastic stories do help little Lucius.]

4

Courting in the Evening
"If You Want to Woo,
Bring Along a Chair"

"Ed ancora che d'Agosto fosse, postosi presso al fuoco a sedere, comincio con costei, che Nuta avea nome, ad entrare in parole."

["And even though it was August, having sat by the fire, he began to talk to her, whose name was Nuta."]

Boccaccio, *Decameron*, the Sixth Day, Novella 10

"Dicendo che al suo contado tornar si voleva e quivi consumare il matrimonio, chiese commiato al Re."

["Saying that he wanted to return to his countryside, and there consummate the marriage, he asked leave of the King."]

Ibid., the Third Day, Novella 9]

After the children had been put to bed by their mothers, the young people came to life. It was generally at that time of night that one sang *stornelli* and *rispetti*,[1] monostrophic love songs, which whether originally Tuscan or not were most popular,[2] mainly because they were tied to daily courting rituals and expressed the various stages in the development of a love without being too explicit or causing embarrassment. On the one hand, the singers managed to express their feelings and show off their singing ability or poetic qualities of improvisation, while, on the other, they were able to pretend to sing without reference to the sentimental situations of those present, because the *stornello*, or folk song, "goes like this."

As in many other genres of folklore, love songs acted as impersonal carriers of very personal communications.[3] For those in love, Tuscan musical folklore provided a code of communication, some established texts, the possibility of improvising others quite easily, and the opportunity to communicate one's feelings without exposing oneself to the immediate disapproval of the "guardians" of etiquette and moral rules.[4]

The *veglia* was a regular and prolonged social occasion during which the young could meet legitimately. Courting and the general social integration of the young were carried out in the presence of chaperons. One had to speak metaphorically so as to avoid even the most benevolent disapproval. There was also the problem of not making a fool of oneself in front of one's peers. A young man who publicly drew a blank with a girl was exposed to the sarcasm of his friends; moreover, other girls could then retort that "they did not want those rejected by others." Therefore, one always tried to "tread softly" by first testing the girl's intentions very cautiously. The girls were careful in their replies to the young men; they tried to "throw them off balance" and make them speak clearly and openly.

Courting by singing often started during the day, in the open, when the young were working in the fields or walking in the woods with the animals. Sometimes the young people even climbed on trees, so that their voices could be heard from farther away:

And the wheel turns and spins.
From the top of the hill one can see the sun,
And there are young girls,
And there are young girls,
And the wheel turns and spins.
From the top of the hill one can see the sun,
And there are young girls
With young boys talking about love.[5]

Before speaking openly, they sang, and the man was the first to start, often with a compliment:

You have eyes as black as pepper,
Lips as red as the cherries.
May God make you good; cause beautiful you are.[6]

And also:

O God of Gods,
You seem the most beautiful to me.
Oh, how dear you are to my eyes.[7]

Every night you come in my dreams,
tell me beautiful one why do you do it,
tell me beautiful one why do you do it
and who comes to you when you are asleep.[8]

Brushwood flower,
What pretty little feet, what a lovely gait,
What a beautiful little girl with great refinement.[9]

Sometimes the singer was more poetic:

When you were born, a garden was born;
one could smell it from far,

one could smell it from far,
especially the smell of jasmine, and even the earth started trembling.[10]

When you were born, a beautiful flower was born,
The moon stood still,
The stars changed color.[11]

Or more daring:

You have the black eyes [or brown, blue, green, etc.] of a fairy,
You attract lovers like a magnet,
And you are born, O beautiful one, to make me die.[12]

Sometimes the song constituted an explicit declaration:

Little flower,
You lovely thing, I am in love with you.
You lovely thing, I am in love with you.
I would give my life for a kiss from you.[13]

Little flower . . .

To this type of song, often sung within hearing distance of the
girl, she replied by serving the singer with the same sauce, and
often with a refusal, which put down the category to which the
suitor belonged:

Lily flower,
I do not want a peasant as a boyfriend,
I want a man from the city; it is nicer.[14]

Sometimes the woman sings, seriously or jokingly, about her desire
to marry a factory worker and change status:

> I don't want a peasant, I don't want to cut grass,
> I don't want a bricklayer, I don't want sorrows,
> I don't want a gambler who'll win or lose,
> I want somebody working at the Ginori factory. [15]

More often, the stereotyped refusal was sung even if the young
man was to her liking. By doing this the girl showed that she was
not one of those who would flirt with anyone:

> I do not listen to the young men of today,
> They vie with each other in making fun of girls. [16]

Or the classic:

> Men are false and deceitful,
> They have only one soul yet a hundred hearts. [17]

Or else:

> Pear blossom,
> Pears are good and the peels are sour,
> Pears are good and the peels are sour,
> Men are false and women are sincere. [18]

Another one:

> Clover flower,
> Young lad you are mistaken,
> Young lad you are mistaken,
> The grass of want has not yet been sown. [19]

In other replies there was a tone of open challenge, a malicious
note, and a warning not to underestimate the girl:

> Flowering peaches,
> I have made fun of nineteen lovers,
> I have made fun of nineteen lovers,
> And if you are teased as well, that will make twenty. [20]

In the fields, the vineyards, and the woods, one could hear voices resounding and rebounding.[21] Naturally, this type of singing required that one be in the right place at the right time. There are many songs inviting the girl to the fountain, the meeting place of all traditional cultures:

> Flower in the shade,
> Pick up your jug and go to the fountain
> And I'll wait for you there, shining star.[22]

> Apple blossom!
> Come to the fountain; I shall speak to you
> And love's sail will rise.[23]

Other songs give credit to the fountain's function:

> To the water, to the water, to the new fountain,
> Who does not know how to make love, learns there,
> And who is without a lover, finds one there.[24]

> And little brunette, my little brunette,
> If you take your pitchers and come along
> We shall go to the fountain together,
> We shall go to the fountain together.
> And little brunette, my little brunette,
> If you take your pitchers and come along
> We shall go to the fountain together,
> And we shall be able to speak about love.[25]

Before accepting a similar invitation, the girl could ask the singer on the other hillock to give his name, address, and so on, pretending not to have recognized him:

> In the middle of the sea I cut myself,
> A little fish said, "Ouch!" to me,
> I hear your voice, and I do not know who you are.[26]

Sooner or later, the girl might agree to meet the young man at the village fountain. Many of my female informants confessed to me that they often emptied their water jugs in the sink, behind their

mother's back, so as to have an unquestionably legitimate excuse
to go out and fill them up. "So much water in my house has never
been consumed as when I was having an affair with Vitaliano."
Even the acceptance of the invitation was done metaphorically. Two
of the most common songs of assent are:

> Little flower,
> of all the flowers that will blossom,
> of all the flowers that will blossom,
> the flower of my love will be the most beautiful.[27]

> I want to love you as long as the world is world,
> until stones will start flying in the air,
> until they will find the bottom of the sea.[28]

As one can see, these folk songs may appear to have very ambiguous meanings, but when I asked my informants how they could
be sure that the song's message had been understood, they all replied: "Make no mistake. Those who want to understand, understand!" "A word is enough to the wise!"[29] In any case, if she
wished, the girl could be even more explicit:

> When I see you appear on the hill
> I fall in love with your gracefulness,
> Your beautiful eyes are the death of me.[30]

Or even risqué:

> I'm born for kisses and those I want,
> like people in love exchange them.
> I want them on my lips and on my hair,
> then I close my eyes and wherever they go, they go.[31]

> Don't send me kisses by mail anymore
> Since on the way they lose their flavor.
> If you want to give them to me, give them in the mouth
> So you'll taste what love is.[32]

Apart from toiling in the fields and journeying to the village fountain, other opportunities for preliminary meetings were furnished

I'm born for kisses and those I want . . .

by mass, fairs, and balls. Fairs took place about once a month in the villages, and practically all the families of the surrounding country-side came along.[33] While heads of families, agents, and middlemen were doing business, the young inspected hawkers' wares, listened to storytellers, watched puppet shows, and got to know young people of the opposite sex. Young men also went to the fairs to eye the girls,[34] and vice versa. The bolder men struck up conver-sations at lunchtime while eating on the grass (very few were "nap-kin people," who could afford to eat in *trattorie* [small restaurants]) or when strolling around the village. The young men and women went around in separate groups. One "strayed" only rarely to be able to meet more privately. Very subtle passes were made in order to escape the attention of parents or even friends and to gain, di-rectly or indirectly, such basic information as "to whom they [the girls] belonged" and where they lived. The same activity took place in the church square on Sunday mornings after late mass, which one most often attended to have a look around and to be seen. The same thing happened on a smaller scale at the afternoon re-ligious functions. Women who wanted to display their virtue went to the early mass to avoid even the modest worldliness of the late mass. Famous couples like Dante and Beatrice, Petrarch and Laura were known to have exchanged amorous glances in church or after the service; criticism or praise of a woman's behavior in church is widespread in the literature of the elite as in folklore.[35] Some *stornelli* sung in the evening ironically or sarcastically refer to such moments:

When you go to mass
you keep your book in your hands,

you glance at your boyfriend
and he glances back at you.[36]

Little chap with the black hat
Which you hold in your hand while walking in the church:
My little chap, be less vain![37]

The following is more biting and speaks about a girl with an artificially "fortified" bust:

O little girl with the boots
Up in church you tap your heels;
You're showing a lot of tits
But they're not yours.[38]

In church, in the church square, or in religious processions one
could always meet up with friends. This occurred also on solemn
feast days and those dedicated to patron saints. During the processions the women were grouped together and the men "behind, with
the band," but when the procession had reached the far end of
the village, it made a U-turn, so that one could pass alongside and
exchange glances during that occasion as well.

In this way, before meeting up in the evening, the young men
and women could look each other over, get to know each other,
and speak to each other in public and private. For this reason, the
evening songs started once again, or continued, the lines of "an
old story" which the girl often insisted should be furthered at the
veglia in front of her family:

Little jujube flower,
If you want to make love, bring along a chair.
The stones are slippery in the woods.[39]

Beneath the window there is mud;
Do not come along with silk shoes.
If you want to make love, come inside the house.[40]

To go *a seggiola* was the common way of saying "to go courting
in the evening." In fact, when one went visiting neighbors' homes
in the evening, one took along a chair to sit on (children had a small

chair or stool).[41] If the "boyfriend" had come a long distance and without a chair, the girl could "save the place" next to her. A very well-known *stornello* speaks about this custom, which was a demonstration of affection:

> And when you used to come to my home,
> The best seat was yours.
> Now that you no longer come, I have given it away.[42]

> Flower in the lawn,
> I kept your place for a while,
> I kept your place for a while,
> You didn't come and I've given it to someone else.[43]

Conversely, a girl could accuse a young man of having changed seats in order to sit near another girl, which was interpreted in the system of folk sociometrics as a betrayal (GG 209).

The first songs of the evening sometime talked about greetings and often repeated the greeting gesture that the couple made when arriving.

> I bid you a good evening with a song
> And I greet you, silver palm,
> That amongst other beautiful ones are most beautiful.[44]

Other songs, in sextets or octaves, provided the reply which the girls could choose to sing:

> You are as welcome, O young man,
> As the weekly feast day;
> You are more handsome than a lily of the valley,
> Your woman may be proud of it.
> If I were her, I would be proud
> To have such a handsome man, despite my ugliness.[45]

Stornelli were often sung in alteration with *rispetti* and octaves. The singer could show to whom the song was directed by looking at the person in an eloquent way before, during, or immediately after the song;[46] sometimes this was declared in a loud voice—rising up from one's seat, "This is for you, Zaira"—depending on whether the song contained a public or private message. Looking over collections of popular Tuscan songs, it is easily recognizable that their contents cover without omissions all the possible situations of courting and love.

At this point in the *veglia* all the young present could ask questions, give answers, accuse each other, justify themselves, and declare publicly or privately their sentiments. Besides reciprocal complimenting of each other (one could also say *"farsi i rispetti"* [*"rispetto* equals respect"] and declarations of "kindness and beauty" of the man or the woman, songs often had binding counterpropositions:

I am more fond of you than my own mother.[47]

was the closing line of various *stornelli*. Another went like this:

I want to love you until the end of the earth.[48]

At other times the girl could take the initiative, even complaining to him and accusing him of very little daring:

In Rome they have given us a new Pope.
The world turned around in the other direction:
Now it is the woman who has to make declarations to the man![49]

In fact, indecision could lead to unexpected preventive replies:

Little chick-pea flower,
You have been boiling for a long time and yet never cook.
From now on it's all well understood.[50]

Or:

Young man going to spend the evening out,
Tell me for whom you feel passion.
If it is for me, you are mistaken.[51]

Sometimes coded messages were more complex. Palmira told me that, when she was young, she and a suitor quarrelled. So someone else starting courting her and visiting her regularly in the evenings. She neither encouraged nor discouraged him so as to convince her "boyfriend" that she was interested in making peace, and quickly so. When a reconciliation took place, he took to visiting her in the evening once again. Now there was the problem of her other admirer, who was also there. Having fixed her gaze on the latter, Palmira sang:

> I had a green horse and joy,
> I used to keep it tied up in a field
> And slowly the rope became knotted.
> The heart returns to where it is in love.[52]

I had a green horse and joy . . .

The effect was immediate; the first wooer smiled at her from the corner in which he was sitting. The other rose suddenly, made for the door without saying good-bye, and never came back again.

However, the refusal was not always accepted in holy peace; and so one passed from *rispetti* (respect) to *dispetti* (spite), and from love songs to squabbles or "stings." The dialogue became disputation and a verbal duel following the typical pattern that included all the resources, subtlety, and malice of the proverbial Tuscan sarcasm (one of the best known *stornelli* ends with "we all have the art of mockery").[53]

> O little girl with the beautiful eyelashes,
> All passersby compare you to an angel.
> Everybody wants you but nobody takes you.[54]

This is one of the most common *stornelli* and was sung by a certain Baroncelli (one evening in Staggia in January 1974) to a girl called Gilda who, apart from him, had refused several suitors. Gilda did not lose her composure and replied:

Why do you come visiting in the evenings
If you have a lady friend?
You are wearing out the soles of your shoes.

Gilda in fact was right because Baroncelli was "half involved" with a girl in Salivolpi. Baroncelli did not turn a hair and immediately answered back:

I come when I feel like it.
I am not forbidden to come here.
You're not the one who pays for my shoe soles.

So she, with a malicious smile, looking at Baroncelli's shoes, which were badly worn at the heel, countered:

Weather, don't rain,
Baroncelli has weak shoes.
He hasn't got the money to buy a solid pair.[55]

That exchange ended in a jovial fashion. But in other contexts one could be really insulting. Here are some choice examples:

You have acquired yourself a little woolen dress,
You first wore it for the nine-days functions,
And you're the raggediest old woman in the village.[56]

You have acquired yourself a little woolen dress . . .

Pea flower,
I found you amongst a lot of parrots.
You are all pecked by birds.[57]

Flower that has been born,
It is useless for you to paint your chops,
It is useless for you to paint your chops,
Your raggedly old face cannot be hidden.[58]

You have acquired a tulle dress
To cover the hump on your back,
To cover the hump on your back,
You are ugly, badly wrinkled, and covered with blisters.[59]

"Ricotta-cheese" flower,
Your mummy when making your mouth
Took the measurements from an old slipper.[60]

Little flower,
You have black eyes, a yellow face,
And he who marries you will get a bad deal.[61]

Sometimes, to gain incisiveness, the *stornelli* were sung in sequence
without refrain:

But go jump into the sea
with the express train if you want to please me,
jump more than 100 meters under
since nobody is keeping you from doing it.

But go jump into the sea . . .

And when I'll have read it
in the paper, you know what a big sorrow!
I'll eat a steak,
I'll drink a glass of wine, seven of punch, and a coffee.

And I carry in my pocket
a good knife, all ready to cut,
to cut the heart to you
If you leave me, asshole you and your mother.[62]

Or else one would sing an appropriately antagonistic refrain:

And I'd like to see you fried in a pan,
especially your shoulder bone,
especially your shoulder bone,
the liver, the hip, and the bowels.

Bren, bren, bren, I can stay away from you.
Bren, bren, bren, I can stay away from you.

In my window there's a brick missing,
why do you come around, son of a bitch,
why do you come around, son of a bitch,
since for you I've got no passion.

Bren, bren, bren, I can stay away from you.
Bren, bren, bren, I can stay away from you.

Born of a vile person, blood of a snake,
don't gossip about me, you no-good,
don't gossip about me, you no-good,
anyway I'll keep my honor anytime.

Bren, bren, bren, I can stay away from you.
Bren, bren, bren, I can stay away from you.[63]

The impact of similar types of *stornelli* is not easy to evaluate without knowing the contextual situations, but there were times when it was extremely serious. Rubieri reports that in March 1815, at Antella, the seventeen-year-old Enrichetta Micheletti, "abandoned by

And I'd like to see you fried in a pan . . .

her lover, was so badly stung by the *stornelli* that were thrown at her by either fortunate rivals or jealous suitors that she tied a stone to her neck and drowned in a washhouse." [64] Tiffs also took place among those of the same sex. In this case the songs could reflect the competition between two or more men in acquiring the graces of a woman, or that of girls interested in the same man:

> Lupin flower,
> There were four of us dreaming of the same man,
> There were four of us dreaming of the same man,
> And everyone was drawing water to her own windmill. [65]

In the songs one could also make accusations:

> Blossoming spike-lavender,
> Don't you remember the kisses I gave you?
> Don't you remember the kisses I gave you?
> You behaved like Judas and betrayed me. [66]

> You wounded my heart with stinging nettle
> and made it bleed all over.
> To stay with you, one must really suffer,
> because you are so phony in your speech. [67]

And the reply:

> Dittany flower,
> You were my first love and you will be the last,
> You were my first love and you will be the last,
> And one can say this is legitimate love.[68]

At other times the accused could admit his responsibility and affect nonchalance:

> When I came to see you I did it as such
> And not because I wanted to make love,
> And not because I wanted to make love,
> I did it so that I could pass an hour with company.[69]

And the other could answer back:

> The grass in my garden has yielded hay;
> If I was fond of you I wouldn't have left you.
> I have always kept you as a "filler."[70]

In these popular songs there were also references to ends of romances. In such circumstances one usually chose to appear nonchalant and detached; in this way one could also show availability to accept new relationships:

> Yesterday evening my girlfriend left me,
> This evening I'll eat with more appetite,
> Tonight I'm going to have a relaxed sleep.[71]

> When you left me, I cried,
> I dried my eyes with my white handkerchief;
> As soon as you were out the door, I laughed.[72]

> Straw flower,
> And you thought to lead me by a bridle!
> By a bridle one leads a mare.[73]

> And you tell everyone I'm yours!
> Tell me, at which fair did you buy me?
> Dig a hole and jump in it.[74]

> When you were coming to make love
> you were saying I didn't know how,
> you were saying I didn't know how,
> now I learned and I won't go back with you.[75]

"Love without quarrel molds" says a proverb that undramatizes lovers' quarrels. Both in real life and in the *stornelli*, reconciliation usually follows:

> Little flower,
> Let me sing as I am happy,
> Let me sing as I am happy,
> I have made peace again with my love.[76]

The family often obstructed these romances promoted by courting in the evenings. In traditional Tuscany, at least in more recent times, the interference of the family or more exactly of those with the *patria potestas* was shown not so much in the direct choice of husband or wife for their sons or daughters but, above all, in the practice of their powers of veto.[77] Instead of trying to bring about marriages, much more time was spent on preventing those judged as being inconvenient or inopportune for some reason, maybe the "family name" or the personal qualities of the prospective husband or wife. Thus, there were people who had to sing:

> Flower of garnet,
> It's not my fault if I left you,
> It's not my fault if I left you,
> It was my mom, she didn't go for it.[78]

> Dear little brunette [or blonde, or Beppino, etc.] I cannot love you,
> Because my parents are not happy about it.[79]

Other folk songs were addressed to those opposing the relationship, especially to future mothers-in-law, as in these *stornelli*:

> O mother-in-law do not get angry;
> Your son will not have me;
> And even if he'd want me, I will not have him;
> I don't want to disturb the family.[80]

I went to the woods to make firewood
to burn my poisonous mother-in-law.
When she starts, she never stops!

Or this refrain:

And spin and turn
My mother-in-law is a snake.
If she'd get a stroke
she'd stop bitching.[81]

And before, you were coming with the rain or the winds,
Now you don't even come when the sun shines.
Since your parents are not happy with it,
We won't be able, dark-haired one, to make love.[82]

Another example:

And my mother doesn't want me to love you,
Make her happy and don't come here anymore.[83]

A common refrain goes like this:

Mummy doesn't want it nor does daddy,
What are we going to do, what are we going to do,
Mummy doesn't want it nor does daddy,
How are we going to be able to make love.

Daddy doesn't want,
Mother neither,
I've cried so much
and Heaven knows it![84]

However there were folk songs with a more optimistic content:

Mummy doesn't want it and daddy is thinking about it,
Patience is needed, patience is needed,
Mummy doesn't want it and daddy is thinking about it,
One needs patience to make love.[85]

Another one goes like this:

> My parents aren't happy, nor are yours;
> Tell me, beautiful, how much do we love each other?
> Let's love each other wholeheartedly; we'll win.[86]

Opposition was sometime overcome through the mediation of a priest or matchmaker or through the perseverance of the young couple. But, on other occasions, it led to the breaking off of relationships, recriminations, or other melodramatic threats:

> Miserable parent, what do you think about it?
> Don't you want to give your daughter to me?
> Don't you remember your past life?
> Didn't loving seem sweet to you?[87]

> Treacherous parent, what do you think about it?
> Why don't you want to give me your daughter?
> I want to do the slaughter of the innocents,
> The test will be made with my dagger.[88]

Sometimes the young man in love, as proof of his good, honest, and unselfish intentions, declared that he wanted the woman and not her dowry, as in this old *rispetto*:

> And what have I done to you, evil widow,
> To have made you decide not to give your daughter to me?
> I have asked you for neither fields nor vineyards
> And not even a pair of oxen to work for me.
> I have asked you for neither silver nor gold,
> Give me your daughter or otherwise I shall die.
> I have asked you for neither gold nor silver,
> Give me your daughter and I shall be happy.[89]

Other folk songs threatened drastic solutions, such as eloping:

> And if my [your] parents are not happy,
> We can take a little gig and go to Pisa,
> Up to the high altar and we get married.[90]

Fir tree branch,
If you don't give me your daughter,
If you don't give me your daughter,
I shall marry her in a wood without a priest![91]

Despite such bold intentions, in real life very often the girls replied in the same way as the girl in Gradi's novel: "I shall stick to what my parents wish me to do,"[92] and married, as in the last line of the folk song:

When mummy and daddy will be happy.[93]

Whether the couple made "love in secret," or "love at home," or had done the *toccamano* (that is, the explicit agreement between the families with the official engagement and the choice of the wedding date), the couple almost always had to undergo the test of a journey on his part and the consequent separation before the marriage took place. The departure could be caused by various reasons and the young man could stay away quite a long time. The most common circumstance was military service. In many folk songs the women lamented that "my lover has gone under the flags."[94] Sometimes this was the lament:

Victor Emmanuel, what are you doing?
You want all the best of the youth,
And what will you do with the old ones?[95]

Folk songs expressing men's farewells were very popular:

Good-bye, good-bye, good-bye,
Beautiful little brunette, good-bye!
And before leaving
I would like to give you a kiss!
A kiss for my daddy,
A kiss for mummy!
A kiss for my beautiful
And then I'm going to the army![96]

Other journeys were made to Maremma, Casentino, north Africa,

From the front in World War I, a war picture sent to a fiancée (courtesy of Vanna Bianciardi, Brussels).

From home, a 1930 portrait in a romantic mood "for your eyes only" (courtesy of the Biblioteca Comunale degli Intronati, Siena).

European countries for working purposes, and farther afield, even America. Seasonal and temporary emigrations caused by a necessity to find work were preceded by promises and good-byes. Precise references to these departure customs, which later often served as qualifying marriage tests, are to be found in songs:

> You, handsome, in Maremma, and me in the mountains! [97]

Or else:

> I cannot remain an hour without you,
> And yet I shall have to remain so long on my own![98]

The girl, while singing, would turn to the man, asking him to be constant in his affection:

> You will have chances of making love;
> Be merry, but don't give your heart away.[99]

The man could do likewise:

> And if I should die and do not return,
> Look after your virtue with downcast eyes.[100]

On leaving, the man pledged his word and, symbolically, his heart:

> And if I leave, I shall leave my heart
> Which you can have until I return.[101]

The girl asked the date of his return:

> Young man, when are you coming back?[102]

The date could be indicated in a song:

> And I replied to her in a few words:
> My return shall be when God so desires;
> And then I gave a humble reply:
> I shall return between May and April.[103]

In the songs, one could hint at marriage on one's return. In fact, the journey often had the purpose of putting aside savings to "put up a house" and get married:

> I shall return, I shall return, do not doubt it;
> My dear, do not be afraid,
> Because in a short time you will see me come back;
> Because I always keep your image imprinted on my mind.
> And so, beautiful, I shall stop loving you
> When I am dead and buried. [104]

The woman could sing about her weeping and her prayers to God for his speedy return, but sometimes her sorrow was overcome by the generous desire expressed with poetic gentleness to wish her lover a pleasant journey:

> So go, may God speed your way,
> And may your return be sweet happiness!
> And go, may God look after you,
> And for you, may clear water turn into wine;
> May God give you an easy path,
> And for you, may clear water turn into wine. [105]

In Tuscan folklore sung in the evenings, there were also a number of texts dedicated to separation and distance. The *rondinelle*, invocations to the swallows, were common songs also found in the folklore of other areas, as shown in a famous essay by Pitré. [106] In the Tuscan folk songs one asked the swallow to carry a message to a distant love. Here is a version, perhaps the most famous and widespread, collected by Tigri:

> O swallow flying in the sky,
> Come straight back and do me a favor,
> And give me one of the feathers on your wings
> So that I can write a letter to my love.
> When I have written it and done it beautifully,
> I will give you back the feather, O swallow;
> When I have written it on white paper
> I'll give you back the feather that you're missing;

When I have written it on gold paper,
I'll give you back the feather and your flight.[107]

In this way the folk song comforted those who were far away from each other. From the context of the *veglia*, it was clear to whom the singer's thoughts were addressed. The parents, relations, or friends of the missing person would make a note of it and pass it on. Sometimes someone would interrupt the singers to ask for news of those absent, and someone would read letters from the absentee which had been autographed or given to a "scribe" at the fair to write out or compose. He asked the name of the woman, the color of her hair, and some other brief description; then he would pour out octaves which were sometimes sung or read publicly at the *veglia* with the praise of everybody.[108] The lover left behind would grab at the first opportunity to write personally or get someone else to write a suitable reply, and in the meantime would sing:

If someone is going to Maremma, let me know,
As I want to send a letter to my love.[109]

Other times, the girl would sing *rispetti* like the following, the most famous of all Tuscan folk songs, against Maremma:

They all say, "Maremma, Maremma!" . . .

They all say, "Maremma, Maremma!"
To me, it seems a bitter Maremma.
The bird that goes there loses its feathers.
I lost there someone who was dear to me.

Maremma, Maremma, may it be accursed.
May Maremma be accursed, with those who love it.
My heart is always trembling when you go there
Because I'm afraid you'll never come back.[110]

In this way, the time of separation passed, and then came the moment when one sang:

And I happily welcome you home,
And what I doubted has no grounds for doubt,
And I rejoice in welcoming you home.[111]

The spring flower has returned!
Who wasn't here before has returned!
The fruit on the tree has returned!
And when I've got my love, I've got everything![112]

However, the homecoming was not always a happy event. As a rule the man first inquired about the girl's behavior, his family and friends being his sources of information; he only continued his relationship with her once he was assured that she had behaved well and that "nothing had been said about her." Normally one had more faith in one's family and friends than in the girl herself. Sometimes one chose to take one's revenge because of the girl's misbehavior. This could be done through the words of a song sung at one of these evening meetings, blackening the girl's name in front of everybody present:

Before I'll be willing to marry you . . .

Before I'll be willing to marry you
black snow will have to fall from the sky
and mountains will have to walk,
the sun will have to raise at night only.[113]

And crickets eat the dry grass,
With Rosina I tore the papers
and then I left her . . . and whoever wants her can have her.[114]

Sometimes the accusation was more explicit and direct:

When I loved you, so did many others,
Now they have discovered your failings,
That you are the mistress of all scoundrels.[115]

In these rare cases, the folk song represented the sign of the end
of the relationship, the vendetta-punishment, and man's superiority signified by sarcasm, spite, or irony:

I learned it from my friends:
you had a pink ribbon in your slips,
the garters were pink also,
and in the middle of the bust a ribbon this large.

You flirted a bit with everyone,
and you swore eternal love to everyone,
and you kept evil inside your heart;
they all thrusted it inside you.[116]

When I used to visit you, you were a wench,
Now I no longer come, you have grown a crest,
As a girl you had a child.[117]

The same happened if, on his return, the man found that the girl
no longer wanted him or had found someone else:

And you boast of having left me,
But I will boast about something else;
I took your face in my hands and kissed it;
For the others, you are a girl, but for me, you were a wife.[118]

As the reader will have gathered from the preceding examples—limited to the essentials—the folk songs lent expression to all phases of courtship, and they catered to any individual situation.

It is also possible—grouping the enunciative contexts and knowing the singers' personal stories—to classify the folk songs in chains of syntagmatic types, corresponding to the development of events in the lives of the persons concerned in the folk song. Some of the most common patterns among the many possible ones are the following:[119]

I

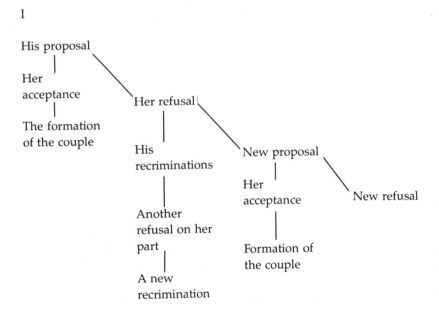

His proposal

Her acceptance

The formation of the couple

Her refusal

His recriminations

Another refusal on her part

A new recrimination

New proposal

Her acceptance

Formation of the couple

New refusal

II

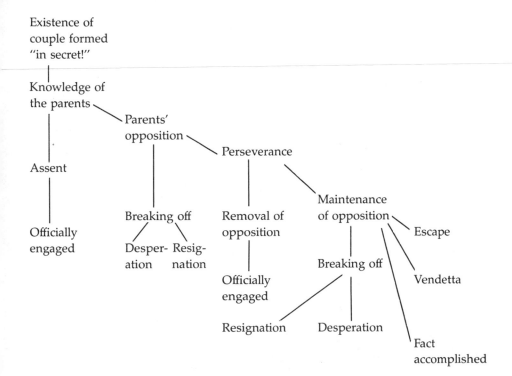

Existence of
couple formed
"in secret!"

Knowledge of
the parents

Parents'
opposition

Perseverance

Assent

Breaking off   Removal of   Maintenance
opposition   of opposition   Escape

Officially
engaged   Desper- Resig-
ation   nation

Officially
engaged   Breaking off   Vendetta

Resignation   Desperation

Fact
accomplished

III

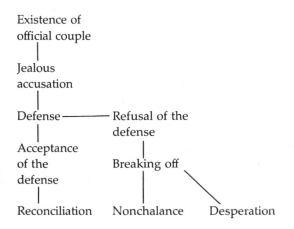

Existence of
official couple

Jealous
accusation

Defense————Refusal of the
defense

Acceptance
of the   Breaking off
defense

Reconciliation   Nonchalance   Desperation

IV

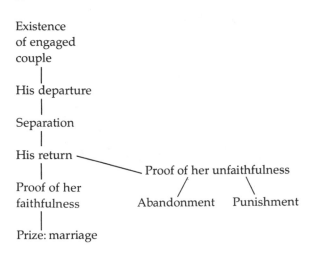

Existence
of engaged
couple
|
His departure
|
Separation
|
His return
| Proof of her unfaithfulness
Proof of her   /   \
faithfulness   Abandonment   Punishment
|
Prize: marriage

At the *veglia*, the older people tended to maintain control of the situation even during the singing. As we have seen, folk songs could have ambivalent contents, functions, and meanings. Texts expressed typical situations and the most important problems of the group, but the strategies that were proposed and the positions that were reflected in the songs themselves were not necessarily the official and dominating ones of the group. Folk songs, *rispetti*, and octaves sung by the young sometimes proposed solutions that were unorthodox and of open rebellion:

> O God of Gods,
> Because of Beppino, yesterday I was beaten up,
> And for his sake I would go through it again.[120]

> O mother, O mother, don't give me an old man;
> don't give him to me, because it's a shame;
> give me a young man, someone who is well awake at night![121]

Or referring to someone who was not favored by a mother:

> I want a husband of my own choice
> Because it's me who has to be with him, not her.[122]

Or referring to someone that her family would have liked for her or, even, turning to the boy:

If you and I are happy, everybody's happy.[123]

Other rebellious songs threatened escape or a marriage "in the woods without a priest."

During such songs, the older generation kept quiet and let the singing continue, so that the young relieved their feelings and rid themselves of their aggressions and frustrations in a harmless way (one evening an old man from Greve whispered to me, "A dog that barks doesn't bite,"[124] while a young man was singing, "We shall put it to the test with my dagger"). Sometimes, however, one could balance the potential danger of the text with appropriate comments in opposition to the connotations of the text. This I observed one December evening in 1973 at Montevarchi when Giacco Ferruzzi wanted to sing "that of the shepherd," which he considered one of the rarest and most beautiful pieces of his repertoire.

> "Listen my dear love and my love very dear to me,
> When you go away I want to come with you."
> "What do you want to do with me, beautiful brunette,
> Fresh rose and poor rose;
> What do you want to do with me,
> Beautiful brunette who's leaving?"
> "Cut grass for your horse, handsome shepherd,
> My dear love and my love dear to me;
> Cut grass for your horse, but I want to come with you."
> "What are you going to reap with, beautiful brunette,
> Fresh rose and poor rose;
> What are you going to reap with,
> Beautiful brunette who's leaving?"
> "With a sickle, handsome shepherd,
> My dear love and my love dear to me;
> "With a sickle, but I want to come with you."
> "If Children are born, beautiful brunette,
> Fresh rose and poor rose;
> "If children are born, beautiful brunette,
> Fresh rose and poor rose;
> "They will be mine and yours, handsome shepherd,

My dear love and my love dear to me;
They will be mine and yours, but I want to come with you."
"Where are you going to change them, beautiful brunette,
Fresh rose and poor rose;
Where are you going to change them,
Beautiful brunette who's leaving?"
"In the Jordan River, handsome shepherd,
My dear love and my love dear to me,
In the Jordan River, but I want to come with you."
"What will you call them, beautiful brunette,
Fresh rose and poor rose,
What are you going to call them,
Beautiful brunette who's leaving?"
"Children of a shepherd,
My dear love and my love dear to me,
Children of a shepherd, but I want to come with you."
"If you pass the mountains, beautiful brunette,
Fresh rose and poor rose;
If you pass the mountains, how are you going to do it?"
"With the help of God, handsome shepherd,
My dear love and my love dear to me;
With the help of God, but I want to come with you." [125]

Listen my dear love and my love very dear to me . . .

After the necessary compliments, someone began saying that
shepherds still existed and that they passed by that part of the countryside. Then one word led to another. [126] One man said, "Wherever
they had passed, something was always missing," indirectly accusing them of theft. Another said that they even robbed each other;
a third mentioned that one shepherd had killed another whom he
had caught red-handed stealing from him. An old woman remarked

that they lived "wildly" without ever seeing anyone, "like animals."
An old man then commented with a sneer that they "know animals
well, come on!" When I asked for an explanation, my neighbor
replied in lowered tones, "People say that they even have relations
with animals," and someone else exclaimed in a loud voice, "Eh,
the little ewes!" Many people giggled. Other than its literal meaning of "small sheep," *pecorina* can also mean "coitus from behind,"
and in that context suggested that the shepherds came into contact
with the sheep that way. [127] Whether consciously or not, in this way
the comments had balanced any positive impact made on a young
public by the words of this folk song in which the girl in love wanted
to be together with the handsome shepherd at all costs, as sometimes occurred in reality. The group wanted to show the other side
of the coin to those who at a later stage might have been involved
in a similar situation, and by so doing had unconsciously repeated
their ethnocentric affirmation of superiority over shepherds. [128] Then
one could sometimes hear stories of individual or group fights between peasants and shepherds, of course with the former getting
the upper hand. [129]

Another "other" group was that represented by fishermen. The
group belonging to the Tuscan agricultural culture were also preju-
diced against them, particularly with regard to mixed marriages
between the two groups. In the following text, found in Lecchi
in 1974, the prohibition to make love to "fishermen who go out to
sea" is explicitly expressed:

"O country girl standing on the cliff,
Come down into my boat.
To tell you all the affection that I have for you
From the depths of my heart, I would like to give you some advice,
You are beautiful and dear, I like you so much,
If you make love to me, I will bring you great pleasure."
"I cannot love you, O handsome fisherman . . .
I cannot love . . . Where is the whore mother of the . . . [Member of the
    audience: "Shut up."]
I cannot love you, O fisherman of the waves
Because I am poor and you are great.
I was born in the mountains amongst the foliage
Where the chestnuts and acorns are born. And then?

[Member of the audience: "The snow . . ."]
Ah, The winter snow falls, you know.
I have no clothes to make love to you."
No! It's wrong! [Member of the audience: "Alright!"
   Member of the audience: "Now he speaks and says to the girl, 'I'm a
   fisherman . . .'"]
"Ah! I'm a fisherman and carry a cloak
To cover you completely with coral
With which I'll take you to the dance."
Alright? [Member of the audience: "Yes."]
"Dressed and bridled, you will look lovely.
If you make love to me, it will bring you great pleasure."
"I cannot love you, O handsome fisherman
Because I could be beaten up by my mother.
She doesn't want me to make love
To fishermen who go out to sea.
Among winds, and storms, they could flood."
[Member of the audience: "Drown!"]
"For this reason, O handsome youth, I cannot love you." [130]

O country girl standing on the cliff . . .

The rule that the girls had to learn at the *veglia* was the same as
that applied to the young men: "buy your wine and wife nearby"
["*donna e vino comprali dal vicino*"] and "choose your wife and oxen
from your own homegrounds" ["*donna e buoi dei paesi tuoi*"].[131] So
the girls were also taught not to choose a husband from another
area, that is, foreign to the group to which she belonged. As in
the preceding cases, the prohibition could include fishermen and
shepherds, subcategories of the more general category of "foreigners," that is, "those from outside." Folk songs like the following
were sung against foreigners:

Vine branches and grapes
And, as my mother always said,
Love of a foreigner lasts a short time. [132]

A proverb specifies:

A foreigner's love lasts a short time.
The country changes and so does the venture. [133]

A *rispetto* from Casentino proposed an explanation:

Love from foreigners lasts a year,
Because they already have a girl at home;
Love from foreigners lasts a month,
Because they already have a girl at home;
Love from foreigners lasts a day,
Because they already have a girl in their land. [134]

After the singing of the young, the older generation began to
sing and the songs fell in line with the official values of their generation. While the topics remained the same—love, engagements,
journeys, homecomings—the possible developments of plots and
their endings were reduced to the suitable ones. Explicit morals
also appeared as in this story, without a title, heard in Lecchi in
November of 1973:

"Since you got back
Why didn't you come to see me?
Just think, my treasure and beloved,
That one day you left me here pregnant.
You told me that I was pretty.
Now just take a look at your little girl.
Give her little sweet face a kiss.
She calls out 'daddy' day and night."
"Go away from here.
You know that I don't want to see you anymore.
I want to embrace Bruna,
Who is much more beautiful and richer than you.
Go away. My heart says
I will live happily with her."
"Understand that in no way

You can persuade me.
You will see that you will not be happy,
Horrible cruel man, if you take her.
And you will see that I will show you a thing or two
And where I find you I will skin you alive.
And you will see that I will show you a thing or two
And where I find you I will skin you alive."
One day the little dressmaker
Left with her baby
And waited one morning
Until the vile deceiver went out.
He was married to his beautiful one.
She ready armed with a revolver
Came out of a corridor and in a rage
Fired three shots and killed the deceiver.
She was arrested.
All the people started shouting,
"She took her revenge
And we all want her to be freed."
Young men, I want to warn you
Not to betray young girls.
If not, they will send you to your burial.
They will avenge themselves without being afraid. [135]

Since you got back . . .

In this case the moral of the group wishes to impose itself not only
on the individual but also on the rules of society, and it is clearly
pronounced superior to these rules. In this way the group disap-
proves of he who "betrays," that is, leaves a pregnant girl to marry
another, and approves of the person who wreaks "just revenge"

on her own against the official laws of society but in accordance with the unwritten code of honor.

However, there are also many stories with a happy ending like that of Lisetta. This version was given in October 1973 by Palma Anichini at San Sano.

Sing, sing Lisetta, until you are married . . .

"Sing, sing Lisetta, until you are married;
Sing, sing Lisetta, until you are married."
"I don't want to sing or laugh, my heart is overwhelmed;
I don't want to sing or laugh, my heart is overwhelmed.
My love has gone to war, who knows when he'll be back;
My love has gone to war, who knows when he'll be back.
If I knew the way, I would like to go and find him;
If I knew the way, I would like to go and find him.
By asking I shall find the way;
By asking I shall find the way."
Halfway there she met a handsome young man;
Halfway there she met a handsome young man.
"Tell me, O tell me young man, where do you come from?
Tell me, O tell me young man, where do you come from?"
"I come from a place where the sun never sets;
I come from a place where the sun never sets."
"Tell me, O tell me handsome young man, have you seen my first love?
Tell me, O tell me handsome young man, have you seen my first love?"
"Yes, I have seen him, but I didn't recognize him;
Yes, I have seen him, but I didn't recognize him.
Three soldiers were taking him to his burial;
Three soldiers were taking him to his burial."
Lisetta fell to the ground, having fainted from great grief;
Lisetta fell to the ground, having fainted from great grief.
"Cheer up, cheer up Lisetta, I am your first love;
Cheer up, cheer up Lisetta, I am your first love."

Arm-in-arm she took him back to the village;
Arm-in-arm she took him back to the village.
When they arrived in the village, all the people appeared at their windows;
When they arrived in the village, all the people appeared at their windows.
"Here is Lisetta, having found her first love;
Here is Lisetta, having found her first love." [136]

Here everything happened for the best. Lisetta passed the qualifying test, having shown extreme sorrow when she heard the false news about his death. With him she made a triumphant entrance into the village community. Everyone was at the windows as in the case of real marriages, for which this image was perhaps a picturesque functional equivalent.

As the older generation slowly took over the performing at the *veglia*, the young once again became the audience and started communicating by means of glances. [137] The glance was of capital importance in a situation where verbal and gestural expressions were in some way subjected to censorship. Consequently, folk songs often talked about eyes, little eyes, "lively eyes," "beautiful eyes," eyes of a fairy, eyes that shine and "that seem like two little, round mirrors." Others begged, "Do not look at me because you are consuming me," or pled pity against murderous eyes that have captivated:

My eyes met yours;
Yours were more beautiful and put me in bonds.
[*I miei occhi co' vostri s'incontrorno:*
I vostri eran più belli e m'allegorno.]

One who was in love never took his eyes off the person he loved. The woman's eyes had to be more modest, lowered and passive, following the rest of her behavior, typical of an "honest" girl. Instead, men's eyes were more active, in a series of subtle gradations, from a "slightly shining" eye to one which was *manucano* [eater], in which case he devoured the girl with his eyes. He could "undress the girl with his eyes," throwing more "love torches" than Nencia of Barberino, [138] or wink to hint at an invitation or sign of understanding:

Fennel flower,
I am not happy unless I look at you;
I am not happy unless I wink at you. [139]

But in the long run, love was not communicated well through
glances, and here once again the girl invited the man to speak more
clearly or "pronounce himself":

Fennel flower,
A word in one's ear is worth more
Than a hundred thousand winks. [140]

By "taking a look" at the girls in the village or at the singsongs,
one often ended up by "giving one's word." Seeing is believing. [141]

5

The End of the *Veglia*
"The Right to Ask and the Obligation to Refuse"

"Le femine a niuna altra cosa, che a far questo e' figliuoli, ci nascono, e per questo son tenute care . . ."

["Females are born for no other reason than to have children, and it is for this that they are held dear . . ."]

Boccaccio, *Decameron*, the Fifth Day, Novella 10

"Colei sola è casta la quale o non fu mai da alcun pregata, o se pregò non fu esaudita."

["She alone is chaste whom no one ever asked or, if asked, was never satisfied."]

Ibid., the Second Day, Novella 9

To this point it has been argued that the *veglia* is an organized time for talk, and because of this focus on community expressivity, we have seen that the casual and the spontaneous often break into the more formal and even ceremonial chains of expressive items of tradition. In adult-child interactions, as in courtship, the interaction is primarily of the conversational and casual sort; when games or performances break out, however, there is a strong thematic continuity, so much so that the event itself was thought of by the Tuscans as *vegliatori*, a performance event. Thus, interactional flow which, by conversation, is focused on the content of the talk can, by the conventions of the occasion, become a performance or a genre. The switch involved here is simply to agree to bring stylistic matters (like singing, dancing, or self-conscious storytelling) into the open, thus telling everyone that play is in process.

Nowhere is this division between spontaneous talk and self-conscious performance more important and more difficult to describe effectively than in expressive interchanges about the doings of others.[1] For what may begin as chit-chat or news easily becomes gossip, scandal, even slander. This is especially so when these doings are embodied in stories, proverblike utterances, or even songs. In theory, of course, there is a clear distinction between moralizing talk about others one knows and others one does not know or cannot have known because they lived so long ago, but in practice the *vegliatori* perceived—as my informants repeatedly explained— a continuum between stories of those present at the *veglia* and stories of those absent, between stories of people alive and stories of people passed away. The *veglia* itself, in other words, transcended "normal" conventions of space and time; it was a performative event that in itself gave different degrees but the same kind of reality and truth to *all* that happened within the borders of its interaction ritual.

"The young man and the young girl of the common folk both looked for a heart with which to understand each other: they found it; they understood each other; and they comprehended each other by singing; the wishes, the contrarieties, the loves, the homages, the joys, the sullenness—all had poetic interpretations. They wanted to be married; even this wish they expressed in rhyme; they married. What had they left to sing about? . . . The singing ceased with the occasion and rightly so." This is what Ermolao Rubieri wrote on the end of the season of love songs.[2]

Assertions of the same kind are found in the folklore texts themselves:

The woman when she is singing wants a husband,[3]

says a refrain, and the story of Lisetta reported in the last chapter begins:

"Sing, sing Lisetta, until you are married."[4]

The time of singing is before and not after the wedding.

The love songs were, in fact, part of courting. This is clear not only in everyday life but also in the development of the *veglia*. When courting stopped, so did the singing. When at the end of the *veglia* the elders took the floor again, the tone and topic changed; the emphasis shifted to maintaining the family units, rather than the formation of the couples.

Once they had resumed the control and conduct of the *veglia*, the elders proceeded to maintain it until the end. In the majority of cases, the part of the *veglia* that the elders dedicated to themselves was the last. Each of the three age groups into which the *vegliatori* were divided (children, young adults, and elders) had their favorite stories. Individually, the elders might prefer some particular fable of love or magic related in the first two parts of the *veglia*, especially if the events of the protagonists repeated the happy cases of their own lives or compensated for their past misfortune with a happy ending. However, in general, the elders liked and were more interested in the "stories of married people," in which the protagonists confronted situations with which the narrators or listeners who were "old" (that is, "adult" with positive connotation, deriving from age and experience) had to deal regularly at that stage of their life.

Consequently, toward the end of the *veglia* the narrators recounted pitiful cases, the events and vicissitudes of marriage. Such tales also provided examples both pertinent and didactic to the "young" (that is, not married but of marriageable age) about the possible future familiar crises and their possible development and results.

They narrated many such stories, either in recited verses or in sung verses (octaves but also sextains and quatrains) or in prose. The more famous were also represented in folk dramas, such as the Maggi or the Bruscelli, and were mentioned or quoted in *rispetti* or *stornelli*; their presence in many diverse genres of folklore indicates their primary importance for the familiar system that produced or accepted them.

One of the stories that my informants agreed was among the nicest was that of Genoveffa. The version that follows is of Sidonia Fanetti, Casentinese, as she recounted it in 1974:

It is Genoveffa, then but, . . . I remember very little, eh then! This girl, I don't remember if she is a king's daughter or if she is of a . . . but anyway, yea, of Brabante; I think Genoveffa was of the house of Brabante. She marries this king, this prince. This very young girl, Genoveffa. But there is a cousin that is also in love with this Genoveffa, but she refuses him. Then the husband has to leave for war, and this cousin remains home. Then till . . . when the husband leaves, Genoveffa is pregnant. But he succeeded in insinuating in the mind of the parents that this girl is like a . . . a witch, like a sorcerer, that she is bad, anyway that she can do all wrong, and that she would give birth to a beast. Instead she gives birth to a child, she gives birth to a good child, a nice child, a nice child, and then they do not know what to do to rid themselves of the baby and they send . . . to this husband, a box with . . . an ugly creature and they tell him that this very bad woman did this . . . this ugly creature and that . . . and they do not know how to get rid of it. Then he gives orders that this woman be killed. And when she is able to walk, naturally the hunting guard, . . . the king, in short, the queen, the mother gives orders to this hunting guard that this girl be killed. And she says, "No, don't kill me!" She tells him, no . . . "Kill me but not my son." Then he tells her to go far away. He says, "I will bring you far away," and he kills a deer that . . . because . . . to bring the eyes, because the queen, . . . the queen mother wants the eyes. To bring the eyes [A female listener "Of the woman!"]. Of the woman, of course, of Genoveffa. And this boy . . . and then this poor girl goes far away with this baby, in a forest. It is night, poor girl, she is afraid, hears all the night noises of the animals and hears . . . anyway she recommends herself and prays to God, this baby is hungry, then she stopped by a large oak, say, this oak is split, there is a hole. And she enters inside the hole in the oak because she is cold. In this . . . hole there was a female deer, who had a baby deer who was dead. And this deer, it is like . . . like a miracle: she stuck out her . . . her breast to this child. This baby starts to suck, and there this . . . from one day to the other and . . . this female deer is a mother to this baby and she becomes an inseparable companion of this Genoveffa. The years go by, and this boy grows, and . . . he lives in a savage stage. The mother taught him many things, she taught him that his father is a king, anyway, of . . . of the kingdom where they live, but for reasons that are not clear she tells him, anyway, she was sent away, and she teaches . . . he becomes very good for . . . always in company of this deer, in the use of the bow, in short, and dresses with animal skins. The mother eh . . . occasionally they find dead animals and the mother makes clothes and sews them with weed, in short with liane . . . with all that the forests can offer in vegetables. Then years go by and the prince . . . the king comes back from the wars. And naturally they presented him with the eyes of this . . . this woman. But then he is horrified, and repents. Now, I do not remember if . . . during a hunt, this cousin is wounded, and then before dying he reveals the secret and the . . . the wrong he has committed. And he inveighs against the mother, telling her, "You all have been evil," and he goes in search of this woman. That is, the hunting guard tells him of the place where . . . and during a day of hunting the king ordered a large hunt, and the king goes and follows this deer. This deer goes, goes, and goes, ahead, ahead, ahead, and ahead and takes him . . . and takes him nearly to . . . near the oak . . . in short, to the home in the oak where this woman is, where Genoveffa is with her son. And the king shoots at the deer, and this . . . and wounds her. And he sees . . . come out of this oak grotto a woman with this big boy, that were crying. So he comes near and says,

"Why," he says, "are you crying?" And she says that "this was our bene-factress," She says, "this—as to say—she has helped us to live many years." Then the king asked them who they were. And this woman tells him that she is Genoveffa. He says, "Genoveffa?" "Yes," she replies, "that the pity of a servant did not kill as the king had ordered, and this is the son." So then the king kneels in front of her, asks her forgiveness, and brings her to his kingdom, and like this . . . and . . . he brings her . . . home . . . and . . . they are married again. And then she is queen and the son at the death of the father . . . will be . . . after many studies, really, he is made to study . . . and becomes king. [Vegliatore: "And the moth-er?"] [Other vegliatore: "Yes, it is like this."] And the mother . . . I do not remember if the king punishes her, I think so. They put her in prison . . . something like this. [Vegliatore: "Or they send her away."] Yes, yes, either they burn her or send her away, I think something like this. I remember something like that . . .[5]

This story, which we might call with all due redundancy "suc-cessful succession," presents the simplest rendering of the family-romance narrative, the boldest statement of the to-the-death ri-valries implicit within this family system. It is, then, the Tuscan embodiment of the Oedipean drama, rendered in overt formal de-velopment. The resonances within the conflict of mother-in-law and daughter-in-law are so openly stated they almost resist further symbolic analysis. Genoveffa refuses a suitor who in the absence of her husband takes revenge, slandering her. We have to note that in real life the birth of monstrous children was considered to be a malediction and punishment with regard to the woman, while the resemblance of the newborn to the father was considered to be a positive sign of blessing. The folk belief, in Tuscany and else-where, presumed that if in the moment of conception the woman thought of the husband the newborn would have his features. The monstrous children were caused by the fact that the woman, in the moment of conception or during the pregnancy, had fixed her mind on an animal or desired the meat of an animal. Raffaele Corso reports a case from a Tuscan source in the sixteenth century in which a woman of Pietrasanta gave birth to a girl, "savage with camel hair, because when she conceived, she was looking at an image of Saint John."[6]

Genoveffa's husband believes his family and condemns his wife to death. The queen mother asks expressly for the eyes of Genoveffa who, saved, is to regress to the more innocent state, comparatively speaking closer to the natural state within this familiar complex. She will emerge from this through the recognition of both herself and her son. She will then pass on to a new and definitive social state, reaffirmational marriage with the king, whom the son will succeed at the proper time. At the symbolic level of the narrative, it is possible to find a relation of opposition between Genoveffa and her mother-in-law. The latter provokes the death sentence of Genoveffa with the false proof of her incapacity to have a normal child; in addition, she orders a "symbolic castration." Both facts caused the elimination of Genoveffa from her husband's life, which Genoveffa finally re-enters after presenting the male heir. It is then that the queen mother is punished, burned, imprisoned, or estranged.

This sequence, so resonant of other renderings of the family romance in narrative form is, in fact, a precise projection of the life dramas within the patriarchal Tuscan family. In this system a bride did not definitely acquire her status in the new family until she gave birth to the first male child and, by doing so, assured the continuity of the patriarchal family. The birth of the firstborn made her pass from the status of companion to that of "mother of my children," at which time she achieved the same status within the extended family and community as her mother-in-law had. In the life of her husband, she usurps the place of his mother but through what is regarded as a natural progression. At this point, there is a tendency for the husband to call his wife "mother" rather than by her Christian name, as a sign of her change of status and as a reminder to his mother that having a child transforms all relationships from the dependency point of view.

That the *old mother* does not give up so easily all of the time is reflected in the fact that the story of Genoveffa continues to be narrated, sung in octaves, represented at the Tuscan *Maggi*, and also printed in longer and "pretentious" versions, many of which were found in the books sold at the fairs, where they were tacked on walls by the ballad and story singers.[7]

The motif of the unjust accusation of the bride is one of the most common in the texts of Tuscan folklore concerning married couples. However, the ending is not always happy as in Genoveffa's case: often, as in the most popular among these stories, the "Pia de' Tolomei," there is a tragic end. The story of the Pia has a historic foundation: it is mentioned by Dante in the *Comedia*.[8] It is more than probable that the story was handed down from his time without interruption in Tuscan folklore in various forms. There were also many folk re-elaborations in verses, tempered by oral traditions which, at the same time, dynamically contributed to their evolution. Famous among the many was an elaboration by Sestini in the form of a "poetic novella."[9] There were also many versions printed in pamphlets and handbills.[10] In the last century the foreman of the Florentine printing house Salani noted that they printed up to seventy thousand copies a year.[11] Another famous version was that sung by Giuseppe Moroni, nicknamed Niccheri, an illiterate "extemporaneous poet" of the second half of the nineteenth century.[12] Even today, the story of the Pia is printed, sung, narrated, and acted out.[13] The version in chained octaves in a pamphlet printed in 1972 rapidly sold out,[14] just as the ones of a century ago did.

The story of the Pia follows diverse versions in the Tuscan folklore. Besides the canonical version in which the Pia died of deprivation in the castle of the Pietra where her husband had imprisoned her, there is another version in which Pia is killed by a keeper of the castle who pushed her from the bastions.[15] According to another traditional version collected by Hooker[16] in the zone of the castle of the Pietra, the Pia committed suicide. The story in one form or another is known to everyone in the area; the sung version in octaves coexisted with others in prose. Not all *vegliatori* knew the entire story in verse, of course. At times, the story was narrated in a shortened hybrid form, with verses and prose interchanged. The following is one of such versions, collected near Brolio in 1974 at the *veglia* of the Cennis. Maria Cenni recounted it for her husband, Sestilio, for me, and for the other six or seven *vegliatori* on that cold evening with "the moon that entered through the window."

MARIA CENNI: *The story of the Pia of Tolomei was beautiful! but now . . . Before, yes, I knew it. I knew plenty of them!*

ALESSANDRO FALASSI: *The Pia. Siena made me, Maremma destroyed me . . .*

SESTILIO CENNI: *You knew it!*

MARIA: *Yes, eh, I don't remember!*

AF: *Not even some of it?*

MARIA: *Because it says: A gentleman from Siena. Wait. Siena fought against the Maremme. Florence was fighting against Volterra. There was no place where there was not war. . . . Wait . . . Florence fought against Volterra . . . Ah. The Pia of Tolomei married a gentleman that was not from Siena. And from the Pietra, he was called Nello. And they were married. Then she said: war erupted. Goddammit . . . ! I don't remember . . . He left. Left for the war. I do not remember now. In conclusion . . .*

AF: *Yes, but when he left for the war, what happened?*

MARIA: *He left, right. So she remained. She remained and then there was Ghino who gave her trouble, right. Because this Ghino, he liked this lady and . . . and . . .*

SESTILIO: *He was his friend!*

MARIA: *It was really his friend who betrayed him. So he went to see her at night. But she did not want him, right. Then they were in war together with Ghino; and Ghino told him, "I am going home." So he said, "If you are going home, go to see my wife." He said, "Yes, I will go," he said, "to say hello to your wife."*

SESTILIO: *He really was looking forward to this! [The* vegliatori *laughed.]*

MARIA: *But . . . he went, but he never told her what he did or how she was, do you understand. So when one night when he went to see her, she did not open the door, right. She did not open. But she had a brother, she had a brother, and this brother used to go to see her, too. He was also at the war. Then one night this Ghino was so bad and he knew that her brother went to see her, too; he told him he said, "You, Nello" (when he came back, when they met again he told him), "You think that your wife is an honest woman," he said. "You will see that your wife betrays you." "I don't believe it," he said, "that my wife may betray me." "I'm telling you that your wife," he said, "is betraying you. If you want to come to see," he said, "I . . . after ten o'clock in the evening . . ."*

SESTILIO: *"I will prove it to you."*

MARIA: *"I will prove it that another man is going to see her," he said. "But how?" "Yes." Then they dressed, both of them, and put themselves in hiding in the garden to observe. Around ten o'clock or eleven she . . . the doorbell rang and her brother . . . brought her news of her husband*

*. . . so she came down and opened the door, right in her nightgown.
So he saw this, that she went to open, and that she was in a nightgown . . ."*

SESTILIO: *They did not know that it was her brother . . .*

MARIA: *They . . . he . . . he knew it. Ghino knew it because he was
mean.*

SESTILIO: *He knew it!*

VEGLIATORI: *And they remained caught at it!*

MARIA: *Eh! and, well, they left. He said, "I wouldn't believe that my
wife would do this," but now he said to him, "I almost believe it."
Ghino said, "Did you see, you did not believe it, I proved it to you."
So then he returned to the war . . . no, and he returned to the war.
Then when the war was over, Pia was at home waiting for him. Eh,
so then at night he left and went home. He rang the doorbell. She
heard an . . . a persistent bell sound. So Pia said, "This is my beloved
Nello and . . ." poor woman [breaking out in tears], I was amused,
but also sorry, when I knew this story . . . When I was little . . . well
. . . So she said, Nello in his fury broke the cord from the bell . . . He
rang the bell with such fury that he broke the rope and chain from
the bell. Yes, he pulled out the bell completely!*

Pia said, "This is not my beloved one."
Pia went to embrace him.
And Nello, he shook his sword.
She said: "What is wrong? What is wrong, Nello?

Because you lost lately, the next time you will win again."

SESTILIO: *"You will be the winner."*

MARIA: *"You will be the winner." Nello shook his sword and did not say
a word. Then at night she talked to him, but he did not respond. At
a certain point he said: "I will have to bring you in a large castle. Tomorrow morning we will saddle the horses and we must . . . and we
must leave. You must come with me." "Where are you bring me," she
said, "where are you taking me?" "You will see where I am bringing
you," he said; "You will come with me." So he went down the stairs . . .
to the doorman and told him, "At such and such an hour, you will
saddle the horses, because we are leaving." He brought her to a castle.
Now I do not remember the name of this castle, but he brought her
to a castle.*

SESTILIO: *But it was beautiful!*

MARIA: *Then at five o'clock in the morning, they left, and . . . mounted their horses and left. The . . . doorman had prepared everything, and so on and on and on, they went to this castle. He said to this custodian of the castle: "Look," said he, "here I am leaving the horses, and then, give us each a bed, and tomorrow at five you leave the door open and you saddle the horses because I have to leave but the lady will remain here." He said, "You do not let her go out, never and never!" The servant obeyed and did not let her go out. Then in the morning she could not sleep, because she said, "From this and that I heard say that the castle was habitated by witches." She said, "Holy mother, I hear say from this one and that one that the castle is witched." She was afraid, she couldn't sleep. So that little by little, after a while she fell asleep around five o'clock in the morning. When she went to sleep a little, he took the horses and went away.*

SESTILIO: *And away he went!*

MARIA: *And away he went, so that when she woke up, he was gone. She went to open the door. There was a castle guardian. She said, "Where is my husband?" "Madam, your husband is gone and you must stay here." She said, "Why must I stay here?" "Yes," he answered, "you must stay here for a few days." So this poor woman was desperate, and she waited a day or two . . . but ended up staying there forever . . .*

SESTILIO: *But this, this is not a fairy tale, this is a real fact. This is the truth.*

AF: *It's the truth, eh!*

VEGLIATORE: *Yes, yes, eh, but really we know that, eh, also . . . also Dante in the* Divine Comedy *and . . . and he said on purpose: "Siena made me and Maremma destroyed me." Because she . . . why . . . Siena made her, she was born in Siena, and died in Maremma . . .*

SESTILIO: *Eh, yes, yes!*

MARIA: *It's true, it's true.*

VEGLIATORE: *Eh, Palazzo Tolomei is still there in Siena.*

MARIA: *Eh, sure! The Palace of the Pia of Tolomei of the Sienese land.*

VEGLIATORE: *Yes, yes, continue!*

MARIA: *[Excitedly] Married a gentleman that was not from Siena. And he was called Nello from the Pietra and she married him. So then to finish, uhmm . . . so that she always wanted to go out, but the castle guardian prevented her from doing so. One day, she waited and she became very thin . . .*

VEGLIATORE: *Do you drink also [pouring the drinks]?*

VEGLIATORE: *Yes, yes.*

VEGLIATORE: *Easy, easy, I have to go home . . . enough, enough, enough.*

MARIA: *When her husband returned, he met a friar on his way. But not a friar, a Capuchin.*

VEGLIATORE: *A Capuchin.*

MARIA: *Eh, he found a Capuchin who said . . . and he gave him a ring, to this Capuchin. He said that he had left his wife in the castle; "when you will go to this castle, you give her this ring." So then this Capuchin after more . . . I think six months, she stayed there. Six months, yes. So then when he arrived near the castle, he went to greet this lady, but she was already sick, poor woman; she couldn't stand by herself and so he gave her this ring telling her that her husband had left it for her. She accepted the ring. Then the guardian of the castle started to let her go out a little, because she felt so bad, she was ready to die. So then Ghino . . . "I wish you die." I feel like crying!!! [She cried.]*

SESTILIO: *Isn't she stupid!*

MARIA: *It is . . . the truth, really, it's as if I knew her, it's true [she dried her tears]. How does the story go now, I don't remember. Now, that man was so mean, he was so bad, that afterward he repented. In repenting he said, "Why, this woman has been six months in this castle and now she is dying," so he repented. Then he said, "I want to go see her." And while . . . No, on the contrary, he said, "I want to go see her husband." And while . . . No, on the contrary, her husband, while he was going to see the husband, he found a wild beast on his way who wanted to devour him. So he fought with this animal. In the meantime the father told the husband:*

> "She was your wife but also my daughter;
> Let's go to see her for once."

So they left, took the horses and left to go to the castle. When they were on the road, they found the wild beast and Ghino who was about to be eaten by the wild beast. Ghino was still alive. So he said, "Take your wife away from that castle because she is innocent." I wish you die [she cried], I . . . I feel like crying. I can't help it!

SESTILIO: *[With affection] Why do you cry!*

MARIA: *No, really, I wish you die, I . . . uuh! For me . . . I've always liked this story; and then. So he said. So they took the horses and went*

*away . . . went away. Eh! And . . . wait, eh. Ah, they heard a bell
ringing. They met a little girl in the street, they heard this bell ring.
He said, "We heard a bell," they said to this girl; then she answered,
"It is a rare sound. Yes," said she. "It's for a woman who has been
in the castle for six months, it's twenty-four hours that she is dead.
Anything else I cannot tell you dear sir." So they arrived at the castle
and found her dead. But I . . . I do not remember everything, because
when I sing . . . when I knew it, it made me cry, and better I do not
think of it. But anyway, it is beautiful . . .*

Unfortunately, I could not obtain any information about the narrator's life that was particularly noteworthy to establish specific parallels or points of contact between her life and this narrative. It
seems, however, that her first husband was particularly jealous and
that he physically abused her. It is possible that in the story there
were invested sentiments and individual remembrances; anyway,
more than one Tuscan refrain confirms the concrete realization
of this possibility:

> Be careful not to do like Nello
> Who let Pia die of sorrow;
> He imprisoned her for six months in a castle
> Without reason or motive.[17]

And another one said:

> I want to go in the Maremme
> Where Pia of Tolomei went;
> I want to stay with the beautiful ones
> And I want to die like she died.[18]

In any case the sincere tears that forced Maria to interrupt the narration several times showed at least sensitivity and a profound
attachment to the story of the unhappy wife; the same sentiments
were demonstrated when Beatrice del Pian degli Ontani, the most
famous folk singer of nineteenth-century Tuscany, proceeded to
sing her octaves in tears.[19]

The story of Pia has many points in common with that of Genoveffa, such as the departure of her husband, the perverse plot of the

bad man, the unjust punishment inflicted on the bride, and the final re-establishment of the truth. However, the sequence of the redeeming maternity is missing. The story has a sad ending. We could, at this point, speculate that the bride, who was not expecting a baby (or, even "worse," who was sterile), is less necessary to the narrative than the fertile one. The mother-in-law/daughter contrast is lacking in the story of Pia, and if one wished to compare the stories of Pia and Genoveffa, one could suggest that the mother of Nello is not present because she is not structurally necessary. The opposition between the two women does not exist, "because" Pia is not expecting an heir and therefore she does not threaten the role of her mother-in-law.

Other narratives recounted cases of unfaithful wives or monstrous mothers who killed their children or enjoyed a lover while the husband was far away at wars or working. But the husband returned and took justified revenge upon the woman. A typical example of such narrative developments occurs in the story of Gabriella. The version that is related was collected in 1973 at Figline Valdarno.

> I will sing about this beautiful woman
> With her small girls and her husband,
> By name she was called Gabriella,
> And of an atrocious and dissolute event
> About two girls in the tender age
> Who were called Giulietta and Giuseppina.
> About two girls in the tender age
> Who were called Giulietta and Giuseppina.
> Ulisse said: "My dear Gabriella,
> Here I am without work or an occupation.
> Now I must leave and go away,
> I am called to go to work in France.
> If I don't leave, we will make debts
> And when they are made, we cannot pay them."
> Gabriella answered, "My dear Ulisse,
> Remember me and the little girls;
> You leave here the three of us without money;
> I do not earn and they are so little."
> Ulisse said, "I will think of it even [when] dead

And the first money I earn I will send to you."
In fact he left for France.
He was a mechanic and went to work in a factory,
And at six lire a day plus a few tips.
He sent sixty lire for the first fifteen days
To the wife, telling her,
"Eat and drink with the girls, my dear."
He sent money to his wife, telling her,
"Eat and drink with the girls, my dear."
After a while she frequented
A young man, her first lover.
In a very short time she found herself pregnant.
Then Ugo said, "Let's terminate our relationship."
She said: "My little Ugo, do not abandon me!
I will put the two girls in a convent,
You will make the papers so we can run away.
Meanwhile take this gold and this silver;
My husband sent it to me.
We will go to America while he is not here.
My husband sent it to me.
We will go to America while he is not here."
Between themselves they had established
To leave together, but fatal destiny,
A letter from her husband
To Gabriella and brought by the postman
Telling her that he was returning, and she
Wanted to kill the girls and run away with her lover.
She took a knife and slaughtered Giuseppina
While the poor girl was sleeping.
She threw her in the toilet piece by piece,
While at this time Giulietta awoke,
Saying, "Barbarous woman without heart,
You killed Giuseppina and I will tell father!"
Saying, "Barbarous woman without heart,
You killed Giuseppina and I will tell father!"
At this time she went near her
And grabbed her by the hair;
With the same knife she killed her
And she threw her also in the toilet.
After the massacre she heard knocking at the door.
She thought it was her lover and ran to open the door.

When she saw that it was her husband
She became very pallid in the face,
And he saw the blood all over the floor.
"What is this blood, this is quite a revelation.
Whose blood is this?" he immediately asked.
"It's the blood of the girls killed in fury."
"Son of a bitch," he said, "iniquitous and wicked."
He took a dagger and thrust it into her heart.
Gabriella fell to the floor dead,
And Ulisse went to report it to the police
With the delegate and two Carabinieri,
Having seen and evaluated.
It was a just vendetta.
This good father was allowed to go free.
He gathered the pieces of the little girls
Killed by the barbarous mother.
This is an example never to be followed.
Women think a little
When the husband loves you,
Never change lovers.[20]

I will sing about this beautiful woman . . .

Once more the moral of the group is affirmed over the justice of society, and a man remains free after a justified vendetta.

Another example of the same pattern is illustrated in the story of Lea:

"Tell me, beautiful Lea, where is your husband?
Tell me, beautiful Lea, where is your husband?"

"My husband is in France, I wish he would never come back.
May the ground that holds him sink.
May the sun that illuminates him blind him.
May the ship that carries him sink."
"Quiet, my beautiful Lea, quiet, there is your husband!"
"Forgive me, dear husband, I will not do it again."
"I will not forgive you, I want to cut off your head."
Her head went flying, the room thundered.
"I will make a tomb with thirty-six bricks."[21]

In this narrative the husband gives the just punishment to the wife, whom he finds unfaithful upon his return.

The same test is found in the narrative in verses called "the false pilgrim,"[22] or "Bernardo's story." Bernardo left for the war, left his wife—"after seven years she could remarry." He returned after seven years, in disguise, and put his wife to a test; and because she had not recognized him, she refused his advances. So then he made himself known, she gave him his just welcome, and the two reunited.

The narrative structures appear consistent:

The husband leaves.
The fidelity of the woman is put on trial in his absence.
The husband returns.
The woman is punished or rewarded according to how she behaved.[23]

All the narrative developments can be considered variations or complications of this primary structure: when the woman is accused unjustly, she is punished unjustly and the truth is later established, followed by a "prize." The reconstitution of the couple is her prize. It is also significant that the reconstitution of the couple is always considered to be a prize for the wife and never a prize for the husband, as the *stornello* says:

Bitter flower,
The liberty of man is worth a treasure,
The liberty of man is worth a treasure
and that of the woman a penny.[24]

Equally, the married man is never put to any test at his return, nor does anyone expect that during his absence he has been faithful to his wife. As in the stories, so it is in reality. In fact, in rural Tuscany, it happened that husbands left, often for long periods of time. They could absent themselves for reasons of war or, more commonly, for seasonal work, occasionally in Maremma or in other places, even out of Italy.[25] In these cases the major part of the women "held on to their virtue with low eyes."[26] They often dressed in mourning and waited.[27] Usually, upon his return the first thing the husband did was gather information from his parents and friends about the behavior of his wife.[28] If it seemed that the wife had behaved herself well, he "rewarded" her by returning to her; otherwise, he punished her without listening to her reasons. He never related his conduct or behavior during his absence, nor did the woman expect that during his absence the husband would behave like "San Giovanni," that is, "without deceptions."[29]

In fact, contrary to the last *stornello*, the faithfulness of the man was not worth a penny, but that of the woman was priceless and could not be broken for any reason whatsoever, not even to save the husband's life. In the story of Cecilia the issue is clearly presented and played out, and a clear moral is stated without any ambiguity. Cecilia gives herself to the captain who is going to execute her husband in exchange for his life. The husband is hung nevertheless and she sees him as she awakens in the captain's bed. Breaking the rules of official morality, indicates the story, does not pay even in material terms.[30]

At the *veglia*, people also talked about the absentees. The narratives of traditional folklore did not mechanically or uniterruptedly follow in the diverse parts of the *veglia*. Between one story and another, between one song and another, they talked "about the more and the less." It is the constant comment of any observer that the elders always talked about "relatives." It was enough just to mention a name not immediately recognized by all; immediately, someone would ask "who" or "who is he?" or something similar. The elders furnished the explanation: "Cecco of Cicali, the one that married a niece of Paglino that lived at Garbina." Or "Carlo of Milanesi, the third son of Cellole that married a girl from Villarosa whose name was Losi as a single girl, the cousin of Losi of Cennino, the ones that now live at Malafrasca." Since a person had to be attached by report to the group in order to be placed, they traced

briefly a rudimentary genealogy and an approximate system of kinship. The elements necessary to know a person were "to whom
he belonged," that is, the descendant, the parentage; whom he had
married, and with whom he had become kin; and, finally, "where
they were from," where his family lived. Through this information
—the same that the count asked of Cenerentola in the narrative
and that the young men asked the girls in their courting at the
real dances—the individual was reduced to a group, the individual
to the familiar (familiar signifies "of the family, pertinent to the
family" and also "known, well known"). An individual changed
from "not known" to "well known" when he or she was inserted
in the web of the kinship between the families which constituted
the group to which everybody belonged and the known social universe. Such a process constituted in the Tuscan *veglia* the functional
equivalence of the recitation of genealogies very common in certain
African cultures,[31] and elsewhere. In cultural contexts that are post-
industrial and mass-oriented, one can similarly consider the search
for common acquaintances between persons who have recently
met.

An unknown person who came to the *veglia* was obliged to establish identity in the same manner. Many times at *veglie* in the zone
of the Valdelsa or of Chianti, I was interrogated by my hosts, who
did not know me. The questions were always the same: they asked
me "to whom do you belong," "what was your mother's maiden
name," "who did your grandfather marry" until—in the areas
where my ancestors were known—we found some point of contact
that my interlocutor discovered with triumphant satisfaction or with
commotion: at the Valle they told me that my father "liked the
daughter of Gavurre of San Donato"; Lucia told me with tears in
her eyes that she had held my mother in her arms when she was
a baby; and an old man of Pievescola insisted on showing me a
worn-out molar with a filling that my grandfather applied "around
fifty-two years ago. Uhm! At this time you were not even in the
mind of God." Then he wanted to know, "since your grandfather
had two girls," which one was my mother; then he asked news of
my aunt; then he asked who had married my mother; then who
was the father of my father; then where was our home; then if I
had brothers or sisters; then if my sister was married; with whom;
where was my brother-in-law from; and where did they live. Then

after a satisfied sigh—he had in fact situated me exactly in a familiar system that in one point at least had met with his—he asked me what I wanted to know and helped me as best he could.[32]

In this way, at the *veglia*, the individual about whom they talked or with whom they were talking was finally given a proper kinship role and thus situated in the organization of the family—that was considered the most significant modality among all the distinctive social features of the group. And so from the individual through the "familiar" they reached their "universal," the maximum of generalization that was possible in the cultural microcosm within which one was required to think and represent the individual.

Those absent were often talked about, gossiped about, or even slandered. This type of conversation usually started after the children had been sent to bed, generally toward the end of the evening, though it was not always limited to this time period. These scandalous or malicious exclamations were almost always preceded by "It's said that . . . ," "They say that . . . ," or "They heard it said in town that . . ." Thus, personal responsibility for affirmations of the above nature was avoided. A person about whom "there was nothing to say" or of whom "no one had ever heard anything" was better than somebody "talked about," a "chatterer." Typical subjects for gossip could be stories of intrigues and affairs; of a family in a suburb near Quercegrossa, the husband of which had to move away because his wife was "said to frequent the priest"; of a woman who put salt in the doorway of another in order to give her the Evil Eye; of a farmer who stole from his neighbors; of a head of family who spent all his earnings "on the street," in taverns or with prostitutes; of a girl who was secretly seeing a married man; and sometimes of tavern doings. It is significant that it was toward the evening's end that the censorship was somewhat relaxed; with the children gone to bed, an extra word or so was allowable. Women, more than men, were the targets of these slanders because for them, even among their own sex, the norms of accepted behavior and the moral codes were much stricter and more rigorous.

One of the many such stories I heard at the *veglie* was that of a mother who had locked her small daughter in the house to go "who knew where" (to her lover, it was implied) while "you could hear the child crying from the street." Another was of a husband who

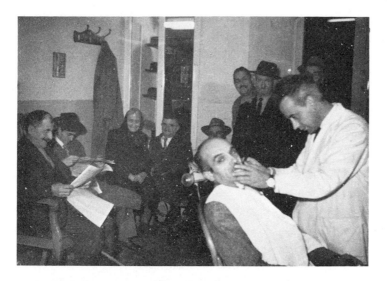

In the village, the gathering places that served for the exchange of gossip were traditionally the barber shop and the pharmacy (courtesy of Camillo Soderi and Anna Bianciardi).

had been heard complaining that his wife's shopping money was no longer enough. He had been heard saying: "Once you brought such good pieces of meat home. Now you don't bring anything," and the narrator explained in part (and part he left to the imagination) that the reason for the change was that the wife was no longer the lover of the town butcher, and that the "good pieces of meat" had been payment for services to be guessed at. One told of an ambitious woman, forever renewing her wardrobe and forever being in debt. "You play so rich but you can't pay," as a verse in a folk song went. Another woman was accused of always buying herself new dresses and of sending her children out "with patches on their seats" or "barefoot" or "with their shoes tied with broomstraws" (that is, without even laces). Another was said to have an affair going with a married neighbor. One morning his wife went to the city, either to the market or else to the doctor. Everyone saw her leave. But a couple of hours later, the adulteress knocked on the open door and said in a loud voice, "May I come in, Mrs. X?" after which she entered as if her lover's wife were at home. Instead, only her lover was there. After "they had done as they liked," the woman came out just as if she had been visiting her friend and not her friend's husband. In closing the door, she exclaimed in a loud voice (so that the neighbors could hear her), "Goodbye now, Mrs. X!" And everyone was giggling over the unsuccessful deception. Other facts were cited, such as in the story of a child of the town who was heard complaining: "Mommy, why don't you take me to the woods anymore? Before you took me there every day!?" and who was cut short with a smack from his mother. Then, with half-phrases, it was explained that the reason behind those trips to the woods was not the "fresh air" found there but, rather, a certain worker in the construction yard nearby. His work being over, the trips to the woods were suspended.

Ambiguity, half-sentences, and half-truths which gave free rein to the imagination and preconceived interest of whoever was listening were characteristic of this kind of gossip. The cultural function of the gossiping done at these evening gatherings was of a primary and essential importance, as has been noted in studies of various cultures.[33] These various insinuating remarks operate as a cohesive element inside a group. First of all, because they are given "in confidence," they are important bits of news reserved to the members of that group. The telling and the listening demonstrate and signify that those present form a definite, specific, and exclusive group. Second, gossip constitutes a method for defining and maintaining the group standards of official morality.[34] The behavior of each and every member of the group is thus subject to the critical scrutiny and moral judgment of that same community. Approved behavior is that prescribed by the roles—once more those of the family— assigned by that specific culture. As Gluckman has aptly observed, "For when you gossip about your friends to other mutual friends you are demonstrating that you all belong to one set which has the duty to be interested in one another's vices as well as virtues."[35]

The evening was over after everyone had said, performed, or listened to his or her part. Those who lived far away and had to walk or ride their bicycle home would often take their leave before the actual breaking up of the party. Frequently, the younger members would try to prolong the occasion, as it was one of their few chances for a get-together. The hosting head of the family could go to bed before all the guests had left, but his wife had to wait until the very end, in part as her duty of hospitality and in part to chaperon the teenagers and young unmarrieds. This continuous control was necessary for the good name of the family and, contrary to what might be assumed, was considered legitimate and necessary even by those so chaperoned. The girls wanted their suitors to see that theirs was a respectable home, and the young men who came with serious intentions wanted to be reassured that the girl of their choice had "good habits," that is, the habit of being carefully watched over. This "habit" produced a wife "as she should be," docile and amenable to a similar control exercised in the new family structure she would enter. Mothers' broadmindedness and permissiveness were stigmatized in songs.

> You twist it and play the peacock
> And to turn it you need a rope,
> And, pretty one, I kissed you on the stairs
> And your mother held the candle for you.[36]

Several verses express the same attitude:

> I enjoyed myself visiting you,
> Gossipy rumors telling you,
> Under your mother's eyes kissing you.[37]

> Little rue flower,
> Your mother is so scrupulous
> She's brought you the boys home.[38]

Little apple flower,
The mother makes love, the daughter learns:
She teaches her how to be a hypocrite.[39]

The young men themselves were very critical of mothers who were
bad examples for their daughters. If anything, they would only
try to think up tricks for prolonging the *veglia* or escaping their
surveillance but never to eliminate it. Someone who came with a
watch (very few had them) would set it back an hour or two in
order to deceive the housemother, who would ask the time and then
disperse the company believing it to be midnight when in reality
it was one or two A.M. Occasionally, they used other strategems.
Rosa told me about when Gino arranged to have some friends of
his let the sheep belonging to the family he was visiting loose. The
mother was the only one left watching over the daughter, and when
she heard the sheep in the fields she ran out to herd them back
to their stall. Thus, for once, the two young people were alone
together for a little while. Nonetheless, these were the exceptions
that proved the rule. In fact, even in a system of double standards
one had to maintain and support the official rules in order to get
around them. This attitude is illustrated in the common Tuscan
saying, jokingly or seriously attributed to girls:

Mummy! Cecco is touching me!
Touch me, Cecco, since Mummy is not watching!

And a girl displaying often this attitude is referred to as a *Cecco-
toccami* ["Cecco, touch me!"]. The term is a joking one, but with
the behavior of mothers, official aspirations of group morals, Tuscan
folklore was much stricter. An inattentive or permissive mother
was soon known and stigmatized as one who "tucked her daughter
into bed," that is, who helped her daughter into bed with the men.
     Some young men, in a poetic vein, would take their leave singing:

I wish you good night by my singing
And I greet you, silver palm,
who are the most beautiful of all.[40]

Silver flower!
Oh, come on, now, don't take offense;
It's the last song I sing.[41]

The girls very rarely accompanied their suitors to the door. Occasionally, if it was a dark night, the mother or father might tell their daughter to "give him light down the stairs" and then the girl would accompany the guest to the threshold on the first floor, whereupon he took his leave. Generally, they never went further than a "See you on Thursday—or Saturday—or Sunday"; sometimes there was an affectionate or loving phrase whispered in addition, after which the young man set out for home.

The return home was not without its dangers; not so much for those returning in groups as for the young man going home alone. Every now and then, someone would hide behind a tree or large bush in order to frighten those who passed by, either by screaming and shouting or else by dressing up in a white sheet and appearing out of the dark suddenly. During the evening, the solitary passerby had probably listened to stories about places where "one heard" or "one saw" strange things. These places were almost always nearby abandoned churches or graveyards or thick woods through which one had to pass for a shortcut. Often taken for supernatural beings or the ghosts of the dead, these apparitions were usually produced by the young men of the area who would place themselves in position and await the intruder who had gone to the *veglia* and courted a girl they were jealous of for one reason or another. They did not want a girl from their group or area to go off with a man from another, thus limiting their own range of selection; women, like everything else of value, were a limited good. I have been told of many, many cases of "stone throwings," of heavy hurlings of rocks, even stonings,[42] partly symbolic and partly real (but more real than symbolic according to the victims), against an unfortunate who had visited a home someone did not want him to visit. Sometimes the ambush was a true aggression: the victim had a "sack placed over his head," after which he was beaten up well, with threats of worse torments to follow should he ever dare return to that particular place. On other occasions, while hiding, they resorted to throwing rotten eggs or large bottles filled with sludge or excrement which broke on the victim, wounding him and soiling his suit (which was most probably his only good one, donned especially for the party). Another punishment was to "impale" the victim, that is, to run a "stick up his sleeves." The agressors would run a stick through the sleeves of their prisoner's coat and across

his shoulders, tying his wrists to the ends of the stick. Thus cruci-
fied, the unfortunate visitor had to return home, being unable to
free himself on his own. These aggressions constituted real and
definite tests of courage, analogous to those that the heroes in the
folktales had to pass to free the princess and thus win her hand.
In reality, as in the fairy tales, the young men risking these am-
bushes could resort to force of cunning in order to get through
the ordeal successfully. They could "play the fox," returning by a
different route each time, or they could stop and affront the danger.
Corrado told me about having encountered one of these youthful
ghosts, near the cemetery of Radda. His response was to shout out,
"If you're dead, I'm not afraid; and if you're alive, now I'm going
to beat the hell out of you." The ghost ran off and Corrado followed, captured, and recognized him. It was an acquaintance who
was jealous of Corrado because of the girl he was courting. In telling me this story, perhaps somewhat elaborated due to my presence
and that of his wife, who was listening with a satisfied air to the
tale of how her husband had overcome physical and metaphysical
tests for her, Corrado explained that he then punished his rival:
"I pummelled him like bread. . . . But some would have been
scared; there have even been some who died of fear."

Thus, the goings-on after the party furnished material for new
narratives, between the real and the fantastic, which would be included in the discussions held at the next *veglia*.

6

The *Veglia* Dance
"Dance Too, Adonis,
Since Everyone Is Dancing"

*"Il re, che in buona tempra era, fatto chiamar Tindaro, gli comandò
che fuor traesse la sua cornamusa, al suono della quale esso fece fare
molte danze."*

["The King, who was in a good mood, sent for Tindaro and ordered him to take out his pipes, to the sound of which he ordered
that there be many dances."]

Boccaccio, *Decameron*, the Sixth Day, Conclusion

*"Appresso questo, fatto venire de' lumi e vino e confetti, e alquanto
riconfortatisi, comandò che ogn 'uomo fosse in sul ballare."*

["After this, having sent for lights and wine and refreshments,
and when everybody felt better, he commanded that every man
dance."]

Ibid.

The season of winter *veglie* was closed by the "Carnival *veglie*," more modernly called Veglioni, or Big Vigils, which progressively replaced the other *veglie* dedicated predominantly to narratives and the types of folklore discussed previously. With the exception of Lent, one danced throughout the year: for example, on Easter Monday; to celebrate the threshing of the grain, in mid-August; on patron saints' days; at the farm *veglia*,[1] the party which the farmer gave in his villa for his sharecroppers, accepting invitations in turn to go to *veglie* given by them; Old Year's Day; and sometimes at weddings and on other occasions. Regardless, Carnival was the traditional season for dance parties.

After Epiphany, which concluded the passing from one annual cycle to the next ("Epiphany takes away all the holidays" ["*La Befania tutte le feste la porta via*"]), the Carnival balls started. These had the characteristics of time *ad limina*, destined to renew the community and its constituents by means of the coincidence of contrary behaviors and the suspension or overthrowing of the rules that governed the lives of the community for the rest of the year.[2] ("During the Carnival season any joke is good" ["*Carnevale ogni scherzo vale*"];[3] "the one day of the year when the old woman dances" ["*un dì dell'anno, la vecchia in ballo*"];[4] "during the Carnival, husbands are worth cardoons without salt" ["*tanto vale il cardone senza sale / quanto far col marito il Carnevale*"].[5]) This period of "leave" in the broad sense dates back with certainty at least to the Roman Saturnalia;[6] maintains fixed morphological features, such as music and dance as mood elevators and masquerade as a sign of reversal behavior; and is of such general importance that all social classes and age groups have always participated in it, in various roles and forms.

The most simple type of dance *veglia* took place in patriarchal houses, in the same large kitchen which up until now has created our stage setting. In the case of these dance parties, it was no longer the head of the peasant's family who invited the guests but, as a rule, the group of unmarried men who invited unmarried women. These young men first of all had to ask the head of the family for permission to use his kitchen. They then saw to engaging an accordionist. There was rarely more than one accordion; however, occasionally there was also a mandolin, a violin, a guitar, or some wind instrument. The young men invited women, with the tacit understanding that they would come accompanied by their mothers or by chaperons. The men also provided refreshments: sweet wine, punch, sherry, or cherry juice served with homemade pastries, a jam tart, or roasted chestnuts, and almost always the traditional *cenci* of sweet pastry fried in olive oil, covered on top with icing, and sprinkled with very white powdered vanilla. Sometimes there was also whipped cream in cone-shaped cornets, cooked on the hearth fire by the housekeeper with a long iron mold in the form of tongs. Sometimes the home where the party was being held furnished the refreshments, taking care of all the organization and preparation. These, however, were dances for friends and acquaintances and were not public and open to anybody. One of the guests could bring along a friend, provided he accepted full responsibility for his guest's behavior, running the risk of not being invited again if his guest did not behave properly. In rare cases an uninvited guest would turn up, asking permission to join the dance. Only if they understood that they knew him was he welcomed. On the whole, to be accepted into the party, one had to have some friend in common with the other members of the *veglia*; that is, one had to be at least marginally a member of this group. The kitchen was cleared, with the table moved against a wall to accommodate the buffet; the stools were also lined up against the walls. The women sprinkled water on the kitchen floor. They then swept it and sprinkled salt over it. This last operation was a ritual one in that it created a ritual space. The rational explanations that I elicited were "to be able to dance better," "to be able to slide more easily," and "to prevent dust," but, as others told me, it was also done to keep away witches.[7]

The fire crackled happily in the hearth, the guests arrived, and the musician as a rule placed himself on the seat above the kneading trough in which the bread was made. The older generation sat comfortably by the fireside or along the walls, and the dancing started.

Polka

The first dance of the evening was always a polka. The men asked the women to dance ("figure" was the term used for the female dancing partner). The girls usually sat next to their mothers or on their laps. The dancing was often started by the head of the peasant's family or by one of the hosts who served as the *capoveglia* (head of the *veglia*) in this type of *veglia* as in the others. The polka played by the musician on the kneading trough was in the traditional 2/4 time, as in the accompanying score, recorded at a *veglia* in 1973 in Buonconvento. The polka, like all the dance tunes played during the *veglia*, lasted from five to ten minutes, depending on the preferences of the musician and the instructions of the *capoveglia* and couples; all the dancers, in fact, had their own favorite dance and their own favorite partner, and one could try to make a dance one was enjoying last as long as possible, both with a signal or a verbal exhortation like *"Va'vai!"* ["Go, go!"], *"Séguita!"* ["More!"], and *"Dell'altro!"* ["Go on!"]. The couples moved in a clockwise direction around the kitchen, one behind the other, performing a series of rotations and revolutions right until the end. When the music stopped, the man accompanied the woman "to her place" and symbolically handed her back to her mother or chaperon, after having thanked her and invited her for another dance later on, but not usually for the next one. Dancing together for a number of dances in a row indicated a strong interest on behalf of the man, reciprocated by the woman, and one was careful to conceal even a liking for someone right from the beginning so as not to expose oneself to restrictive countermeasures by the girl's parents, or to gossip. So they changed partners and passed on to the next dance, which was always a mazurka. "La Regina Taitù" ["The Queen Taitu"], shown here, was recorded from a performance by Dario Tanzini, of Fonterutoli, who by now has played it for half a century. The movement of the mazurka, in 3/4 time, was accelerated in comparison to that of the polka; that is, it was a faster dance.

Mazurka

The progress of acceleration continued with the third dance, which was always a waltz, again in 3/4 time but faster moving than the mazurka. The example was recorded at the same *veglia* in Fonterutoli. The basic sequence of the dance party ended with the quadrille, which, in 6/8 time, was the fastest moving dance. Shown here is a typical example. The quadrille was the most important and complex of all dances at the *veglie*,[8] and the number of those who danced it was close to the number of participants at the party; everyone wanted to dance the quadrille. It was also considered the most suitable dance for talking to and courting from closer quarters the girls in whom one was interested. It was, moreover, the most varied, amusing, and lively of the dances because of the changing of partners and the greater number of steps with their unforeseeable combinations.

The *capoveglia* placed himself in the center of the hall, while the couples formed a circle around him with the men on the inside and the women on the outside. When the music struck up, the *capoveglia* started to "give orders to" the quadrille, calling out the

Waltz

Quadrille

different dance figures with a stentorian voice. The first was always "*A spasso!!*" ["Walk!!"]. All the couples set off walking in a clockwise circle. The *scena a braccino* could then follow, in which the two partners locked left elbows, and from that position they turned 360°. Then he could call out for the *gran scena* (corresponding to the American "grand right and left"). The men set off from their initial position on the inside circle; the women, on the outside. The men moved in a clockwise direction; the women, in a counterclockwise one. To start the dancing, the man took the woman in front of him by the left hand and gave her a thrust so that she took his place on the dance floor, he in turn taking her place on the outside circle. He then took the right hand of the woman in front of him on the inside circle and changed places with her. They continued in this way until the male dancer returned to his original partner, having done the round. In this way, every man met all the women present and vice versa. Other common commands were "a round of polka" or "of mazurka" or "*di valtzer*" [of waltz]. The musician then changed time and the couples danced around the hall before returning *a spasso*, or in a quadrille. Or the *capoveglia* could say, "Young ladies inside!" The couples would then change places, with the men on the outside and the women on the inside. When he shouted "Circle!!" they formed a circle, with the men and women alternating and moving in a clockwise direction with the man in front and the woman behind. At the command "The young lady in front!!" the man and woman changed places, continuing to move around. Another *a spasso* brought the couples back to their positions at the beginning of the dance. *A spasso* was also resorted to by the person commanding the quadrille whenever the couples would make a mistake, mixing up the positions and the couples. When he shouted "Change!!" every man left his partner for the partner of the man in front of him, putting his arm around her waist and guiding her clockwise around the circle. This was followed by another "Change," and once again they exchanged partners. Often the *capoveglia* clapped his hands to indicate the moment when they had to exchange partners. At each handclapping, one had to move up a place to a new partner; two claps indicated two places and so on until one came side by side with one's original partner.

Even if the various movements of the quadrille were substantially the same, the names given to them by the person making the calls were very varied, changing the figures. For each movement, each region or even smaller area had a different name, and this made the dancing problematic for those who were ignorant of the local terms. At Pianella, for instance, a position with a man and woman back-to-back with their hands on their heads was called *zigulinè*. At the command of *Cincirinè*, the couple made a semicircle, holding each other by the hand. Other commands were improvised, such as *"Drecho la conca, drech' i' telaio, drecho la concha, drech' i' telaio!!"* ["Behind the oil jar, behind the spinning wheel!"]. This was heard at Salivolpi and ordered the dancers to move behind the kitchen furniture. There is a version at Volpaia of another very common movement whereby at the command of *Pronti pe' lo zighede* ["Ready!"] the dancers moved *a spasso*, side by side with each other. The man took the left hand of the woman with his right hand, and vice versa, thus forming a cross. When the order *Zighede!!* was called out, the couple turned 180°, still holding hands in crossed position, and went *a spasso* in a counterclockwise direction. At the order *Zàghede!!* they made another 180° turn and continued the *spasso* in a clockwise direction. To mark the end of the quadrille, the "commander" took the hand of each partner in a couple, breaking the circle and shouting out: "Refreshment time!!!" or "Take her for a drink." This guided the dancers toward the kitchen table, transformed into a buffet, where one "stuffed oneself" with whatever there was, usually with great gaiety, as related in the last century by Tuscan writer Giusti: "What wonderful times you used to have! Every half century there was some sort of dance party with a couple of off-key violins, a plate of biscuits, and a flask of *vin santo*."[9] At this point the hat was passed around, in which the men deposited their share to pay for the musician and the refreshments if these were not offered by the host. During refreshment time, the girls usually appeared reluctant and modest, and the men had to urge them to eat and drink. A girl who proved to be a great eater or a big drinker did her image as a future wife and housekeeper no good. The woman who "ate more than she earned" would be a bad companion; one would rather marry a woman who "ate like a bird." After the break, dancing started again with another polka followed by a mazurka and so on, cycle after cycle, until the end of the evening, with the very rare exception of some other, more ancient dance, such as the *battibellico*, the *volpe*,[10] the *trescone*,[11] the *stropiccione*, or the *monferrina*,[12] nearly always danced only once during the evening, serving as a distraction or a virtuoso demonstration.

Trescone

Sometimes the dance party was held on the paved area in front of a barn or in a farmhouse, and on these occasions the landlord invited all his farm workers to join his other guests.[13] This habit, other than obeying the laws of reciprocity and the necessity for contact among those with common interests, had the function of annulling social distances once a year. Farm workers, peasants, and landowners became only dancers; the landladies and the workers' wives were merely classed as women. On these occasions one could decide to show some secret fancy for someone which, if reciprocal, would encourage gossip and allusions to the point of exciting stories at the next *veglia*. They would talk about a ranger who went out with the landlady, a worker who had eloped with the landlord's daughter, the owner's son who was having an affair with a farm girl from Uzzano or Calcinaia, or about illegitimate children sent to the orphanage in Florence or put out to nurse in the Casentino area, famous for its wet nurses, and recognized later on by their father and finally invited to share his affluence. Folk narratives included not only stories that were fantastic and made to sound true, but also real events which became exemplary and fantastic stories. Real life facts had a tendency toward the fantastic, and fantasy toward real life. The folklore even here maintained its characteristic of mediation between the real and the fantastic by means of the true-plausible and the true-possible.

Another type of dance party was sometimes held in the villages on Sunday after the religious service, from about four until eight. On this occasion the girls from the village and surrounding countryside gathered, without their ever-present mothers taking part and without having told them, together with the young men from the village and the peasant boys.[14] It was usually a group of young men who arranged for the hall, the refreshments, and the musician, dividing the expenses and sometimes making the men pay an entrance fee.[15] The women, however, as in all traditional meetings, did not have to pay an entrance fee. These dance parties were jokingly called *carconie* [crowded], because one ended up dancing in a crowd, or *fumicaiole* [smoky], because there was only the uncertain and smoky light of oil lamps. ("In the light of the oil lamp every peasant woman looks beautiful" ["*Al lume di lucerna, ogni rùstica par bella*"]).[16] One went to these dances with a sense of secrecy and of breaking a prohibition. As a rule, these dances were organized without the permission of the *carabinieri*, which was theoretically always necessary for a public dance. But had they asked permission, everybody would have known about the dance and the "guardians" of the girls would have had to come. The girls' excuse to be sent to the village was to attend religious functions, after which one danced in secret. Sometimes they danced instead of going to church and attended the *veglia* with a vague sense of committing a sin, a feeling of guilt, and an attitude of complicity with those present, none of whom, for one reason or another, had permission to be in that situation. The girls from the surrounding countryside would have told their parents that they were going to a church service followed by a walk in the village. The village girls would say the same. Almost always the girls made sure they were seen by some acquaintance of their parents so as to have an "alibi" in case of possible questioning by their families. The parents of the girls from the surrounding countryside did not want their daughters to meet village boys on these occasions. The latter, as a rule, did not have honorable intentions; otherwise, they would have visited the girls in their own homes. Nor did their sons have much to gain. The village girls were no good at working in the fields and were "flirts," "pretentious," and badly brought up. The parents

in the village considered it a drop in status if their sons mixed
with the farm girls, whom they considered "boors," "unrefined,"
"crude," and so on. "To have a peasant in the home" was not their
greatest hope, and these gatherings could cause this to result. Many
blason populaire anecdotes derived from this feeling: there are stories
about girls who arrived in cowhide shoes and peasants who danced
in shoes with nails in the soles, making the noise of a team of oxen,
while the villagers were naturally "more refined" and "more distinguished."

The *fumicaiole* did not have a chaperone, and the group of peers
settled controversies and arguments that sometimes finished in
brawls either inside or outside the hall. The dances were the same:
the polka, the mazurka, the waltz, or the quadrille. The couples'
behavior, however, was relatively freer; one could speak more freely, one could offer to walk the girl part of the way home, one could
arrange a date in the woods, or one could be free with one's hands.
The girls, however, knew how to take care of themselves, and
breaking the rules had to follow the rules of rulebreaking. At Castellina they still speak about a *fumicaiola* in the 1930s when a young
man was touching the behind of a young girl under the pretext
of guiding her in the dance. She admonished him in a loud voice:
"Your damn hand!!! Gino!! Your damn hand!!!" In this context, the
mano morta, or "dead hand," was a hand placed on a forbidden
part with the excuse of the dance and pretending that nothing was
amiss. The young man would then boast to his friends about having touched some girl's breasts or behind, and to have found it
"hard" or *mollicone* [squashy]. Or he could boast about having
placed his genitals near hers during the dance. His friends in turn
would have asked the usual questions, like "What did she do?"
"Did she go for it?" and received proverbial replies like "Poor thing,
she is so hungry that she can't wait any longer." Even if this dance
lacked the formal control of the older generation, there was a more
decentralized and treacherous one, that of the peers' gossip. At the
fumicaiole, as in the folktales, "the man has the right to ask, the
woman the duty to refuse," and the girls did not forget this even
while going out and returning home with the young boy who took
their fancy.

The most complete and complex form of dance party, containing
all the elements of the dance *veglie* mentioned before, plus some

others, was the *veglia* held in the village or small town for "members
and families." Almost all the villages had a "party society" or "club"
formed by representatives of practically all the families in the village.[17] This society organized *veglie* reserved strictly for its members
and their families and for occasional guests who were, once again,
the direct responsibility of the members who accompanied them.
These special parties were traditionally held three times per Carnival and marked the most important days of it, ending the winter
party season with which we are concerned. The most important
days were the Thursday of the Carnival period (or *giovedì grasso*),
the following "Carnival Sunday," and the "Carnival Tuesday," during which one danced until midnight when the church bell tolled,
indicating the end of the dance and the Carnival season and the
beginning of penance and Lent. On other occasions the societies
could organize dances that were open to the public but with an
entrance fee. This practice has expanded over the last few years
to include parties for children, summer dances, evenings for ama-
teurs or holiday makers, New Year's Eve parties, *pentolacce* for mid-
Lent, et cetera. But underneath the diffusion of dances throughout
the year which is the logical result of their commercialization, there
is a symbolic-ritual value that is still clearly discernible in the three
Carnival dances organized by the closed village communities for
their members.

On these occasions many musicians, even ten or more, were
chosen from the municipal band. There were drums, violins, accor-
dions, bass clarinets, trumpets, and bugles. Before going to the
hall where the dance would be held, the band made a tour of the
village, playing as it went along. In this way it let all the villagers
know about the forthcoming dance. In the dance hall the members
of the band took their positions on a raised platform, decorated
with vases borrowed from villagers, some of whom were entrusted
with the decoration of the hall. At the entrance was a cloakroom;
the buffet was prepared in a separate hall. The tables were placed
all around the hall, with the chairs and benches along the walls.
The young men without a table remained standing near the orchestra so as not to block the view of those seated. To be allowed at
this *veglia*, the boys had to be at least eighteen years of age, and
the girls had to be at least past the stage of puberty. The parents

A little Carnival Queen at a *veglia* in 1893; the handwritten note says "My doll at age 6" (courtesy of Zoe Mazzuoli).

decided when their daughters were old enough to go dancing, making their debut in society. Entrance was forbidden to those who were too young or not members of the group. They were thrown out with little formality. Before the Carnival festivities, a dance school was held twice a week so that the more elderly and experi-

A fat Romeo posing in his costume at a masquerade in 1860 (courtesy of
Lucia Rossi-Ferrini).

enced dancers could teach the young men "under fire" for the first
time, who were known as "young cocks" or "young fowls."

The men had to wear a dark suit, which was either double-breast-
ed or worn with a waistcoat. They wore black patent leather shoes
and white gloves "to avoid too much direct contact with the wom-
en dancers." [18] The girls arrived escorted by their mothers or aunts,
sometimes in a coach, "so as to avoid dirtying their shoes and
clothes," like Cinderella, and just like her, they tried to look as different and transformed as possible with regard to their everyday
appearance. For each of the three dances, they flaunted different
outfits which no one was supposed to have seen beforehand. These
were prepared in great secrecy at home or by the dressmaker. The
wealthier and more ambitious of the female sex displayed family
jewelry and different hairstyles. The jewels were lent by mother
or grandmother after long warnings and stories about their enormous monetary value and in particular about their affective value:
"This brooch belonged to my poor old grandmother who gave it

The Chianti band before playing at a *veglia* of the Carnival in 1897 (courtesy of the Falassi family).

to me when I got married, and her aunt gave it to her when she died so be careful not to lose it." Often Cinderellas or protagonists of "Donkey Skin" presented themselves at balls with dresses decorated with "the sun, the moon, and the stars," or "of gold, of silver, of pearl." In reality the women's outfits were often decorated with chains, bracelets, earrings, brooches, and necklaces in gold, silver, or pearls. The aesthetic of these gowns and those described in the tales was after all not so very different; it was only the fairy tale descriptions that made them appear that much more glittering. The emphasis, always, was on transformation: from the everyday to the festive and from the dull and worn to the new and bright and shiny. The message of transformation and the renewal of vitality is, after all, a simple one to dramatize, but none could be more profound, especially when the change was part of such a calendared, emotionally prepared for, and heightened time. The stuff of fairy tales was not very removed from the unusual events of everyday life.

A new-style band, with snare drums and majorettes, before a *veglia* in Poggibonsi in 1978 (courtesy of M.o Salvatore Cintorino, Siena).

Underscoring this theme of dressing up and transformation was the focus on wearing the right shoes, by even the most under-classed of the participants. These *veglie* were frequented by girls from the surrounding countryside who often had to walk quite a few kilometers to attend. Many wore their old shoes and scarves, carrying their good shoes and accessories in a parcel. Once in the vicinity of the village and on a good road, they put on their good shoes, leaving the others in a bundle under an oak tree. On their way home, they would collect their old shoes. The young boys often resorted to similar contrivances. Many have told me about a certain "Gambine di Casalta" ["Little Legs from Casalta"], who carried stone slabs in his pocket which he carefully placed over stretches of mud and puddles of water, passing over them without dirtying his shoes.

The person chosen to open the dance was the *caposala*, a respected man with a deep knowledge and understanding of the customs and mentality of the villagers. He was often a "reveler" and good danc-

Members only: a *veglia* in the late 1920's (courtesy of the Biblioteca Comunale degli Intronati, Siena).

er[19] and was entrusted with making sure the evening ran smoothly, doing the calls for the quadrille and saying the "good-night to the musicians," so ending the dance. The basic dance sequence was the same as that of the other dance parties: the polka, the mazurka, the waltz, and the quadrille. Variations according to time and place were often inserted in the sequence but without subverting it. They could, for example, dance three rounds of the polka, the mazurka, and the waltz, followed by a quadrille. Recently they have added new dances after the waltz, such as the *sciotisse*, the tango,[20] the *fostrò*, the *onesteppe*, and so on. Anyway, as the informality of the names suggests (Giusti, indeed, calls it *soarè*),[21] social functions and meanings of this *veglia* have remained substantially the same.

The music of the latest tunes was also reduced to a more traditional familiar dimension. Frequently one danced to the rhythm of melodies of a very varied origin. An English traveler taking part in a dance about the time of the First World War observed an orchestra made up of a mandolin, a violoncello, and guitars playing the war melody of "Tripoli, bel suol d'amore," probably in the rhythm of a polka.[22] This was a common practice. One of my informants, Gostino, told me how at a dance at San Rocco a Pilli after the Second World War the couples danced for at least a quarter of an hour to the sound of the "Bandiera Rossa" (the Communist anthem), played as a polka. When he turned to the leader of the band asking him why they were playing that particular piece and for such a long time, he stopped directing for a moment to reply, "Young man, this is what we do at San Rocco." He then carried on directing with renewed vigor, moreover singing at a polka beat: "Avan-tio-po-po-lo . . ."

This process continues today, since new social reality in Italy seems to cause the production of new texts and possibly new genres, more or less oriented toward politics or pop music.[23] At the dances for the Communist Festival dell'Unità, now held annually, I have heard the refrain of the Communist anthem played on a polka tune, followed by one strophe on the quadrille tune and a second strophe on a tango and so on. The text, due to folk poet Eugenio Bargagli, provided a dramatized, idealized illustration of the life of Italy's most prominent Communist leaders of this century, Antonio Gramsci[24] and Palmiro Togliatti:

> Right on with the people
> out for revenge!
> The red flag
> shall triumph!

Right on with the people [first four lines only] . . .

> Antonio Gramsci founded the Party,
> fighting side-by-side with the workers.
> He chose a red flag among all colors,
> and today it's a color that triumphs still.

Sickle and hammer and rising star;
this is the party of freedom!

In nineteen twenty-one the fascists of the Duce
started the march on Rome
with clubs and rifles, and they plot
to arrest Antonio.

   Right on with the people
   out for revenge!
   The red flag
   shall triumph!

Antonio Gramsci was arrested
and tortured under the clubs.
They had no remorse
and he had to die of tortures.
We had to undergo twenty years of fascism,
massacres, and shootings at the workers!

But Togliatti emigrated to Russia.
He had to finish his studies.
He always struggled for the Party.
It's the Party that every day goes further ahead!

   Right on with the people
   out for revenge!
   The red flag
   shall triumph!

Antonio was questioned many times
and he was asked to change ideals
and often he was hit and abused,
but he answered, "Who does evil, pays for it."
He died, murdered in his prison cell
under the evil people of the treacherous Fascism.

But Gramsci's own doctrine
penetrated upon the workers,
and it taught to defend the colors,
the colors of freedom!

Right on with the people
out for revenge!
The red flag
shall triumph!

Togliatti was a model student,
he conquered the scholarship,
he became strong and very intelligent,
and he always fought for the Party.
He fought in September of '44
when there was the surrender of Fascism.

But Togliatti came back to do his part
at the head of the workers
against the Fascism and the exploiters.
Nobody shall stop this struggle!

Right on with the people
out for revenge!
The red flag.
The red flag.
Right on with the people
out for revenge!
The red flag
shall triumph![25]

Yet at regular *veglie* these texts are very uncommon, because of their political, ergo divisive, character. The *veglia*, on the contrary, was a ritual of community integration that tended to minimize all differences, including political ones, among participating members.

Before the orchestra started playing, a young man went up to a girl, asking her, "Shall we dance?" or "Young lady, allow me this dance?" Sometimes, if he did not know the girl, he asked the mother's permission to dance with her daughter, a small sign of respect in line with the proverb that generally warns, "He who wants a fig must lower the branch; he who wants a girl must flatter her mother" ["*Chi vuole i fichi abbassi i rami, chi vuole le figlie accarezzi le mamme*"].[26] Courtesy demanded that all the girls present at the party be asked to dance at least once by each boy. If a woman was married or engaged, the man had to ask the permission of her

husband or fiance before inviting her to dance, otherwise an argument might ensue. As in the case of mothers or aunts, they had
the power of veto, but they used it only if he who invited the woman
to dance was a good-for-nothing, a rascal with bad intentions, or
a wooer explicitly disliked by her family prior to the *veglia* in question. In these cases they made firm bargains: "Listen, if you dance
with Corrado, I'm going to take you home." With the exception
of these unusual cases, the girls had to dance with everybody. A
refusal had to be justified; for instance, one could say, "I've already
been asked," [27] in which case the young man could insist, asking
for the next dance and so on. "I'm tired" was a suspicious reply
and like the above-mentioned one, did not exempt one from having
to accept a dance later on. If a girl refused a man by saying that
she had already been invited when she had not, or if she said she
was tired yet accepted the invitation of someone she preferred afterward, trouble was caused. On rare occasions, the man carried out
his threat and slapped her. Normally the *caposala* intervened, forc-
ing her to accept the invitation or punishing her by making her
sit out for one or more dances, while drunk or impolite men were
asked to leave the hall. The women could only resort to a sort of
passive resistance, as this old *rispetto* depicts vividly:

> I'll teach you what the girls do
> if they dance with somebody half-heartedly:
> They go around the dancing floor all stiffened up;
> they pretend that their feet hurt.
> But when they dance with the one they want
> they have no wings, yet they fly!
> And when they dance with their lovers
> they look like some poisonous snakes!
> And when they dance with their favorite ones
> then their feet do not hurt any longer. [28]

The rule was that everybody had to dance with all and sundry,
and the *caposala* could encourage this fundamental principle of the
veglia, calling out, "Commitments are forbidden!!" so that no one
could dance more than one dance with a particular partner.

   In addition to the *caposala*'s duties as "matchmaker," his function
as keeper of law and order was equally important. He had to call

the *carabinieri* if there was a big brawl, which, however, was un-likely among people who had had family ties for generations. Other than guaranteeing the general principle of the mixing of the two sexes, the *caposala* more or less discreetly directed the specific practi-cal applications of it. He did so by replying to specific questions which he was discreetly asked: "But is she engaged?" "But hasn't she got anybody?" "Wasn't she going with someone from Colle?" or "Who is that young lady dancing with that man over there?" Sometimes the intervention of the *caposala* was more direct, as in "*Ballo a i' canto*" ["Dance to the singing"]. On that occasion, having climbed onto the platform, he gave a man direct instructions to dance with a particular girl. These were given in extemporary verses like the following:

> This dance is no good
> If Beppino doesn't come over here.
> It would be much better
> If Beppino came over here.[29]

Beppino then went to the foot of the platform and the girl who was to partner him was invited to dance:

> And this dance is no good
> If Rosa doesn't come over here.

Sometimes, having taken the girl by the hand, he directly called over her partner for the next dance:

> Adonis is also invited to dance,
> Dance too, Adonis, since everyone is dancing,
> And this includes the beautiful and the ugly.[30]

This versified pairing has taken place exactly in the same way for centuries, as we can see from a manuscript account of a folk dance held at Rovezzano in 1552. There the head of the dance, *colui che impone*, sang verses beginning:

> This dance is no good [*Questo ballo non sta bene*]

and matched partners ordering:

And you [name of the dancer], my companion,
go nearby your desired one
and there remain.[31]

Sometimes, before the *veglia*, a young man or woman would approach the *caposala*, confiding in him about a secret fancy and expressing the wish to show it indirectly to the person concerned. One could say, "Oh, take care to make me dance with her please." In this case the *caposala* could "matchmake" without saying a word or he could describe the entire underhand intrigue in public. If the couple concerned were chatting, he could sing verses like the following:

Look how beautiful she is,
And it was only yesterday that she said to me,
"I want Francesco Bernabei
If he wants a dance around the hall!"

Consequently, everybody, including Francesco Bernabei, knew about the beautiful girl's fancy for him when they were invited to dance together, and they also knew that she had pressed for the dance the day before. I had just recorded the preceding verses in person at Fonterutoli when I was called up to dance with this other impromptu rhyme with the same rhythm as the preceding one:

I would also like him to join in.
I hope she won't stone him.
I beg the son of Mr. Falassi
To have a dance around the hall![32]

In the verse concerning me, as in the preceding ones, there is a reference not only to the person but especially to the family, which was considered to be the most important element of the social personality of the *vegliatori* and of their relationships within and outside the *veglia*.

On other occasions the *caposala* started dancing with a girl whom he later on handed over to a young man with whom she would then dance. He then took a second girl whom he handed over to another young man. This snowballed until everybody was on the dance floor. He could then repeat the operation with the men, finding a female dancer for each of them. It was always the *caposala* who announced the various dancing competitions that were arranged about halfway through the evening. There were different types of competitions and they were held for different dances. The competition could be arranged to choose the couple that was best at the waltz, the polka, the mazurka, or any other dance. The *caposala* surveyed the participating couples from the platform, and at the end of the dance judged, with the help of the band leader or some other personality, the best couple, who was presented with a prize. In other competitions every couple was given a number tag which the woman wore so that the couples could be identified by number. The dancing started, and from the platform the judge called out the number of the couple worst at dancing, in this way signalling them to leave the floor and take their place among the audience. At the end there was only one couple left on the floor. They made a demonstration swing around the hall, afterward receiving the prize. Another dancing competition was the *stroncagambe* [leg breaker], which nearly always involved a waltz that the couples danced until exhausting their energy. The last couple on the floor, still dancing when the legs of the others were "broken" with fatigue, won the competition through sheer persistence more than skill.

Other than the dancing competitions, at some stage during the *veglia* games[33] were held. The principle of these was the formation of couples and the allotment of a penalty to the person who remained "unpaired." An example was the dance with the handkerchief. Two women started dancing together until they found themselves in front of a man, where one of them dropped a handkerchief. The man picked it up, exchanging it for one of the women, and started dancing with her. The other woman took the handkerchief and went in search of another woman with whom she repeated the previous operation and so on. At the *caposala*'s signal the orchestra stopped playing, and the woman who remained with the handkerchief in her hand received a penalty, which nearly always consisted of saying or doing embarrassing things, such as kissing someone she did not know or making love declarations to an old man. After the penalty a pair of men took the handerchief and the game was repeated the other way round. Another dance game was the "dance with the broom." A man started dancing with a broom while all the other men were dancing with women. Still dancing, he approached a couple, beating

the broom handle on the ground and leaving it balancing precarious-
ly. Without letting it fall, the male partner in the couple left his partner
to catch the broom. In this way the man first dancing with the broom
had exchanged it for a woman and his successor repeated the operation and so on until the *caposala* stopped the music and alloted a
penalty to the unpaired man with the broom in his hand. This could
then be carried on with the women dancing with the broom instead
of the men.

Other games were held without music, such as "The Flask and the
Candle." The *caposala* chose a girl who was made to sit on a stool
beneath the orchestra, and he gave her a flask and a lit candle. He
then chose three young men, often her courters or men she fancied.
Next, he lined them up in front of her. The three of them then bowed,
paying homage to her. At this point the girl handed the flask to one
of the three, who thus *faceva fiasco* [was a fiasco—pun on the word
fiasco, or flask]. Another received the candle, which symbolically left
him to "play gooseberry" [pun on the word *candela*]. The girl then
rose to dance with the third man, thus showing her liking for him.
The game could be repeated with the men and women exchanging
roles. This was one of the most popular games and was commonly
considered to be a real indicator of the sentiments of the participants:
"I want to see if Attilia gives the flask to Corrado."

Another game was "*alle coppie*" ["The Couples"]. On one side of
the hall four women stood in a circle, and on the other five men
arranged themselves in a circle. The two circles moved around until
the *caposala* clapped his hands. The men ran across the hall to fetch
the women. The man who remained by himself received a penalty,
after which the game was repeated with five women who had to
partner four men. Naturally, one always tried to pick or be partnered
off with the person one fancied without making it too obvious. The
couples thus formed then danced, with possible aftereffects of jeal-
ousy and chidings: "You let yourself be picked by Bistino, that no-
good jerk!" Another very popular game was "Cat and Mouse." The
dancers lined up in many parallel queues about a meter apart. The
caposala then chose a man and a woman to be at the head of each
row. At the agreed-upon signal, the man had to chase and catch the
woman, who was running between the rows. The game then ended
with the capture of the woman or the manifested incapacity of the
man to catch her. Often the people forming the obstacle stretched

out a hand or an elbow to block the path of the man or woman, and the spectators derived amusement from seeing whether the women wished to be caught or not. The *caposala* could choose any combination: a husband and wife, an engaged couple, a girl and a suitor of hers whom she found undesirable, a very young girl and an old man, or a young boy at his first *veglia* and a *donna fatta* [mature woman]. The connotations attributed by the spectators and participants to this game changed each time and it became a pantomime of married life, courtship, or a rite of passage. At my first *veglia*, the *caposala* humorously said to me, "Let's see if you can catch a woman," and he made me tire myself out for at least a quarter of an hour behind the most agile woman in the hall. A couple of times I was on the point of getting hold of her, but I was held back by men who guffawed, "Eh, you can't make it!" This type of symbolic test of one's càpacity to conquer a woman formed part of the ritual of attaining manhood for the boys. At this age one could go dancing, get married, or go to brothels. One could, in short, "take up with a woman" in all contexts, and there were times, as on this occasion, when one symbolically had to show that one was capable of performing with masculine skill and endurance.

Almost all the games mentioned previously could be played as part of the quadrille, which in this type of *veglia* was even more ceremonious than in the preceding ones. At the *veglie* for members and families, one invited the girl in whom one was most interested to dance the quadrille. "I had her to myself for all the quadrille" was a comment that demonstrated a strong, explicit, and reciprocated interest of a young man. The nomenclature of the figures and the number of participants of these *veglie* differed from the simpler ones. The hall was much larger than the country kitchen and one could see as many as forty couples dancing in it. The *caposala* started with *Alò, Alé, Alèi,* or *Anavan le premié*.[34] Practically all the orders were given in this kind of bastard French which everybody, including the *caposala*, had to strain their ears to understand. But it made the dance "refined" and gave it a "certain tone." And as the famous *caposala* Corrado del Nano explained to me, "It's enough just to understand one another." As always in a family, one ended up by understanding maybe with the help of a tug from the *caposala* for a couple that was late, with some bungler's expulsion from the dance, or with the providential *A spasso!!*—sometimes reinforced by a "Goddammit" from the *caposala*, who always wanted "things to be done in the proper way." The *scena a braccino* was called *grascè*;[35] the *a spasso, promené*. Other figures were the *alame* [the allemande of American square dancing], *ro* [the *rondò*], the *pirule* [the *zíghede* mentioned before], the *changé la dà*[36] to indicate girl swapping when dancing, the *all'arriè* to mean backward, the *ballonzé*[37] to make the couples dance about on the same spot, the *galoppé* to indicate the *a spasso* at a gallop, and the *sorge* to make the men take the women in front of them. Often the quadrille finished with the *scutiscià*[38] [*queue de chat*] or *gomitolo* [ball]. The couples held hands in a ring that wound into a ball in the center of the hall. When they were all crowded together, the first dancer to lead the brigade to the buffet emerged from the center of the "ball," making his way under the raised arms of the others, either straight away or after the *remercì le da*,[39] a "thanksgiving" to the women performed with a bow, always "French style."

For the buffet, which was held in another hall, they sat at small tables, relaxing after the fatigue of the quadrille. One could at last speak without the direct control of one's parents, who usually remained out of sight in the dance hall and commented, "Did you see how she moved close to him!" "But what a noise Elvira was making!" "Tillo bounced like a rubber man," "That boy from Quercesola is as loose-joined as a puppet," and "My daughter hasn't missed one dance!" Besides commenting on the dance itself, the elders engaged in conversation, bringing the group up to date on events while maintaining and revitalizing its communication network. At the buffet, one could override the family veto. A girl who was not supposed to dance with a certain young man would see to it that she was invited by a friend of his so that she could meet up with him at the buffet. While having some punch, a *vin santo*, a sweet wine, an *amarena* [cherry syrup], or a citron water, one spoke about this and that but above all about the affairs of the heart, continuing the conversation later on in the hall.

> Beautiful clover,
> As from that evening when I saw you dancing
> You made me lose my brains.[40]

They also asked for explanations: "I saw you dangling after Rosa"

or "I saw you getting sweet with Aleandro." When changing partners during the quadrille, one tried to partner as long as possible
the prettiest girls, while the ugly ones were discarded as quickly
as possible. This clogged the lines and caused backslapping, or,
if one danced with one's head covered as in the quadrille described
in the last century by Tuscan writer Fucini, a "clonk" on one's top
hat helped to speed up the movement.[41]

The ways of striking up a conversation were rather restricted in
number, such as "Signorina, where are you from?" "Who are your
parents?" "What is your name?" and "What is your surname?"
These are the same ritual questions, almost word for word, that the
prince or the count asked Cinderella in the fairy tales related previously. And in the same tone as "'Un so!" ["I do not know" in
Tuscan] the replies, as in the tales told about Cinderella, could be:
"O proà a 'ndovinare!" ["Oh, try to guess!"], "Un te lo dico perché lo
so icchè tu fai" ["I'm not going to tell you because I know what you
do"], "Tu mi 'eni a fa' la posta!" [You're coming to trip me up], and
"Lo so icchè tu voi" [I know what you're after]. The man could per-
sist: "I shall be good to you. I shall be like a foot for your shoe."
"I'm a serious-minded boy. I work all day in the fields; your father
knows that. We are always in the fields together." "Are you coming
to dance on Saturday?" "Are you going to religious functions?"
"Are we going to see one another?" "Are you coming back on
Thursday?" The girls always hesitated before replying, even if they
liked the young man, so as not to show that they were too interested
and to throw them off balance, pe' vedere di portalli allo scalino di
casa [to see that their intentions were right from the beginning]. They
could reply, "I don't know; I think so," "I hope so," "If my mother
lets me go," "If my sister looks after the animals for me," and "I'll
think about it." One passed with caution from the formal voi or
lei to tu when one wished to reduce the social distances which were
supposed to be maintained at the veglia. This was illustrated at a
buffet during the Carnival season in 1966 when a forward young
man turned to his immediate neighbor at table: "Would you like
a little spumante?" "Mah . . ." The young man persisted: "I've
drunk only some of it. Do you mind drinking some from my glass?"
—taking the "mah" to indicate a discreet assent. "Well . . . to tell
the truth, I mind," she said. "I hardly know you . . ." "Let me introduce myself! Viligiardi Remo!" exclaimed the young man openly.

"Nepi Alba!" added the girl, shaking the hand that he extended. She then drank tranquilly from the glass, unconsciously renewing the Roman tradition of the *mercipotum*, the beginning of couple solidarity by ritual drinking from the same glass.[42]

About a quarter of an hour after the quadrille, the orchestra struck up another polka and the couples returned to the hall to start the *soaré* once again. Often at each *veglia* and at least once during the Carnival season, they organized the *reginetta*, the forebearer of today's beauty contests. During the *veglia* the men bought a quantity of "tickets," or coupons, from the buffet or the *caposala*. At the beginning of each dance at least one was given to a girl, who kept it in her hand. While she was being invited or during the dance itself another young man might come along, offering a greater number of tickets. The man who had first invited her then had to take part in a sort of auction for the girl or else hand her over to the newcomer. In general one "paid" more for the quadrille than any other dance. Toward midnight all the girls handed their tickets to the *caposala*, who counted them and then awarded the title of "Little Queen" to the girl with the greatest number of tickets, offering her a prize as a souvenir, such as a bracelet or brooch. The little queen then danced with the young man she fancied the most, usually the one who had given her the largest number of tickets. It was as a rule a waltz which they danced alone. Sometimes the little queen did not have the inclination and so she danced with the *caposala* or her father. It sometimes happened that a girl out of spite for an enemy handed over her tickets to a third woman so that the latter won. The men could also make alliances among themselves so as to prevent "electing" an outsider instead of a girl from the village, or it could happen that some young man wanted to show off his great economic power by offering an astronomical number of tickets to a girl with whom he wanted to win favor.

Toward midnight most of the mothers took their daughters home. Sometimes they danced until dawn, not, however, on the last day of the Carnival season. Until World War I, approximately, a while before midnight a masked man dressed in a black ceremonial suit with tails, walking cane, and top hat appeared on the floor, greeted by the applause of the audience, and danced the last dance. He was the Carnival in person. At midnight another man entered the hall, dressed with a long gray *spolverina* [duster] to which were attached

A *reginetta*: the belle of the ball in a peacock's costume in 1930 (courtesy of the Biblioteca Comunale degli Intronati, Siena).

smoked herrings. He was the impersonation of Lent and was booed by the dancers because he closed Carnival.[43] At exactly midnight the church bell sounded (Don! Don! as in the story of Cinderella quoted previously) and the orchestra stopped playing. Lent started and the season of *veglie* came to a halt. The following day in church the usual ritual sermon against the sin of dancing would be delivered. In the past decades, up to 1960 approximately, the Catholic church has been particularly severe, at least in theory, against public dances, which were seen as potential pretexts for pagan behavior and sensual pleasure. As were the polka, mazurka, and *valzer*, the *dances tournantes* were stigmatized as endeavors of "dubious morality" in the last two centuries. The same happened for the tango, considered obscene because "the man put his leg in between the woman's legs!" after the famous dancer Pichetti performed it privately in front of the Pope himself. In certain parishes, priests were instructed not to bless the homes of those who held public dances and to cancel the saints' feasts if the parishioners intended to organize a dance.[44] At Castellina they still remember how Monsignor Profeti, during the years between the two world wars, used suddenly to uncover the statue of Our Lady of Sorrows with the seven swords stuck in her heart, preaching, "Look! The eighth was inflicted by you last night at the dance!" So the *veglia* had its last penalty on the following day, which was the first day of Lent.

The Tuscan dance party concluded the season of *veglie*. It shared and summed up the characteristics of the ritualized meeting of the community on the occasion of the formation of couples. After all, like the engagements of marriages, dance was per se an agreement regulated by measure: dance was one of the expressive means of the group solidarity. At these dances one "shortened" the time of courtship. The engagement periods ran roughly like this: at the time of these Carnival *veglie* one got engaged, in Lent one never got engaged, and during the rest of the year one could get engaged. The dance party had the function of forming new couples.[45] This took place according to a mechanism of exchange based on reciprocity. The families "gave" their marriageable daughters and "received" in exchange wives for their bachelor sons. We are dealing with an application of the principle of the circulation of the women-object, one of the bases of a great number of cultures.[46] This exchange took place according to a specific code of signs. The dancers danced around the hall, in front of the entire community, which functioned as overseers, organized in a "club" of members or a closed group of neighbors and acquaintances. Outsiders were excluded on principle. The group taking part in the *veglia* had to coincide with a group which could provide suitable husbands and wives. In the first three dances, one went to "fetch" the woman, usually from the mother's knee, to dance with her in front of everybody and then take her back to her mother. The men had to invite all the women to dance; the women had to accept a dance with everybody. The women's duty was stricter. By doing this the group of men showed their right "of proprietorship" with respect to the women. The only women excluded from this duty were the *impegnate*, which meant "that they are dancing with someone else," but it could also be taken to mean "engaged" or "married." The only women who could refuse were those already assigned to one of the men in the community. For the already existing couples, dancing meant stating to the group both the persistence and the stability of the "fixed couple," the *coppia fissa*. The quadrille, in turn, summed up the *veglia* and all its dances. As Duff-Gordon remarked, "The Italians have typified the way of courtship—old as the world—in their country dances."[47] The spectators were standing or sitting around the hall, facing inward and delimiting the space; the men were in the center of the hall, and the *capoveglia*, head of the group of men, was in the exact center. The men controlled the inside space, which was more important than the marginal space occupied by the women. One started by proposing to a woman who interested one; then one danced, making her "pass through the hands" of everybody and "having in one's grip" the women of all the others. At the end, one returned to one's original partner, but only after the group's basic principle—the possession of all the women by all the men—had been exemplified with exact symmetry. Then one could "take away" the woman to the buffet to eat and drink without her family being present any longer. The basic structure was therefore:

1. Woman requested from the group.
2. Woman shared by the group.
3. Woman granted to a single member of the group.

There was also a progression of dances, from couple dances to contra- (or square) dances—thus the paradigm of breaking up the community into duos, then its reassertion of community in the describing of the figures on the floor. The power here, of course, was in mixing up the whole crowd, making them dizzy, testing social order only to reassert it—after sufficient interactions had taken place to make a new coupling arrangement possible. This was one of the few ways of getting the girls safely out of their own homes into an environment of change. This exchange was only made more overt in the auction dance, the monetary gains of which went to the group sponsoring the event. The fact of internal antagonism also was illustrated by the monetary auction to "elect" the little queen, symbolic of the competition in real life to "acquire oneself" a woman and make her "queen of the home." Thus ended the *veglia* and so it ended in everyday life.

7

The Outcasts' Counter-*Veglia*
"Women, the Tavern, the Dice"

". . . a'micidiali dannati dalla ragione, andando essi alla morte, è dato ber molte volte del vino."

[". . . the murderous men damned by reason, as they go to death, they are given wine to drink many times."]

Boccaccio, *Decameron*, the Eighth Day, Novella 7

". . . affermavano il bere assai . . . essere medicina certissima a tanto male . . ."

[". . . they affirmed that drinking much . . . was a very certain medicine for such an evil . . ."]

Ibid., the First Day, Introduction

In Tuscany, as in so many places, an important distinction was made between the home, the place of privacy, and places outside the house where more public gatherings could be held. This distinction becomes especially important when, as in the *veglia*, the home is opened up for a celebration, one which shares many of the characteristics of public congregations but which must nonetheless, as I have been arguing, depict the ideal of community order in celebration. The home, then, is the place for both sexes and all ages to come to enter into festivities, but always under the firm control of the heads of the group that gathers.

The public place of meeting most in contrast to the home was *la bettola*, the drinking place, the retreat both in the everyday sense and during the *veglia* for the men who did not subscribe so fully to the monitoring of behavior. It is in this public and male environment that a festive world alternative to the *veglia* was to be encountered.

Not all men went to the special evening gatherings, either those held in the family or those held for Carnival time. There were always some who went to the wine seller's bar or to the innkeeper's tavern in order to "wait for the time for bed." The *bettola*, as indicated by its literal meaning,[1] was a place one went basically to drink. Its signboards ("Wine shop," "Wines," "Wine store," and others) proclaimed its purpose. The bar was also a shop but only secondarily; one went there to drink wine more than to buy it. The inn, however, just as did the historically older tavern,[2] offered food and board as well; both can be considered the precursors of today's hotel restaurants.

The inside was always furnished in the same way. There was always a marble counter, underneath which were the enormous bottles of the house wine and the bottles of wine for special occasions (which was drunk rarely and then only by the wealthiest patrons). The host almost always had a particular bottle of the best wine which he poured out only for his clients of consequence (he himself was often one of these) and for strangers he deemed of importance. Sometimes he began by serving his special wine, falling back on his cheaper variety when his customers had drunk so much they were no longer able to distinguish with any great precision what they were drinking. On top of the counter were the quarter, half, and full liter containers; all measures were filled on the spot. Next to these were the *gòtti*, the characteristic Tuscan wine glasses into which one poured three fingers of wine at a time, and as often as possible. Clients sat on benches placed along the walls or on four-legged round stools with a hole in the middle placed around marble-topped tables.

One could go to the inn in the morning and in the afternoon for "a quick glass and away," but more often one went for the evening, after dinner. There were those who drank alone at the counter, but it was more usual to sit at a table and drink with the others. If someone came alone, it was always easy to start a conversation. Drinking was considered a social activity, even if of a very particular kind: "He who won't drink in company is either a thief or a spy" ["*Chi non beve in compagnia, o è un ladro o è una spia*"]. "Come on for a drink!" or "I'll pay!" were invitations offered frequently to colleagues, friends, and those one wanted to get to know better. The proposing of a drink was an offer one could not refuse, and it tended to create a special atmosphere of reciprocity and familiarity. "Let's go for a drink together" was synonymous with friendship, community spirit, and understanding. Another joking refrain was "Let's go hide among the branches" or "Let's go to the branchy bushes." These expressions derived from the word *frasca*, a leafy branch usually taken from the acacia, which was used as a signboard for the inns and taverns and which was exchanged with a new one as soon as it began to fade. *Frasca* (or branch) is also the origin of such proverbs as "Good wine needs no branch" ["*Il vino bono 'un ha bisogno di frasca*"],[3] which literally translates into "a good inn is known to all and needs no publicity." Figuratively, it can be understood as "An all-around good girl does not need to put herself on show to be appreciated." Similarly, "He who does not want the tavern, let him remove the branch" ["*Chi non vol l'osteria, levi la frasca"*],[4] which (the literal sense having been lost) probably means "He who does not want problems should begin by not seeking them out." This popular etymology explains the name *malafrasca*, which was given to many small, run-down inns of ill-fame. The branch remained on the doors of the inns until after the First World War, at which point it was progressively replaced by painted and, still later on, neon signs.

Among the patrons of the inn, wine acted as a connecting agent; that is, it was the catalyst of the group. "With a glass of wine you make a friend" ["*Con un bicchier di vino si fa un amico*"];[5] and "Men are like tiles: they drink each with the other" ["*L'òmini so' come e' tegoli: si danno da bere uno all'altro*"].[6] Indeed, the existing system in these inns was not that every member should pay for himself whenever he took a drink, but rather for each to pay in his turn for the entire group. As in English, it is referred to as a *round*, and one going drinking was referred to as "doing the rounds." At the end, each member of the group had paid for what he had drunk, but in a way that strengthened the ideas of equality and solidarity. One ended up by drinking as much as the others (which was often a great deal) but without having to face each glass wondering about how much one could afford to drink. Local customs provided for any small drinking debits or credits. If one had his drink paid for, he was obliged to return the favor. If he got up before the rounds had been completed, he would declare, "Oh, well then, I owe you drinks." This counted as his acknowledgment that he would take care of his share the next time. If someone did not want to obligate himself, he would try to turn down an invitation to drink by saying that he had just had one or that he did not feel well. The exchange of wine thus had an explicit nature, regulating social contacts and indicating degrees of familiarity.[7] One of the most natural approaches to an unknown at a nearby table was "Do you want a drink?" "Would you like a drop?" "Want to taste this?" or "Do you care to try this?" A refusal was regularly interpreted as a rejection of an offer of friendship.

In these *bettole* one could also find something to eat, but usually just as an accompaniment to the drinking; one ate a bit so as not to drink on an empty stomach. The most common "dishes" were hard-boiled eggs, alone or with chicory; liver pâté sandwiches; and various kinds of salami. Naturally, there was no water: "Better muddy wine than clear water"; "Water pains, wine sings" ["*Meglio vin torbo che acqua chiara*"; "*L'acqua fa male e il vino fa cantare*"]. Sometimes, Bacchic poems were sung:

> Only toward good men
> [Chorus] Like us, like us.
> Let generous wine be poured.
> [Chorus] Fill up, fill up.
> Water's for the perverse.
> [Chorus] And the flood, and the flood did show it![8]

> By Bacchus, this is a good wine.
> It's been a year under the vine leaves.
> I picked the grapes and put them in the vat
> and made them prisoners in the barrel.
> I pierced the barrel with the little screw
> and put it in the glass to decant it
> and give it its bright colors,
> and it warms up the heart of those who drink it.[9]

> Drink, drink, comrade,
> or else I'll kill you.
> Don't kill me, comrade,
> Since now I shall drink![10]

> Comrades, let's fill,
> let's fill the glass.
> Let's drink and let's sing.
> Pleasure is short-lived![11]

Water was antimatter in the philosophy of the tavern: "It doesn't even taste of fresh water" meant "It doesn't taste of anything." "Water's for washing" or "With water, I wash my feet [or my ass]" were the drinkers' traditional responses to those who for some reason offered them water. Urination was said "making water." This contrasted "water," the waste liquid expelled from one's body, with "wine," a liquid good to drink and consumed by the body: "Good wine makes for good blood" ["*Buon vino fa buon sangue*"].[12] Giusti, an occasional patron of the tavern himself, collected many proverbs which contrasted wine with water, such as "Those who will mix water with wine deserve to drink water [or the sea] with their heads down" ["*Quei che con l'acqua mischia e guasta il vino merta di bere l'acqua (o il mare) a capo chino*"].[13] Some of the more common "antiwater" proverbs are: "Baptized wine's not worth anything" [*Vin battezzato non vale un fiato*"];[14] "May God take water from him who doesn't want wine" ["*A chi non piace il vino, Dio gli tolga l'acqua*"];[15] and the advice "Drink wine and let the water go to the mill alone" ["*Bevi il vino e lascia andar l'acqua al mulino*"].[16] In Tuscany, wine is considered to be a primary source of sustenance and nutrition, as much and more than bread: "He who has bread and wine is better off than his neighbor" ["*Chi ha pane e vino sta me' che il suo vicino*"].[17] More than a century ago, some Tuscan peasants explained to a passing English traveler that wine was for them nutrition, drink, and shelter: "Our wine was food, and drink, and covering to us."[18] An old inhabitant of Greve in Chianti, commenting on an advertisement for a type of Chianti which reproduced Louis Pasteur's aphorism "Wine is the healthiest and most hygienic of all drinks," said to me: "Our old ones knew that by themselves. So much so that my poor uncle died of good health." He was referring to the cirrhosis of the liver caused by too much drinking which took his uncle to the grave.

Drinking in the taverns or inns was effectively different from drinking at other gatherings or at meals. At the home *veglia*, drinking was measured, balanced, a subordinate factor. "Good wine makes tales long" accords with the precepts of biblical folklore from Ecclesiasticus: "Temperance in drinking is the health of body and soul,"[19] "Wine drunk moderately gladdens the spirit and heart,"[20] and "A good life for a man means wine used sobriously; you will be sober if you drink with moderation."[21]

One went to the inn, however, to drink and to drink a lot. The limits of tolerance passed, wine became potentially dangerous, an ambivalent element by which one measured himself against the others to see who could hold the most. Testifying to the ambivalent nature of wine are various toasts, such as the following:

> Wine, little wine,
> You're good and you're beautiful.

Sometimes to my head you get.
You're an ugly rascal,
And I'll send you to jail.[22]

After having recited these lines, the extemporary poet would proceed to empty his glass in one swallow and thus send the wine
to the "prison" of his stomach. The drinkers willingly accepted the
dangerous friendship with wine, following the old adage: "A drunk
says to wine: I forgive you the evil you do me for the good you
show me, and for the love of your good taste" ["*L'ubriaco dice al
vino: io ti perdono il mal che mi fai per il ben che mi dai e per amor
del buon gusto che tu hai*"].[23]

Together with the praises of wine, Tuscan folklore also presents
numerous warnings and advices against excessive drinking: "To
guzzle without restraint a long time one doesn't last" ["*A trincar
senza misura, molto tempo non si dura*"];[24] "He who has wine for a
friend has himself for an enemy" ["*Chi del vino è amico, di se stesso
è nemico*"];[25] "A man of wine is not worth a dime" ["*Uomo di vino
non vale un quattrino*"].[26] Besides the danger to one's health, excessive drinking also brought on financial ruin; it was said of a good-
for-nothing that he "drank it all," meaning that he spent all his
money in the bars. "A prodigal wine-drinking swill won't have
either bakery or mill" ["*Prodigo e bevitor di vino non fa né forno né
mulino*"].[27]

In any case, such proverbs were out of place in taverns. An old-
timer from Geggiano once advised me thus: "If you want to hear
that sort of thing, you had better go see someone with an ulcer.
Here, you'll only hear the other sort, like

Empty the glass that's full,
Fill the glass that's empty,
Never leave it full,
Never leave it empty."[28]

The rounds were made clockwise, unless someone in the group
was more important than the others. In such a case, the man serving
began with the more important member of the group and then started on the round of the others.

Probably the most famous of all proverbs about wine is "Truth is in wine" ["*La verità è nel vino*"],[29] the Latin "*In vino veritas*," which is in its turn a derivation from the Greek. Many other proverbs from Tuscan folklore express similar concepts, proposing wine as a philosophical substance which leads to a real knowledge of basic values and of the true aspects of men and things. "Wine going inside, good sense coming outside" ["*Vino dentro, senno fuora*"];[30] "Wine and scorn make plainer each and every disdainer" ["*Vino e sdegno fan palese ogni disegno*"];[31] "Where wine can, silence can't" ["*Dove può vino non può silenzio*"];[32] "When Bacchus triumphs, thought flees" ["*Quando Bacco trionfa il pensier fugge*"];[33] "Wherein enters wine, exits knowledge" ["*Dove entra il bere se n'esce il sapere*"];[34] "After drinking, each wants to tell his thinking" ["*Dopo bere ognuno vuol dire il suo parere*"].[35] Those opinions given when full of wine, however, are not the best: "That which from wine is opined is never from a sound mind" ["*Consiglio in vino non ha mai buon fine*"].[36] The truth of the tavern, consequently, was never of the best kind but rather of the kind that stung. A friend from Ama once told me that "a man is known in his drunkenness," paraphrasing in part the adage according to which "a man is known in three circumstances: when he's angry, when he has to pay, and when he drinks" ["*L'uomo si conosce in tre congiunture: alla collera, alla borsa e al bicchiere*"].[37] For my friend and many others, drunkenness produces different effects, depending on the personality of whoever it is who gets drunk. Here follows a rough sketch of various drunken types according to my informants from Ama.

After having drunk too much, some work themselves into a state of anger, which resolves itself in verbal and physical aggressivity: "In San Donato, they get into fistfights every night before going to bed." Others, usually introverted types, become overly talkative, "getting hold of your ear [and] won't let go." Others, usually sad and morose, become exhilarated. Still others dissolve in tears, "opening the floodgates." My informant himself was telling me that just the other night he had had to stay up over an hour with his friend Vito, who, drunk as "a roof tile," was embracing him and crying out between his hiccups, "O Giovannino, don't leave me, I don't have anybody but you in the world, don't abandon me, don't leave me alone, stay here, don't go away . . ." All this without any specific reason for distress on Vito's part. Everything was going as well for him as it always had. He had not suffered any recent shock or tragedy; he was really 'doing just fine.' When on a drunk, one ends up by being that which in normal life and society he cannot be.

There were also well-defined customs, not for how much to drink, but for what and how to drink it. One was never to mix white and red wines. "White and red, take me home" ["*Bianco e nero conducimi a casa*"] meant that if one drank both kinds he would undoubtedly be unable to get home on his own. The pouring out of the wine was an act of courtesy, and, as mentioned, the rule was to fill the glasses on the table clockwise. On the chance that there might be a drop of preserving oil or a piece of cork left in the top of the bottle, whoever was pouring began with his own glass, filling it just enough so as to remove the foreign matter. Then he turned to the person immediately on his left and continued around the circle until he had served everyone. At a certain point during the pouring, he might change the hand with which he was holding the bottle or flask from right to left. This was done in order not to pour out "as a traitor." The folk explanation of this tradition is that, in olden times, if one wanted to knife the person sitting next to him he needed free the arm farthest from his victim. And so, he would use his left hand in pouring to the left, his right to the right. With his other arm free he could wield his knife more easily and more effectively: swinging his weapon around in a half circle, he could place the full force of his arm behind his thrust. Consequently, to pour out in this way "as a traitor" allegedly signified hidden hostility.

If the group of drinking companions was small, only two or four, they usually ended up playing cards. The cards used were the Tuscan deck of forty, divided in four suits: Hearts, Diamonds (sometimes called "coins" or "bricks"), Spades, and Clubs. Each suit went from one to seven, plus the face cards: the "hunchback," or Jack, was worth eight points; the "woman," or Queen, worth nine; and the King, or "royal," worth ten. Ludovico Zdekauer, basing himself on, among other sources, a Florentine Provision of the twenty-third of March 1376,[38] conjectures that the modern deck of cards is a Tuscan invention. Whatever the historical origin of cards and card games may be,[39] their major importance during the get-togethers in the taverns and inns is an established fact. Card games were rarely played during other kinds of gatherings, and, anyway, it was only the men "who knew how to hold the cards in hand," "who

At the *caffè*, the modern counterpart of the tavern, drinking wine and play-ing cards (photo by Mario Salvi, Siena).

really knew how to play their cards right." Figuratively, this expres-sion has come to mean "to know the rules of behavior in a given situation" or "to know how to resolve a problem," that is, to be culturally and socially competent. A woman or boy who wanted to play cards or in a broader sense to meddle in others' affairs was regularly informed that "to be able to play, one had to have held the cards in hand" ["*per giocare, bisogna aver tenuto le carte in mano*"].[40] The figurative meaning of this expression confirms the positive value of experience: in card playing, as in other areas of traditional Tuscan culture, the rule was that women and boys did not even "know how to hold the cards in hand."

The card games played in the inns and taverns, and more recently in rural bars and cafés, are many. Nonetheless, the most important and common are Scopa, Briscola, and Tressette, and their variations.

It is significant that these three card games and their closest derivatives have always been considered "permissible" or "legal." It indicates their profound consonance with the basic values of the culture which gave rise to, accepted, and adapted them. In any case, they are all games based not on chance but on experience and good memory. The one who could remember all the cards which had already been played usually won. Whoever played first considered himself "under," or at a disadvantage. Whoever "spoke" or played afterward was obliged to respond but could do it with the advantage of "experience" or, rather, the knowledge of the other players' cards. He still had "his hand to play" when the others had already "put their cards on the table." Within the limits of the possibilities of the cards he held in his hand, the last player to "speak" decided who would win the hand. More than the others, he could "take it or leave it." In any case, in order to win, each card that was played was subjected to, modified by, or needed the support of the cards played next. The players of those had the advantages of knowing the card played and of speaking afterward (compare "he who laughs last laughs best" ["*ride ben chi ride l'ultimo*"]). In Scopa, "to take" was better than "to put down" on an empty table, that is, to have to speak first.

Similarly, without any reference point, at the end of Briscola, one tried to take the trump, rather than go to "the deck." The known card was trump, good in any case, the known being more sure than the unknown. Moreover, for each hand there was a limited number of points at the disposition of the players. Every point one did not make went to his adversaries, according to the most general and basic principle of limited good, of "*mors tua, vita mea*" ["your death, my life"]. Every gain was obtained only at the expense of the others; the number of points necessary to win was defined beforehand and could not be surpassed. Once the maximum number of points was reached the game was over. Whoever lost did not pay in proportion to the points he had made or to the distance he had put between himself and the other players. The only possible exception was a total loss; then the one who had made no points might have to pay double because in effect he had not even begun to play. It can be said, however, that the stake at these games was always very small. It was almost always "the candle" (the modest charge for the renting of the cards) or a round of drinks which brought the drinking rounds mentioned above into the card playing ritual. Further, it also included the game in the traditional system of daily reciprocation of an economy based on natural exchanges and not on money. For this reason, Scopa, Briscola, and Tressette might also be played at the family *veglia*.

Other than these games, considered "permissible" and legal, there were many which were held to be illegal, officially not permissible, and through the centuries stigmatized in various ways by common morality, the Church, and civil authority. The list of forbidden games given out by the chief of police in every province is nearly identical throughout Tuscany. In its actual form it derives from the "Text of Laws of Public Security" made in 1931, which forbids minors of eighteen years and under from playing cards and which forbids anyone from playing games of chance. This list, which all shops wherein cards are rented to the clients are obliged to display, is made up as follows:

List of Forbidden Games
1. Battifondo of ninepins, with betting
2. Ninepins in the Corner
3. Cappotto with stick and billiards
4. Cassetta, or Carrettella
5. Bazzica
6. Morra
7. Macao, or Nine
8. Piattello, or Mercante
9. Toppa, or Zecchinetta
10. Seven and a Half
11. Fifteen, Twenty-One, Thirty, and Forty
12. Thirty-One and Thirty-Five (named Pezzente)
13. Dice
14. Primiera a Invito, or Bambara
15. Biribissi
16. Ecarté
17. Bassetta
18. Bestia
19. Roulette
20. Tre Carte

21. Tombola with scorecards
22. Naso
23. Pharaoh
24. Barriera
25. Tagliare
26. Mazzetti
27. Lasquenet
28. Passatella
29. Poker
30. Foot Ball Star of Time
31. Ramino

Pinball machines and fishing with a mechanical crane have been added in their turn. Included in the above notice are excerpts from Articles 718–723 of the current Penal Code which provide for the punishment of transgressors by fines or by arrest, depending upon the gravity of the offense.[41] It is worth noting that games of chance, according to the Penal Code, are those "wherein the scope is of profit, and winning or losing are entirely by chance, or nearly so."

Traditionally, these games were played in the tavern, despite the above prohibitions. Thus, the tavern also became, for gambling, the "other," the forbidden place. Many of the tavern patrons shared, even if only more or less consciously, the tart, mocking, bitter wit of Cecco Angiolieri,[42] self-declared poet of the antivalues: tavern (the bar of his times), "questionable" females, and dice (the game of chance which consumed time, life, and property). A confused spirit of visceral protest and a sort of instinct toward angry self-destruction came into play as well, as exhibited in Niccolò Machiavelli's famous letter to Vettori, which follows in part. (Machiavelli was himself a frequent patron of the Tavern of Sant'Andrea in Percussina, where he alternated gambling with the writing of *The Prince*.)

> Having eaten, I return to the tavern; there I find the host as customary, a gravedigger, a miller, and two bakers. With these I entangle myself for the whole day, and we play at *cricca*, at *tricche-trach*, wherein are born a thousand contentions and infinite spites with injurious words; and more often than not, one quarrels for a coin, and it is not rarely that we are heard screaming as far as San Casciano. Thus, wrapped in between these lice, I drag my brain out of its mildew,

Machiavelli's Tavern, still run in the old style at Sant'Andrea in Percussina, with the gathering area around the fireplace (courtesy of the Serristori Estate).

and vent my spleen for the malevolence of this my fate; and I will feel glad that it crushes me in this way in order to see if it may feel ashamed of it at all.[43]

According to public and religious morality, card playing in the taverns was a totally negative endeavor. "Cards belong to the Devil" ["*Le carte sono del diavolo*"][44] and the ancient "Dice belong to the Devil" ["*I dadi son del diavolo*"] emphasize the negative aspect, as does "Where cards are played, there the Devil amuses himself" ["*Dove si gioca, il diavolo ci si trastulla*"].[45] The tavern was also the topical place of the Devil and not without reason. "Gambling has the Devil in its heart" ["*Il gioco ha il diavolo nel cuore*"].[46] "Gambling is war" ["*Il gioco è guerra*"].[47] Gambling, as far as public morality was concerned, led to loss of time and money and, moreover, was often the cause for fights between friends and for blasphemy. In the philosophy of folklore, it is not possible to win in games of chance. Indeed, "He who doesn't want to lose doesn't play" ["*Chi non vuol perdere, non giochi*"][48] and "He who wants to have his money back, let him not play again" ["*Chi si vuol riaver, non giochi più*"].[49] Games of chance were thus outside the system of limited good, wherein at least what one person lost, another one would win. Here only loss and its irreparability are considered: "He wins a lot who doesn't play" ["*Assai vince chi non gioca*"];[50] "He who plays loses his place" ["*Chi va al gioco, perde il loco*"];[51] and "Don't start gambling if you don't want trouble" ["*Non ti mettere a giocare, se non vuoi pericolare*"].[52] This type of proverb demonstrates how gambling was considered a social loss. In effect, it was, insofar as its logic was directly opposite to that of the hegemonic values. Playing for money was condemned, and money won by gambling was "marked," dirty, bad. Often the winner himself spent his winnings immediately in an irrational and showy manner. Money, according to a saying attributed by the folk to Saint Francis, is "the Devil's dung." It is logical, therefore, that the Enemy deposits it on the large pile ("The Devil always defecates on the large pile" ["*Il diavolo caca sempre sul monte grosso*"])[53] to increase the property of the already rich.

The concept of limited good sustains in fact the economy of exchange typical of the traditional Catholic worldview, which for centuries condemned banking, usury, and the accumulation of money in general. Consequently, "out of the ordinary" wealth had to come from a pact with the Devil, or at least from some sort of connection with him. "In order to be rich, you have to have a relative in the Devil's house" ["*Per esser ricco, bisogna aver un parente a casa del diavolo*"].[54] Up until the Renaissance, bankers were regularly excommunicated, and with reason if it is the Devil who lends money. ("The Devil lends money for twenty-five years at the most" ["*Il diavolo presta i danari per venticinque anni al più*"].)[55] And interest is no less than his son: "Interest is the son of the Devil" ["*L'interesse è figlio del diavolo*"].[56]

The only form of redistribution of wealth encouraged by Tusco-Christian folklore is charity, a categorical absolute, recommended by the prescriptive proverb "Charity is good even when offered to the Devil" ["*La carità è fatta bene anche al diavolo*"]. Instead, whoever gives, demanding at the same time to control the use and scope of his gift, as did Weber's Calvinistic Protestant, or who wants it back again, should it be spent badly or for some other reason, behaves wrongly and will not recover his ungenerously given money.

"He who gives and then takes back finds himself on the Devil's rack" ["*Chi dà e ritoglie, il diavolo lo raccoglie*"].[57] Contrarily, "He who gives of his own will be repaid by God" ["*A chi dona del suo, Dio gli ridona*"].[58] Charity is not to be argued about; it is irreversible.[59] Whoever disputes it or inverts the beneficent downward flow, such as a poor man who gives to a rich one ("When the poor give to the rich, the Devil has himself a good laugh" ["*Quando il povero dona al ricco, il diavolo se la ride*"]),[60] touches on the ridiculous and dangerous. Besides, a just reward awaits the poor in the next life: "Better to be in heaven in rags than in hell in richly embroidered clothes" ["*Meglio in paradiso stracciato che all'inferno in abito ricamato*"].[61]

The condemnation of gambling and, consequently, of the tavern (and in more recent times of its derivative, the café) is thus consonant with the traditional Catholic worldview. Gambling and the tavern, particularly in the rural areas whence come these proverbs, provided the occasions, rare though they were, for meetings, social encounters, exchanges of ideas, and potential contacts outside the Church and religious rites. The community or the group that gambles together has a general tendency to stay together, even when the game is over.[62] Fountains, water sources, and other crucial centers for encounters in small towns are almost always near Church buildings. The tavern, source of wine, basically came to represent a social center in competition with the Church, a possibility of social life alternative to that offered officially by the family and other official institutions.

Furthermore, at the gambling table, relatively important sums of money change hands rapidly, as a result of a risk, an investment, or aleatory good luck. And "He who admits to the existence of luck denies God" ["*Chi confessa la sorte, nega Dío*"].[63] Altogether, in a trivial manner, as it may be, gambling was a potential contribution to the formation of that capitalistic mentality of the entrepreneur which Thomistic economic theory forbids and condemns as its dangerous opposite.

Cards have taken on a metaphorical importance from their objective value. In folk speech, "Let's put our cards on the table" means "Let's speak clearly," as "to play with the cards face up" means "to act openly." Someone who has a secret resource has "an ace up his sleeve," while he who has used up all his possibilities

has "played out his hand" and is left with "the low cards." Someone who has a stroke of good luck "has made a *primiera* with three
cards." An ideal solution is an "ace," and someone who acts in
a way contrary to his own interests "plays at *vinciperdi* ["*who wins,
loses*"]." Whoever uses methods judged excessive in respect to the
"stake," that is, to the advantage he can hope to obtain, may be
told ironically, "Oh, you're playing the low cards." On the other
hand, whoever, starting off at a great disadvantage, loses to someone at a disadvantage is told, "You lost the ace to the two!" And
someone who does not have power or authority "counts as much
as the twos in a trump" or "is a low card."

Marriage as well is seen as a metaphorical game: "He who loses
at this game, loses for three"; that is, he loses everything, the entire
stake.[64] The game Primiera also had a more precise sexual significance: to play Primiera was a euphemism for courtship or, more
specifically, for coitus. It was often used in this sense in such verses
as the following:

And I passed over Dante's gate.
I saw Beatrice as a prisoner.
Pretty brunette's kisses were my bait
And with the prettiest I played Primiera.[65]

Or:

The port of Leghorn has a waving flag:
I touched your tits, my dear,
I touched your tits, my dear.
And on your breast, I did Primiera.[66]

Come on, handsome dark-haired, let's play cards.
We have to play the games that I know.
We'll play Briscola and Primiera.
If you need a heart, I'll give you mine now.[67]

Some cards had a specific and individual metaphorical value.[68]
The King of Diamonds represented the paternal figure and wealth,
and in certain parts of Tuscany he was allowed the special value of
an extra point in the game of Scopa. I have been told that, even
in places where he was equal to the other kings, when he showed

up in a hand he was always greeted with pleasure as a sign of good luck, whatever game was being played.

The favorite card of those who played Seven and a Half (similar to Twenty-One) was instead the Queen of Hearts, "the Crazy One." In this game she was worth as many points as whoever held her wanted, and whenever she showed up, the deck was afterward reshuffled. She was the card that could be "coupled" with any of the other points. In the Tuscan card decks she is pictured as a blonde and holds a red rose in her hand; the players read her as a woman "of heart, of the sense," who gives herself to everybody. The Queen of Spades, instead, is her opposite, "an obstinate woman," bizarre and refractory, who gives herself to no one. The "black man" was the Jack of Spades, who lent his name to a fearful being in children's lullabies. He was, moreover, the most undesirable card in Black Man, one of the more common games played at evening gatherings. Whoever had him in hand at the end of the game was the only loser. The black man was left on his own as he could not be paired with any of the mother cards in a deck purposely reduced to thirty-nine cards. Figuratively, it means a man without a woman, "a spade," with negative connotations. When someone ended up in bad company or in an ugly situation from which others had saved themselves, it was said of him, "He's been left with the black man in his hand."

The King with his long white beard and scepter, the Queen with her rose, and the Jack with his unsheathed sword were also interpreted as the old father, woman, and youth. Perhaps these interpretations betray to some degree the players' obscure psychological invested feelings. A complete enquiry into popular Tuscan card reading, based on the face cards, should be able to demonstrate how the twelve face cards in the deck were invested with special meanings and became established categories according to familiar roles (father, mother, son), distinguished successively in positives and negatives (Hearts and Diamonds being positive, Spades and Clubs negative), and opposed in pairs (Hearts to Spades, Diamonds to Clubs) with a strong opposition (Hearts-Spades) mediated by a weaker one (Diamonds-Clubs).[69] Thus, a woman having her cards read who uncovered a Jack and three low clubs was told, "*Fiori, fiori, fiori*. And they're all *fiori* from the black man."[70]

There was hardly ever a card game that did not finish in arguments. Frequently, at the end of a game, the loser tried to show that he had only been unlucky, that he had not lost because of another's skill. And so, they verbally replayed the whole game, discussing the possible results had each hand been played differently. Often one player would direct bitter resentment and furious words to his partner. When one lost, it was necessary to save face, and this could be done only by demonstrating that it was one's partner who had lost the game through stupid mistakes, while one's own superior ability would have normally brought certain victory. Card games thus divided the pairs of partners previously joined in solidarity, because in losing they reacted according to the logic of *"mors tua, vita mea."* As someone had to be at fault, clearing oneself automatically meant throwing the blame on another. Occasionally, when it became very serious, there were accusations of cheating made against opponents ("You saw my cards!") or against spectators ("You're telling him what I have in my hand!"). At this point, punches were likely to be thrown. More usually though, the contenders limited themselves to "rosaries" of blasphemy, characteristic of "anyone who is baptized, Christian, and Tuscan." In all taverns there were signs which warned, "A decent man neither spits nor blasphemes," or, more tersely, "Don't blaspheme." More recently signs began to appear reading, "Pope John says: dearest children, don't blaspheme," updating Mussolini's "Don't blaspheme for the honor of Italy." [71]

It is significant that these streams of blasphemy were called "rosaries" and the single blasphemous phrase "candle stubs." [72] It was also common to do a parody of Christian prayers and formulas. For instance, "In the name of the father" became

Neither debts
Nor credits,
Neither wife
Nor children.
Amen!

O Holy Virgin,
pray for us.

became:

> O Holy Virgin,
> mind your business.

The parody of the Creed began:

> I believe in
> God Father,
> Omnipotent,
> a little to
> man, to
> women not
> at all.

All these often trite parodies were jokingly called "services."[73] Such designations place these texts in the well-defined position of being the antithesis of the real prayers and rosaries told at the family gatherings, led by the head of the household, who acted as priest. Prayers were recited in many families every evening and in all Tuscan homes during the first days of November, around All Saints' Day. As for the candle stubs, real candle stubs and lamps were kept lit in front of pictures of the Holy Family, the Baby Jesus, the Madonna, and old Saint Joseph.

One of the tavern jokes was to have someone repeat *"Accidenti a San Frascheggio sulle mura di Viareggio"* ["Damnation to San Frascheggio on the walls of Viareggio"] until his tongue became twisted and he came out with *"Accidenti a San Francesco,"* which blasphemy would set the whole group off in laughter.

Tuscan blasphemy is principally directed toward God (God dog, God executioner) and toward the Madonna (Whore Mother, Mother Prostitute, Sow Mother). In common use today is the ancient *Diàmine* which has now lost its original blasphemous meaning of *"Diabule Domine"* [Devil Lord].[74] This sort of blasphemy seems to follow a certain dialectic logic insofar as it unites a positive term (God or Madonna) with a negative one (executioner, whore, etc.). In Thomistic Catholic logic, on the other hand, good and evil must always be held rigorously apart, carefully distinguished, and separated. Blasphemy therefore attacked both theological and logical systems.

Aside from automatic blasphemy, inserted naturally in discussions and consequently devoid of theological value, more blaspheming was done in the taverns than elsewhere, from anger, from existential agony, from a need to let it all out. As Gostino tried to explain to the old Monsignor Profeti of Castellina, "God instituted blasphemy so that the man could vent himself." This demonstrates admirably the validity of popular Tuscan religiosity along with Sartre's philosophical statement that blasphemy is a religious and theological proposition. *"Nier le dogme . . . c'est être fou et le déclarer"* ["To deny dogma . . . it's to be a fool, and to declare it"].[75] In fact, blasphemy is called in Tuscan folk speech *resia*, that is, heresy, an incorrect theological statement.

Obscene language was also an important part of the songs that accompanied the downing of wine during the nights at the tavern. Indeed, "tavern talk" or "inn language" is synonymous with obscenity in folk speech. The vulgar cants of Italian university students are called *osterie* [bars]. At family gatherings one had to speak in metaphors and euphemisms, with "a crooked tongue" or, indeed, with one's "mouth closed." At the tavern, however, the language was coarse, "at full mouth," "wide-open," "mouth-filling," "mouth-rinsing," and kept all one's companions in tears from laughing. At family reunions, urination was spoken of as "a little need" and defecation as "a need." These verbal taboos in reference to bodily functions were deliberately ignored during the meetings in the taverns where the clients would join in songs like the following, which was recorded in the area of Siena in 1972.

Come on brothers, run, run near
To eat the turds in the field here.
  Like manna fallen from the heavens,
  Like manna fallen from the heavens.
Turds here, turds there, turds everywhere
When you shit,
When you shit,
Turds here, turds there.
When you shit
You have to strain.
  And we like the liquid shit
  Because it splashes,

Because it splashes.
And we like
The liquid shit
Because it splashes
Here, there, and everywhere.
Long live the turd,
Big, round, and ripe.
It comes out the ass
In quantity.
Turds here, turds there
When you shit.
When you shit
You have to strain.
   I cleaned up my butt
   With a green cypress leaf,
   But the shit stayed there just the same,
   Stuck to the hairs of my ass.
   Poor ol' me, poor ol' me.
   I'm covered in shit
   From head to foot.
   Long live the turd,
   Big, round, and ripe.
   Long live the turd
And he who knows how to make it.
Shit here
And shit there.
When you shit
You have to strain![76]

After the song, interjections and explanatory comments followed, frequently becoming a contest among the singers once the subject had been "uncorked." The night I heard the above song, the singers felt they had to explain to me: "It's a little pornographic, you know, but after all, everybody shits . . . ," "Whoever doesn't, dies!" "The Pope shits, too!" "Well, you know, I'm a little fussy about shit. Once I found a hair in it and I threw it all away." At that moment, a middle-aged woman appeared at the door looking for her husband, and this immediately stirred up a torrent of commentary: "Here she is, come for the hors d'oeuvres!" "Oh, Francesca, you heard shit mentioned and you peeped in right away!" "You heard us from your home and came to eat a crust!" "Look, she got here just in time for dessert!" The woman disappeared on the spot without saying a thing, and the man sitting next to me, looking at her unusually large buttocks, elbowed me and commented with a traditional joke: "With that ass, if she farts in a sack of confetti, it's gonna be Carnival for six months." [77] The group continued by telling me that they had sent the song to the San Remo Festival. "And do you know, they didn't accept it! With all it cost to send it!"

Next, two men of the group, quite tipsy, began to waltz while the others clapped hands, singing out, "Let's drink, drink, drink . . ." The man playing the part of the woman gave a showy imitation of the abandoned mannerisms of a female of the zone, famous for being "if not chaste, at least cautious." Thus, among the antitheses of the tavern, dances between men, with one of the two imitating the more or less vulgar gestures of a certain kind of woman, were occasionally to be found. "Anyway, all women are sluts!" exclaimed a man at a nearby table. Then, realizing he had caught the attention of some at neighboring tables who knew him well (he had just received a romantic blow), he recovered himself. Making a joke of it and involuntarily passing from the particular to the universal, he said: "Perhaps my sister not so much . . . but, no, they're all whores!" The "antidance" finished up amid general jesting, the "woman" having behaved in a manner exactly opposite to the code of discretion peremptory at all proper dances.

Next came the time for the telling of the various "hits" made at the proper dances. "I ran into one from Milan, she came up to me . . . We were dancing, then I changed position, and she said, 'I could feel it better before.'" Another told how he would start dancing by taking four steps forward and four backward for several times. Then, after his partner had learned the step, when she came forward on the fourth step, he would go back only three so she would come up against his genitalia: "That's how I got my prick next to her." A third related how he rubbed up against a somewhat silent dancing partner who, having accepted the initial contact with his genitalia, after a while said, "Do you mind . . . your watch chain's pressing me . . ." "And who had a watch!! Much less a chain!" And they all burst into laughter. [78] Still another told of when he went to a dance at Ama. He invited a girl who was sitting down and seemed quite attractive to dance. When she got up, she was twice his size and answered, in a rough voice, "Let's go," beginning to bounce him around the dance floor in an "antidance" that she led.

Thus women were thoroughly roughed up in these masculine chatterings. This misogynous factor in the tavern gatherings was of primary importance. In tavern songs, woman is openly attacked, ridiculed, and insulted as whore. Female behavior in the chants and texts of tavern folklore is always the opposite of that which is publicly acceptable. In other forms of gatherings, the woman was always discreetly reserved; in these texts she takes the sexual initiative. The language, here, is openly sexual as opposed to the customary proper speech of the *veglia*. At the other gatherings, every woman "acted like a saint"; in the taverns, woman is the stereotype of the prostitute, complement of the Virgin in the concept of the "ideal" woman in Tuscan folklore. Singing in falsetto, tavern regulars imitated young women imploring,

> Mamma, I want a husband
> Who'll put his finger
> Where I like it.[79]

One of the favorite songs was that of the Chimney Sweep, popular also in other parts of Italy. Here is one variation which I collected in Castiglion d'Orcia in 1973:

> Throughout these little streets
> You can always hear
> The voice gay and clear
> Of the Chimney Sweep.
> [The chorus repeats all four lines.]
> From a window peers
> A pretty little miss
> Who with a gentle voice
> Calls out to the Chimney Sweep.
> [Chorus repeats.]
> First she invites him in,
> Then she gives him a seat,
> And next to drink and eat,
> All for the Chimney Sweep.
> [Chorus repeats.]

And after he's eaten
And drunk from the rim,
The hole she shows to him,
The hole of the chimney.
[Chorus repeats.]
"I'm sorry my young man
That my chimney is so narrow.
Oh, my poor young man, and how
How will you ever get up?"
[Chorus repeats.]
"Don't you worry my good lady.
I know how to work and get paid,
For I'm an old hand at this trade
Of up and down the chimney."
[Chorus repeats.]
And four months later
The moon is growing
And people are asking
About the Chimney Sweep.
[Chorus repeats.]
And nine months later
Is born a little baby
And there ain't no maybe,
He's just like the Chimney Sweep.
[Chorus repeats.][80]

Throughout these little streets . . .

Most texts stigmatized sexual liberty on the part of a woman, for it
was weighed for its immediate consequences, the visible evidence
of a disgraceful pregnancy.

You've got yourself a striped dress.
You got it with your thighs,
You got it with your thighs.
But it's too tight, your tummy's growing.[81]

A variant of the third line goes:

From morn to eve, your legs spread [or "wide"]

There were also many traditional narrative jokes on this subject, such as the one of the mother with two small children sitting in a train compartment who turns to her children and says, "You see, dears, if this gentleman would only sit with his legs together, we'd have more room." To which the man answers, speaking to the children, "You see, kids, if your mother had only kept her legs together, then we'd all have more room here." An irregular pregnancy (a disgraceful situation for which the man was not to be blamed because "she should have been more careful") was cause for many jokes which were at the same time self-justifications of a traditional privilege. One other story went:

A woman once had two daughters, one of whom was married but unable to have children. The mother prayed for grace so that her daughter could have a baby. But her unmarried daughter had one instead. And then the mother said, "They've made a mistake, they misunderstood me . . ." MORAL: Women are no good, not even for praying to the saints.[82]

The same philosophy was also found in a *stornello*, sometimes even sung at the family *veglia*, alluding to some premature and inopportune pregnancy.

Flower of reed,
All my day spent by the crib,
All my day spent by the crib,
I've no husband yet I'm called mother.[83]

Drinking songs against marriage were sung in Tuscany, as in many other regions of Italy. The men of the taverns saw marriage as the end of freedom, the beginning of troubles, a leap into the dark:

"Woman, woe; Bride, bills; Wife, worry" ["*Donna, danno; sposa, spesa; moglie, maglio*"].[84] These songs were spaced between stories about married men who were not allowed to go out after dinner, who had to stay home to watch over a dishonest wife, or who had wives who "had put the pants on," who "ruled with the rod." These stories were a form of consolation for those who for some reason or another, because forbidden by their family or master, because of lack of money, or because refused by the woman or her family, had been unable to find a wife. Indeed, many came to the tavern "to drink in order to forget" a broken engagement as much as an unsuccessful marriage. For these men who retreated to the solidarity of the group of their male friends, folk songs against marriage were important, such as the following invoking one's good mother as opposed to the bad wife:

If I choose a peasant
She'll always be gathering straw;
She'll become a tar, rough, and raw.
Mamma mia, what'll I do.

If I choose a pretty one
She'll always be in front of the mirror;
She'll become a flirt.
Mamma mia, what'll I do.

If I choose a tenant
She'll always be out getting wood;
The Guard'll find her and get her pregnant.
Mamma mia, what'll I do.[85]

If I choose a peasant . . .

The rejection of marriage brought the conversation to women, seen as negative and dangerous beings, and to the essence of the double standard. Thus, tavern philosophy advised one "to let the others marry" and to get involved with a woman only for sexual necessity. Often, at the tavern, stories were whispered about housewives who went not only with their husbands but also with the husband's brothers who were bachelors, because in some patriarchal families not all sons could take a wife. "One bell's enough for the whole church" was one of the sarcasms which accompanied these stories. The "clever" man, thus, was supposed to watch out for the honor of his own wife and sisters and at the same time to seduce other men's women, a behavioral pattern based once again on the dichotomy of the Virgin/Prostitute which furnished the guidelines for classifying women in all contexts. Consequently, the drinking songs exhorted one to let others marry while enjoying the privileges of being male along with those of being a bachelor. They brought the following verse of Cecco Angiolieri up to date but did not modify its essence.

> I'll keep the women young and light
> And leave the others the old and raggedy.[86]

Into this uninterrupted chain fall the drinking songs, such as the following which tells the story of Bista, in the version of Piancastagnaio on Mount Amiata.

> Bista had a wife and a pretty one, too.
> [Chorus: "Drink, drink . . . up to the end.]
> And he'd only been married awhile,
> Yet marriage brought him troubles:
> A misery he had not dreamed of.
> Whenever he came at night
> Down on the floor he found her.
> Oh, my God, what woe,
> To bed without dinner he had to go.
> To his Catherine he would say,
> "Make yourself prettier, pray,
> I want to kiss you."
> But she calmly kept on snoring.

"I want to kiss you."
But she calmly kept on snoring.
So Bista went to his friend and said:
"Listen to what I say.
Well, don't be unhappy,
I'll sell her to you for fifty lire.
Well, don't be unhappy,
I'll sell her to you for fifty ones."
And now that Bista is all on his own,
He feels he has become a bachelor,
For all his troubles he has left behind,
And he walks as if he had found a fortune.
He tells his friends:
"Listen to what I say,
Whoever wants to avoid strife
Takes a woman always and never a wife.
Whoever wants to avoid strife
Takes a woman always and never a wife." [87]

Bista had a wife and a pretty one, too . . .

In public morality, tavern women either were whores or behaved
as such, not only as experienced by the men in the tavern, but also
as evoked in their songs, full of the machismo of its members.

To make love at night
With a babe who was all right

In a secret house
Who let herself be kissed,
From a blow job of five pesos
I got the clap.
I'd have been better off
Masturbating myself with passion.[88]

Other rhymes which were sung or recited touched on specific services. The following is a fragment referring to a prostitute:

Oh, may God freeze you over in hell.
I saw you fucking under the oak.
Unhood it to me, engrave it,
And put it aslant, Zaira,
Otherwise I won't give you a lira.
My balls are of sugar,
My gun is with me.
If you want to taste the muscle
Come to bed with me.[89]

The name Zaira could be substituted with that of a woman known by all in order to increase the laughter and, implicitly, to emphasize the concept that "all women are whores." The payments mentioned in these songs are so low as clearly to be charitable contributions rather than compensations. The allusion to onanism, aside from its obscene and humorous aspects, repeats the idea of male privileges. Often when speaking of one who had a worthless, wretched, or rascally son, it was said, "Poor ol' man, it would have been better if he'd masturbated rather than conceived a son like that."

Those who were more or less unhappily married had the consolation of singing songs like "Cara Rosina," which confirmed the superiority of the male and his right to supreme authority over house and family. The following is a fragment from "Cara Rosina," the best known and most frequently sung, as it mentions the most crucial points.

And the roads you make me ride,
Cara Rosina, cara Rosina,
And the roads you make me ride,
Cara Rosina, you'll have to pay for.

For this is my home and I command here,
And every day I want to know,
For this is my home and I command here,
And every day I want to know, who comes and goes.[90]

The tavern was not a place a "lady" could visit, much less join in the gatherings held there. "Woman of the tavern" is synonymous with "woman of ill-repute," and, indeed, the tavern was one of the few places in the countryside where these women could be found occasionally. Also, sympathetic innkeepers would frequently give rooms to clandestine couples, whether unmarried or adulterous. Thus, the innkeeper became a negative middle man, the antithesis of the head of the family, who favored the "regular" formation of couples, that is, of theoretically chaste engagements and theoretically faithful marriages. "A country innkeeper is either assassin or thief"; "Host or enemy—it's all the same" ["*Oste di contado, o assassino o ladro*"; "*Oste e nemico è tutt' uno*"].[91] These and similar proverbs are strongly indicative of the heavy negative aspect of the innkeeper as a host figure. The negative connotation of the host figure held for the women of his family, who helped out around the tavern as well.

Don't ever try to deal with
Hosts' daughters or millers' horses.[92]

Another antithesis to the official code of behavior which the taverns produced was the lie. The continual effort which the storytellers in family *veglie* put forth in order to ensure their listeners that what they were relating was pure fact, or at least based on fact, or else metaphors for true facts, was occasionally put aside during the reunions at the tavern, where one could play at "who can shoot the biggest [lie]." Sometimes they ended up in contests of who could lie the best. Among these, the most bizarre, ingenious, and hyperbolic lies left the tavern walls and were requested of storytellers on other occasions. They became part of the patrimony of the community, which, in adopting them, began to elaborate and vary them until they passed into the folklore.

Among the favorite stories of my childhood were those of the prisoners returning after the Second World War. Livio of Mondo often told "the one about the cow," a "narrative lie" invented in a tavern around 1948, one that I heard several times around 1950. The story referred to the internment in India of Livio and many of his Italian comrades. Their food was of the worst, particularly because of the absolute lack of meat for "religious reasons." The cows, sacred animals to the Indians, wandered around the fields in absolute liberty. Then, one day, "just listen to what I thought up." Having procured through important and secret friendships a stick of dynamite, he stuck it up the rectum of one of the sacred cows. He lit it, and then ran for cover just in time, followed by a few friends he had let in on the secret. "Boom!"—an explosion that made the earth and the windows of their huts tremble. The cow flew up in pieces, "the biggest was like this" (and he showed us the dimensions with gestures). And then away they all ran toward their feast of meat, "already roasted" from the explosion. Thus, thanks to Livio, at least once in the prison camps of India they ate well. And when someone asked: "But what did it taste like? Was it as good as ours?" Livio answered: "Even better. After all, it was blessed! Just like lamb at Easter here."

Another "narrative lie" from the same period and area I heard from Gostino Bartalini, a soldier on the African front during the Second World War. We often asked him to tell us about "when I was fighting the war in Africa." One day, they were out "on a reconnaissance patrol" when they heard strange noises coming from a clearing in the forest. On drawing closer, they were astonished to realize that it was someone singing. "And so, cautiously coming to this open space," they saw where the singing was coming from. "It was a rattlesnake with its head straight up, singing *Aida*. Ta ta ta ta ta, tara tatà tà tà, tara tatà tatà . . ." And he started to sing the triumphal march from Verdi's *Aida* in full voice.

An important series of antithetical texts which were sung and passed down at the county tavern are those of a specific sociopolitical content.

> It's striking eight, but it'll be nine,
> And my children they're fasting still.
> And courage, but who can bear it.
> Infamous society, give us to eat.

Long live courage, but who can bear it.
Anarchy would defend it.
Long live courage, but who can bear it.
My children are hungry, they're asking for bread.

I too want to wear the Socialist clothes.
Red is beautiful, the banners are red,
And the day of the revolution will come,
And infamous society you will have to pay.

Life is lovely, and honor is lovelier still.
I love my wife, I love my family.
But long live courage, whoever can bear it.
Infamous society, give us to eat.

The jails are full of Socialists.
Watch out, cruel and abusive government,
For the day of the revolution will come,
And you, infamous society, will have to pay.[93]

It's striking eight, but it'll be nine . . .

These protest songs turned on religious institutions as well as on society and government.

And when I die, I don't want any priests.
No priests, no friars, no *paternosters*,
No priests, no friars, no *paternosters*.
All I want is a Socialist flag.[94]

A complete study of the songs of protest sung at the inn would require a full-scale inquiry;[95] for this present account, it is, however, worthwhile noting that these protest cants against society and religious institutions formed an important part of the tavern repertoire. In a recent book, Roberto Leydi notes that most of the events that happened in the taverns were adapted from other occasions of non-orthodox gathering and community interaction.[96] And it is indeed true that the tavern, the place of "the other" and center of resistance to the hegemonic values dominant in official culture, constituted the most ideal place and entity for the reception of "heretical" ideas, the antithesis of the official values of other gatherings. The tavern was also a meeting place for the first political dissidents, who found themselves in a position of contrast with respect to the culture of official values. Before the creation of political organizations or, on a more diffuse level, of an alternative Socialist and Communist sub-culture, before co-operatives, cafés, and "houses of the people" existed in Tuscany, one of the most important meeting places for the early Socialists was the tavern or inn.

It was at the tavern that the few travelers who passed through the countryside, off the main roads of communication, stopped. Before daily newspapers and other forms of mass media reached these rural areas, only rare and often spotty distorted accounts of news from the cities and other far-off places arrived in the country-side via the tavern. Along with news, the travelers brought stories of their own experiences and ideas. Piero Bargellini has advanced the hypothesis, suggestive even if not documentable, that early Christianity arrived in Tuscany and in Florence by way of the roads and late-night reunions at the taverns and wherever else "the horses and the Christians" rested themselves for the night. Going to the tavern to find out the news and to meet "strangers" was common practice for centuries. Niccolò Machiavelli wrote, in 1513: "Then I transfer myself on the road to the inn: I speak with those who pass by, and I ask about the news from their places; I learn many things, and I note the varying tastes and diverse fantasies of men."[97]

Among those who passed by, and who had the greater "fantasy," were the extemporaneous poets who went from here to there for the fairs. They sang in rhymed octaves, improvising in the country and in the town squares, at public ceremonies, and whenever they were invited to any kind of gathering. One of these was often at the tavern meetings. The poet would speak a little, tell a few stories, and ask questions about the people of the place. [98] After having sung some tales and rounds and "improvised" a few rhymed octaves chosen from his repertoire as being most suited to that particular public, the poet or his friend, "the shoulder," passed the hat around or tried to sell the sheet with the text of the recently sung story for a few coins. Thus, the clients could take the text home with them, and if there was someone in the family group who could read, he repeated it aloud until the others had it memorized. And it was thus that the more curious, successful, enjoyable tales passed from the town square to the family kitchen and vice versa, that the facts of daily life which these extemporaneous poets gathered from the taverns were included in their repertoire to complete the communication cycle in both directions.

Among the favorite songs were the "contrasting octaves," which were improvised by two antagonists on a chosen theme and which lasted until one of the two "gave it up," declaring himself beaten by being left without words, by getting mixed up, by "leaving the field," or by accusing his opponent of "having let out a whopper." The two antagonists could take the parts of the hare and the hunter, the sun and the moon, man and woman, city and country dweller, and so forth. An example of poetic contrast in rhymed octaves follows. Gino Ceccherini sang both parts to me in a tavern near Tavarnelle in 1972, after having explained to me that he often recited it in public at Communist festivals of the Unità, where he went with Elio Piccardi. Thus, this particularly successful contrast poem from an improvisation became a fixed text.

> A peasant worker who came from this plain
> Said to his master: "I want to go away,
> For the life here requires too much strain,
> And to share cropping I have to say nay.
> You wait for the grape until it's mature.
> I double your harvest and your savings for sure,
> And then half the crop you take from the farm,
> And you still have the courage to do me harm."
>
> "And so you'd go to become a hodman.
> O Pasquale, you're really pretty dumb.
> Change one master for another if you can.

You'll just be controlled by a brother bum.
And winter, you know, it's hard and cruel.
You have neither trick nor trade, you're a mule,
And you'll go some months doing nothing.
Oh, yes, you'll have trouble finding anything."

"I know they've made you a cavalier,
A commander with a medal of gold.
You've got your hand in all the pots near here,
And you take your break from another's hold.
You've aligned yourself with powerful groups,
And you all attack us farmers in troops,
Enemies of all of the rural castes,
It's all right for you as long as it lasts."

"Of farmers such as you I have no fear,
Nor of the tempest with its harsh rough wind
Because stubborn fools I can find around here.
For every one I lose, a hundred I find.
Whether in the mountains or on the plain,
If the land is not worked it gives me no pain.
No, it's leasing out does not me dismay.
I can lose nothing, for the State will pay."

"We've formed a syndicate, O master mine,
And landowners like you will soon be fried.
For I've worked honestly and you can't pine
Because for decent pay to ask I've tried.
Because of me the hard times you've survived.
I've paid your taxes whene'er they arrived.
You'd pick on the dead if ever you had a chance."

"I have always been on top of the heap.
I'll always be one of the noble lords.
I go to the beach with all of my keep,
Eating of the best, away from the hordes.
As for my expenses of heat and light,
Your back-breaking work pays for those all right.
You wait for the rise of the Kremlin sun,
But big fish always eat the little one."

"O master, the farmer's gotten smarter.
He thinks of more than the breadbasket now.

No more will he take to your farm for barter
The grain he's reaped, his capons, his sow,
With his hat in his hand, bending his legs,
Meanwhile building up your reserve of eggs.
I've got to fifty-eight and that's no mean,
And even if I steal more, it's no sin."

"Whatever, it's little enough you're worth.
We can buy the peasants we need on sale.
We eat and we drink and we're full of mirth,
Even 30 percent keeps us all hale.
Now you want meetings and a syndicate.
There's only one hope left in your rut,
And that's to see the sun of your future.
You'll have a lot of suffering from your cure."

"O master, you'll be destroyed someday,
The day the bell tolls for all such as you.
What Lenin did, to you I surely can say.
He freed the slaves from their chains, so must you.
Listen then, if it won't bore you too much,
For I'll tell you of Mao, of Castro, and such.
Their masters and rulers they mangled.
Many they took and from trees they dangled."

"It seems to me that you're telling a tale
By talking of that kind of person here.
However rough the times, they can only fail
In Italy, those types are far from near.
The clever ones make the dumb ones pay,
And that's something you don't like to say.
You'll always need a whip for your ass.
It's not right that we be ruled by the mass."

"Master, I know why these things you say.
Your workers now are taking a bath.
Once they used to come for their pay
With heads bowed, on their knees, up the path.
Now their ideas from China they say,
And your debts no longer will they pay." [99]

Other texts, called "stories in octaves," commented more specif-

A peasant worker who came from this plain . . .

ically on an important event of macrohistory, reducing it to a more accessible dimension. A famous example is this story of Hitler and Mussolini, which was printed on a leaflet sold by its author, Antonio Gramigni, at fairs and in the *bettole*.

> For the ambition of those two unhuman ones,
> one from Rome and the other from Berlin,
> we all had a dog's life,
> from the oldest to the youngest one of us.
> They wanted to hold the world in their hands;
> they were competing to see who was the more murderous.
> They formed Nazism, Fascism,
> but today the day of justice has come.
>
> They spread enmity in the world;
> one person couldn't trust his neighbor.
> Where before there had been friendship,
> then it was the kingdom of hate.
> They threw all of us in the mud.
> They deceived us with violence.

Better if we weren't even born:
we would not have had to face such disasters.

Those shameless people renegaded
even families and parents,
but for those who were the persecutors
today it will be trouble
because the ones they persecuted
now will make them pay for what they did:
when they had the club in their hands
they lost control over their brains.

Very often there were violences;
they were out for trouble;
like adolescents they behaved.
They were going around at night
and knocked on many doors
to abuse many people,
and they gave us purges of castor oil
to let us sit in the outhouse all the time.

But today you are the ones who must be worried;
today violence and abuse are over;
these evil facts do not happen any longer;
people want justice and to punish you;
your graves are not far away
and ready to receive you properly.
We will put in them also Farinacci,
and we will say, "A bunch of buffoons died."

And now with your lies you'll get nowhere.
You don't hold even a square meter of land;
your mightly Empire has crumbled.
All over you were trapped and defeated
by Russia, America, and England.
And you were screaming and yelling
like a peddler of pots at a market;
now you must pay for when you had the Pact of Steel.

Buy this story you all, innkeeper or baker.
I'll sell it to you, it's for all seasons.

And the more you read and study it
you'll get satisfaction from it.
The older people and the children alike will cry.
Now I'll stand up, I'm thirsty from singing.
I was never one of the bad poets,
and poet Gramigni gives greetings to you. [100]

Not all of these "stories in octaves" or "contrast songs" were learned or repeated continuously. Some of the more inventive and successful ones, however, passed into the local folklore, and certain verses sometimes became proverbs or were sung by themselves. One of these is the story of Pasquino, also in octaves, which can be sung either as a "contrast" by two singers or as a whole song by one person. In the complete version a farm worker who disagrees with his master reaches the point where he wants to fight and completely sever relations. His wife, however, goes to serve the master; thus, with an act of surrender, the terms of which are somewhat ambiguous, Pasquino resigns himself to relative well-being through the efforts of his wife. Here is the end of the story, according to a version collected in the Arezzo area in the 1960s:

"If this is true, it's no use arguing more.
Morning and evening you'll send her to me.
Cooking my bread and meat will be her chore,
As well as cleaning all my rooms, you see.
She can also look after my washing, for
Then I'll give you my keys, one, two, three.
And so a barrel of wine will be all yours,
Plus a big sack of grain filled from my stores."

And so Pasquino left in a humble way.
He married Anna and his ambition ceased.
He was as light-hearted as a donkey in May
When on the flowering plants he's allowed to feast.
And so Annina in the feminine way
To serve master and husband is leased.
To and fro she runs from one to the other.
She could take care of an army without much bother.

My friends, here the story must come to its end.
Whoever marries, from Pasquino must learn.

He, in taking a wife, no longer had to fend.
His bread and wine for him both did she earn.[101]

This story is in line with the antifeminism of the texts previously reproduced. It is significant, however, that the bitter finale of this song, wherein Pasquino is "dishonored," is often omitted or forgotten. All my peasant informants remembered the following lines:

He gave himself over to God with open arms,
And spoke with his eldest son about possible harms.
"Give me my sacks," was Pasquino's will.
"I'll beat the master or I'll go to the mill."[102]

By such an operation of significant selectivity, one remembered the part of the song favoring one's own social group.

The counter-*veglia* of the excluded ones lasted longer than the other types of *veglia*, and often it was the cock's crowing which signalled its end. At this point, all drank the "stirrup cup" (this name, it seems, was acquired from the fact that, in olden times, cavaliers often drank their last drink with one foot in the stirrup, ready to mount their horses and be off). "Don't be on your way unless your mouth tastes like wine"; "Shoes and wine are the road's line" ["*Non ti mettere in cammino se la bocca 'un sa di vino*"; "*Suola e vino fanno far cammino*"]. Thus, the drinkers took the occasion for the last toast and mug, preparing themselves to leave for home and for the problems they would find awaiting them there, that is, the rage of the head of the family if they were bachelors or that of their wife if they were married. Often, the more fortunate, those who did not have to account for themselves to anyone or whose wives were either heavy sleepers or resigned to their circumstances, would accompany home their less fortunate friends who pretended to be carefree about what was to come. Whoever returned home drunk or high was often received with fists and screams by other relatives who had stayed at home for the family *veglia* and woke up or stayed up for the late-night scene. And so, one's friends waited listening at the door, for frequently the shouting inside could be heard out on the street. There were dramatic mothers who reached for their children to scream at their husbands: "Wicked wretch! You go out the door and leave me alone with this poor creature!" Others took the rolling pin in hand and then shouts like "Ouch!" "No," "What're you doing? Stay still! Don't!" were heard. Some husbands were able to slip into bed without waking their wives, and the next morning under questioning they would argue about the exact time when they had come in: "What time did you get in last night?" "Oh, probably it was around two . . ." "I woke up at two and you weren't here." "Well, I didn't look at my watch, but it was around then, I'm sure . . ." And so on, thus, bluffing it out. These encounters, particularly when won by the husband, would be repeated to friends the next night at the tavern, reinforcing in this manner their sense of solidarity as a group of outcasts and men. Among these stories, one which is repeated frequently in tavern folklore, is the one about the husband who came in late and was telling his sleepy wife that it was only one o'clock when the clock in the bell tower rang out four times. And so the husband screamed at the clock: "All right, we've understood! Keep your trap shut, big mouth." In another version, the husband has just claimed that it is ten o'clock when the bell rings out one o'clock. "Ten o'clock, huh, you bum!" comments the wife angrily. And he calmly replies, "You expected the bell to ring zeroes too?" My favorite, however, is the one about E. M., who came home from a card game with friends about five in the morning, when dawn was just beginning to break. He succeeded in getting in and sitting down on the bed without awakening his wife, and he started to undress as best he could in that position. He woke her, however, just as the bell tower was striking five. "I felt my blood run cold," he said later, telling the story. But her only comment was: "O E., what are you doing? You're not getting up this early, are you?" And with great presence of mind, he saved himself by saying: "You're right, B. You know what? I'll go back to bed." And so, he finished getting undressed in peace and went happily to bed to sleep like a log. Thus in life as in the stories, "With a good wit he saved his honor." And an evening begun "with songs and highs" for once did not end "with pains and cries."

8
Conclusions

"*. . . ma avere infino a qui detto della presente novella voglio che mi basti, e a coloro rivolgermi ai quali l'ho raccontata.*"

["But having up until now spoken about the present novel, I want this to be enough, and I would now like to turn my attention to those to whom I told it."]

           Boccaccio, *Decameron*, the Fourth Day, Introduction

"*Nondimeno me n'è pure una rimasta da raccontare, nella conclusion della quale si contiene un si' fatto motto, che forse non ci se n'e alcuno di tanto sentimento contato.*"

["Nevertheless, I still have one to tell in the conclusion of which is contained a saying, that perhaps we have not as yet been told of such a sentiment."]

           Ibid., the Sixth Day, Novella 9

The *veglia* as we have seen it has lasted over five hundred years without losing its function or its meaning. As Vico suggested, the reason why popular traditions were born and maintained by entire nations for "long spaces of time" comes from the fact that "they must have had public motives of truth," and more truth resides in a collective creation than in an individual one.[1]

The *veglia* has been the main social occasion in which social roles and values have been discussed and transmitted in rural Tuscany; folklore has provided for centuries the means and messages of such crucial communicative events; the texts we have analyzed include all the classic functions of communication: emotive, referential, poetic, phatic, conative, metalingual.[2] Not all such functions are present in each text, nor are they evenly distributed when they occur in a text; but on the whole the folklore we have analyzed presents itself as a flexible and complete metalanguage, a complete system of communication.[3]

Folklore does not exist in a timeless dimension, but rather in a concrete process that is part of a ritual meeting held in the heart of a cultural group, definite in time and space.[4] The Tuscan texts I have discussed can receive their specific final sense only from the cultural microcosm that uses them, which is made of elements and systems of another substance, such as ideological, social, and underlying economic structures.[5] Consequently, I have maintained this explicatory principle: these facts derive their quantitative and qualitative characteristics *from the fact* that there are specific individual characteristics within both their performative and their cultural contexts. Accordingly, the contents of the texts have not been interpreted as ritual survivals pertaining to preceding cultural stages,[6] but, rather, as elements more or less metaphorical of their contemporary cultural stage. If the texts, and especially the narratives among them, present elements referring to past cultural periods, one can say the same about the culture itself, which at every given historic moment presents itself as an extraordinarily complex organic unity of factors with different historical age, stratified and integrated to various degrees among themselves. As there are "historical" elements of a different age in culture, so in folklore there are "metaphorical" elements referring to historical elements of different age, but which remain present or operating in contemporary texts, at least at the unconscious level, by means of symbolic investments. In its whole, the folklore of a culture is homologous with it, while every single text or part of it is analogous to a segment of it, at a level which can be conscious or unconscious, literal or metaphorical; their correspondence is either direct or inverted.

The folk themselves are aware of the strict correspondence between folklore and culture; in fact, narrators and listeners constantly commented to me that a truth, literal or metaphoric, resides in these texts:[7] "They are stories, but they are true." "They are true facts." "They seem all rather true to me." One could observe that the narrators and listeners very often made precise analogies with events in their own lives. At other times one could observe how mechanisms of the unconscious came into play: in these cases the narratives provide the means of dramatization to situations blocked at the conscious level.[8] In any case, the people at the *veglia* clearly identified with the roles of the tale characters.

Similarly, scholars have held that valid inferences can be drawn from the "secondary system" of folklore and correlated to social structures or to other aspects of cultures. Fisher, from a sociopsychological point of view, affirms that in this sense narratives, vis-à-vis psychological texts, do not present any disadvantage with regard to stability, representativity, and interpretability.[9] In the same sense, Von Franz, from the point of view of Jungian psychology, asserts the representativity of folk narratives with respect to profound individual and collective psychological mechanisms.[10] Moreover, from specific structural characteristics of narrative sequences peculiar to specific cultures, it is possible to infer particular historic characteristics of the cultures themselves;[11] from the fact that specific narrative sequences are limited to particular cultural areas, one can maintain that their presence or absence is an effective index of the limits of the area in question.[12]

Without exception, the reality to which the texts refer is the family in its patriarchal, patrilinear model that is diffused throughout rural Tuscany where they were collected. Larger sociological units remain external and are consciously refused: we have seen narrtives in which "the people" free a father who has killed his unfaithful wife or a girl who has killed her unfaithful fiancé. Family above society: in fact, "society" in the Tuscan countryside was often used to mean a group of patriarchal families, equal among themselves yet singularly independent and sovereign.[13] Because of the objective preeminence of the family in the historical and sociological reality in which these texts exist, the dimension of explanation that I have chosen is the family "isotype," which accounts for contents and structures in a broader and more coherent manner than any other to be found in the texts.

The family provided the sociological frame, and, within it, the performative frame to the texts. Performers and audience were family members, friend of the family, and prospective family members. The audience identified with the tale characters, who were usually mentioned by family role, such as "the son of the king," "the mother," "the daughter." Even the king of the tales was seen in his role of father, in his home, and "At home everyone is the King" goes the proverb as if to draw closer the two roles.

It is not surprising then to find that in Tuscan folklore the most frequently found narratives concern family values and the formation of families. I am referring not only to my own collection: the texts and collections accessible to scholars are numerous and impose certain quantitative considerations along the same lines. Generally speaking, in Tuscan folklore one rarely finds animal fairy tales (Aarne-Thompson Tale-Type 1–299), religious ones (AT 750–849), or those with the stupid Ogre as protagonist (AT 1000–1199). There are also relatively few traditional jokes and anecdotes (AT 1200–1349). After examining a rather large number of folk narratives, D'Aronco concludes in his index that in Tuscany the magic-romantic and love tales have had extraordinary popularity; the frequency of these seems exceptionally high compared to the repertoires of other regions and cultural contexts.[14]

The same can be said for sung narratives and Tuscan musical folklore, "regurgitating with love and passion" as Cocchiara observed[15] and as, a century before, Capponi also observed with some regret: "It is a historic fact of no mean significance, in my opinion, that all the songs are love songs. It is true, in a way I am sorry about it; but we are made like this, and you could not model us along your own lines." [16] But what other contents should we expect to find in a folklore genre which was practically the one and only means of socially approved communication between lovers or prospective lovers? Furthermore, with the help of appropriate ethnographic data it is possible to see how the sequences in which these love folk songs were sung have a structural pattern of the same kind as the folk narratives, a pattern whose focal point is the conclusion in an engagement or a marriage, that is, a socially approved status. Singles, especially women but also men, were socially disapproved of in many ways. In folk speech they were called *pinza* and *pinzo* [spinster] with a negative connotation; in the narratives they were always the bad or the unfortunate characters; in the singing they were the object of sarcastic rhymes; in most of the games Tuscans played at the danced *veglia*, they were the losers of the game and had to undergo the *"penitenza,"* a symbolic punishment that could be avoided only by having a companion, that is, being a part of a couple; in the popular card game Omo Nero [Black Jack] the losing card was the odd Jack, the only one that did not have a match.

In fact, the only genres of folklore in the *veglia* that were not directly related to courtship and marriage were the rhymes, riddles, and lullabies directed to children. This folklore, however, also concerned socialization, only at a deeper level of logic and semantics. In the opinion of my informants, children learned through folklore the names of things (definition), the differences between two things (disjunction), and that two words could rhyme or have the same sound or a very similar sound (implication); they could be told one thing for another (metaphor); they could be shown that one word may mean several different things (polysemy). They were also shown "how to put things together" (syntax) and that "there was the good and the bad in the world" (morals). Along with these rudiments, children were presented with the tales of love and magic, where they were shown what was awaiting them in their culture: rites of passage, youth, courtship, engagement, marriage, family, inheritance at the death of the old ones. This appears clearly if we consider the group of tale-types most common in Tuscan folklore: a few of them have been already exemplified and discussed in Chapter 2, but mainly in their performative aspects; here, instead, we have to consider the structure of the few tale-types that have constantly proven to be the most widely popular every time folklorists have collected folk narratives in Tuscany[17] and see them in the light of the corresponding role structures in the traditional Tuscan family.

In the stories of Donkey Skin and of the Princess and the Frog (AT 925 and 440A), one deals with the refusal of incest, or the primary founding act of culture,[18] from the point of view of the woman and the man. It is worth noting that an inversion occurs in the narratives: "the fairy" and the father want to marry the prince and the princess, respectively; the initiative with regard to the complexes of Oedipus and Electra dealt with by the narrative is turned around and attributed to the parents. There is also a shift in the nature of the relationship desired, which changes from a sexual relationship to "marriage." With the refusal of an incestuous marriage the two protagonists precipitate into a state of latency (animal form, journey) from which they will emerge by means of qualifying trials. Having recovered their human individuality (that is, having passed from Nature to Culture), they marry a prince and a princess, respectively. The differences between the two narratives are also significant: in the beginning of the one dealing with the woman, the death of the mother is represented as the symbolic equivalent of the separation from the mother in reality. At the end the father is forgiven. One could infer that Electra's complex is considered relatively less serious than Oedipus'. In the narrative regarding the man, the maternal figure is presented in the disguise of a fairy. Probably, the mother-son constellation, being the most important in reality that the narrative represents, involves and demands a longer journey and a stricter censorship before arriving at the level of consciousness. In reality the process followed by individuals to Culture followed analogous phases of development: for the woman, it was the refusal of her mother, then that of her father, followed by a period of latency, then the attainment of maturity by means of passing qualifying tests, and finally marriage; for the man, it was separation from his mother, a period of latency, then the attainment of maturity by means of passing qualifying trials, and then marriage.

Other narratives furthered the argument focusing on qualifying trials. Dealing with women, an example is AT 402, in which a girl, bewitched in the form of an animal and in competition with other girls, passes the qualifying tests of cooking, sewing, weaving, keeping the house in order, rearing animals, and good grooming. Having recovered her human form, she marries a prince. The same thing happened in reality: Tuscan girls had to learn exactly the same things before being ready for marriage. A second example is AT 403, in which two adolescent stepsisters are compared. The good one, through her choice of modest objects and her good manners, acquires a star on her forehead; the bad one, because of her ambitious choices and bad manners, acquires a donkey's tail on her forehead, remains a spinster, and is always made fun of, while the other marries a prince. In real life the same good qualities were considered fundamental for the conclusion of a good marriage.

For men, the qualifying trials for marriage in the narratives could consist of defeating the rivalry of their brothers, winning a joust, giving food or clothing to bewitched girls (AT 408), or fathoming a riddle. In reality there could be rivalry with others for the hand of the same girl, the ritual answers to give to her family while asking for her hand, or the food and clothing to give as gifts (and the implicit promise of feeding and clothing the woman) before receiving assent to marriage.

In the narratives the element of competition for marriage both for men and women is often present, sometimes in family circles or sometimes among equals. The same thing took place in reality; not everyone could get married, and marriage was "limited good": who found a husband or wife did so at the expense of others. Moreover, in the narratives the good always married and the bad did not. In narratives and in reality, marriage was a sign of grace and a happy ending for the good ones, a positive status and value.

The basic mechanism for the balanced functioning of the cultures is the application among its members of the principle of reciprocity, which articulates the specific obligation of giving, receiving, and repaying.[19] This principle is illustrated by a series of narratives that metaphorically appear to regard the concept of circulation of women-objects.

In AT 425A a widower father robs a rose from the garden of a monster who forces him to give his daughter in replacement. The monster, transformed into a prince, then marries her. Assuming the rose-woman equivalence, very common in Tuscan folklore, one can hypothesize in these narratives the presence of a paradigmatic example of the circulation of woman-object. Who takes a rose belonging to someone else has to give his daughter in replacement. The very use of the symbol (rose=woman) exemplifies the principle of equivalence.

The same principle occurs in AT 313, in which the object is stolen before the birth of the daughter and is given back when she reaches adolescence, that is, marriageable age. In AT 301, one of the most common in Tuscany, he (a wizard, a monster) who has robbed someone else's garden flowers or fruit holds the same number of girls prisoner, one or more of whom will be freed and married by the same number of princes or sons of the victim of the robbery.

The same principle, the circulation of the woman-object, was at the basis of the dances at the *veglia*. Observing the sequence and the context, it is possible to see how the function of the formation of couples was completed with the execution of a kinetic text that constituted a ritual of distribution and integration.[20] Each man had to invite all the women to dance and each woman had to accept a dance with whosoever invited her. In the quadrille, in everybody's opinion the dance with the greatest amount of semantic information, the dancer took the girl who interested him most from the maternal "bosom" where she was seated and took her into the dancing circle. He then had to "give" her or let her be "carried," "handled," and "held" by all the other men in the group before getting her back at the end of the dance. In the meantime he himself had to "hold," "handle," and "change" all the women in the group. On the whole, the men exchanged among themselves the women-objects to which they showed a sort of property right in a perfectly symmetrical manner. After the syntagmatic recitation of the principles of property and circulation, every individual was allowed, at the sign of authority (the *capoveglia*, or person in charge of the dance), to lead the woman away (to drink or eat at the buffet, where customarily the daughter was kept far away from her mother). The same general principle of property appears clearly in ritual customs relating to courting and marriage.

The stoning of a visitor from outside the groups affirmed their

right of property and preemption with regard to the woman who
the victim wanted to take away. In the *serrata* [roundup] the young
people of the bride's home village blocked the street between her
home and his to show that they would not let her out; the groom
gave the group a symbolic price and in this way he could take the
woman with him[21] and conclude the symbolic *deductio* [abduction].
In folk speech one can see traces of the same conception: for a woman "to be of someone" meant "to be the wife of," "the daughter
of," but the expression literally means "to be the property of." In
traditional Tuscan the terms tended to be synonymous:

> O mother, mother,
> when I grow up I won't be yours any longer.
> I'll belong to that handsome
> blond boy, if he takes me away![22]

> I belonged entirely to father and mother.
> Now I belong to Beppino, if he takes me.[23]

Similarly, at the marriage all the friends of the groom brought
presents and gave the ritual kiss to the bride.[24] (Sometimes as a
wedding present one gave the bridal couple a booklet of folk narratives with a happy ending—occasionally even specially printed—
wishing them "to live happily ever after," another explicit proof
of the close bond between tales and family!) The bride had to "touch
the hand" of each of her brothers-in-law (repeating the gesture by
which she became engaged to her husband)[25] and cook for a week
in her new home not only for her husband but also for all her new
in-laws.[26] Another form of collective ownership of the woman was
implied and commented on by the saying "a bell is sufficient for a
nation" ["*una campana fa a un popolo*"],[27] with which one asserted
metaphorically that a housewife had sexual relationships with her
bachelor brothers-in-law, in addition to her husband.

A whole series of folklore texts showed this conception of the
woman and implicitly tended to maintain it. One of the most common proverbs directed at men is "*moglie e buoi dei paesi tuoi*" ["wives
and oxen from your own backyard"].[28] In fact the group maintained
a higher level of cohesion and equilibrium if its members married

among themselves. If too high a number of men and women married outside the group, this brought about a reciprocity, the symmetry of which was difficult to control. From the point of view of stability of the group it was important that there be possible husbands for the women. It was even more important for the men to have as many women as possible from which to choose a good wife. A series of narratives discussed and assessed different possibilities in this respect. We have already seen examples that in text or context advised women against choosing as lovers or marriage partners foreigners, shepherds, or fishermen. AT 955, which is very common in Tuscany, shows by means of a "demonstration to the contrary" how marriages with people from other places end badly, in opposition to marriages with one's own neighbors which, instead, have a happy ending. In these narratives a girl marries an "unknown gentleman who is mysterious and handsome" but who is later found out to be a leader of murderers. The woman then flees and marries a prince. This sort of "divorce" and second marriage shows that the first marriage was so wrong it did not count, for all practical purposes. The bad man tries to harm her but is killed. The opposition of the two husbands is significant: the good one is always a king's son (of Spain, England, or Portugal, etc). We never know anything about the bad one. The narrative can be considered as a metaphor of nuptial customs and of the attribution of positive and negative qualities: the mysterious gentleman to whom she is married without anyone knowing anything about him turns out to be a leader of murderers; the other, who we know comes from a well-to-do family, proves to be a good husband.

A series of narratives often dealt with the engagement period; they were not metaphorical and contained explicit "morals" of the prescriptive type. Narratives of this type always include an account of the journey[29] made by the man, his return, the tests qualifying one for marriage, and marriage given as a prize (or denied as a punishment) to the woman. In reality, as in the tales, journeys made by the men were common and usually due to military service or seasonal emigration. To the contrary, one very seldom heard of journeys made by women, either in reality or in the tales unless in the case of emergency, such as the search for "her first love." The woman waited and during the separation had to pass tests of faithfulness to her promised lover far away. If, when put to the test (sometimes arranged by the fiancé himself in disguise), the girl proved to be faithful, he married her. If, instead, she was unfaithful, even in the case of plausible reasons, he would not accept her. The man's duty, in narratives as in reality, was to keep the promise he made to the girl at his departure. He who returned and changed fiancées or even worse, left the girl he was previously involved with, maybe even leaving her pregnant, found himself in the grave, and rightly so, as is explicitly declared by the moral that governed both reality and the stories.

Marriage, a rite of passage par excellence,[30] had different psychological implications for the bride and groom. AT 709, for example, refers to the psychological situation of the woman in which a vicious mother, jealous of her daughter, tries to kill her. The girl runs away and marries a prince, and the mother is burned to death. This narrative development can be considered a metaphor for the mother-daughter conflict, solved by the marriage of the daughter who in this way eliminates her mother from her life. It should be noted that in traditional Tuscan weddings the mother of the bride did not go to the church for the ceremony; her presence and the ritual were mutually exclusive.

And the groom's mother? As far as narratives are concerned, AT 707, which is very common in Tuscan folklore, treats this theme. The development is the following: in the absence of a king, the queen has children, at least one of which is a male. The king's mother then sends a message to her son saying that the queen has produced animals or monsters. The queen is banished, and her mother-in-law orders her execution. The king then returns and finds and recognizes his wife and children who have been miraculously saved. He is reunited with them, and his treacherous mother is burned to death. In the previous case the bride's mother was burned in connection with her daughter's marriage; in this case the groom's mother is burned because the bride gives birth to a baby boy. Passing on to consider Tuscan culture, it appears that the only way in which a bride acquired a definitive status with her in-laws was by bringing babies into the world, particularly males. "Salute e figli maschi" ["health and male children"] was the most common traditional blessing addressed to the bride and groom at the wedding. Only with the birth of her first baby boy, which guaranteed the continuity of the patriarchal family, did the wife replace her mother-in-law with respect to her husband, becoming a mother herself. In narratives the mother-in-law was burned; in reality she lost status. A Tuscan folk saying expresses clearly the fact that mother-in-law and daughter-in-law were in complementary distribution:

> My mother-in-law to be, I'll be your daughter-in-law:
> I'll enter the home, and you'll exit from it.[31]

Her son often started calling his wife "mother." The fact that the woman did not become fully a part of her new family with marriage but rather with maternity is confirmed by the fact that, if the wife did not bear children, on her death her dowry was restored to the family into which she was born.[32]

On the contrary, nothing happened to the fathers of the characters in narratives, neither before nor after the marriage. Even fathers with incestuous desires were forgiven and invited to the marriage. Narratives repeated, "He must also be happy," and, in fact, the person in question always tried to take the future bride or groom away from the father, but also had to be assured of his assent to the wedding. In narratives, paternal authority was respected under any condition, as it had to be in reality.

With marriage the woman was entrusted with the "morality" and "honor" of her new family that she had to maintain, often in the absence of her husband. The sociological reality of the husband's absence from home because of military service or seasonal work corresponded to the psychological reality of a family constellation with an absent father. In the absence of her husband, the wife could be "tempted" by other men, but it was the wife's duty to remain faithful to her husband. We have considered some typical examples of this in narratives, the collation of which is significant:

1. (Gabriella) Lea accepts.
   Her husband returns.
   The truth comes out.
   (Gabriella) Lea is killed.

2. Pia refuses.
   Her husband returns.

The truth is re-established.
Pia dies.

3. Genoveffa refuses.
Her husband returns.
The truth is re-established.
Genoveffa lives and is "remarried" by her husband.

The truth is always re-established at the return of the husband, but the happy ending takes place only if the woman, besides being honest, gives birth to a male child. It is important to note that the woman in the wrong, or even suspected, is punished, while the man who tempted her gets away without any penalty except God's. In the story of Pia, Ghino is considered a negative figure because he deceives his friend, not because he tempts Pia. "The man has the right to ask" was the moral in narratives, and in reality he had the same privilege. In narratives "the woman has the obligation to refuse" temptation as she had in real life, so that at the end of her life she could be complimented by the traditional Latin epitaph:

Casta vixit, lanam fecit, domum servavit
[Lived in chastity, wove the wool, kept the home]

These are some of the parallel developments of stories performed at the *veglia* and real-life stories of the people present at these evening gatherings, of rites of passage and tale-types. These are some of the most important "theorems hidden in the poems" of the *veglia* and of families in traditional Tuscany.

In Tuscan folklore a system of coherent values was articulated, part of a worldview[33] that included time and space, and within these, roles and dimensions, both individual and social. The first part of the *veglia* was centered on the formation of subjects capable of assuming social and familial obligations; the second part concerned the stipulation of reciprocal contractual obligations; the third part regarded their preservation and the sanctions related. The group of children learned cultural competence in the first part of the *veglia*; the group of youngsters learned performance in the second part; the group of elders taught both groups.

The basic coherence appearing in the *veglia* does not, however, mean that its folklore was univocal.[34] Together with values, contents, solutions, and preferred developments proposed and imposed by the dominating culture, there were others which were disapproved of, advised against, and punished; side by side with the prescribed and the probable, one found the not prescribed and the possible: that which constituted the alternative, the rest, the countervalues, the negativity, the protest, the opposition. Part of the nonorthodox texts were admitted in the family *veglia* and balanced by the context. Depending on the occasion, these nonorthodox texts were the exception that confirmed the rule or the unspecified negation that affirmed its existence or a bad example in answer to which a good example would be produced or the satire that responded to reality without ultimately affecting it. Another series of prohibited concepts was thrown into the unconscious dimension of culture from which they emerged as signs, symbols, and metaphors of what existed in it.[35] The greatest part of these texts, however, were assigned to the anti-*veglia* at the inn. There, along with the "anti-texts," one found the individuals who for some reason did not have a *veglia* to attend. To maintain its equilibrium, in fact, the culture knew how to foresee, provide, and circumscribe forms of expression and meeting places to integrate symmetrically nonetheless those who could not, or did not want to, or were not supposed to be integrated into the system of the *veglia* and of the family. My informants themselves indicated to me the system of oppositions they perceived in that respect. As for participants we have:

Veglia	Anti-*Veglia*
Capoccia [patriarch]	*Oste* [innkeeper]
Cozzoni [middle men]	*Ruffiani* [ruffians]
Donne oneste [honest women]	*Donne disoneste* [dishonest women]
Famiglia [family group]	*Uomini* [group of single men]

And for the performances we have:

Veglia	Anti-*Veglia*
Verbal censorship	Obscenity
Moderate drinking	Drunkenness

Permitted games	Forbidden games
True stories	Lies
Praise of women	Misogyny
Praise of family	Hatred of family rules
Praise of religion	Antireligious protest, blasphemy
Politeness	Aggressiveness
Concord	Discord
Praise of institutions	Social protest

Culture prevented the external formation of true alternatives to its own existence, whether ideological or existential, by permitting within itself antivalues which were a mirror image of the official ones. By so doing, it assured itself a long existence and a stable balance for centuries. From what has been seen in the texts and contexts one can derive in conclusion the following proportion:

Individual		Collective	
Individual life cycle	Individual tale : version	Rites of pas- : :sage of the life : cycle	Tale type

From this one derives the other:

Culture		Folklore	
Individual life cycle	Rites of pas- : sage of the life: cycle	Individual tale : version	Tale type :

This means that the texts taken all in all were homologous with their contexts. In particular, narrative structures were analogous to those of the rites of passage and the system of the characters' roles was analogous to that of the family roles present in the performative and cultural contexts.[36]

The same can be said of the constraints and controls that regulated the performances of the folklore at the *veglia*. One form of control was to quote a balancing counterexample to match and exorcise the dangerous text proposed to the audience; a second one that we have analyzed was a frame of negative contextual comments; a third one was the singing of a *ritornello*, a fixed-form refrain that the whole group of *vegliatori* sang each time one individual singer had sung his *stornello*. Famous *ritornelli* are:

L'amore è come l'ellera	[Love is like ivy;
dove s'attacca more	it dies where it attaches itself
così così il mio core	in the same way my heart
mi s' è attaccato a te.	attached itself to you.]

Love is like ivy . . .

Or else:

Cogli la rosa	[Pick the rose
e lascia star la foglia	and let the leaf go.
ho tanta voglia	I have a great desire
di fare l'amor con te.	to make love to you.][37]

Pick the rose . . .

The *ritornello* reduced each individual statement and performance within the fixed frame of the one sung by the group: the individual merged into the group.

The performance of narratives obeyed the same principle. The structure of the tales was given and the creative freedom of the narrator was limited to the form and the length to be given to the traditional canonical development. No narrator could ever save Pia in the story (if anything, one could try to make her die differently), or pardon Lea, or find a husband for Cenerentola's sister. The audience energically protested to any change that narrators would make on the structure ("It's not that one!" "It does not go like this!" "You don't know it!"). Similar social constraints existed in real life. Individuals could live their lives as they pleased, as long as they did not touch on the family structures and undergoing constraints. Nobody could avoid punishing an unfaithful wife, or marrying a girl one had "compromised" in front of the group, or leaving a fiancée who was "the lover of an army," or "going to the vegetable garden to get the cabbage" if the father was sick. Individuals in the culture, like narrators in the *veglia*, had the freedom to make up their story as they liked it, as long as everything would fit into its place at the end.

These controls aimed at maintaining the equilibrium inside the family itself, as well as the coextension of this to the farm, the productive unit which cyclicly assured them of their subsistence. One took a wife if and when it was necessary for, or at least compatible with, the progress of the farm,[38] and for the same reason one needed manual labor, that is, children, much better if male. However, one had to be sure not to have too many or too few with respect to the size of the farm which had to produce enough for the farmer, his family, and the owner. The latter explicitly controlled the size of the peasant family by exercising over the marriages of the sharecroppers, both men and women, the power of veto and sometimes that of command.[39] Peasants usually asked the owners permission before they were married; the owner traditionally gave the bride the "dowry gift" in money or linen. The owner could insist that the men get a wife if in his opinion the family needed more women and children, or he could insist that the peasants marry off their daughters, his basic criterion and interest being whatever he believed to be the optimum exploitation of the farm. In cases of disagreement, the owner could always give the sharecroppers the *"disdetta"* [termination of contract] and have them vacate the farm. In a final analysis, it was the economic structures that formed the family structures and roles that we have considered in rural Tuscan culture and in its folklore.[40]

After having existed for five centuries, the *mezzadria* [going halves] as an economic institution is disappearing in Tuscany.[41] Its death seems to have decreed the end of the traditional Tuscan family.[42] The new family is a nuclear one, residing usually in one-family living quarters in suburban or urban settings:[43] almost all husbands and a good number of wives earn a fixed salary. The change of the economic structures has brought about the change in the family structures. With the reduced extension of the family, the principles of authority, the economic and decisional powers, the relationships between men and women and between the generations are being rapidly reconsidered. Because of these changes, and moreover with the penetration of mass media and literacy into the Tuscan country-side, the culture to which we have referred is shifting from very stable to very rapidly changing. After the ongoing changes in economic and sociological structures, those who in the future will study the same cultural universe that has constituted the object of our discussion will be able to record new forms and contents, structures, and modalities in folklore texts.[44] The *veglie* that I have described are becoming more and more rare in Tuscany, but that does not imply the "death of folklore," rather the continuation of its everlasting evolution with new texts, enunciative contexts, and ideologies of reference. Folklore remains a profound heritage of cultural man because it originates from his worldview and his social being. The existence of folklore remains immutably bound to the very existence of Culture whose journey it has always shared, and guided for its part, in the dialectic relationship between tradition and situation.

Appendix of Italian Texts

1. THE WORLD BY THE FIREPLACE

Ref. n. 19   Sta' sul fuoco quando è sera
a grattar la sonagliera
se vuoi aver la pelle intera.

Ref. n. 41   La carne fa la carne,
il pane mantiene,
il vino fa buon sangue,
il pesce fa le vesce,
e l'erba fa la merda.

Ref. n. 50   La massaia che va in campagna,
perde più che la 'un guadagna.

La massaia che sta a ca'
che guadagna non lo sa.

La roba sta con chi la sa guardare.

Il meglio boccone è quel del cuoco.

Ref. n. 52   Troppi cuochi guastan la cucina.

O ragazzina
ma quanti giovanotti tieni in trama
ma quanti giovanotti tieni in trama
i troppi cuochi guastan la cucina.

Ref. n. 55   Madonna benedetta d'i' castagno,
fammi la grazia i' mi' marito accechi,
e non possa vedere i' mi' guadagno,
Madonna benedetta d'i' castagno!

Ref. n. 65 Escì fuor lupo dal bosco
colla faccia nera nera
portò via il più bel caprin
che la pastora aveva . . .

Ref. n. 94 Portami la tua torcia bell'e accesa
la paglia da bruciare ce l'ho già io . . .

L'uom è il fuoco e la donna è stoppa,
viene il diavolo e gliel'accocca.

Fior di ginestra
dove s'è acceso il foco pe' una volta
dove s'è acceso il foco pe' una volta
sempre un po' di scintilla e la ci resta.

2. FAIRY TALES FOR THE YOUNG AND THE OLD

Ref. no. 14 La casa del mio amore è in un bel piano
e davanti alla porta in un giardino
ci nasce un albero di melograno.

Ref. n. 24 Le manine delicate
quante cose sanno fare!
San lavare, san stirare
e la mamma accarezzare!

Canini gattini e figliol di contadini
sono bellini quando son piccini.

Ref. n. 39 Sette a letto
sette sotto a i' letto.
Sette a letto andiamo
e sette a casa rimaniamo.
Ragazzi, andate a letto.

Ref. n. 40 A letto a letto, disse Marco vecchio,
e chi 'un ha letto, vada sotto a un letto.
A letto a letto, disse la farfalla,
e chi 'un ha letto, dorma nella stalla.

3. BEDTIME AND CHILDREN'S FOLKLORE

Ref. no. 3 "Petuzzo, va' nell'ortuzzo
a pigliare il cavoluzzo

perché il babbo è malato."
"Io no che 'un voglio andare!"
"Allora dirò alla mazza che ti dia.
Mazza dai a Petuzzo
perchè 'un vol anda' nell'ortuzzo
a pigliare il cavoluzzo
perchè i' su' babbo è malato."
"Io no che 'un voglio dare!"
"Allora dirò al foco che ti bruci.
Foco brucia la mazza
perchè la mazza 'un vol dare a Petuzzo
perchè Petuzzo 'un vol anda' nell'ortuzzo
a pigliare il cavoluzzo
perchè i' su' babbo è malato."
"Io no che 'un vo' bruciare!"
"Allora dirò all'acqua che ti spenga.
Acqua spengi i' foco
perchè i' foco 'un vole bruciá' la mazza
perchè la mazza 'un vole da' a Petuzzo
perchè Petuzzo 'un vole andá' nell'ortuzzo
a piglià il cavoluzzo
perchè i' su' babbo è malato."
"Io no che 'un voglio spengere!"
"Allora dirò a i' bove che ti beva!
Bove bevi l'acqua
perché l'acqua 'un vòle spenge' il foco
perchè i' foco 'un vole bruciá' la mazza
perchè la mazza 'un vole da' a Petuzzo
perchè Petuzzo 'un vole andá' nell'ortuzzo
a pigliare il cavoluzzo
perchè i' su' babbo è malato."
"Io no che 'un voglio bere!"
"Allora dirò alla fune che ti leghi!"
"Fune lega i' bove
perchè i' bove 'un vole bere l'acqua
perchè l'acqua 'un vole spengere i' foco
perchè i' foco 'un vole bruciá' la mazza
perchè la mazza 'un vole da' a Petuzzo
perchè Petuzzo 'un vole andá' nell'ortuzzo
a piglia' il cavoluzzo
perchè i' su' babbo è malato."
"Io no che 'un vo' legare!"

"Allora dirò a i' topo che ti roda.
Topo rodi la fune
perchè la fune 'un vole lega' i' bove
perchè i' bove 'un vole bere l'acqua
perchè l'acqua 'un vole spenge' il foco
perchè i' foco 'un vole bruciá' la mazza
perchè la mazza 'un vole da' a Petuzzo
perchè Petuzzo 'un vole andá' nell'ortuzzo
a pigliá' il cavoluzzo
perchè i' su' babbo è malato."
"Io no che 'un voglio rodere!"
"Allora dirò a i' gatto che ti mangi!
Gatto mangia i' topo
perchè i' topo 'un vol rode' la fune
perchè la fune 'un vol legare i' bove
perchè i' bove non vole bere l'acqua
perchè l'acqua non vole spenge' il foco
perchè i' foco non vol bruciá' la mazza
perchè la mazza 'un vol dare a Petuzzo
perchè Petuzzo 'un vole andá' nell'ortuzzo
a piglia' il cavoluzzo
perchè i' su' babbo è malato."
Disse i' gatto: "Mangio, mangio!"
Disse i' topo: "Rodo, rodo!"
Disse la fune: "Lego, lego!"
Disse i' bove: "Bevo, bevo!"
Disse l' acqua: "Spengo, spengo!"
Disse i' foco: "Brucio, brucio!"
Disse la mazza: "Do, e do!"
Disse Petuzzo: "Vo, e vo!"

Ref. n. 8   Io me ne andai per una strada stretta
incontrai la Mena Ciuffetta.
La mi chiese la fetta.
La fetta l'andai a prendere alla madia;
la madia mi chiese la farina;
la farina l'andai a prendere dal mugnaio.
Il mugnaio mi chiese il grano;
il grano l'andai a prendere nel campo.
Il campo mi chiese il concio;
il concio l'andai a prendere dal bove.
Il bove mi chiese il fieno;

il fieno l'andai a prendere nel campo.
Il campo mi chiese la falce;
la falce l'andai a prendere dal fabbro.
Il fabbro mi chiese il lardo;
il lardo l'andai a prendere dal maiale.
Il maiale mi chiese le ghiande;
le ghiande l'andai a prendere alla querce.
La querce mi chiese il vento;
il vento lo portai alla querce.
La querce mi diede le ghiande;
le ghiande le portai al maiale;
il maiale mi diede il lardo.
Il lardo lo portai al fabbro;
il fabbro mi diede la falce.
La falce la portai nel campo;
il campo mi diede il fieno.
Il fieno lo portai al bove;
il bove mi diede il concime.
Il concime lo portai al campo;
il campo mi diede il grano.
Il grano lo portai al mugnaio;
il mugnaio mi diede la farina.
La farina la portai alla madia;
la madia mi diede la fetta;
la fetta la portai alla Mena Ciuffetta.

Ref. n. 9   Tre pulcini andando a spasso
incontrarono la volpe
che andava passo passo
leggiucchiando il suo giornale.
"Buona sera signorini,
e di bello che si fa?"
"Giacché mamma è andata fuori
siamo usciti dal pollaio."
"Bravi, bravi per davvero!
Voglio stringervi la mano!"
E d'un tratto s'appressò
e glu-glu se li mangiò.

Ref. n. 10   La Befana vien di notte
con le scarpe tutte rotte
col vestito alla romana.

Viva, viva la Befana!

La Befana liscia liscia
entra in casa e fa la piscia,
se la fa nella sottana;
brutta, sudicia la Befana!

Ref. n. 11   Sotto il ponte di Baracca
c'è un bambin che fa la cacca.
La fa dura, dura, dura,
e il dottore la misura.
La misura a trentatré
e a star sotto tocca a te.

Ref. n. 12   C'era una volta Cecco Rivolta
che rivoltava i pantaloni.
Se la fece nei calzoni
la su' mamma lo brontolò,
e per dispetto ci ricacò.

Ref. n. 14   Maria Teresa la pisciò in Chiesa.
Il Priore la brontolò
e per dispetto ci cacò.

Ref. n. 15   Povero Cecco, povero Cecco.
Ha fatto la cacca, la piscia a letto.
La su' mamma l'ha brontolato;
povero Cecco s'è ammalato,
s'è ammalato forte forte,
povero Cecco è andato a morte.

E ci aveva una campana
tutte le notti la suonava,
e ci aveva un campanello
e suonava pure quello.

Ref. n. 17   Sette vecchie le andavano a Roma.
Sette borse le avean per una.
Ogni borsa sette nidi,
ogni nido sette uccelli.
Fate il conto quanti son quelli?

Ref. n. 20   Io ci ho una cosa
che ha tanti anelli e non è sposa.

A una finestraccia
c'è una vecchiaccia;

gli tentenna un dente
e chiama tutta la gente.

Il giorno si guardano,
la notte si baciano.

Sotto il letto ci ho un omino bianco
che sta con una mano sul fianco.

La mamma diventa secca infino all'osso;
il figlio balla e cresce a più non posso.

La va giù, la ride; la vien su, la piange.

Indovina indovilena: chi ha i' bellico nella stiena?

Ref. n. 21   Qual'è quella cosa che ha un occhio nella coda?

Cento sorelle stanno a sedere;
l'una con l'altra si danno da bere.

Ref. n. 22   Ci ho un campettino lavorato lavorato;
non c'è passato ne bovi né aratro.

Ref. n. 23   Io ci ho un lenzuolo tutto rattoppato;
non c'è passato né filo né ago.

Ref. n. 24   Più se ne leva, più cresce.

Nasce con le corna; vive senza corna, e muore con le corna.

Qual'è quella cosa che quando lavora si tira dietro le budellina?

Prati verdi, stanze rosse, frati neri.
Chi c'indovina gli dò tre poderi.

Ref. n. 25   Cruda la 'un si trova, e cotta la 'un si mangia.

Cotta si mangia, e cruda non si trova.

Mangia per il corpo e caca per le rène.

Ref. n. 26   Ruggieri è in camera, sospira e lacrima.
Stai zitto Ruggieri, che t'accetto volentieri.

Ref. n. 27   Tutto il dì sta alla finestra,
e la sera se ne leva.

Ref. n. 28   Voi siete indovinellista e vi credete:
trovatemi una vecchia che abbia un mese.

Io ci ho una sala bella bella

tutta foderata di raso rosso
con tutte le poltrone bianche d'osso
e nel mezzo una donna che balla.

Ref. n. 29 O sette o otto
sotto un cappotto.

Ref. n. 30 Pentola piena che vien per ripa
con quattr'occhi e quaranta dita.

Ref. n. 32 Nerellino sta impiccato,
Rossellino gli dà nel culo.

Ref. n. 33 Io ce l'ho e ce l'ho bella;
ce l'ho sotto la gonnella.
Se qualcuno me la tocca
gliela batto nella bocca.

Ci ho una borsina
cucita alla rinfranta
spaccata nel mezzo
e a chi me la tocca
gliela butto nella bocca.

Ref. n. 34 Maddalena sta distesa,
Patanocco sta attaccato.
La Rosina giù di sotto
va nel culo a Patanocco.

Ref. n. 35 Pelosa di fuori, pelosa di dentro;
alza la gamba e mettila dentro.

Ref. n. 36 Vai per un sentiero
trova un omino nero;
càlagli i pantaloni,
màngialo in due bocconi.

Ref. n. 37 Torno da Milano
con una cosa in mano
se trovo la mi' amorosa
gliela infilo nella pelosa.

Ref. n. 38 Lo metti dentro, è duro;
lo tiri fuori, è molle.

Ref. n. 39 Il Papa ce l'ha ma non l'adopra.
La Signorina non ce l'ha ma lo vorrebbe avere.

La Signora ce l'ha e l'adopra quando vuole.
La vedova ce l'aveva e l'ha perso.
Che cos'è?

Ref. n. 40   Ce l'avete un po' di liscoso
per dare a i' mi' peloso
un po' di cotto tra muro
quattro coccole di culo
il sugo di gambe torte
e un po' di bianco delle coscc?

Ref. n. 41   Sopra un albero ci sta una monaca.
Viene il vento e gli alza la tonaca.
Bella robina si vede alla monaca!

Ref. n. 42   Pancia in fuori,
uccello penzoloni.
Chi non l'indovina
son dei bei coglioni.

Ref. n. 43   Un vecchierello
in un campicello
butta giù i calzoni
e fa veder l'uccello.

Ref. n. 44   Io ci ho un cazzo lungo un braccio
e un coglione più leggero attaccato.
Vuoi che te lo dia quando l'ho adoprato?

Ref. n. 45   Dondolin che dondolava
tra le gambe lo parava;
piglia, piglia il coltellino
per tagliarlo il dondolino!

Ref. n. 47   Grande e grosso lo vorrei
in carne viva lo metterei
L'Arcivescovo lo tien sì caro
che tutta la notte lo tiene in mano.

Ref. n. 48   Piccol il toglio
e grosso lo voglio;
più ch'egli cresce,
men mi rincresce.

Ref. n. 49   Prima di farla non si pòle avere
e dopo fatta la 'un si pòl godere.

Ref. n. 50   Nasce tra due montagne,
              vive senza pelle,
              muore cantando.

Ref. n. 51   Nasce, muore. Non si vede, ma si sente.

Ref. n. 61   Fate la nanna coscine di pollo
              la vostra mamma v'ha fatto i' gonnello,
              ve l'ha cucito torno torno,
              fate la nanna coscine di pollo.
              Fate la nanna possiate dormire
              il letto vi sia fatto di viole,
              il materasso di piume gentile,
              il capezzale di penne di pavone
              e le lenzuola di tela d'Olanda;
              fate la ninna e poi fate la nanna!

Ref. n. 62   E se il gallo non cantasse,
              la campana non suonasse,
              e se il giorno non venisse,
              anco un po' ti cullerìa.
              Fai la nanna, anima mia!

Ref. n. 63   Ti aleggino d'intorno i sogni belli
              che fan vedere ai bimbi il paradiso.
              Gli angioli del ciel ti son fratelli;
              li vedi, me lo dice il tuo sorriso.

              Dormi, dormi, fai la nanna,
              tesorino della mamma.
              Scorre il fiume e fa cià-cià
              e il bambino dorme già.

              Dormono i fiori, dorme l'uccellino,
              dormon farfalle e tace ogni rumore.
              Dormi anche tu nel bianco tuo lettino
              e sogna della mamma il grande amore.

              Stella stellina
              la notte s'avvicina
              la fiamma traballa
              la mucca è nella stalla,
              la mucca e il vitello,
              la pecora e l'agnello,
              la chioccia e i pulcini,

ognuno ha i suoi bambini,
ognuno ha la sua mamma
e tutti fan la nanna.

Ref. n. 64   Fate la nanna e fatela con Dio!
Fatela voi, che la farò pur'io.
Fate la ninna, e fatela la nanna!
La bimba è bella e l'è della su' mamma;
della su' mamma e del su' babbo ancora.
Questa bambina è nata in buon'ora.
Nata in buon'ora, ed in buon'ora sia
l'ora che tu nascesti, anima mia!

Ref. n. 65   E' stato il vento
a buttare giù la canna,
bambino fa' la nanna
la mamma vuol dormì.

Ref. n. 66   Nanna eri, nanna eri,
stavo meglio quando 'un c'eri.

Ref. n. 67   Nanna era, nanna era,
questo bimbo anno 'un c'era.
Se non c'era anco quest'anno,
e' non era punto danno.

Ref. n. 68   Presi marito per usci' da' guai
ed ora ci so' dentro più che mai.
Presi marito per resta' da me
e ora invece di due noi siamo tre.

Ref. n. 69   Ninna, oh! ninna, oh!
Questa bimba a chi la do!
La darò alla su' zia
che la bimba la butti via,
che la butti in quel piazzale
dov'è scappato quell'animale.
Ninna, oh! ninna, oh!

Fai la nanna, che tu crepi,
che ti vengano a piglia' i preti!
Ninna, oh! ninna, oh!
Questa bimba a chi la do?
La darò alla su' mamma
che gli canti la ninnananna

la darò all'Omo nero
che la tenga un giorno intero.
Ninna, oh! ninna, oh!

Ref. n. 76   Nanna, oh, nanna, oh,
questo bimbo a chi lo do?
La darò all'Omo nero
che lo tenga un giorno intero.
Nanna, oh, nanna, oh,
questo bimbo a chi lo do?
Lo darò alla Befana
che lo tenga una settimana.
Nanna, oh, nanna, oh,
questo bimbo a chi lo do?
Lo darò al buon Gesù
che lo tenga un anno e più.
Nanna, oh, nanna, oh,
Questo bimbo a chi lo do?
Lo darò alla su' mamma
che gli canti la ninnananna.

Ref. n. 77   Ninna, nanna, la malcontenta!
Babbo gode e mamma stenta;
babbo va all'Osteria
mamma tribola tuttavia;
babbo mangia il baccalà;
mamma tribola a tutt'andà
babbo mangia le ballotte,
mamma tribola giorno e notte;
babbo mangia i boccon bòni
mamma mangia gli stranguglioni.

Ref. n. 78   Fai la nanna, bambozzolo mio,
che tu faccia le braccia grosse,
che tu leghi quell'omo cattìo;
fai la nanna, bambozzolo mio!

Ref. n. 79   Dolce sonno dal cielo scendi e vieni,
vieni a cavallo e non venire a piedi,
vieni a cavallo su un cavallo bianco,
dove cavalca lo Spirito Santo,
vieni a cavallo, su un bel cavallino,
dove cavalca Gesù Bambino.
Falla la nanna, ne li dolci sonni!

Mamma ti canta, e tu bambino dormi!

Ref. n. 80   Fai la ninna, fai la nanna!
Il bambino è della mamma,
della mamma e della nonna,
di Gesù e della Madonna,
della mamma e della zia,
di Gesù e di Maria.

Ref. n. 81   Pussa via, canaccio nero!
Il mi' bimbo 'un te lo vo' da'
Lo vo'dare a i' Dio d'i' cielo;
Pussa via, canaccio nero!
Pussa via, canaccio bianco!
Il mi' bimbo 'un te lo vo' da'
Lo vo' dare allo Spirito Santo!
Pussa via, canaccio bianco!

Ref. n. 82   Nanna, nanna, nanna, oh!
il bambino a chi lo do?
Se lo do alla Befana
me lo tiene una settimana.
Se lo do al bove nero
me lo tiene un anno intero.
Nanna, nanna, nanna fate
il bambino addormentate!
S'addormenti nella culla
con Gesù e con la Madonna!

Ref. n. 83   Ninnananna, sette e due,
il bambino gli ha le bue,
dalle bue guarirà
e Gesù l'aiuterà.

Ref. n. 85   Angiolin bellin bellino,
con quel capo ricciolino,
con quegli occhi pien d'amore,
Gesù mio vi dono il cuore,
ve lo do e ve lo dono,
Gesù mio vi chiedo perdono.

Ref. n. 86   Alzando gli occhi al cielo
di Gesù m'innamorai.
Feci l'atto pe' salire
Lui mi disse "Non venire;

vatti prima a confessare
se vuoi l'anima salvare."
Quando fui confessato
da una voce fui chiamato:
"Vieni, vieni peccatore,
giorno o notte, a tutte l'ore!"

Ref. n. 87   Nanna ieri, nanna ieri,
e le sporte 'un son panieri;
e i panieri 'un son le sporte,
e la vita 'un è la morte,
e la morte 'un è la vita
la canzone è già finita.
Nanna, oh, nanna, oh,
e il bambin si addormentò.

Ref. n. 88   Uno due e tre!
Il Papa non è Re,
Il Re non è Papa.
Chiocciola non è lumaca,
lumaca non è chiocciola.
Paleo non è trottola,
trottola non è paleo.
Cristian non è Giudeo,
Giudeo non è Cristiano.
Pan di miglio 'un è di grano,
pan di gran non è di miglio.
Farfalla non è grillo,
grillo non è farfalla.
Letto non è capanna,
capanna non è letto.
Zucchero non è confetto,
confetto non è zucchero.
Grasso non è strutto,
strutto non è grasso.

4. COURTING IN THE EVENING

Ref. n. 5   E rigira e rifrullala la ròta
di punta ar poggio ci si vede 'r sole,
e le ci sono le ragazzine
e le ci sono le ragazzine.
E rigira e rifrullala la ròta

di punta ar poggio ci si vede 'r sole,
e le ci sono le ragazzine
coi giovanotti a parlare di amor.

Ref. n. 6   Avete gli occhi neri come il pepe,
i labbri rossi come le cerage,
vi faccia bòna Dio, ché bella sète.

Ref. n. 7   O Dio de' Dei,
la più bellina mi parete voi.
Oh, quanto cara siete agli occhi miei.

Ref. n. 8   Tutte le notti in sogno mi venite
ditemi bella mia perché lo fate
ditemi bella mia perché lo fate,
e chi ci vien da voi quando dormite.

Ref. n. 9   Fiore di stipa
che bel piedin, che bella camminata,
che bella ragazzina tutta compita.

Ref. n. 10   Quando nasceste voi nacque un giardino
l'odore si sentiva di lontano
l'odore si sentiva di lontano
e specialmente quel del gelsomino
anche la terra cominciò a tremare.

Ref. n. 11   Quando nascesti voi nacque un bel fiore
la luna si fermò nel camminare,
le stelle lo cambiarono i' colore.

Ref. n. 12   Avete gli occhi neri della fata,
li amanti li tirate a calamita,
a pe' fammi mori', bella, se' nata.

Ref. n. 13   Fiorin fiorino
di voi bellina innamorato sono
di voi bellina innamorato sono,
la vita vi darei per un bacino.

Ref. n. 14   Fiorin di giglio
i' damo contadino non lo voglio
lo voglio cittadino gli è più meglio.

Ref. n. 15   'Un voglio un contadin, 'un vo' far erba,
'un voglio muratore, 'un vo' dolori,
'un voglio giocator che vinca o perda,

lo voglio della fabbrica Ginori.

Ref. n. 16   I' non do retta a' giovanotti d'ora,
canzonan le ragazze fanno a gara.

Ref. n. 17   E l'omini so' finti e traditori
hanno un'anima sola e cento còri.

Ref. n. 18   Fiore di pera
la pera è bona e la buccia l'è amara
la pera è bona e la buccia l'è amara
e l'omo è finto e la donna è sincera.

Ref. n. 19   Fior di trifoglio
giovanottino vu' pigliate abbaglio
giovanottino vu' pigliate abbaglio,
non è ancor seminata l'erba voglio.

Ref. n. 20   Peschi fiorenti
ho canzonato diciannove amanti
ho canzonato diciannove amanti,
e se canzono voi saranno venti.

Ref. n. 22   Fiore d'ombrente
prendi la brocca e vattene alla fonte
e lì t'aspetto' stella rilucente.

Ref. n. 23   Fiore di mela
vieni alla fonte, ti darò parola
e lì si scioglierà d'amor la vela.

Ref. n. 24   All'acqua all'acqua, alla fontana nòva:
chi non sa fa' all'amore, ci s'impara,
e chi non ci ha l'amante, ci si trova.

Ref. n. 25   E morina la mia morina
e se le prendi le brocche e vieni,
noi anderemo alla fonte assiemi
noi anderemo alla fonte assiemi.
E morina la mia morina
e se le prendi le brocche e vieni,
noi anderemo alla fonte assiemi
e noi potremo parlare di amor.

Ref. n. 26   Nel mezzo de lo mare mi tegliai'
un pesciolino mi rispose "Ohi!"
Sento la voce, ma non so chi sei.

Ref. n. 27 Fiorin fiorello
e tutti i fiorellini fioriranno
e tutti i fiorellini fioriranno,
quello dell'amor mio sarà i' più bello.

Ref. n. 28 Ti voglio amare finché mondo è mondo,
finché le pietre se n'andran volando,
finché del mare troveran lo fondo.

Ref. n. 30 Quando ti vedo su i' poggio apparire
il tuo passo mi fa innamorare,
i tuoi begli occhi mi fanno morire.

Ref. n. 31 Son nata per i baci e voglio quelli
come l'innamorati se li danno.
Li voglio sulla bocca e sui capelli,
poi chiudo l'occhi e dove vanno vanno.

Ref. n. 32 Non mi mandar più baci per la posta
che per la strada perdono i' sapore:
se tu me li vuoi dare dammeli in bocca
così lo sentirai cos'è l'amore.

Ref. n. 36 Quando vai alla Messa
lo tieni il libro in mano
la dai un'occhiata al damo
e lui la rende a te.

Ref. n. 37 Giovanottino dal cappello nero
e su per Chiesa lo tenete in mano
giovanottino mio, fatene meno!

Ref. n. 38 O ragazzina dagli stivaletti
e su per Chiesa lo battete il tacco:
vu' fate tanta cioccia, e non son vostre.

Ref. n. 39 Fiorin di giuggiola,
se vuoi fare all'amor, porta la seggiola
lo senti su quel sasso ci si sdrucciola?

Ref. n. 40 Sotto la mi' finestra c'è la mota,
non ci veni' con le scarpin di seta:
se vuoi fare all'amore, vieni in casa.

Ref. n. 42 E quando tu venivi a casa mia
la meglio seggiolina era la tua,
ora 'un ci vieni più, l'ho data via.

Ref. n. 43   Fiore di prato
il posto per un poco l'ho tenuto
il posto per un poco l'ho tenuto.
Non ci veniste, e a un altro gliel'ho dato.

Ref. n. 44   La buonasera ve la do col canto
e vi saluto voi, palma d'argento,
che tra le belle lo portate il vanto.

Ref. n. 45   Siate lo benvenuto, giovanetto,
come la festa della settimana;
siete più bello d'un fiore mughetto
e se ne può tener la vostra dama.
E se foss'io, me ne vorre' tenere
d'esser sì brutta, e sì bel damo avere.

Ref. n. 49   A Roma ci hanno dato un Papa nòvo
il mondo s'è girato all'incontrario:
tocca alla donna a dichiararsi all'omo!

Ref. n. 50   Fiorin di ceci
è tanto che tu bolli e mai non cuoci;
da ora in poi ci siamo bell'e intesi.

Ref. n. 51   Giovanottino che alla veglia andate,
ditemi la passion per chi l'avete?
Se l'avete con me, ve la sbagliate.

Ref. n. 52   Avevo un cavallino verde e gioia
me lo tenevo nel campo legato;
e gira e gira la fune s'annoda,
il cuore torna dove è innamorato.

Ref. n. 54   O ragazzina dalle belle ciglia,
ognun che passa a un angelo v'agguaglia:
tutti vi voglion ma nessun vi piglia.

Ref. n. 55   Perché la sera a veglia ci venite
se la ragazza tanto ce l'avete?
Le suole delle scarpe consumate.

Ci vo' venir quando mi pare e piace.
Queste parte le non mi son proibite.
Le suole delle scarpe 'un me le fate.

Tempo non piovere
il Baroncelli ci ha le scarpe debole,

non ha i quattrini pe' compralle stabile.

Ref. n. 56   Te lo sei fatto il vestitin di lana.
l'hai sei rinnovato alla novena,
e del paese sei la più Befana.

Ref. n. 57   Fior di piselli
io t'ho trovato in mezzo a' pappagalli
se' tutto bezzicato dall'uccelli.

Ref. n. 58   Fiore che nasce
e' inutile ti tinga le ganasce
e' inutile ti tinga le ganasce
il muso di Befana 'un ti sparisce.

Ref. n. 59   Te lo se' fatto i' vestitin di tulle
pe' ricopritti i' gobbo tra le spalle
pe' ricopritti i' gobbo tra le spalle.
Se' brutta, frinzellosa e pien di bolle.

Ref. n. 60   Fior di ricotta
la vostra mamma per farvi la bocca
l'ha preso la misura a una ciabatta.

Ref. n. 61   Fiorin fiorello
avete l'occhio nero, il viso giallo,
e chi vi sposerà farà un bel bollo.

Ref. n. 62   Ma vatti a butta' in mare
col diretto se vuoi far piacere a me;
buttati più di cento metri sotto
che nessuno ti trattien.

E quando sul giornale
l'avrò letto sai che pena che mi vien:
la mangio una bistecca
lo bevo un gotto sette pònci ed un caffè.

E in tasca ce lo porto
un bel coltello fatto apposta per taglia',
per taglia' il cuore a te
se m'abbandoni, bucaiolo te e tu' ma'!

Ref. n. 63   E ti vorrei vede' fritto in padella,
massimamente l'osso della spalla
massimamente l'osso della spalla,
il fegato il picchiante e le budella.

Bren, bren, bren, posso stare lontan da te.
Bren, bren, bren, posso stare lontan da te.

Alla finestra ci manca un mattone,
o che ci vieni a far nato d'un cane
o che ci vieni a far nato d'un cane,
tanto con teco non ci ho la passione.

Bren, bren, bren, posso stare lontan da te.
Bren, bren, bren, posso stare lontan da te.

Nato d'un vile e sangue d'un serpente,
non mi levar più chiacchiere ignorante
non mi levar più chiacchiere ignorante,
tanto l'onore lo conservo sempre.

Bren, bren, bren, posso stare lontan da te.
Bren, bren, bren, posso stare lontan da te.

Ref. n. 65   Fior di lupino
èramo in quattro a corteggiare un damo
èramo in quattro a corteggiare un damo
e ognun tirava l'acqua a i' su' mulino.

Ref. n. 66   Spigo fiorito
non ti ricordi i baci che t'ho dato?
Non ti ricordi i baci che t'ho dato?
T'hai fatto come Giuda e m'hai tradito.

Ref. n. 67   Con un pugnale m'hai ferito il cuore
e me l'hai fatto tutto sanguinare
a star con te bisognerà soffrire,
perché sei tanto farso nel parlare.

Ref. n. 68   Fiore di díttamo
sei stato il primo amore e sarai l'ùrtimo
sei stato il primo amore e sarai l'ùrtimo,
e questo si può dire amor legittimo.

Ref. n. 69   Quando venìo da te faceo pe' fare
e non faceo pe' fare all'amore
e non faceo pe' fare all'amore,
facevo pe' passare un'ora insieme.

Ref. n. 70   L'erba del mio giardino ha fatto fieno,
se ti volevo bene 'un ti lasciavo,
te t'ho tenuto sempre pe' ripieno.

Ref. n. 71   Iersera la ragazza m'ha lasciato:
                  stasera mangerò con più appetito,
                  stanotte farò un sonno riposato.

Ref. n. 72   Quando tu mi lasciasti, io piangevo;
                  colla pezzola bianca m'asciugavo;
                  non eri fuor dell'uscio che ridevo.

Ref. n. 73   Fiore di paglia
                  e ti credevi di menarmi a briglia!
                  A briglia ci si mena la cavalla.

Ref. n. 74   E vai dicendo a tutti che son tua.
                  Dimmelo a quale fiera m'hai comprato?
                  Buttati in una buca, disperato!

Ref. n. 75   Quando venii da me a fare all'amore
                  tu mi dicevi non sapevo fare
                  tu mi dicevi non sapevo fare,
                  ora ho imparato e non ci vo' venire.

Ref. n. 76   Fiorin fiorino
                  lasciatemi cantar che lieta sono
                  lasciatemi cantar che lieta sono,
                  ho rifatto le paci col mi' damo.

Ref. n. 78   Fior di granato
                  'un è stata colpa mia se t'ho lasciato
                  'un è stata colpa mia se t'ho lasciato,
                  è stata la mi' mamma 'un ha voluto.

Ref. n. 79   Cara morina non ti posso amare
                  perché i miei genitor non son contenti.

Ref. n. 80   O socerina non ve la pigliate
                  tanto il vostro figliolo non mi piglia
                  e se 'un mi piglia lui, io non lo piglio:
                  non voglio disturbare la famiglia.

Ref. n. 81   E' so' stato n'i' bosco a fa' la legna
                  pe' brucia' la mi' socera maligna,
                  e la 'unn'e smette più con quella lagna.

                  E gira e gira e frulla
                  la mi' socera è un serpente
                  gli pigliasse un accidente
                  smetterebbe di brontola'.

Ref. n. 82   E prima ci venivi all'acqua e ai venti
ora 'un ci vieni alla spera del sole
ma quando i genitori 'un son contenti
come si fa, morino, a fare all'amore.

Ref. n. 83   E la mi' mamma non vole che l'ami;
falla contenta e più non ci venire.

Ref. n. 84   Mamma non vole babbo nemmeno
come faremo, come faremo.
Mamma non vole babbo nemmeno
come faremo a fare all'amor.

Babbo non vole
mamma nemmanco
ho pianto tanto
e il Cielo lo sa.

Ref. n. 85   Mamma non vole babbo ci pensa,
ci vuol pazienza ci vuol pazienza.
Mamma non vole babbo ci pensa
ci vuol pazienza a fare all'amor.

Ref. n. 86   I miei non son contenti, i tuoi nemmeno.
Dimmelo, bella, con che cuor ci amiamo?
Amiamoci di cuor, la vinceremo.

Ref. n. 87   Perfido genitor, come la pensi
che la figliola 'un tu me la vuoi dare?
Dei tuoi passati tempi 'un ti rammenti?
Non ti parava bello a te l'amare?

Ref. n. 88   Vile d'un genitor, come la pensi?
Perché non mi vuoi dar la tu' figliola?
La strage la farò dell'Innocenti!
Col mio pugnale si farà la prova.

Ref. n. 89   E che t'ho fatto, vedova maligna,
perché la tu' figliola 'un mi vuoi dare?
Io non t'ho chiesto né campo né vigna,
neanche un par di buoi per lavorare.
Io non t'ho chiesto né argento e né oro;
dammi la tu' figliola, se no mòro.
Io non t'ho chiesto né oro e né argento;
dammi la tu' figliola e mi contento.

Ref. n. 90   E se non son contenti i miei di casa,
si piglia un calessino e si va a Pisa;
si va all'Altar maggiore e ci si sposa.

Ref. n. 91   Fiore d'abete
se la vostra figliola 'un me la date
se la vostra figliola 'un me la date
La sposero n'i' campo senza i' prete.

Ref. n. 95   Vittorio Emanuele cosa fai?
La meglio gioventù tutta la vuoi,
e poi dei vecchi che te ne farai?

Ref. n. 96   E ciao e ciao e ciao
morettina bella ciao!
E prima di partire
un bacio ti vo' dare!
Un bacio al mio pappà,
un bacio alla mammà,
un bacio alla mia bella
e poi vado militar!

Ref. n. 103   E gli risposi con poche parole:
"La tornata sarà quando Dio vòle."
E gli risposi con parole umìle:
"La tornata sarà tra maggio e aprile."

Ref. n. 104   Tornerò, tornerò, non dubitare
caro mio bene, non aver paura,
ché in breve tempo mi vedrai tornare
ché impressa porto sempre la tua figura.
Allor ti cesserò, bella d'amare
quando morto sarò in sepoltura.

Ref. n. 105   E va' che Iddio ti dia la buona andata
e la tornata sia dolce allegrezza!
E va' che Iddio ti dia felici eventi,
e l'acqua chiara vino ti diventi;
Iddio ti dia felice cammino,
e l'acqua chiara ti diventi vino.

Ref. n. 107   O rondinella che voli per l'aria
ritorna indietro e fammelo il piacere,
e dammela una penna della tu' ala
io scriverò una lettera al mi' bene.

E quando l'avrò scritta in carta bianca
ti renderò la penna che ti manca;
e quando l'avrò scritta e fatta bella
ti renderò la penna, rondinella;
e quando l'avrò scritta in carta d'oro
ti renderò la penna pel tuo volo.

Ref. n. 110   Tutti mi dicon Maremma Maremma,
per me l'è stata una Maremma amara:
l'uccello che ci va perde la penna
io ci ho perduto una persona cara.
Sia maledetta Maremma Maremma
sia maledetta Maremma e chi l'ama.
Sempre mi trema il cuor quando ci vai
perché ho paura che non torni mai.

Ref. n. 111   E ví do il bentornato allegramente,
e quel che dubitavo niente è stato,
e mi rallegro e vi do il bentornato.

Ref. n. 112   Gli è ritornato il fior di Primavera,
gli è ritornato chi prima non c'era,
gli è ritornata la pianta sul frutto,
e quando c'è il mio amore c'è tutto.

Ref. n. 113   Ma come sarà possibile che ti sposi?
dal cielo dovrà cadere la neve nera
e le montagne devono camminare,
il sole dovrà spuntare solo di sera.

Ref. n. 114   E l'erba amara la mangiano i grilli
con la Rosina l'ho strappati i fogli,
poi l'ho lasciata, e chi la vuol la pigli.

Ref. n. 115   Quando t'amavo io t'amavan tanti,
ora t'hanno scoperto i mancamenti:
tu sei la ganza di tutti i birbanti.

Ref. n. 116   E dagli amici lo viensi a sapere
portavi un nastro rosa alle mutande
di color rosa anche le giarrettiere
e in mezzo al busto un nastro così grande.

Con tutti ce l'hai fatto un po' all'amore
e a tutti gli giurasti amore eterno,
e l'hai tenuto il male dentro al còre,

tutti te l'han picchiato nell'inferno.

Ref. n. 117   Quando venìo da te, t'eri pollastra,
ora 'un ci vengo più, t'hai messo cresta;
tu hai fatto un bel bambino da ragazza.

Ref. n. 118   E tu ti vanti perché m'hai lasciato
ed io mi vanterò d'un'altra cosa:
ho preso i' tu' visino e l'ho baciato;
dell'altri sei ragazza e di me sposa.

Ref. n. 120   O Dio de' Dei
e per Beppino ieri le buscai,
e per Beppino le ribuscherei.

Ref. n. 121   O mamma o mamma, non mi dare un vecchio
non me lo dare perché gli è vergogna,
dammelo giovanino e che non dorma.

Ref. n. 122   Il marito lo voglio a modo mio
perché non ci ha a sta' lei, ci ho da star io.

Ref. n. 125   "Senti mio amore caro e caro mio ben.
Ma quande tu va' via voglio venire con te."

"Cosa vo' fa' co' meco bella brunetta
di rosa fresca e rosa meschè?
Cosa vo' fa co' meco
bella brunetta che va."

Fa' l'erba ar tuo cavallo, ber pecoraro,
amor mio caro e caro mio ben;
fa' l'erba ar tuo cavallo ma vo' venire con te."

"Con che la mieterai bella brunetta
di rosa fresca e rosa meschè?
Con che la mieterai,
bella brunetta che va."

"Con la farce da grano ber pecoraro,
amor mio caro e caro mio ben;
colla farce da grano ma vo' venire con te."

"Se nascerà i figlioli bella brunetta
di rosa fresca e rosa meschè?
Se nasce dei figlioli,
come vorai tu far."

"Saranno miei e tui bel pecoraro
amor mio caro e caro mio ben;
saranno miei e tui ma vo' venire con te."

"Dove l'appezzerai bella brunetta
di rosa fresca e rosa mesché?
Dove l'appezzerai bella brunetta che va."

"Nel fiume del Giordano ber pecoraro,
amor mio caro e caro mio ben;
nel fiume del Giordano ma vo' venire con te."

"Come gli farai nome bella brunetta,
di rosa fresca e rosa mesché?
Come gli farai nome bella brunetta che va."

"Figli d'un pecoraro
amor mio caro e caro mio ben;
figli d'un pecoraro ma vo' venire con te."

"Se passa le montagne bella brunetta
di rosa fresca e rosa meschè?
Se passa le montagne come vorai tu far."

Con l'aiuto der Dio ber pecoraro
amor mio caro e caro mio ben;
con l'aiuto der Dio ma vo' venire con te."

Ref. n. 130　"E o campagnola che stai sullo scoglio,
scendi e vieni quaggiù nel mio naviglio,
per dirti tutto il bene ma io che ti voglio
di cuore io ti voglio dare un consiglio:
sei bella, sei cara, quanto tu piaci a me,
se fai con me all'amore, lo provi un gran piacer."

"Non posso amarti o pescator dell'onde,
perché son poverella e tu sei grande;
son nata su in montagna in fra le fronde
indo' nasceva le castagne e ghiande.
La neve d'inverno ci fiocca dèi saper,
non ho neppur vestito per far l'amor con te."

"Son pescatore e lo porto un mantello
per ricoprirti tutta e di corallo;
con quello ti porterò alle feste da ballo.
Vestita, imbrigliata, bella tu sarai te,
se fai con me all'amore, lo provi un gran piacer."

"Non posso amarti o bello pescatore,
dalla mia mamma ne potrei toccare;
nun vole io che faccia all'amore
coi pescatori che vanno per mare.
Tra venti, burasche, potrebbino allagà
per questo, o bello giovane, ma io non ti posso ama'."

Ref. n. 132   Pampani e uva
e la mi' mamma sempre lo diceva
l'amor del forestiero poco dura.

Ref. n. 133   L'amor del forestiero poco dura:
muta il paese e muta la ventura.

Ref. n. 134   L'amor dei forestieri dura un anno
perché la dama al su' paese l'hanno;
l'amor dei forestieri dura un mese
perché la dama l'han nel su' paese;
l'amor dei forestieri dura un giorno
perché la dama l'han nel su' contorno.

Ref. n. 135   "Da quando sei tornato
perché nun sei venuto con me a ritrovà?
Pensa tesoro e amato
che un giorno e incinta mi lasciasti qua.
Me lo dicevi che ero carina
certo ora vedi la tua bambina
Dagli un bacin nel suo visino adorno,
che chiama 'babbo' di notte e di giorno."

"Di qua vattene via
mai più lo sai 'un ti voglio più vedé;
la Bruna voglio abbracciare
che è assai più bella e più ricca di te.
Vattene via. Mio cor lo dice:
colla tua bella starò felice.
Vattene via il core a me lo dice:
colla tua bella viverò felice."

"Guardelo in nessun modi
che persuasa nun tu mi poi fà
vedrai non te la godi
brutto crudele se la vai a piglià.
E lo vedrai te ne farò delle belle
e indò ti trovo ti farò la pelle

e lo vedrai te ne farò delle belle
e indò ti trovo ti farò la pelle."

Bel giorno la sartina
colla bambina bene se n'andò
'spettallo la mattina
ma che sortisse il vile traditor.
S'era sposato con la sua bella;
lei pronta armata di rivortella
da un corridore sortì e con furore
sparò tre córpi e uccise il traditore.

Lei viene e fu arrestata
tutta la gente prencipionno a grida'
dicendo: "La s'è vendicata
e tutti quanti la vogliamo in libertà."
Giovanottini ch'io vo avvertire
le ragazzine di non tradire:
sinnò vi manderanno in sepoltura,
sapranno vendicassi e senza ave' paura!

Ref. n. 136   "Canta canta Lisetta in fino 'un sei da marità'
canta canta Lisetta fino 'un sei da marità'."
"Non vòi cantà né ridere lo mio core è appassionà
non vòi cantà né ridere lo mio core è appassionà.
Mio amore è andato alla guerra chissà quando tornerà
mio amore è andato alla guerra chissà quando tornerà.
Se sapesse la strada lo vorrei andare a trovà
se sapesse la strada lo vorrei andare a trovà.
A forza di domande io la strada la troverò
a forza di domande io la strada la troverò."
Quando fu a mezza strada 'n un bel giovane l'incontrò
quando fu a mezza strada 'n un bel giovane l'incontrò.
"Dimmi dimmi o bel giovane da che parte ne vieni tu?
dimmi dimmi o bel giovane da che parte ne vieni tu?"
"Ne vengo da una parte dove il sole non va mai giù
ne vengo da una parte dove il sole non va mai giù."
"Dimmi dimmi o bel giovane l'hai tu visto il mio primo amo'?
dimmi dimmi o bel giovane l'hai tu visto il mio primo amo'?"
"Io sì che l'ho veduto ma non l'ho riconosciu'
io sì che l'ho veduto ma non l'ho riconosciu'.
L'avevano tre soldati lo portavano a sotterrà'

l'avevano tre soldati lo portavano a sotterrà'."
Lisetta cade 'n terra ma svenuta dal gran dolo'
Lisetta cade 'n terra ma svenuta dal gran dolo'.
"Stai su stai su Lisetta sono io 'l tuo primo amo'
stai su stai su Lisetta sono io 'l tuo primo amo'."
Si presero a braccetto e al paese lo riportò
Si presero a braccetto e al paese lo riportò.
Quando furn'al paese tutto il popolo s'affacciò
quando furn'al paese tutto il popolo s'affacciò.
"Ecco ecco Lisetta ha ritrovato 'l suo primo amo'."
ecco ecco Lisetta, ritrovato 'l suo primo amo'."

Ref. n. 139   Fior di finocchio
non posso stare se non ti riguardo
non posso stare se 'un ti strizzo l'occhio.

Ref. n. 140   Fior di finocchio
val più una parolina nell'orecchio
che centomila strizzantine d'occhio.

Ref. n. 141   Vedere per credere.
Veduto è mezzo creduto.

5. THE END OF THE *Veglia*

Ref. n. 17   Guardati di non fare come Nello
che fece mori' Pia dalla passione;
sei mesi la rinchiuse nel castello
senza motivo e senza una ragione.

Ref. n. 18   Io me ne voglio anda' nelle Maremme
dove l'andò la Pia de' Tolomei'
io me ne voglio stare con le belle
e la morte vo' far che fece lei.

Ref. n. 20   Vi canterò di questa donna bella
con le piccole bimbe e 'r suo marito;
di nome vien chiamata Gabriella,
e di un fatto di atroce e dissoluto
sopra due bimbe della tenera età:
Giulietta e Giuseppina si vennero a chiama'.

Lo disse Ulisse "Gabriella mia
qui io so senza un lavoro un dì occupato,

io qui bisogna parta e vada via
a lavorare in Francia son chiamato.
Se io non ci vado, dei debiti si fa
e quando si son fatti non si possan paga'."

Lo disse Gabriella "Ulisse caro,
ricordati di me e delle bambine
qui tu ci lasci in tre senza un denaro
io non guadagno e loro son piccine."
Lo disse Ulisse: "Morto ci penserò
e i primi che guadagno io te li spedirò."

Come difatti parte pélla Francia
meccanico l'entrò in un'officina
e a un sei lire il giorno più quarche mancia,
sessanta lire la prima quindicina
spedì alla moglie dicendogli così:
"Mangia e bevi mia cara insieme alle bambin."

In poco tempo lei lo praticava
un giovanotto 'r suo primo amatore
di nome questo Ugo si chiamava
e a trovalla veniva a tutte l'ore;
in poco tempo incinta si trovò
allora disse Ugo: "Cessiamo questo amor!"

Gli disse "Ughino mio non mi abbandonare
queste bambine io le metto in convento;
farai le carte noi si possa scappare,
'ntanto prendi questo'oro e quest'argento.
Il mio marito lui lo ha mandato a me,
noi s'anderà in America in mentre lui non c'è."

Così tra loro l'ebbano stabilito
ma di partire insieme il fatal destino:
una lettera scritta l'avea 'r marito
a Gabriella la portò il postino.
Sente che torna, per non si far trova'
vòle uccider le bimbe, con l'amante scappar.

Prende un curtello e scanna Giuseppina
dorce ner sonno di lei poveretta,
a pezzi la gettò nella latrina
e in qui' mentre si sveglia Giulietta
dicendo "Donna bàrbera e senza cuo'

t'hai ucciso Giuseppina, ar babbo lo dirò."

Allor mentre di lei la s'accostava
di per un dei capelli te la frenava
cor solito curtello l'uccideva
e giù a pezzi anch'essa la buttava.
Fatto la strage, bussare lei sentì,
credea fosse l'amante, corse subito a aprì.

Quando ella vedde gli era 'r suo marito
lei diventò più tetra nella faccia,
e il sangue che lo vide sopra l'impiantito.
"Che è questo sangue, questo l'è una gran traccia.
Che sangue è questo?" subito dimandò.
"E'il sangue delle bimbe, uccise nel furo'."

"Razza d'un cane, disse, uniqua e fella."
Prende un pugnale e glielo mise ar cuore.
A terra cade morta Gabriella,
e Ulisse gli è andato a avvisa' 'r Pretore
cor diligato e dei carabinier.
Visto e considerato, giusta vendetta gli è.

Fu posto in libertà questo buon padre,
ma delle bimbe lui levati i pezzi
fatti da questa bàrbera sua madre.
Questo è un esempio che nessun s'avvezzi.
Donne pensate un po':
Quando il marito vi ama
mai non cangiate amo'.

Ref. n. 21   Dimmi mia bella Lea il tuo mari' dov'è
Dimmi mia bella Lea il tuo mari' dov'è?
"Il mio marito è 'n Francia, potesse mai torna'.
La terra che lo porta potesse sprofonda';
il sole che lo illumina potesselo acceca';
la nave che lo porta potesselo annega'."
"Zitta mia bella Lea, zitta, c'è il tuo mari'."
"Marito mio, perdono, non lo farò mai più."
"Non vo' perdoni io, la testa vo' taglia'."
La testa fece un balzo, la sala rimbombò.
"Innalzerò una tomba con trentasei matton."

Ref. n. 24   Fiorino amaro
la libertà dell'uom vale un tesoro

la libertà dell'uom vale un tesoro
e quella della femmina un denaro.

Ref. n. 36   La rigiri e fai la ròta
e pe' giralla ti ci vòl la fune,
e pelle scale bella ti baciavo
e la tu' mamma ti reggeva il lume.

Ref. n. 37   Quando venìo con te mi divertivo
diverse paroline ti dicevo
sotto gli occhi di mamma ti baciavo.

Ref. n. 38   Fiorin di ruta
la vostra mamma fa la scrupolosa
i giovanotti ve li porta in casa.

Ref. n. 39   Fiorin di mela
la mamma fa all'amor, la figlia impara,
e poi gli insegna a far da bacchettona.

Ref. n. 40   La bonanotte ve la do col canto
e vi saluto a voi, palma d'argento,
che tra le belle lo portate il vanto.

Ref. n. 41   Fiore d'argento
Su, non ve lo prendete per affronto,
e' l'ultimo stornello che vi canto.

6. THE *Veglia* DANCE

Ref. n. 25   Avanti o popolo
alla riscossa
bandiera rossa
trionferà.

Antonio Gramsci fondò il partito
lottando a fianco dei lavoratori
scelse bandiera rossa tra i colori
oggi è il colore che trionfa ancor.
Falce e martello e stella rinascente
questo è il partito della libertà!

Nel Ventuno i fascisti del Duce
iniziaron la marcia su Roma
con manganelli e moschetti si trama
di dovere Antonio arrestar.

> Avanti o popolo
> alla riscossa
> bandiera rossa
> trionferà.

Antonio Gramsci venne arrestato
e torturato sotto i manganelli
senza nessun rimorso furon quelli
ed in prigione ·gli toccò a morir.
Vent'anni di Fascismo si subiva
massacri e spari sui lavorator!

Ma Togliatti in Russia emigrava
i suoi studi doveva fini',
per il Partito lui sempre lottava,
è il Partito che avanza ogni dì!

> Avanti o popolo
> alla riscossa
> bandiera rossa
> trionferà!

Antonio fu più volte interrogato
e gli fu chiesto di cambia' ideale,
e spesso era percosso e maltrattato
ma lui rispose "Paga chi fa il male!"
Moriva nella cella assassinato
sotto i malvagi del Fascio traditor.

Ma di Gramsci la sua dottrina
penetrava sui lavorator
ed insegnava a difende' i colori
i colori della libertà!

> Avanti o popolo
> alla riscossa
> bandiera rossa
> trionferà!

Togliatti era un modello di studente
la borsa lui di studio conquistava,
divenne forte e molto intelligente
e pel Partito sempre lui lottò.
Lottò in settembre del Quarantaquattro
quando del Fascio la resa ci fu.

Ma Togliatti tornava a far parte
alla testa dei lavoratori
contro il Fascismo e gli sfruttatori
questa lotta nessun fermerà!

Avanti o popolo
alla riscossa
bandiera rossa
bandiera rossa.
Avanti o popolo
alla riscossa
bandiera rossa
trionferà!

Ref. n. 28   V'insegnerò come fanno le citte
quando ballan con un malvolentieri:
se ne van per la sala ritte ritte,
fanno le viste d'aver male a' piedi.
Ma quande ballan con chi voglian loro,
non hanno l'ali, eppure piglin volo;
e quande ballan coi su' innamorati
paian tanti serpenti avvelenati;
e quando ballan coi su' favoriti,
allor dal male i piedi son guariti.

Ref. n. 29   Questo ballo non va bene
se Beppino qua non viene
meglio è meglio sarà
se Beppino qua verrà.

Ref. n. 30   E anche Adone gli è invitato a i' ballo.
Balli anche Adone, tanto ballan tutti,
e ballan quelli belli e quelli brutti!

Ref. n. 32   Guardala come l'ha bella
e anche ieri me l'aveva detto:
"del Bernabei voglio Francesco,"
se vuol fa' un giro di sala!

E anche a lui gliela vo' dare
speriamo che non gli tiri i sassi:
prego il figlio del Signor Falassi
se vuol fa' un giro di sala!

Ref. n. 40   Trifoglio bello

da quella sera che ti vidi in ballo
tu mi facesti perdere i' cervello.

7. THE OUTCASTS' COUNTER-*Veglia*

Ref. n. 8   Sol per uomini dabbene
              [coro] come noi come noi
              generoso il vin si versi
              [coro] fallo pieno fallo pieno
              l'acqua è fatta pei perversi
              [coro] e il diluvio e il diluvio lo dimostrò.

Ref. n. 9   Corpo di Bacco questo l'è un buon vino
              è stato un anno sotto le frondiere.
              La colsi l'uva e la messi nel tino
              e nella botte la feci prigioniere.
              La botte la bucai col succhiellino
              e a dichiarar la misi nel bicchiere
              per darglieli li suoi vivi colori,
              e questo è un vino che riscalda i cuori.

Ref. n. 10   Bevi bevi compagno
              sennò t'ammazzerò.
              Non m'ammazzar compagno
              adesso beverò.

Ref. n. 11   Colmiamo compagni
              colmiamo il bicchier,
              si beva si canti,
              fugace è il piacer!

Ref. n. 22   Vino vinello
              sei buono e sei bello
              a volte tu mi vai al cervello;
              brutto briccone
              ti butto in prigione.

Ref. n. 28   Vuota il bicchier che è pieno,
              riempi il bicchier che è vuoto;
              non lo lasciar mai pieno,
              non lo lasciar mai vuoto.

Ref. n. 65   E l'ho varcate le mura di Dante
              l'ho vista Beatrice prigioniera,

delle morine n'ho baciate tante,
colla più bella ci ho fatto primiera.

Ref. n. 66   Il porto di Livorno fa bandiera:
te l'ho baciate le poppine, o cara,
te l'ho baciate le poppine, o cara,
sopra il tuo petto ci ho fatto primiera.

Ref. n. 67   Vieni, morino, vieni si gioca a carte:
si deve fare i giochi che so io,
si giocherà a briscola e primiera
e se ti manca un cuore, ti dono il mio.

Ref. n. 73   Né debiti
né crediti
né moglie
né figlioli
Ammene!

O Santa Vergine
pensa per te

Io credo in Dio Padre Onnipotente,
agli uomini poco
e alle donne niente.

Ref. n. 76   Su fratelli accorrete accorrete
qui nel prato la merda a mangiare
come manna caduta dal cielo
come manna caduta dal cielo.

Merda di qua, merda di là . . .
Quando si fa la cacca
quando si fa la cacca . . .
Merda di qua, merda di là
quando si fa la cacca
bisogna ponzar!

E a noi ci piace
la merda squacquera
perché spillacchera
perché spillacchera.
E a noi ci piace
la merda squacquera
perché spillacchera
di qua e di là.

Viva lo stronzo
bello e maturo
evviva lo stronzo
e chi lo sa far.
Merda di qua
e merda di là,
quando si fa la cacca
bisogna ponzar!

> Mi sono pulito le chiape
> con un ramo di verde cipresso,
> ma la merda è rimasta lo stesso
> attaccata ai peli del cul.
> Povero me, povero me,
> son tutto nella merda
> da capo ai piè.

Ref. n. 79   Mamma voglio marito
che mi metta il dito
dove piace a me.

Ref. n. 80   Per questi vicoletti
si sente ognor cantare
la voce allegra e bella
dello spazzacamin.
[il coro ripete i quattro versi]
S'affaccia alla finestra
la bella signorina
con voce graziosina
chiama lo spazzacamin.
[il coro ripete]
Prima lo fa entrare
e poi lo fa sedere
dà da mangiare e bere
allo spazzacamin.
[il coro ripete]
E dopo aver mangiato
mangiato e ben bevuto
gli fa vedere il buco
il buco del camin.
[il coro ripete]
"Mi spiace giovanotto
che il mio camino è stretto

povero giovanetto
come farà a salir."
[il coro ripete]
"Non dubiti signora
son vecchio del mestiere
so fare il mio dovere
su e giù per il camin."
[il coro ripete]
E dopo quattro mesi
la luna va crescendo
la gente va dicendo
dello spazzacamin.
[il coro ripete]
E dopo nove mesi
è nato un bel bambino
assomigliava tutto
allo spazzacamin.
[il coro ripete]

Ref. n. 81   Te lo sei fatto il vestitino a strisce
te lo sei guadagnato con le cosce
te lo sei guadagnato con le cosce,
il vestitino stringe la pancia cresce.
[variante: dalla mattina a sera gambe ritte]

Ref. n. 83   Fiore di canna
tutto il giorno con i piedi alla culla
tutto il giorno con i piedi alla culla,
non ho marito e son chiamata mamma.

Ref. n. 85   Se la piglio contadina
starà sempre a far lo strame
mi doventerà un catrame
mamma mia come farò.

Se la piglio un po'belloccia
starà sempre allo specchietto
mi doventerà un pennecchio
mamma mia come farò.

Se la piglio piglionale
stara sempre a far la legna
trova i' guardia, me la impregna,
mamma mia come farò.

Ref. n. 87   Bista aveva una moglie e bella assai
[coro: béi béi béi fino alla fine]
era da poco che s'era sposato:
i' matrimonio gni portò de' guai,
una miseria nun s'era sognato.
Quando a casa ritornava
stesa 'n terra la trovava.
Oddio che pena
e Bista andava a letto senza cena.
La spoglieva poveretto
poi se la portava a letto.
Oddio che pena
e Bista andava a letto senza cena.
Gni diceva "Caterina
falli un poco più carina,
ti vo' baciare"
ma lei tranquilla ne stava a russare.
"Ti vo' baciare"
ma lei tranquilla ne stava a russare.
Disse Bista a quell'amico:
"Senti un po' quer che ti dico:
non t'avelire,
ti dò la moglie pe' cinquanta lire.
Nun t'avelire,
ti dò la moglie pe' cinquanta lire."
Ora che Bista gli è rimasto solo
gni par d'esse' dovento un giovanotto'
della miseria nun porta più dòlo,
gni par d'avéllo vinto un terno al lotto.
Va dicendo a quell'amico:
"Senti un po' quer che ti dico:
chi nun vòl guai
pigli la donna sempre e moglie mai.
Chi nun vol guai
pigli la donna sempre e moglie mai."

Ref. n. 88   Fare all'amore di sera
con una bimba discreta
in una casa segreta
e che si lasci baciar.
Mi son chiappato lo scuelo
con un pompin cinque pesetas

era meglio una sega
fatta con mucha passion.

Ref. n. 89   O Dio ti diacci
t'ho visto far l'amor sotto le querci
Scappucciamelo, scalpellamelo
strapazzamelo Zaira
sennò la mezza lira
stasera 'un te la dò.
Le palle l'ho di zucchero
il fucile l'ho con me,
se vuoi assaggiare il muscolo
vieni a letto con me.

Ref. n. 90   E le stradelle che tu mi fai far
cara Rosina, cara Rosina,
e le stradelle che tu mi fai far,
cara Rosina le devi pagar.
E questa è casa mia e qui comando io
e ogni dì voglio sapere.
E questa è casa mia e qui comando io
e ogni dì voglio sapere chi viene e chi va.

Ref. n. 92   Figliole d'osti e caval di mugnai
'un te n'impicciare mai.

Ref. n. 93   Battan l'otto ma saranno le nove
i miei figlioli son digiuni ancora,
ma il coraggio, ma chi lo sa portare;
infame società dacci mangiare!

Viva il coraggio, ma chi lo sa portare,
l'anarchia la lo difenderebbe,
ma viva il coraggio, ma chi lo sa portare,
i miei bambini han fame, chiedon pane!

Anch'io da socialista mi voglio vestire,
bello gli è il rosso, rosse le bandiere,
ma se verrà i' giorno della rivoluzione,
infame società dovrai pagare!

Bella è la vita, più bello l'onore,
amo mia moglie e la famiglia mia,
ma viva i' coraggio, ma chi lo sa portare,
infame società dacci mangiare!

Dei socialisti è piene le galere,
bada governo, infame maltrattore,
ma verrà i' giorno della rivoluzione,
infame società, dovrai pagare!

Ref. n. 94   E quando mòio io, non voglio preti,
non voglio preti e frati né paternostri
non voglio preti e frati né paternostri,
la voglio la bandiera dei socialisti.

Ref. n. 99   Un contadino di questa pianura
disse al padrone "Che voglio andar via
perché la vita si fa troppo dura
non posso lavorare a mezzadria.
Aspetta l'uva quando l'è matura
e mezza se la porta in fattoria;
io gli raddoppio il frutto e il capitale
e ha sempre il vizio di trattarmi male."

"Vorresti andare a fallo i' manovale,
Pasquale, tu se' poco intelligente
tu ci hai un antro padrone, i' caporale,
ti riguarda i' lavoro l'assistente.
L'inverno sai gli è perfido e brutale,
quarche mese starai senza far niente,
te nun hai né arte e né mestiere
la sarà brutta 'n tutte le maniere!"

"Lo so che l'hanno fatto cavaliere,
commendatore con medaglia d'oro;
lei la vol bene a tutte le bandiere,
la mangia il pane dell'altrui lavoro.
S'è associato alle potenti schiere
nemiche delle forze del lavoro,
e tutti contro quest'agricoltura:
tutto l'anderà ben finché la dura."

"Io de' contadini 'un ho paura,
né alla burrasca e quando tira i' vento,
di certa gente colla testa dura
ne perdo uno e ne ritrovo cento.
Tanto in montagna come sia in pianura
di allogare i poderi 'un mi sgomento;
se quarcheduno rimarrà sfittato

lo fo mai conto, pagherà lo Stato!"

"Padrone, s'è formato un sindacato,
i padroni saranno digià fritti,
uno che onestamente ha lavorato
è suo dovere chiedere i diritti.
Ora che il tempo nero gli è passato
bisognava subire e stare zitti
e al contadino far pagar le tasse;
lei piglierebbe il morto, ritornasse."

"Fo sempre parte alle persone grasse
e sarò sempre un nobile padrone,
parto pe'i' mare colla prima crasse
e i meglio ristoranti all'Abetone.
Quanto i' metano sia la luce e i' gasse
pagherà sempre chi piega i' groppone;
hai voglia d'aspettallo i' Kremlino!
i' pesce grosso mangia i' più piccino."

"Padrone, ha rinfurbito il contadino,
non va più col paniere e colla sporta,
e i capponi e presciutti di suino
in fattoria più non le riporta.
Cappello in mano e faglielo l'inchino
e d'ova fresche mantené la scorta.
Al cinquantotto so' digià arrivato,
e poi a ruba' di più nun è peccato."

"L'è sempre poco icché ti s'è assegnato
i contadini si comprano all'asta,
si mangia e beve, 'un s'è mai lavorato
anche i' trenta percento a noi ci basta.
Hai voglia a fa' i comizi a i' sindacato
e solo una speranza t'è rimasta,
e di vedello il sol dell'avvenire
io dico t'arai tanto da patire."

"Padrone, un giorno gli potrà finire,
se per tutti sonasse le sirene,
Lenin che fece glielo posso dire:
agli schiavi gli sciolse le catene.
Se 'un gli dà noia di stare a sentire
di Mao e di Castro gli faró le scene:
fecion la distruzione dei padroni

e qualchedun lo messon ciondoloni."

"Mi par che mi racconti i paragoni
di porta' certa gente sulle scene
ai tempi crudi come ai sollioni
questo regime in Italia non ci viene.
I furbi che fan le spese ai più coglioni
e l'è una cosa 'un ne starebbe bene:
pe' somari ci vol sempre la frusta,
comandi e' contadini nun è giusta."

"Padrone, qualche cosa lo disgusta,
vedere i contadini fare il bagno,
la fin del mese vengon colla busta,
se vestissero sempre di fustagno!
Invece veston di panno cinese,
a' vagabondi 'un voglian far le spese!"

Ref. n. 100   Per l'ambizione di due disumani
uno di Roma l'altro di Berlino
s'è fatto tutti una vita da cani
da i' più vecchio insino a i' più piccino.
Volean tenere il mondo con le mani,
faceano a gara a chi era i' più assassino,
formarono Nazismo, Fasci e Milizia:
oggi è venuto i' giorno di giustizia.

Nel mondo seminaron nimicizia,
uno d'un altro 'un si potea fidare
indove prima c'era l'amicizia
collera e odio ci venne a regnare.
Ci buttarono tutti nell'immondizia,
con violenza ci vennero a ingannare,
era meglio se 'un s'era nemmen nati,
a tali scempi 'un ci s'era trovati.

Rinnegaron codesti disgraziati
parenti amici e perfino i genitori,
ma per quelli che sbirri sono stati
d'ora in avanti saranno dolori;
perchè quelli che hanno perseguitati
li faranno pagare i loro errori:
quand'ebbero per le mani i' manganello
lo persano i' controllo d'i' cervello.

Ogni poco avvenìa quarche duello
che loro se l'andavano a cercare
dappertutto facevano bordello
e di notte si misero a girare;
andarono a chiappare questo e quello
bussarono alle porte ben serate.
Ci purgaron la sera e la mattina
per farci andar più spesso alla latrina.

Ma ormai e' s'avvicina il vostro giorno,
oggi abusi e violenze son finiti
questi fatti malvagi 'un han ritorno,
ché ognuno agogna a vedervi puniti
con un viaggio senza mai ritorno,
i sepolcri per voi son ben puliti:
ci metteremo insieme Farinacci
diremo "E' morto un branco di pagliacci."

E con le tue menzogne più 'un tu ciacci,
tu 'un sei padrone d'un metro di terra
il tu' Impero è ridotto in calcinacci
la Russia con l'America e Inghilterra
da ogni parte le t'han teso i lacci,
nel mare come in cielo ed anche in terra
E tu gridavi come un pentolaio:
sconta quande tu' avei il Patto d'acciaio.

Comprate questa storia, oste e fornaio
e se in ogni stagion la studierete
ve la vendo d'agosto e di gennaio
soddisfazione ce la troverete,
co i' più piccino piangerà il su' aio.
Or m'alzo, dal cantar mi sento sete
Tra i poeti non fui dei più maligni
e vi saluta il poeta Gramigni.

Ref. n. 101   "Se è ver cotesto, più non si ragioni.
Da me la manderai sera e mattina
a cucinarmi i' pane e e' maccheroni,
far le faccende in camera e in cucina.
a riguardarmi camicie e carzoni,
le chiavi d'i' granaio e di cantina;
e io di vino te ne dò un barile,

un sacco t'empierò di pan gentile."

Parte Pasquino con parola umìle
sposa l'Annina e cessa ogni appetito
allegro come un asino in aprile
quando vede i' tarpogliolo fiorito.
L'Annina con maniera femmenile
prima serve i' padrone e poi i' marito
svelta va su e giù franca e sfrontata,
la basterebbe a servilla un'armata.

Amici qui la storia è terminata
Chi piglia moglie impari da Pasquino
che con la serva s'ebbe anche l'entrata
e non gli mancò più ne pan né vino.

Ref. n. 102   A Dio si raccomanda a larghe braccia
e col figlio maggiore si consiglia.
"Datemi i sacchi" risponde Pasquino
"o bastono i' padrone o vo a i' mulino."

8. CONCLUSIONS

Ref. n. 22   O mamma mia
e quando cresco non sarò la tua,
ma d'i' biondino, se mi porta via.

Ref. n. 23   Fior di giunchiglia
e prima ero d'i' babbo e della mamma
e ora son di Beppino, se mi piglia.

Ref. n. 31   Sòcera mia, sarò la vostra nòra:
io entrerò in casa, e voi vu' andrete fòra.

Notes

1. THE WORLD BY THE FIREPLACE

1. See the *Vocabolario degli Accademici della Crusca* (Venice, 1729), II, 505, entry *veglia*.

2. See Egidio Forcellini, *Lexicon Totius Latinitatis* (Padua, 1940), IV, 989, where the significant civil, military, religious, literal, and metaphorical meanings of *vigilia* are enumerated.

3. Carlo Battisti and Giovanni Alessio, *Dizionario etimologico italiano* (Florence: Barbera, 1957), V, 4001, entry *veglia*.

4. Pietro Fanfani and Cesare Arlia, *Lessico dell'infima e corrotta italianità* (Milan: Carrara, 1881), p. 501, entry *veglia*.

5. On this type of sacred wake, which has its roots in the medieval popular theater, see Arnaldo Rava, *Teatro medievale: L'apparato scenico nella visita delle Marie al Sepolcro* (Rome: Coletti, 1939).

6. *Capoccia* is the father of the family, who governs and administers the finances (see Pietro Fanfani, *Vocabolario dell'uso toscano*, p. 224, entry *capoccia*).

7. *La massaia* (the housemother), wife of the head of the family or rarely of his brother, is the custodian of the household goods and guardian of the house; see the *Vocabolario della Crusca*, I, 736, entry *massaia*.

8. *Pigionale* (*pigionavolo o pigionavole*) is he who has no land but pays rent and works "for third parties"; see the entry *pigionale* in Fanfani, *Vocabolario*, p. 719.

9. *Cozzone*, a middle man who tries to arrange marriages or to sell horses and anything; see *cozzone* in *Vocabolario della Crusca*, I, 321, and *cozzone* in Fanfani, *Vocabolario*, p. 311. One of Giovanni Boccaccio's most famous characters, Andreuccio da Perugia, is a *cozzone* of horses (*Decameron*, II, 5).

10. *Treccone* (in Sienese also *treccolone*), technically a wholesaler of food-stuff; see *Vocabolario della Crusca*, II, 485.
11. Temistocle Gradi, *Racconti*, p. 16.
12. Giuseppe Giusti, *Raccolta di proverbi toscani* (newly amplified and published by Gino Capponi); on p. 321, Giusti reports the censored version, "La sera leoni e la mattina babbioni."
13. Fanfani, *Vocabolario*, p. 364, entry *erba*.
14. Ibid., entry *frasca*, p. 401.
15. Ibid., entry *fascinotto*, p. 376.
16. Giusti, *Raccolta di proverbi toscani*, p. 140.
17. For the dependence on the division of time in a rural culture with respect to the antithetical couple, day/night, see Giuseppe Lisi, *La cultura sommersa*, p. 77.
18. Giusti, *Raccolta di proverbi toscani*, p. 140.
19. Ibid., p. 141. Another proverb cited by Giusti exhorted one to enjoy the fireplace and the *veglia* rather than going out:

    Stay by the fire when it's night
    to scratch the collar of the guitar
    if you desire to save your life (p. 141)

    See Appendix for Italian text.
20. Niccolò Tommaseo, *Dizionario della lingua italiana* (Turin: Unione Tipo-grafico-Editrice, 1861–79), III, part 2, p. 1049, entry *pipistrello*. Debtors "who could not leave the house during the day for fear of being arrested" were likewise called bats.
21. Pietro Fanfani, *Una fattoria toscana*, p. 91.
22. Boccaccio, *The Decameron* (Harmondsworth and New York: Penguin Books, 1972), p. 472. The expression also has a double sexual meaning; see the three expressions at the entry *cencio* in *Vocabolario della Crusca*, I, 237. See Appendix for Italian text.
23. For the concept of limited good, see George M. Foster, "Peasant Society and the Image of Limited Good," *American Anthropologist* 67 (1965):293–315. A different attitude is shown, paradoxically, in the story of the great train robbery: one of the bandits thanked the hand-cuffed conductor who had given him a light (P. Fordham, *The Robber's Tale* [New York: Popular Library, 1965], p. 88).
24. Giusti reports a more complete version in which men or women reveal themselves to be persons of little value when they have to "light the lamp or the fire" (*Raccolta di proverbi toscani*, p. 100).
25. Contagious magic is that which operates a transfer of quality or property through contact and contagion; see J. G. Frazer, *The Golden Bough*

(New York: Macmillan, 1935), I, part 1, pp. 52–54, 174–214.

26. Angelo de Gubernatis, *Storia comparata degli usi natalizi in Italia e presso gli altri popoli indo-europei* (Milan: Treves, 1878), p. 2. See also H. J. Rose, "Ancient Italian Beliefs Concerning the Soul," *Classical Quarterly* 24 (1930):129–135.

27. See Fanfani, *Vocabolario*, p. 864, entries *scaldamano* and *scaldino*.

28. Ibid., entry *caldanella*, p. 202.

29. Lina Duff-Gordon, *Home Life in Italy*, p. 48.

30. Fanfani, *Vocabolario*, entry *fornello*, p. 399.

31. "*Molto fumo, e poco arrosto*" they say, "*di chi tanto presume, e poco vale*"; see the entry *arrosto* in *Vocabolario della Crusca*, I, 108. For other texts, see Charles C. Doyle, "Smoke and Fire: Spencer's Counter-Proverb," *Proverbium* 18 (1972):683–685.

32. Lisi, *La cultura sommersa*, p. 23.

33. The comparison, used also in metaphoric sense, between coal fire and wood fire is reported by Tommaseo in the *Dizionario della lingua italiana*, entry *fuoco*, II, part 1, p. 960.

34. Of the first proverb, Giusti reported a cognate: "*Buon fuoco fa buon cuoco*" (*Raccolta di proverbi toscani*, p. 309). The second is reported in the same collection (p. 100). See Appendix for Italian text.

35. Boiled and roasted, as basic terms mutually exclusive in opposition, are introduced by Claude Lévi-Strauss in *Structural Anthropology* (New York: Basic Books, 1963), p. 87:the roast being the sexual manner; the boiled, the nutritious way to prepare the food. The categories of "fried" and "grilled" (correspondent to the Tuscan *sgrillettato*) are discussed by the same author in the *L'Origine des manières de table* (Paris: Plon, 1968), pp. 409–410. For the culinary fire as a mediator of Nature and Culture, see the diagram in Lévi-Strauss, *The Raw and the Cooked* (New York: Harper & Row, 1969), p. 294.

   For a descriptive-functional morphology of the culinary elements, see instead Walter Hough, *Fire as an Agent in Human Culture* (Washington, D.C.: United States National Museum, 1926), pp. 30–52, where there are also listed the different modalities of application of heat in the kitchen.

36. For the tasting as a ritual, see Lisi, *La cultura sommersa*, pp. 24–25.

37. See Umberto Mannucci, *Bisenzio tradizioni e cucina*. There are many recipes among the less elaborate and more interesting, a good number of which have their cultural context of preparation and consumption. Giovanni Righi Parenti in *La cucina degli etruschi* lists recipes of Arezzo, Siena, and Grosseto, many of these dating back to ancient times, with their histories and legends. See also Waverly Root, *The Food of Italy*, pp. 25–70, and Janet Ross and Michael Waterfield, *Leaves from Our Tuscan*

Kitchen (updated reprint of the 1899 edition). Another interesting set is in Duff-Gordon, *Home Life in Italy*, pp. 72–88; there can be found recipes for minestrone, bread soup, green soup, *maccheroni*, rice *alla artigiana*, mush, cod fish, *tortelli*, chicken and rabbit *alla cacciatora*, vegetables, egg flip, dark pudding. For a more complete guidebook, see Luigi Carnacina and Luigi Veronelli, *La cucina rustica regionale* (Milan: Rizzoli, 1974), II, 163–208.

38. Giusti, *Raccolta di proverbi toscani*, p. 308.

39. Ibid., p. 307.

40. Ibid.

41. See Appendix for Italian text. A different version is in the collection of Giusti (ibid., p. 307): "*Carne fa carne, pan fa sangue, vin mantiene, pesce fa vesce, erba fa merda.*"

42. Caterina Longo Kiniser, *Toscana d'altri tempi*, p. 11.

43. Mabel Sharman Crawford, *Life in Tuscany*, p. 162.

44. Ibid., p. 310.

45. Besides indicating the place where food is prepared, "kitchen" signifies also the repertoire of the food and also, specifically, "*minestra, brodo o peverada*," from the Latin *jus*, which suggests a primary nutritive substance and reconverts it to placental maternal liquid. See *cucina* in the *Vocabolario della Crusca*, I, 327.

46. Many proverbs assert the priority of hunger with respect to the refined taste. In this sense the hunger of the table guests was the best ally of the cook: "*La fame è il meglio cuoco che ci sia*," cited in Ubaldo Cagliaritano, *Proverbi toscani*, p. 74, as are "*L'appetito non vuol salsa*" and "*La salsa di San Bernardo* [i.e., hunger] *fa parere i cibi buoni.*" As it appears from this proverb, hunger was one of the main ingredients of the home kitchen.

47. See Fanfani, *Vocabolario*, pp. 390–391, entry *finestra*. Comments Fanfani, "soup and window" in this expression may also mean "two hard choices" metaphorically.

48. "*A mangiar male o bene, tre volte bisogna bere*"; see Giusti, *Raccolta di proverbi toscani*, p. 306.

49. The *cercone* wine got its ironic name from the fact that one really had to look for it (*cercare*) in the leftovers of the grapes in order to make it.

50. The status of the housemother in principle exempted her from the heavy work of the fields. "The housemother that goes to the fields loses more than what gains" says the proverb justifying the housewife that stays "guarding the house" (see Giusti, *Raccolta di proverbi toscani*, p. 101). Instead, "the housemother who attends the house, earns five pennies and doesn't know it" (ibid.), underlying the concrete and economical value of her work. "The goods stay with those who know

how to maintain it" (ibid.)—the abundance derives by entrusting the house to a thrifty housemother. Some advantages had to derive from this position as the proverb insinuates: "The best bite is the one of the cook" (Cagliaritano, *Proverbi toscani*, p. 74). See Appendix for Italian text.

51. See Giusti, *Raccolta di proverbi toscani*, p. 313.

52. "Too many cooks spoil the kitchen"; See Pirro Giacchi, *Dizionario del vernacolo fiorentino*, p. 42, entry *cuochi*. Also Giusti in *Raccolta di proverbi toscani*, p. 55. The traditional refrain:

O young maid,
how many young boys you hold in plot?
Too many cooks spoil the cooking. [Indicates the analogy woman/food as cultural objects]

See Giuseppe Tigri, *Canti popolari toscani*, p. 374. See Appendix for Italian text.

53. "To have the little ladle in the hand" means to be in the position of the housemother, that is, to command and to be a master. See Giacchi, *Dizionario del vernacolo fiorentino*, p. 67, entry *mestolino*.

54. See the *Vocabolario della Crusca*, entry *mestola*, I, 751: "Who can make his part himself will do it well." See also Giusti, *Raccolta di proverbi toscani*, p. 79.

55. See Longo Kiniser, *Toscana d'altri tempi*, p. 74–75. See Appendix for Italian text.

56. Duff-Gordon, *Home Life in Italy*, p. 138.

57. Giusti, *Raccolta di proverbi toscani*, p. 308.

58. Ibid., p. 309.

59. In relating the preceding proverb, Giusti comments, "The blaze after the table" (ibid.). See also Fanfani, *Una fattori toscana*, p. 75.

60. Giuseppe Tigri, *Contro i pregiudizi popolari*, p. 35.

61. The magic-religious significance of the power over the fire is illustrated, with comparative data, by Mircea Eliade in *Rites and Symbols of Initiation* (New York: Harper and Row, 1965), pp. 85–86. For the performance of games with fire as a means to convince the spectators that who performed them participated in "other" dimensions and privileges of reality, see ibid., pp. 95–96. See also his *The Forge and the Crucible* (London: Rider, 1962), pp. 79–86, where he discusses the "Masters of Fire."

62. The house, as an ideal "radial center of the cultivated land, is like a tower that defends culture"; see Lisi, *La cultura sommersa*, p. 79 n. 2.

The proverb *"Né casa in un canto né vigna in un campo"* (Giusti, *Raccolta di proverbi toscani*, p. 102), exhorting one to construct it in the center, expresses the same conception. This constant and specific organization of space has often been individualized as an affinity and a volumetric and aesthetic agreement between the house and its environment, forming a contiguity between architectonic structure and surrounding nature. See, for example, Mario Tinti, *L'architettura delle case coloniche in Toscana* (with drawings by Ottone Rosai), pp. 12–13; Duccio Baccani, "Analisi di un paesaggio agrario: Il Chianti," doctoral dissertation, Facoltà di Architettura, Florence, 1970; Alessandro Falassi, "Spazio significante e veglia nella cultura della campagna toscana," *Granducato* 4 (1976):127–136.

For a survey of Tuscan countryside in the Renaissance, see Gigi Salvagnini, "Agricoltura e case rurali in Toscana alla fine del Cinquecento," *Granducato* 4 (1976):97–126. The equivalence between cultivated land and woods in each *podere* appears clearly in the data relative to the Tuscany of 1830–1930, discussed in Emilio Sereni, *Storia del paesaggio agrario italiano* (Bari: Laterza, 1974), p. 400.

63. This concept is used as a term of comparison between two types of cultures in Alexandre Koyré, *From the Closed World to the Infinite Universe* (Baltimore: Johns Hopkins University Press, 1968).

64. *Inferno*, I, 2, 5. In a Tuscan legend, a character of Dante, Ugo, "the great baron" of Tuscany mentioned in Paradise, XIV, 128, is led by his bolted horse to "a circle surrounded by trees, black and limbed to the top; from a cavern of fire in the middle came red beams of sulphur and of smoke. Out from the cavern came hairy and large-limbed men. . . . That must be the entrance to hell" (see Idilio dell'Era, *Leggende toscane*, p. 71).

65. These are verses of the *pastorella*, a folk song of possibly French origin, collected among others by Nigra, Nerucci, and Giannini; see Appendix for Italian text. For another version, see Giovanni Giannini, *Canti popolari toscani*, pp. 391, 411–412.

66. De Gubernatis, *Storia comparata degli usi natalizi*, p. 72 n. 1.

67. A typical example is in the fairy tale of the beautiful Rosana: In the gloominess and dark of the woods, Lucidio drew a bit of water to the lips of the wicked, dying Sir Bertaccio, but all of a sudden there was a large fire, and the noise of six thousand thunders, and the cursed man was taken away "in body and soul" (see Gradi, *Racconti*, pp. 275–276).

68. The crucifix that we can still see in the church of Spaltenna appeared in the woods in a very miraculous way to a shepherdess devoted to the Madonna. The legend is reported among the tales of Ancilla, an old Chianti woman, in ibid., pp. 242–245. According to another legend, the Virgin Mary appeared in the shade of the centenarian trees to Ugo

of Tuscany and exhorted him to change his way of life (see dell'Era, *Leggende toscane*, pp. 66–68).

69. See, for example, the story of Madre Oliva, related by Maria Pierazzoli, in which mother and son are exposed in the woods, in Giuseppe Pitré, *Novelle popolari toscane*, II, 113–114.

70. See, for example, "the blind" in Angelo de Gubernatis, *Le novelline di Santo Stefano*, pp. 306–308.

71. De Gubernatis, *Storia comparata degli usi natalizi*, p. 124.

72. Dante used *salvatico* for a boorish and rough man (*Purgatory*, XXVI, 69). Boccaccio did similarly in the second story of the fourth day (*The Decameron*).

73. "It is not land to plant a vineyard there"; that is, he is a "man without value." See the entry *vigna* in the *Vocabolario della Crusca*, II, 523.

74. In his penetrating essay, Lisi hints also of the material connection between things and their metonymic logic, both operators of knowledge (*La cultura sommersa*, pp. 554–555).

75. Some Tuscan farmers said so to an American traveler; see Crawford, *Life in Tuscany*, p. 165.

76. Duff-Gordon, *Home Life in Italy*, p. 143.

77. Longo Kiniser, *Toscana d'altri tempi*, p. 15.

78. For a study of the rural Tuscan house in its architectural form and according to geographic distribution, see, for example, the study of Renato Biasutti, *La casa rurale nella Toscana*; and Guido Biffoli and Guido Ferrara, *La casa colonica in Toscana*. Interesting indications are also contained in Bino Samminiatelli, "Case rurali in Toscana," *Le Vie d'Italia* 44 (1938):988–995; and Guido Morozzi, Architettura colonica in Valdarno," *Le Vie d'Italia* 48 (1942):200–208. For a folkloristic approach, see, instead, C. Ferraro, "La casa nel folklore," *Archivo per lo Studio delle Tradizioni Popolari* 16 (1897):153–165, 339–351, 457–472; 17 (1898): 71–98, 193–215. In this last study, we find interesting hints of the popular anthropomorphic conception of the house (the door like a mouth, the windows like eyes, etc); the patriarchal house, in fact, grew with the family: at every wedding they added a room. The men were called "support of the house"; the head of the family, "pillar"; the children, "low roof"; etc. Church and town were seen as multiples of the house.

79. For the function of the stairway in the rural home, see Mario Gramolini, "La scala nella casa rurale," *Rivista di Estimo e Genio Rurale* 5 (1947):40–47, with a series of examples and projects.

80. The meaning of *cucina* in the word *casa* is indicated in Battisti and Alessio, *Dizionario etimologico italiano*, I, 788, entry *casa*.

81. Etymologically, the term derives from late Latin *foculare*, place of the fire, where the fire is kept. See Charles Du Cange, *Glossarium mediae*

et infimae latinitatis (Njort: Favre, 1884), III, 553, entry *foculare*. In the sense of *casa*, family, the term was used in central Italy before 757; see Battisti and Alessio, *Dizionario etimologico italiano*, III, 1674, entry *focolare*. For the cowl of the chimney as "door open night and day," see Lisi, *La cultura sommersa*, pp. 20–21, n. 3.

82. "The oil lamp does not hurt the eyes like the lamps of the master's house that pierce like pins! When you come in from the dark you seem to go blind!" (Longo Kiniser, *Toscana d'altri tempi*, p. 94).

83. Gaston Bachelard, *La Flamme d'une chandelle* (Paris: Presses Universitaires de France, 1970), p. 98.

84. The time of the *veglia*, marked by the burning of the log and by the consumption of oil in the lamp, seems to be of the same gender as musical and mythological times, "machine à supprimer le temps," according to the definition of Lévi-Strauss. The musical time in fact operates under the notes and rhythms on a primary terrain that is the same physiological time of the listener. The music changes the segment of time consecrated to its listening from a diachrony (like the external time) to syncrony closed in itself. The hearing of the musical piece by its internal organization can immobilize the time that passes. Through and during the listening of music, "we accede to a kind of immortality." See *The Raw and the Cooked*, pp. 15–16.

85. The concept of the fire as a substance naturally leaning toward the summit and as an expression of transcendent spiritualities is already in Dante, *Purgatorio*, XVIII, 28–29:

Poi come'l fuoco muovesi in altura
per la sua forma ch'è nata a salire.

Symbolic aspects of the verticality of the flame which is like a "shifter" are discussed by Bachelard in *La Flamme d'une chandelle*, pp. 56–69.

86. See the scheme by Lévi-Strauss in *L'Origine des manières de table*, p. 125.

87. This traditional usage, together with that of putting the umbilical cord of the cats under the stone of the fireplace to make them remain affectionate to the house, is reported by De Gubernatis in *Storia comparata degli usi natalizi*, p. 129.

88. "Pale like cinders" is a similitude of common use. It is cited by Giusti in *Raccolta di proverbi toscani*, p. 368. The recycling of the waste of the fire is discussed, with the relative symbolic value, by Gaston Bachelard in *The Psychoanalysis of Fire* (Boston: Beacon Press, 1969), pp. 32–33, where there is also an elaboration, on pp. 35–38, of the ethnographic data presented by J. C. Frazer in *Myths of the Origin of Fire* (London: Macmillan, 1930).

89. For the *ceppo* [log] in Tuscany, see, for example, Paolo Toschi, *Il folklore* (Roma: Editrice Studium, 1969), pp. 75–76. The Christmas log was kept to be lighted during the year to avoid the bad weather; the usage is recorded by Giacchi in *Dizionario del vernacolo fiorentino*, pp. 35–36. *Ceppo* in Tuscany also means "Christmas present," as noted by De Gubernatis in *Storia comparata degli usi natalizi*, p. 88, where he interprets it as "symbolic of the vegetation of life that we hope to last all year" (p. 113). The relation between the Christmas log and the presents and tips also called *ceppo*, which children receive at Christmas from their elders, is parallel to the relation between the *veglia* log and the entertainment and morals that were received as a gift by the youngsters from the elders.

90. For *ceppo* as a group of houses, see Fanfani, *Vocabolario*, p. 252. *Ceppo* signifies also "origin of the family"; see the entry *ceppo* in the *Vocabolario della Crusca*, I, 283. In a legend going back to the beginning of the 800s, a farmer cut down an old chestnut tree. The trunk fell with a groan and at the split—that is, at the log—appeared an image of the sacred family (see Duff-Gordon, *Home Life in Italy*, p. 344). For the *ceppo* as symbol of marriage, of the pregnant woman, and for the woman as the tree of life, see Raffaele Corso, *Patti d'amore e pegni di promessa* (San Maria Capua Vetere: La Fiaccola, 1925), pp. 53, 62–64.

91. *Vocabolario della Crusca*, entry *ramo*, II, 157–158. De Gubernatis in *Storia comparata degli usi natalizi*, pp. 121–122, gives examples of the metaphorical use of the words *trees*, *branch*, *roots*, and other terms originated in the vegetable world.

92. De Gubernatis, *Storia comparata degli usi natalizi*, p. 121 n. 1.

93. Bachelard, *La Flamme d'une chandelle*, p. 68.

94. In *The Psychoanalysis of Fire* (pp. 43–58), Bachelard analyzes the sensualized fire as a male principle that fertilizes the water, which has feminine substance, and indicates also the specific equivalence spark = seed; seed = spark. Along the same line is the analysis of Géza Róheim in *The Origin and Function of Culture* (New York: Doubleday, 1971), p. 130. The sexual symbolism of the fire is very common in Tuscany folklore and appears clearly in double entendres of the following type.

> Bring me your firebrand well lighted;
> straw to burn I already have . . .
>
> [heard in 1972 at Poggibonsi]

We find the same meaning in such proverbs as "The man is fire and the woman is oakum, comes the devil and lights the spark," in Giusti, *Raccolta di proverbi toscani*, p. 30. The sexual significance of fire in folklore is also presented by De Gubernatis in *Storia comparata degli usi natalizi*, p. 123. But also, in common language, we say "burning with love" or simply "cooked," that is, "taken from the fire of love." Also, in Tuscan tales told during the *veglia*, at times it is the sun, fire par excellence, that with its ray impregnates the princess who is held prisoner in the tower by her parents. See, for example, the version published by Domenico Comparetti in *Novelline popolari italiane*, p. 195. "Give fire to the rag" is a double entendre with a sexual meaning, for "intercourse" is used by the old woman in the story of Pietro di Vinciolo. See Boccaccio, *The Decameron*, p. 472. "Fire," as a synonym for "love," is used also in a popular song:

Weed flower,
where the fire is lit once
always a bit of spark remains.

See Tigri, *Canti popolari toscani*, p. 373. See Appendix for Italian text.

95. "Fire at times is taken for an entire family." See *Vocabolario della Crusca*, entry *fuoco*, I, 531. See also Tommaseo, *Dizionario della lingua italiana*, II, part 1, 960, entry *fuoco*.

96. For the taxes called *casatico* and *focatico*, see Tommaseo, *Dizionario della lingua italiana*, II, part 1, p. 961, entry *fuoco*.

97. Both expressions are cited in the *Glossarium mediae et infimae latinitatis* by Du Cange, III, 533, entry *focus*.

98. For many versions of this game, found in many countries, see Paul G. Brewster, *American Nonsinging Games* (Norman: University of Oklahoma Press, 1953), pp. 46–47.

99. In some rites of passage, the novice was symbolically "roasted" to become a full member of the social group. In the kitchen, as in the rites of the *veglia*, the fire is in the liminal position between Nature and Culture. See Eliade, *Rites and Symbols of Initiation*, pp. 8–9.

100. The fire as a symbolic primary substance already possessed for the alchemists the property to connect the things that were homogeneous and to disconnect those that were heterogeneous. The fire as "terrible divinity," able to contradict itself and then to pose itself as the principal universal explanation, is discussed by Bachelard in *The Psychoanalysis of Fire*, p. 7.

2. FAIRY TALES FOR THE YOUNG AND THE OLD

1. For some of the latest attempts at analyzing such a rich corpus of folklore, see among the Italian works Giorgio Cherubini and Bianca

de'Bernardi, *Analisi strutturale di narrative infantili* (Florence: Sansoni, 1974), and Cecilia Gatto Trocchi, *La fiaba italiana di magia* (Rome: Bulzoni, 1972). Both works include some Tuscan texts. For a more psychological and psychoanalytical orientation, see Bruno Bettelheim, *The Uses of Enchantment: The Meaning and Importance of Fairy Tales* (New York: Random House, 1977).

Among the contemporary Soviet folklorists' work, see Eleazar Meletinski, "Structural-Typological Study of Folktales" and "Problem of the Historical Morphology of the Folktales." They are in Pierre Maranda (ed.), *Soviet Structural Folkloristics* (The Hague: Mouton, 1974), I, 19–51, 53–59.

2. For a general discussion, see Richard Bauman, "Verbal Art as Performance," *American Anthropologist* 77 (1975): 290–311; and Dell Hymes, "Breakthrough into Performance," in *Folklore: Performance and Communication*, ed. Dan Ben-Amos and Kenneth S. Goldstein, pp. 11–74 (The Hague: Mouton, 1975).

3. On the dynamic aspects, see Barbara Kirshenblatt-Gimblett, "A Parable in Context: A Social Interactional Analysis of Storytelling Performance," in *Folklore*, ed. Ben-Amos and Goldstein, pp. 105–130.

4. Gradi, *Racconti*, pp. 264–265.

5. Ibid., p. 253.

6. In Tuscany as well as in rural Sicily, to which Salvatore Salomone-Marino refers in his famous study, storytellers never intended that their tales should be told only to children. The stories, including the "magic tales," were always meant for everyone present, "for adults and children alike." See Salomone-Marino, *Costumi e usanze dei contadini di Sicilia* (Palermo: Andò, 1968), p. 77.

7. The same ritual process is described by Duff-Gordon, an Anglo-Saxon resident near Carrara at the beginning of the century. One Sunday evening the Duff-Gordons had invited Guinigi, a famous storyteller of that region, to a storytelling gathering. Guinigi greeted everyone: "Revered ladies and gentlemen, I am at your service" and, placing himself in the corner near the fire, he repeated that he was at their command; but he obstinately refused to tell a story, saying he didn't remember those that were requested, that by now the children knew them better than their own grandparents, that the children knew more things than the adults did, and that therefore they wouldn't want to sit and listen to fairy tales. After much insisting on the part of the audience, he began to swear on the heads of his grandchildren that he didn't remember one single story; he then offered to procure for his guests a book he had at home: "One hundred and one nights." Then, when everyone had just about given up, he suddenly began in a

stentorian voice to tell a story that had not been requested (see Duff-Gordon, *Home Life in Italy*, pp. 325–326).

8. The motif of the girl who is the only one able to reach the fruit on an enchanted pomegranate tree can be found, for example, in Temistocle Gradi, *Saggio di letture varie per i giovani*, pp. 141–157; it is the story of Isabelluccia (cute little Isabelle). Also see Carl Weber, "Italienische Märchen in Toscana aus Volksmund Gesammelt," extracted in *Forschungen zur Romanischen Philologie*, 1900, pp. 16–19. In Weber's collection the story is entitled "Cenderognola"; it is AT 403A. For the numerical references, I followed Gianfranco D'Aronco, *Indice delle fiabe toscane* (even though the enumeration is often debatable), except where otherwise indicated.

9. Vladimir Propp, *Morphology of the Folktale* (Austin: University of Texas Press, 1968). For the most recent trends derived from this seminal book, see Alan Dundes, *The Morphology of North American Indian Folktales* (Helsinki: Academia Scientiarum Fennica, 1964); Claude Brémond, *Logique du récit* (Paris: Seuil, 1973); Marie-Louise Tenèze, "Du conte merveilleux comme genre," *Arts et Traditions Populaires* 18 (1970):11–65.

10. Vladimir Propp as well as Claude Brémond simplify the analysis, adopting "God's point of view," that is, total information about events. For Brémond, see "La Logique des possibles narratifs," in *Communications* 8 (1966):60–76.

11. For the structural method of reading the plot as a game, see Umberto Eco, "Le Strutture narrative in Fleming," in *Il caso Bond*, by various authors, pp. 73–122 (Milan: Bompiani, 1965). A theoretical discussion is in William O. Hendricks, "Methodology of Narrative Structural Analysis," *Semiotica* 7, no. 2 (1973):163–184.

12. This version, the most common, is quoted by Giusti, *Raccolta di proverbi toscani*, p. 300. A variant from Tuscany —"*la novella non è bella/se sopra non ci si rappella*" ["if you don't recall remembrances upon it"]—is in Gherardo Nerucci, *Sessanta novelle popolari montalesi*, p. 4. See also Giuseppe Cocchiara, *Pitré la Sicilia e il folklore* (Messina-Florence: G. d'Anna, 1951), p. 64.

13. Raffaele Corso, *Reviviscenze: Studi di tradizioni popolari Italiane* (Catania: Guaitolini, 1927), pp. 122–123.

14. See, for instance, the version reported by Tigri in *Canti popolari toscani*, pp. 11–12. See Appendix for Italian text.

15. Just like the prince in the story *la bambola* (collected by Gherardo Nerucci) who, as he looks around for prey, finds instead first a doll, then a wife; see Nerucci, *Cincelle da bambini*, pp. 40–45. A version of AT 707 collected by Ciro Marzocchi is entitled "the king who was a hunt-

er." The prince, because he had become a good hunter, is recognized (or acknowledged) as the king; the queen mother is burned; this is an example of the hunt as a ritual of passage from childhood to manhood (see Marzocchi, "Centotrenta fiabe senesi," manuscript 57, Italian Society of Ethnology). See also "The King Who Went Hunting" (AT 709) in Vittorio Imbriani, *La novellaja fiorentina*, pp. 232–236.

16. For fruit used as a sign and a promise of love, see dell' Era, *Leggende toscane*, p. 145. In the legend of Saint Fina, Fina's "sin" was having accepted two apples from a laughing page who threw them at the girls; he had said to her: "Take them, take them, for when you become a bride!" The branch as a promise of love probably goes back to the Roman "*traditio per ramum*." See Corso, *Patti d'amore e pegni di promessa*, p. 34; for apples and oranges as love gifts, see p. 31.

17. This is AT 440, up to now not collected in Tuscany; see Stith Thompson, *The Types of the Folktale*, FFC, no. 184, 3d ed. (Helsinki, 1961), pp. 149–150.

18. A standard joke involving the princess and the frog symbology is in George Legman, *Rationale of the Dirty Joke* (New York: Grove Press, 1971), p. 443.

19. Reciprocal patterns are also present in Tuscan stories: the young prince-fiancé "kisses his mother," and this makes him forget his fiancée. The acceptance of incest is mutually exclusive with marriage, a ritual that consecrates definitively the entrance of the individuals into the cultural world. Incest and marriage are distributed in a complementary way. See De Gubernatis, *Le novelline di Santo Stefano*, pp. 23–24. This is the story of the three oranges (AT 408) in the Tuscan version. "The mother's kiss" was also the white spot on the horses' jaws, which was interpreted as a sign of shame. Horses with such white spots were not purchased willingly, because they were considered "marked for life." For this custom, see Alan Dundes and Alessandro Falassi, *La Terra in Piazza* (Berkeley: University of California Press, 1975), p. 145.

20. This is a very common story. The salt motif can be found in the story of "The Wooden Horseshoe" (or "The Wooden Shoe") and "The Silver Candlestick" (AT 510 VI); see Pitré, *Novelle popolari toscane*, II, 41, 44–45. The geese guard (AT 923) is among the stories collected by De Gubernatis; *Le novelline di Santo Stefano*, pp. 29–30. In other versions, like that of "The Little Golden Slipper," the girl goes to three balls with three marvelous dresses, making the king and the king's son fall in love with her; see Pitré, *Novelle popolari toscane*, II, 87–94.

21. Glauco Carloni, "Indagine sul gradimento dei più popolari tipi di fiaba

e interpretazione di una singolare censura," extracted in *Aggiornamenti di Psicologia dell'Istituto di Psicologia dell'Università di Bologna*, 1968, pp. 1–19.

22. See Giuseppe Costantini, "Una esibizione singolare," *Lares* 9, no. 6 (1938):475–476.

23. The passing of such qualifying tests and the successive marriage are to be found in many narratives: for "spinning and sewing," see, for instance, "The Little Women of Maialia." The girl spins and sews a shirt for the monster in one day, breaking the spell, and he marries her (Pitré, *Novelle popolari toscane*, II, 161). For "doing housework," see "The Cats" (ibid., I, 61). For "making herself beautiful" see Marzocchi, "Centotrenta fiabe senesi," story no. 121. For "bringing up puppies," see "Capo di becco" in Pitré, *Novelle popolari toscane*, II, 51–56. For "taking care of animals," see ibid., II, 99–100, "Monna Caterina." For "cooking," see ibid., II, 97, the story about Pellicciotto: the girl sends homemade bread to the king; he meets her and marries her. "Pellicinia" instead cures the prince, who suffers from melancholy, by sending him a piece of cake inside of which she has put the ring she had received from him at the ball she had attended in disguise. He recovers and marries her. See Angelo de Gubernatis, "Novelline di Santo Stefano di Calcinaia," *Rivista di Letteratura Popolare* 1 (1878):86. The marriage theme in fact occupies a very prominent place both in culture and in fairy tales. For a discussion of ritual elements adumbrated in fairy tales, see Elezar Meletinaki, "Marriage: Its Function and Position in the Structure of Folktales," in *Soviet Structural Folkloristics*, ed. Maranda, pp. 61–72.

24. Giusti, *Raccolta di proverbi toscani*, p. 347. See Appendix for Italian text.

25. It was the little girls who took care of newborn babies, often carrying them around with them. They began to take care of them around the ages of five or six years. You can meet one of these small babysitters in Duff-Gordon, *Home Life in Italy*, p. 223.

26. Nada's version has no parallel in Tuscan collections.

27. The formula was common. Compare "I will tell you a story, but underneath it is the bare truth" in Idelfonso Nieri, *Cento racconti popolari lucchesi*, p. 21.

28. A list of very common interruptions with a typological summary can be found in Linda Dégh, *Folktales and Society* (Bloomington: Indiana University Press, 1969), pp. 117–119.

29. "Good wine makes a long tale" [*"Buon vino, favola lunga"*] in Ugo Rossi-Ferrini, *Proverbi agricoli*, p. 179.

30. Cinderella is AT 510; "The Beauty and the Beast" is AT 403. A version of the second part originating in the Florentine region was collected

by Temistocle Gradi, with the title "Nina-the-Star and Betta-the-tail." Nina ("Nina" in Italian also means "sister" and is an affectionate term; that is, it means "good sister") behaves in a well-mannered way, she is helpful, and she chooses the ordinary over the luxurious. The fairies reward her with pearls, dresses, and a star in the middle of her forehead. Betta is rude, and she chooses the luxurious over the ordinary. A donkey's tail grows in the middle of her forehead. See Gradi, *La vigilia di pasqua di ceppo*, pp. 20–25. The Palace of Cats, which scratch the rude sister and reward the helpful one, is in a version cited by De Gubernatis, "Novelline di Santo Stefano di Calcinaia," p. 62 n. 1. For a general discussion, see also Gail A. Kligman, "A Socio-psychological Interpretation of the Tale of the Kind and Unkind Girl," M.A. thesis, University of California at Berkeley, 1973.

31. From a psychoanalytical point of view, the symbology can be interpreted as follows: Lina saves her own virginity (she doesn't get scratched) while Betta loses it (is scratched). Lina obtains a visible form of virtue (the star in the middle of her forehead) and Betta a *prolaxum*; one becomes desirable, the other repulsive. Among the fairies' gifts—in other versions gifts from the cats or from the king of the cats—is a symbolic one earned through the test of having to delouse some women and having to choose modest garments; the bad sister only receives bugs and lice, a dress that is ripped, and a monkey on her head (Imbriani, *La novellaja fiorentina*, pp. 186–187). Thus one finds a husband, and the other will remain forever the object of mean jokes; see Gradi, *La vigilia di pasqua di ceppo*, p. 25.

32. Duff-Gordon, *Home Life in Italy*, p. 111.

33. Corso, *Patti d'amore e pegni di promessa*, pp. 42, 45, 46.

34. A typical *exemplus* is "the young girl whose cheeks were all eaten by make-up." In fact, when a woman puts on make-up, she "erased from her face the image and figure of God and in its place she put that of the Devil." See Fra' Filippo da Siena, *Gli assempri*, p. 21. This iconographic stereotype has remained in "edifying" literature up to now. For one such portrait—a stepmother with bleached hair, painted lips, and a painted face who gives indignant orders, who never goes to church, who doesn't ever pray, and who often strikes her stepdaughter—see Remo Manfredi, *Mondo allegro* (Padua: Messaggero di S. Antonio, 1944), pp. 119–127.

35. The story of Cinderella (AT 510) is among the most common and best known in folklore. For a collection of 345 variants in different areas and cultural surroundings, see Marian Cox, *Cinderella* (London: Nutt, 1893). The symbolism of Cinderella has been analyzed over and over again psychologically and psychoanalytically. See, for example, Ben

Rubenstein, "Meaning of the Cinderella Story in the Development of a Little Girl," *American Imago* 12 (1955):197–255; M. Collier, "Psychological Appeal of the Cinderella Theme," *American Imago* 14, no. 4 (1961):399–412; Anna Birgitta Rooth, *The Cinderella Cycle* (Lund: CWC Gleerup, 1955).

For a rigorous analysis, based on mathematics, see Pierre Maranda, "Cendrillon: Theorie des graphes et des ensembles," in *Semiotique narrative et textuelle*, ed. Claude Chabrol, pp. 122–136 (Paris: Larousse, 1973). Maranda discusses the tale at the level of family structures and at the level of the conflictual interaction. The history and a discussion of this well-known tale that has antecedents recorded as early as the eleventh century are in Bettelheim, *The Uses of Enchantment*, pp. 166–183, 236–277.

36. Erich Fromm has analyzed the Anglo-Saxon version of Little Red Riding Hood—Little Red Cap—from the point of view of psychoanalytic theory. See his *The Forgotten Language* (New York: Rinehart and Co., 1951), pp. 235–241. Little Red Riding Hood, not listed by D'Aronco, is AT 333; see Thompson, *The Types of the Folktale*, p. 125.

37. For a detailed story about a girl and her cow, see Elide Lapi Bonifazi, *Maggiolata* (Florence: Pucci Cipriani, 1973), pp. 14–15.

38. This is a version of a tale collected as the "story of the feeble-minded man and the sage" by Gherardo Nerucci. See his *Sessanta novelle popolari montalesi*, pp. 298–302. In his version there are two brothers who at the end get rich. In the version collected by Ciro Marzocchi, with the title "Giucco," it is only Giucco who becomes rich; "Centrotrenta fiabe senesi."

39. See Appendix for Italian text. For another version, see Raffaello Cioni, *Il poema mugellano*, pp. 218–219.

40. Collected from Gilberto Giuntini, in 1978, in the area of Empoli. Such short rhymes usually ended the first part of the *veglia* and, according to my informant, originally had a magic connotation as the number seven in the first one seems to indicate. See Appendix for Italian text.

3. BEDTIME AND CHILDREN'S FOLKLORE

1. Mary Sanches and Barbara Kirshenblatt-Gimblett, "Children's Traditional Speech Play and Child Language," in *Speech Play*, ed. Barbara Kirshenblatt-Gimblett, pp. 65–110 (Philadelphia: University of Pennsylvania Press, 1976).

2. An extensive discussion of this process is in Carol Chomsky, *The Acquisition of Syntax in Children 5 to 10* (Cambridge, Mass.: MIT Press, 1969), and Frank Kessel, *The Role of Syntax in Children's Comprehen-*

sion from Ages 6 to 12 (Chicago: University of Chicago Press for the Society for Research in Child Development, 1970).

3. This cumulative tale is related to AT 2015, the goat who would not go home, and AT 2030, the old woman and her pig. This is the version which I got from an old woman from La Piazza in November 1973; see Appendix for Italian text. The story of Petuzzo is very common; for other versions, see, for example, Giannini, *Canti popolari toscani*, pp. 40–43; Orazio Bacci, *Ninne-nanne, cantilene, canzoni di giuochi e filastrocche, che si dicono in Valdelsa*, p. 89; Severino Ferrari and A. Straccali, *Ninnananne, cantilene e givochi fanciulleschi uditi in Firenze*, pp. 15–18.

4. Giannini, *Canti popolari toscani*, p. 46 n. 10.

5. The chain of obligations as a structural finite system in Tuscan culture is the object of an unpublished lecture by Paolo Fabbri at the Ecole des Hautes Etudes, mentioned by A. J. Greimas in "Un problème de semiotique narrative: Les Objets de valeurs," *Langages* 8, no. 31 (1973): 21–22.

6. For some texts, see, for instance, Lina Eckenstein, *Comparative Studies in Nursery Rhymes* (Detroit: Singing Tree Press, 1968; originally published in 1906). A comparative study is in Robbins Burling, "The Metrics of Children's Verse: A Cross-Linguistic Study," *American Anthropologist* 68 (1966):1419–1441. An analysis from the viewpoint of generative metric is in Jacqueline Guézon, "The Meter of Nursery Rhymes: An Application of the Halle-Keyser Theory of Meter," *Poetics* 12 (1974): 73–111.

7. See Chapters 5 and 7.

8. Collected in Monte Morello (Florence Province), 1978; see Appendix for Italian text. An old version is in Ferrari and Straccali, *Ninnananne, cantilene e giuochi fanciulleschi uditi in Firenze*, pp. 15–18.

9. Collected in Monte Morello (Florence Province), 1978. See Appendix for Italian text.

10. Collected in Shangai, suburb of Leghorn, 1978. See Appendix for Italian text.

11. Collected in Montevarchi (Arezzo Province) 1978. See Appendix for Italian text.

12. Collected in Poggibonsi, 1978; see Appendix for Italian text. A version collected in the Sienese region is in Giovanbattista Corsi, "Ninnenanne, cantilene, filastrocche, storie popolari," *Archivio per lo Studio delle Tradizioni Popolari* 17 (1898):58.

13. The problem of the ambivalence of Italian folkloristic materials is treated at the level of contents by Luigi M. Lombardi-Satriani in *Contenuti ambivalenti del folklore calabrese* (Messina: Peloritana, 1968). Relationships regarding individuals, society, and class structure are investigat-

ed in the essay. The same ambiguity is present in Tuscan folklore in regard to the structure of personal relationships and family roles. On obscene children's folklore, see C. Gaignebel, *Le Folklore obscène des enfants* (Paris: Maisonneuve et Larose, 1974).

14. Collected from Cesare Ricci, in the area of Pisa, in the fifties. See Appendix for Italian text.

15. Ibid., see Appendix for Italian text. A version from Leghorn is quoted by Gino Galletti in *La poesia popolare livornese*, p. 94, and has the following ending:

And he had a bell
Which he rang every night.
And he had a handbell
Which he rang just as well.

16. For a structural definition of the riddle, see Robert Georges and Alan Dundes, "Towards a Structural Definition of the Riddle," *Journal of American Folklore* 76 (1963):111–118. A study oriented toward logic is instead that of Elli Kongas-Maranda, "The Logic of Riddles," in *Structural Analysis of Oral Tradition*, ed. Pierre and Elli Maranda, pp. 189–232 (Philadelphia: University of Pennsylvania Press, 1971); and Elli Kongas-Maranda, "Theory and Practice of Riddle Analysis," *Journal of American Folklore* 84 (1971):51–61.

   A general discussion of the riddle is in Roger Abrahams and Alan Dundes, "Riddle," in *Folklore and Folklife: An Introduction*, ed. Richard Dorson, pp. 129–143 (Chicago: University of Chicago Press, 1972). For a semantic approach, see Tzvetan Todorov, "Analyse du discours: L'Example des devinettes," *Journal de Psychologie Normale et Pathologique* 1–2 (1973):135–155.

17. See Appendix for Italian text.

18. Brian Sutton-Smith, "A Developmental Structural Account of Riddles," in *Speech Play*, ed. Kirshenblatt-Gimblett, pp. 111–119.

19. See John M. Roberts and Michael L. Forman, "Riddles: Expressive Models of Interrogation," in *The Ethnography of Communication*, ed. John Gumperz and Dell Hymes, pp. 180–209 (New York: Holt, Rinehart and Winston, 1972).

20. See Giovanbattista Corsi, "Indovinelli popolari raccolti in Siena," *Archivio per lo Studio delle Tradizioni Popolari* 17 (1898):187, for a version from Siena. I collected this and the following 6 in the area of Monteriggioni; see Appendix for Italian text.

21. Collected in Calenzano, 1977; see Appendix for Italian text. This riddle,

very common in all Tuscany, is mentioned in the reprinted collection with an introduction by Giuseppe Rua in *Archivio per lo Studio delle Tradizioni Popolari* 7 (1888):462 (hereafter cited as Rua). The original from the sixteenth century is in the Biblioteca Marucelliana (Miscellanea, 288, 7) of Florence with the title "Indovinelli, riboboli, passerotti et farfalloni. Nuovamente messi insieme e la maggior parte non più stampati, parte in prosa e parte in rima, et ora posti in luce per ordine d'alfabeto. Con alcune cicalate di Donne, di sententie et proverbi posti nel fine. Opera molto piacevole et bella da indovinare et da far ridere nelle veglie per passarsi tempo."

22. Collected in Calenzano; see Appendix for Italian text. A variant with a "tail" is in Cioni, *Il poema mugellano*, p. 243.

23. Collected in Calenzano; see Appendix for Italian text. A version is in Giannini, *Canti popolari toscani*, p. 73.

24. I collected this and the following three in Fiesole (Florence Province); see Appendix for Italian text. Versions are in Carlo Lapucci, *Indovinelli Italiani*, pp. 11, 55, 1–2, 26, respectively.

25. Collected in Certaldo, 1976, as were the following two; see Appendix for Italian text. Versions are in Rua, pp. 453, 462, 461.

26. Collected in Barga, 1971; see Appendix for Italian text. A version is in Giannini, *Canti popolari toscani*, p. 74.

27. Collected in Barga, 1971; see Appendix for Italian text. A version is in Rua, p. 451.

28. Collected in Buonconvento, 1978, as was the following; see Appendix for Italian text. Versions are in Giovanbattista Corsi, "Indovinelli senesi," *Archivio per lo Studio delle Tradizioni Popolari* 10 (1891):400, 403."

29. Collected in Pian Degli Ontani (Pistoia Province), 1976; see Appendix for Italian text.

30. Collected in Pian Degli Ontani (Pistoia Province), 1976; see Appendix for Italian text. Versions are in Cioni, *Il poema mugellano*, p. 245; Giannini, *Canti popolari toscani*, p. 72.

31. Giannini, *Canti popolari toscani*, p. 107. See also Giuseppe Pitré, "La oscenità negli indovinelli," *Archivio per lo Studio delle Tradizioni Popolari* 15 (1896):753–756.

32. Collected in Castellina in Chianti, 1976; see Appendix for Italian text. A version is in Rua, p. 462.

33. Collected in Panzano, 1978; see Appendix for Italian text. Compare:

I have a little bag sewn double,
open in the middle,
and whoever touches it
I'll stuff it in his mouth.

In Giuseppe Pitré, "Indovinelli toscani," *Archivio per lo Studio delle Tradizioni Popolari* 10 (1891):382.

34. Collected in Castellina in Chianti, 1978; see Appendix for Italian text.

35. Collected in Cutigliano, 1976; see Appendix for Italian text.

36. Collected in Cutigliano, 1976; see Appendix for Italian text. A variant is in Lapucci, *Indovinelli italiani*, p. 35.

37. Collected in Castellina in Chianti, 1978; see Appendix for Italian text.

38. Collected in Cutigliano, 1976; see Appendix for Italian text. A variant is in Lapucci, *Indovinelli italiani*, p. 8.

39. Collected in Cutigliano, 1976; see Appendix for Italian text.

40. Collected in Castellina in Chianti, 1978; see Appendix for Italian text. A variant is in Lapucci, *Indovinelli italiani*, p. 105.

41. Collected in Castellina in Chianti, 1978; see Appendix for Italian text. A version is in Corsi, "Indovinelli senesi," p. 404.

42. Collected in Pietrasanta, 1977; see Appendix for Italian text.

43. Collected in Pietrasanta, 1977; see Appendix for Italian text. A variant is in Gherardo Nerucci, "Storie e cantari, ninne-nanne e indovinelli del Montale," *Archivio per lo Studio delle Tradizioni Popolari* 3 (1884):56.

44. Collected in Pietrasanta, 1977; see Appendix for Italian text.

45. Collected in Pietrasanta, 1977; see Appendix for Italian text. A variant is in Corsi, "Indovinelli senesi," p. 404.

46. Renato Fucini, "Nuovi Sonetti," in his *Tutti gli scritti*, p. 958; it is sonnet 43.

47. Nerucci, "Storie e cantari ninne-nanne e indovinelli del Montale," p. 56. See also Rua, p. 450. I collected the first two verses in Pietrasanta, 1977; see Appendix for Italian text.

48. Rua, p. 455. I collected it in Panzano in 1978; see Appendix for Italian text.

49. Collected in Castellina in Chianti, 1978; see Appendix for Italian text. A version is in Rua, p. 459.

50. Collected in Poggibonsi, 1978; see Appendix for Italian text. A version is in Lapucci, *Indovinelli italiani*, p. 74.

51. Collected in Poggibonsi, 1978; see Appendix for Italian text. A version is in Corsi, "Indovinelli popolari raccolti in Siena," p. 188.

52. For a discussion of this functional aspect of the folkloristic performance, see William Bascom, "Four Functions of Folklore," *Journal of American Folklore* 67 (1954):349.

53. Compare Rua, p. 451:

What is it that tells the difference
between men and women?
          [a beret]

54. This disruption of the "rules of the game" is a simultaneous breaking of the *illusio* and of the codified rules of involvement and interaction. On the subject, see Erving Goffman, *Interaction Ritual* (Garden City: Doubleday, 1967): the "vocabulary of embarrassment" is discussed on pp. 99–104 and the problem of the offense on pp. 113–114.

55. The elements relevant to verbal strategy are underlined by Roger Abrahams in "Introductory Remarks to a Rhetorical Theory of Folklore," *Journal of American Folklore* 81 (1968):143–158. See also Thomas Burns, "Riddling: Occasion to Act," *Journal of American Folklore* 89 (1976):139–165; and David Evans, "Riddling and the Structure of Context," *Journal of American Folklore* 89 (1976):166–188.

56. Mentioned as a "trap" in Corsi, "Indovinelli senesi," p. 399. For other, non-Tuscan, versions of this very common riddle, see Michele Barbi, *Poesia popolare italiana*, p. 138.

59. Various examples are quoted and described by Pitré; see "Dello scioglilingua e delle sue relazioni con l'indovinello e col chiapparello," *Archivio per lo Studio delle Tradizioni popolari* 16 (1897):3–12, and in Corsi, "Indovinelli popolari raccolti in Siena," p. 190.

58. Imbriani, *La novellaja fiorentina*, pp. 567–568. This kind of catch-tale is a standard category in the Aarne-Thompson canon; see, for instance, AT 2200.

59. For a theoretical discussion of answers to riddles, see Dan Ben-Amos, "Solutions to Riddles," *Journal of American Folklore* 89 (1976):249–254.

60. Some general remarks about lullabies are in Bess Lomax-Hawes, "Folksongs and Function: Some Thoughts on the American Lullaby," *Journal of American Folklore* 87 (1974):140–148.

61. Collected in Castellina Scalo, 1978; see Appendix for Italian text. This is one of the most common Tuscan lullabies. A version is in Giannini, *Canti popolari toscani*, pp. 6–7. Sung versions are in A. Virgilio Savona (ed.), *Cantilene filastrocche e ninne-nanne*, Vedette VPA 8092, side B; and Daisy Lumini, *Daisy come Folklore*, I Dischi dello Zodiaco VPA 8157, side B.

62. Collected in Colle Valdelsa, 1977; see Appendix for Italian text. A version is in Giannini, *Canti popolari toscani*, p. 9.

63. Collected in Castellina in Chianti, 1978; see Appendix for Italian text. The first three are among the least common, but the last one is well known; see Cioni, *Il poema mugellano*, p. 217. A sung version is in Dodi Moscati, *Ti converrà mangiare i' pan pentito*, Cetra Lp 291, side A.

64. Collected in Certaldo, 1975; see Appendix for Italian text. A version is in Giannini, *Canti popolari toscani*, pp. 4–5.

65. Collected in Certaldo, 1975; see Appendix for Italian text. This lullaby is somehow related to one of the most famous of Boccaccio's tales;

see Alessandro Falassi: "Il Boccaccio e il folklore di Certaldo" in *Boccaccio Secoli di Vita*, ed. Marga Cottino-Jones and Edward Tuttle, pp. 265–292.

66. Collected in Empoli, 1978; see Appendix for Italian text. A version from Siena is in Giovanbattista Corsi, "Sena vetus," *Archivio per lo studio delle Tradizioni Popolari* 10 (1891):250.

67. Collected in Castelfiorentino, 1978; see Appendix for Italian text.

68. Collected in Empoli, 1978; see Appendix for Italian text.

69. These two very uncommon lullabies were quoted in Corsi, "Sena vetus," pp. 250–251. These versions, still sung in Tuscany, were kindly provided by folk singer Caterina Bueno; see Appendix for Italian text.

70. On these figures, see Francesca Alexander, *Roadside Songs of Tuscany*, pp. 96–97; Alfredo Giannini, *Ninne-nanne e giuochi fanciulleschi*, *nozze* [for the marriage] Saviotti-Bicchielli, Lullabies, nos. 2 and 10; Giannini, *Canti popolari toscani*, p. 9.

71. See Glauco Carloni, "I mostri delle fiabe," *Atlante* 7 (1967):70–77. For a general approach to frightening figures, see John Widdowson, "The Bogeyman," *Folklore* 82 (1971):99–115. A psychoanalytical discussion of ogres is in Géra Róheim, "The Nature of Ogres," in *The Gates of the Dream* 2d ed., pp. 355–405 (New York: International Universities Press, 1970).

72. See Giuseppe Giusti, *Epistolario*, I, 6.

73. Giuseppe Cocchiara, *Il linguaggio della poesia popolare* (Palermo: Palumbo, 1951), pp. 171–173.

74. A very common Tuscan saying says, "better a dead man in the house than a Pisan at the door," including in this way the Pisans among the negative entities which are evoked for children.

75. For the narcotic function of the fairy tales according to the same process, see Carloni, "I mostri delle fiabe," pp. 70–77.

76. Collected in Certaldo, 1975; see Appendix for Italian text. A version is in Dante Priore, *Canti popolari della valle dell'Arno*, p. 141.

77. Collected in Certaldo, 1975; see Appendix for Italian text. For other versions, see Giannini, *Canti popolari toscani*, p. 20; Francesco Corazzini, *I componimenti minori della letteratura popolare italiana nei principali dialetti*, p. 29. Alessandro de Gubernatis, *Le tradizioni popolari di Santo Stefano di calcinaia* (Rome: Forzani, 1894), p. 91; Bacci, *Ninne-nanne*, p. 56; Priore, *Canti popolari della valle dell'Arno*, p. 134. A sung version is in Lumini, *Daisy come Folklore*, side A.

For versions, see Giannini, *Canti popolari toscani*, p. 8; Bacci, *Ninne-nanne*, p. 19. See Appendix for Italian text.

79. Collected in Castelfiorentino, 1978; see Appendix for Italian text. A version is in Giannini, *Canti popolari toscani*, p. 3.

80. Collected in Castelfiorentino, 1978; see Appendix for Italian text. A version is in ibid., p. 4.
81. Collected in Castelfiorentino, 1978; see Appendix for Italian text. A version is in ibid., p. 9.
82. Collected in Castelfiorentino, 1978; see Appendix for Italian text. A version is in ibid., p. 8.
83. Collected in Castelfiorentino, 1978; see Appendix for Italian text. A version is in Cioni, *Il poema mugellano*, p. 216.
84. Teaching children prayers at this time is a centuries-old custom. See Alexander, *Roadside Songs of Tuscany*, p. 340, and Manfredi, *Mondo allegro*, p. 78.
85. Collected in Colle Valdelsa, 1975; see Appendix for Italian text.
86. Collected in Colle Valdelsa, 1975; see Appendix for Italian text.
87. Collected in Calenzano, 1977; see Appendix for Italian text. A version is in Cioni, *Il poema mugellano*, p. 215.
88. Collected in Fiesole, 1976; see Appendix for Italian text. My informant remembered it as a fragment of a much longer sequence. A longer text is in Giannini, *Canti popolari toscani*, pp. 54–56. For other Italian versions, see Barbi, *Poesia popolare italiana*, p. 38. Barbi collected 64 versions of this rhyme. Its length varies greatly: Vittorio Santoli mentions a minimum of 18 verses (known in Pisa and Arezzo) and a maximum of 146 (in Sambuca); see *I canti popolari italiani* (Florence: Sansoni, 1940), p. 115.

4. COURTING IN THE EVENING

1. The *stornello* (sometimes called "flower," or "refrain," or "motet") has various forms. It consists of a single strophe of three hendecasyllables or a quinary plus and two hendecasyllables, with an assonance between the first and third lines of verse and an atonic consonance of the second verse; see Cocchiara, *Il linguaggio della poesia popolare*, p. 35. For the origins of this form of folk poetry, see Alessandro d'Ancona, *La poesia popolare italiana* (Leghorn: Giusti, 1906), pp. 353–362. D'Ancona gives the hypothesis of an Etruscan origin to these *stornelli*. Different opinions are found in Giuseppe Cocchiara, *Le origini della poesia popolare* (Turin: Boringhieri, 1966), p. 95; and Giuseppe Pitré, *Studi di poesia popolare* (Palermo: Pedone-Lauriel, 1872). For a detailed theoretical discussion on the *stornello*, see Alberto M. Cirese, "Revisione di nozioni correnti: Lo stornello," in *Studi in onore di C. Naselli* (Catania: Università di Catania, 1978), pp. 87–107. In common language, my informants also designate as *stornello* a four-line song resulting, according to them, from abbreviation of an octave.

The *rispetto* seems to many authoritative scholars to be "a popular treatment of the octave, developed in Tuscany" (see Santoli, *I canti popolari italiani*, p. 23). The fundamental scheme of the *rispetto* is ABABCCDD, or a tetrastich in alternate rhyme and a repeat in rhyming couplets. The *rispetto* is often considered a variety of the *strambotto* (see ibid., p. 47). According to Santoli, the *rispetto* passed from Tuscany to other regions in central Italy, and then to the north and south (p. 68). According to d'Ancona, the *strambotto* originally came from Sicily but assumed its definitive form in Tuscany, from which it was passed to other regions (see *La poesia popolare italiana*, pp. 323–324). For *rispetti* and *strambotti* in "cultured" literary poetry, see pp. 157–158. Nearly all my informants used the terms *rispetti* and *octaves* indifferently for strophes of eight hendecasyllables sung individually and with the ABABABCC rhyme. D'Ancona "and his talented friends Nigra and Schuchardt" are of the opinion that all the forms of such songs are derived from an original Sicilian tetrastich (see p. 352). For a discussion of this problem, see also Barbi, *Poesia popolare italiana*, pp. 24–34.

2. "The Tuscan peasant thinks of nothing else but love, and when he has lost it, he gives up his faith, his fatherland and everything else": this contrasts popular Tuscan poetry with that of other regions; see Ermalao Rubieri, *Storia della poesia popolare italiana* (Florence: Barbera, 1877), p. 540. Rubieri qualifies Tuscan love poetry as being "moral, kind, chaste, and affectionate" (p. 658), and as regards the content, he finds affection, chastity, and delicacy "which we could gladly call platonic, if we could not more clearly and genuinely call it Tuscan" (p. 626). The fact that Tuscan songs are motivated by love has hit collectors and scholars in the eye. "It is a historic fact, of a certain signification, that all the songs are love songs," wrote Gino Capponi to Tigri, for example (see Tigri, *Canti popolari toscani*, p. xxii). Cioni himself, when arranging his collected folk songs, declared to have followed "the gradual process of amorous passion" (see Cioni, *Il poema mugellano*, p. 14).

3. For the same process in African proverbs, see E. Ojo Arewa and Alan Dundes, "Proverbs and the Ethnography of Speaking Folklore," *American Anthropologist* 66, no. 2 (1964):70.

4. The social control in the performance of *stornelli* could take place by sporadic contextual comments made by members of the *veglia* after each song or, if the *stornelli* were many and sung in succession, by intervening in the performance itself. In the latter case, the group sang the fixed-form refrain. This invariable *ritornello* "framed" the individual invention, statement, and style into the organized, fixed, and

redundant folk song style and performance. For an extensive general treatment of this kind of mechanism, see Erving Goffman, *Frame Analysis: An Essay on the Organization of Experience* (New York: Harper, 1974).

5. Collected in 1973 at Montevarchi; see Appendix for Italian text.

6. Collected in 1973 at Montevarchi; see Appendix for Italian text. For a version, see Tigri, *Canti popolari toscani*, p. 325.

7. Collected in 1973 at Montevarchi; see Appendix for Italian text. A version is in Giovanni Giannini, *Canti popolari della montagna lucchese*, p. 13.

8. Collected in 1975 in Barberino di Mugello; see Appendix for Italian text.

9. Collected in 1973 at Montevarchi; see Appendix for Italian text. A version is in Giannini, *Canti popolari della montagna lucchese*, p. 324.

10. Collected in 1975 in Barberino di Mugello; see Appendix for Italian text.

11. Collected in 1975 in Barberino di Mugello; see Appendix for Italian text. It is one of the best known traditional *stornelli*. See a version in Cioni, *Il poema mugellano*, p. 24.

12. Collected in 1975 in Barberino di Mugello; see Appendix for Italian text. A version is in ibid., p. 323.

13. Collected at San Gusmé in 1974; see Appendix for Italian text.

14. Collected in 1975 in Barberino di Mugello; see Appendix for Italian text. A version is in the booklet *Stornelli nostrali* (Florence: Libreria Editrice Fiorentina, 1973), p. 5.

15. Collected in 1975 in Barberino di Mugello; see Appendix for Italian text.

16. Collected in 1975 in Barberino di Mugello; see Appendix for Italian text. A version is in Tigri, *Canti popolari toscani*, p. 370.

17. Collected in Fonterutoli in 1973; see Appendix for Italian text.

18. Collected in Fonterutoli in 1973; see Appendix for Italian text.

19. Collected in Fonterutoli in 1973; see Appendix for Italian text. A version is in Roberto Leydi, *Canti popolari italiani* (Milan: Mondadori, 1973, p. 164.

20. Collected in Fonterutoli in 1973; see Appendix for Italian text. A version is in ibid., pp. 163–164, where the music is also given. It is one of the most common *stornelli*.

21. The song in dialogue form in the Tuscan countryside also attracted the attention of Corso (see *Patti d'amore e pegni di promessa*, p. 29).

22. Collected in San Sano, 1973; see Appendix for Italian text. A version is in Tigri, *Canti popolari toscani*, p. 326.

23. Collected in San Sano, 1973; see Appendix for Italian text. A version is in ibid., p. 336. In the version collected by Tigri, the third verse reads: "And there the great chain will be broken."

24. Collected in San Sano, 1973; see Appendix for Italian text. A version is in ibid., p. 336.
25. Collected in Montevarchi in 1974; see Appendix for Italian text.
26. Collected at Montevarchi in 1974; see Appendix for Italian text. A version is in Cioni, *Il poema mugellano*, p. 36.
27. Collected at Montevarchi in 1974; see Appendix for Italian text. For a version of this folk song but without the repetition of the second verse, see Giuseppe Cocchiara, *L'anima del popolo italiano nei suoi canti* (Milan: Hoepli, 1929), p. 162. There is another version in Grace Warrack, *Florilegio di canti toscani: Folk Songs of the Tuscan Hills*, p. 34.
28. Collected at Montevarchi, 1974; see Appendix for Italian text.
29. Giusti, *Raccolta di proverbi toscani*, p. 350: "A buon intenditor, poche parole."
30. Collected in Cutigliano, 1976; see Appendix for Italian text. A version is in Cioni, *Il poema mugellano*, p. 40.
31. Collected in Barga, 1971; see Appendix for Italian text. A version is sung by folk singer Dodi Moscati, who also collected it in the same area; see *La miseria l'è un gran malanno*, Cetra 11p 265, side B.
32. Collected in Sesto Fiorentino, 1975. A version is sung in Florentine style in the record by Carlo Buti, *Stornelli fiorentini*, EMI-Columbia SEMQ 201, side A.
33. A list of all Tuscan fairs and markets is printed every year in *lunari*, booklets containing miscellaneous information for farmers. The most famous of these is the *Sesto Caio Baccelli*, published in thousands of copies. See, for instance, *Il vero Sesto Caio Baccelli* (Florence: Ofiria, 1978), in which fairs and markets, divided by provinces, are listed chronologically.
34. The account of the custom to go to the fair to look at women and of the custom of "gallant young men to make the country girls blush" is found in Mannucci, *Bisenzio tradizioni e cucina*, pp. 56–57, 66. For a detailed report of one of such visits that ended in marriage, see Ferdinando Anichini, "Il Mangana," *Notiziario del Chianti Classico* 3, no. 12 (1970):11–12. More rarely peasants went to the cities for the weekly markets there.
35. In a *rispetto* a girl sings to her lover:

> I go to church and cannot bear to remain,
> Nor can I bear to say the Ave Maria;
> I go to church and cannot say a word,
> Because I always have your beautiful name to think of.

See Tigri, *Canti popolari toscani*, p. 70. And, sung by a woman, a *stornello*:

Fennel flower,
How long is that priest going to say Mass?
Outside I have my love who is singing and whistling.

In Giannini, *Canti popolari della montagna lucchese*, p. 30.

36. Collected in Rosia, 1975; see Appendix for Italian text.
37. Collected in Montalcino, 1975; see Appendix for Italian text. A version is in Cioni, *Il poema mugellano*, p. 108.
38. Collected in Sesto Fiorentino, 1978; see Appendix for Italian text. A version is in ibid., p. 97; also see n. 3 on the same page.
39. Collected in Sesto Fiorentino, 1978; see Appendix for Italian text. A version is in ibid., p. 58. In the folk song there is also a hint at the "dangers" of love when the couple remains alone. In fact, talking in everyday language, when one wants to say that some girl is pregnant, one uses the euphemism "his feet have slipped."
40. Collected in Sesto Fiorentino, 1978; see Appendix for Italian text. A variant is in ibid., p. 58. The second verse reads, "do not come with little silk shoes."
41. The use is referred to in ibid., p. 58 n. 2.
42. Ibid., p. 125; see Appendix for Italian text. There is another version in Alfonso Pisaneschi, "Maremma amara," *Il Folklore Italiano* 1 (1926):366. A version is sung in the style of Siena in Gruppo Folk Senese, *E mentre Siena dorme*," Playphone MABL 11004, side B.
43. Collected in Stia, 1977; see Appendix for Italian text. A version is in Giannini, *Canti popolari toscani*, p. 209.
44. Collected in Calenzano, 1975; see Appendix for Italian text. For a version of the last century, see Tigri, *Canti popolari toscani*, p. 321. A sung version is in Alfredo Bianchini, *A veglia in Toscana*, EMI-La Voce del Padrone 3C.051.17622, side B.
45. Collected in Calenzano, 1975; see Appendix for Italian text. A version is in Tigri, *Canti popolari toscani*, p. 58.
46. The glance as a means of communication in determinate social situations is discussed in its different functions in Michael Argyle, Roger Ingham, Florisse Alkema, and Margaret McCallin, "The Different Functions of Gaze," *Semiotica* 7, no. 1 (1973):19–32.
47. Cioni, *Il poema mugellano*, p. 28.
48. Giannini, *Canti popolari della montagna lucchese*, p. 8.
49. Collected in Stia, 1977; see Appendix for Italian text. A version is in Cioni, *Il poema mugellano*, p. 43.
50. Collected in Calenzano, 1976; see Appendix for Italian text. A version is in ibid., p. 47.
51. Collected in 1973 at Panzano; see Appendix for Italian text.

52. Collected at Panzano, 1975; see Appendix for Italian text. Compare the following *rispetto*:

I see a little horse that through sheer joy goes
To the middle of a field where he is tied;
Round and round and the rope gets knotted,
And he always remains in the area in which he is tied;
Man is like this, when he is in love,
He believes to be untied, yet it is now that he becomes bound.
So is man, when he is in love:
He thinks he is unbound but he is tied.

See Giannini, *Canti popolari della montagna lucchese*, p. 131. And also the folk song:

I saw a little horse running for joy
In a green field.
Round and round, the rope becomes knotted once again,
And he always comes back to where he is tied.

It is in Cioni, *Il poema mugellano*, p. 155.
53. Tigri, *Canti popolari toscani*, p. 352.
54. Cioni, *Il poema mugellano*, p. 49. Warrack, *Florilegio di canti toscani*, p. 32. See Appendix for Italian text.
55. The *stornelli* in this sequence are variants of well-known ones; see Appendix for Italian text. The first recalls one by Tigri, *Canti popolari toscani*, p. 347. The second is later quoted by Tigri on the same page. See also Cioni, *Il poema mugellano*, p. 47, for the first two.
56. Collected in Rosia, 1976; see Appendix for Italian text. A version is in Cioni, *Il poema mugellano*, p. 114. The "novena" was a religious function that took place on nine consecutive days before a special holiday.
57. Collected in Sesto Fiorentino, 1977; see Appendix for Italian text. A version is in ibid., p. 110.
58. Collected in Sesto Fiorentino, 1977; see Appendix for Italian text. A version is in ibid., p. 102.
59. Collected in Sesto Fiorentino, 1977; see Appendix for Italian text. A version is in ibid., p. 93.
60. Collected in Castelfiorentino, 1978; see Appendix for Italian text.
61. Collected in Calenzano, 1977; see Appendix for Italian text.
62. Collected in Marina di Grosseto from Eugenio Bargagli, singer of tales, and his daughter Mirella, folk singer; see Appendix for Italian text.

For a recorded version see Mirella Bargagli, *Stornelli a disprezzo*, Combo G128 (45), side A.

63. Collected these *stornelli* from Lucca from folk singer Dodi Moscati; see Appendix for Italian text. For a sung version, see her *La miseria l'è un gran malanno*, side B.

64. See Rubieri, *Storia della poesia popolare italiana*, p. 550.

65. Collected in Barga, 1971; see Appendix for Italian text. The same folk song, but in two verses, is to be found in Giannini, *Canti popolari della montagna lucchese*, p. 88.

66. Collected in Cutigliano, 1976; see Appendix for Italian text. A version is in ibid., p. 45.

67. Collected in Fiesole, 1976; see Appendix for Italian text..

68. Collected in Quercegrossa in 1974; see Appendix for Italian text.

69. Collected in Fiesole, 1976; see Appendix for Italian text. A version is in Cioni, *Il poema mugellano*, p. 116.

70. Collected in Fiesole, 1976; see Appendix for Italian text. A version is in Giannini, *Canti popolari della montagna lucchese*, p. 56.

71. Collected in Cecina, 1975; see Appendix for Italian text. A version is in ibid., p. 572.

72. Collected in Cecina, 1975; see Appendix for Italian text. A version is in ibid., p. 38.

73. Collected in Casciano di Murlo, 1975; see Appendix for Italian text. A version is in ibid., p. 41.

74. Collected in Fiesole, 1978; see Appendix for Italian text.

75. Collected in Pontassieve, 1978, from folk singer Caterina Bueno; see Appendix for Italian text.

76. Collected at Quercegrossa in 1974; see Appendix for Italian text.

77. The distinction is in De Gubernatis, *Storia comparata degli usi nuziali*, p. 65.

78. Collected in Cecina, 1978; see Appendix for Italian text.

79. Collected in Poppi, 1975; see Appendix for Italian text. A version is in Cioni, *Il poema mugellano*, p. 61.

80. Collected in San Quirico d'Orcia, 1976; see Appendix for Italian text. A version is in ibid., p. 61.

81. Both collected in Cecina, 1978; see Appendix for Italian text.

82. Collected in Figline Valdarno, 1976; see Appendix for Italian text.

83. Collected in Figline Valdarno, 1976; see Appendix for Italian text. A version is in Cioni, *Il poema mugellano*, p. 62.

84. Collected in Cutigliano, 1976; see Appendix for Italian text. Both refrains quoted in Alexander, *Roadside Songs of Tuscany*, p. 242.

85. Collected in Mercatale Valdipesa, 1976; see Appendix for Italian text.

86. Collected in Mercatale Valdipesa, 1976; see Appendix for Italian text.

A version is in Cioni, *Il poema mugellano*, p. 63.

87. Collected in Campi Bisenzio, 1976; see Appendix for Italian text. A version is in ibid., p. 61.

88. Collected in Calenzano, 1977; see Appendix for Italian text. A version is in ibid., p. 62.

89. Version collected at Greve in 1973; see Appendix for Italian text.

90. Collected in Campi Bisenzio, 1975; see Appendix for Italian text. A version is in Cioni, *Il poema mugellano*, p. 62.

91. Ibid., p. 157. See also the version in Giannini, *Canti popolari della montagna lucchese*, p. 37. Both are in three lines of verse. My version originates from San Gusmé; see Appendix for Italian text.

92. Temistocle Gradi, *Racconti popolari*, pp. 97–98. The girl replies to the man who is in love with her: "I shall stand by what my family does."

93. Giannini, *Canti popolari della montagna lucchese*, p. 89.

94. Ibid., p. 45.

95. Collected in Pietrasanta, 1978; see Appendix for Italian text.

96. Collected in Montevarchi, 1974; see Appendix for Italian text. For some of such folk songs, see, for instance, Riccardo Marasco, Chi cerca trova: Vita e canti di Toscana, pp. 138–139, 179–183.

97. Tigri, *Canti popolari toscani,*, p. 155. I owe the citations through note 103 to folk singer Caterina Bueno, who collected them in the years 1976–78 while doing a joint project with me for the Italian Radio. All these texts are still sung in the area of Pontassieve.

98. Ibid., p. 153.

99. Ibid., pp. 157–158.

100. Ibid., p. 158.

101. Ibid.

102. Ibid., p. 155.

103. See Appendix for Italian text. Ibid., p. 157.

104. Collected in Cutigliano, 1976; see Appendix for Italian text. See ibid., p. 159.

105. Collected in Cutigliano, 1976; see Appendix for Italian text. A version is in ibid., p. 157.

106. Pitré studied the swallow in the various types of folklore and in various cultures, *La rondinella nelle tradizioni popolari* (Rome: Società Editrice del Libro Italiano, 1941).

107. Collected in Empoli, 1976; see Appendix for Italian text. A version is in Tigri, *Canti popolari toscani*, p. 179. For other *rondinelle*, see Marasco, *Chi cerca trova*, pp. 172–177, and Priore, *Canti popolari della valle dell'Arno*, p. 99. The text and music of another *rondinelle* from the Risorgimento are in Luigi Neretti, *Fiorita di canti popolari toscani*, III, 36–37. A sung version is in Lumini, *Daisy come Folklore*, side A.

108. A choice of such letter texts, sung as imaginary letters or sent in the form of real letters, is in Tigri, *Canti popolari toscani*, pp. 183–192.

109. See ibid., pp. 182, 183; they are the formulaic opening of different *rispetti*.

110. For this well-known text, see the uncommon variant in Marasco, *Chi cerca trova*, pp. 76–77. Compare it to the six-verse version in Niccolò Tommaseo, *Canti popolari toscani, corsi, illirici, greci*, I, 192. Collected in the region of Pistoia; see Appendix for Italian text. Sung versions are in Caterina Bueno, *In giro per la Toscana*, Amico ZMKF 55033, side B, and in Lumini, *Daisy come Folklore*, side A.

111. Collected in Carrara, 1978; see Appendix for Italian text. A version is in Tigri, *Canti popolari toscani*, p. 195.

112. Collected in Pontassieve, 1978; see Appendix for Italian text.

113. Collected in Buonconvento, 1975; see Appendix for Italian text. A version sung in the Sienen style is in Enzo Bini and Giorgio Tancredi, *Da mille serenate*, OLS 5, side A.

114. Collected in Pontassieve, 1976; see Appendix for Italian text. See *Stornelli nostrali*, p. 18.

115. Collected in Carrara; see Appendix for Italian text. A version in Raffaele Corso, *Das Geschlechtleben in Sitte, Brauch, Glauben und Gewohneitrecht des Italienischen Volkes* (Nicotera: Published by the author, 1914), p. 175.

116. A sung version of these two *stornelli* is in Sergio Landini and Maurizio Ferretti (eds.), *Canti popolari della provincia di Pistoia*, PT 01, side B. See Appendix for Italian text.

117. Collected in Pietrasanta, 1977; see Appendix for Italian text. A version is in Cioni, *Il poema mugellano*, p. 74.

118. Collected in Cecina, 1977; see Appendix for Italian text. A version is in ibid., p. 123; also see n. 4 on the same page.

119. For a comparison of syntagmatic elements of the story with the syntagmatic elements of a superstition taken from the same cultural context, see Dundes, *The Morphology of North American Indian Folktales*, p. 106.

120. Collected at Gaiole in 1973; see Appendix for Italian text. It is also found in Giannini, *Canti popolari della montagna lucchese*, p. 31.

121. Collected in Pontassieve, 1976; see Appendix for Italian text.

122. Collected in Piancastagnaio, 1976; see Appendix for Italian text. A similar text is reported by Tigri, *Canti popolari toscani*, p. 360.

123. This verse is quoted in Giannini, *Canti popolari della montagna lucchese*, p. 28.

124. Proverb; see Giusti, *Raccolta di proverbi toscani*, p. 125: "can che abbaia non morde."

125. See Appendix for Italian text. A version of this song exists in Giannini,

Canti popolari della montagna lucchese, pp. 203–207. For more recent versions, see Paolo Toschi, *Poesia e vita di popolo* (Venice: Montuoro, 1946), p. 222; Alessandro Fornari, *Canti toscani*, pp. 128–131; or Ivo Guasti and Franco Manescalchi, *La barriera*, pp. 19–21 for the text and p. 162 for the music. A fragment is in Marasco, *Chi cerca trova*, pp. 83–85. A fragment is sung in Caterina Bueno, *La veglia*, I dischi del Sole DS 155/57 CL, side A. In Tuscan folklore there are various texts in praise of shepherds, and they are often sung by women. See:

Who loves a shepherd loves something;
He returns in May and seems a rose;
Who loves a shepherd loves a beautiful flower;
He returns in May and seems a gentleman.

It is in Warrack, *Florilegio di canti toscani*, p. 60.

126. This type of conversation, held amid noises, "hearsay," eyewitnesses, and oral tradition, is very common at these evening singsongs. A discussion on concepts of noise, eyewitnesses, and oral tradition is to be found in Jan Vansina, "De la tradition orale: Essai de methode historique," *Annales du Musée Royal de l'Afrique Centrale* 36 (1961):22–23. See also Chapter 5.

127. For obscene humor regarding zoophily, see Legman, *Rationale of the Dirty Joke*, pp. 206–216. A large number of texts related by Legman deal with sheep and shepherds.

128. Connected to ethnocentrism is the opposition we/the others; in everyday Tuscan use, the couple "we ourselves/you yourselves" clearly indicates the reciprocal division of both groups. For a discussion on this paradigmatic opposition, see William Hugh Jansen, "The Esoteric-Exoteric Factor in Folklore," *Fabula* 2 (1959):205–211. Jansen discusses not only opposition, but also its different and reciprocal cultural perception in two groups, with examples like "They believe that we believe that they are inferior."

129. See, for a report of such small talk, Alexander, *Roadside Songs of Tuscany*, pp. 127–128.

130. This version was sung right through by an old peasant; see Appendix for Italian text. On other occasions it could be sung by a woman, or a man and a woman, in dialogue form. Another version collected in the same village from a woman contains the verse "I have in my heart a great love for you," instead of the other, less chaste, "If you make love to me, it will bring you great pleasure." Sung versions are in Dodi Moscati, *E rigiramelo i' pensiero*, Cetra 11p 332, I, side A. The ver-

sion is from Certaldo. A version from Sestino (Areszzo Province) is "Canzoniere internaizionale," *Siam venuti a cantar Maggio*, 11p 261, side A; a version from Pistoia is in Landini and Ferretti (eds.), *Canti popolari della provincia di Pistoia*, side B. The large diffusion of this folk song may be partially due to a leaflet printed last century and sold in the squares at fairs by storytellers. See it reproduced in Marasco, *Chi cerca trova*, pp. 89–91.

In a Tuscan version of the "Three sailors that go out to sea," the sailor refuses the offer of the girl's father:

I shall give you my daughter
If you swear
Not to touch her for seven years.

The young couple leave together, but, having arrived half-way, the boat sinks and the girl drowns. So her father concludes:

But even if I had another five hundred,
I would not like to give another one to a sailor.

See Santoli, *I canti popolari italiani*, pp. 130–131.

131. See Giusti, *Raccolta di proverbi toscani*, p. 90. Another group that, as elsewhere, in Tuscany was the object of traditional derogatory comments was that of gypsies. "Child of a gypsy" was a common insult, synonymous to "child of a strumpet," i.e., prostitute. Francesca Alexander noted that, among the Tuscan peasants she met, a number were the outcome of marriages with gypsies. She chose one of these as her model; however, this was a defamatory origin and "she would probably not thank me for saying it" (see *Roadside Songs of Tuscany*, p. 150).

132. Collected in Marina di Grosseto, 1976; see Appendix for Italian text. A version is in Tigri, *Canti popolari toscani*, p. 373.

133. See Appendix for Italian text. Compare Giusti, *Raccolta di proverbi toscani*, p. 30.

134. Collected in Stia, 1978; see Appendix for Italian text. An old version from the same area is in Carlo Beni, *Guida illustrata del Casentino*, p. 79.

135. See Appendix for Italian text.

136. See Appendix for Italian text. There is a recent version by Lisetta, with the last verses missing, in Fornari, *Canti toscani*, pp. 45–47. For an older

version, see Giannini, *Canti popolari della montagna lucchese*, pp. 154–156. In other places, it is called "the return." See also Priore, *Canti popolari della valle dell'Arno*, pp. 171–173. Sung versions are in Bianchini, *A veglia in Toscana*, side B. The mention of the "sun that never sets" could refer to the reign of Charles V, as Fornari suggests, or less precisely to a mythical country, "other" by definition.

137. For a reference to the glance used as an indicator of closeness, see Michael Argyle and Roger Ingham, "Gaze, Mutual Gaze, and Proximity," *Semiotica* 6, no. 1 (1972): 32–49. For the affective connotations, see A. Rubin, "Measurement of Romantic Love," *Journal of Social Psychology* 16 (1970): 265–273. Just as the establishment of a visual contact indicates the beginning of a communication, so the interrupting of it is the most common indicator of the end of the communication.

> She does not find a beauty comparable to her own,
> With her eyes she projects love torches.
> Not only, but also:
> She has bewitching eyes,
> That with them she could pierce a wall.

See Lorenzo de' Medici, *Opere* (Bari: Laterza, 1939), II, 151–152. The image of Magnifico is not, however, far from that in the song collected by Tigri:

> When you enter the church door,
> You light the candles with your eyes.

See *Canti popolari toscani*, p. 22. For an *occhio manucano*, see Gradi, "Studi di lingua parlata," in *Saggio di letture varie per i giovani*, p. 46.

139. Collected in Radda, 1973; see Appendix for Italian text. It is a folk song of approach, sung by the man. A version is in Tigri, *Canti popolari toscani*, p. 133.

140. Collected in Radda, 1973; see Appendix for Italian text. This is a folk song containing a reply to the previous one; as a rule, it was sung by the woman. For a version, see the booklet *Stornelli nostrali*, p. 5. It is also in Tigri, *Canti popolari toscani*, p. 372, and in Cioni, *Il poema mugellano*, p. 44.

141. The *veduto* [having seen] is normally considered more valid than hearsay. The proverb reads that something seen is a hundred times better than something heard through others; see Appendix for Italian text. For the same cultural attitude in a different context, see Alan Dundes, "Seeing Is Believing," *Natural History* 81 (May 1972): 8–12, 86–87.

5. THE END OF THE *Veglia*

1. On the different aspects of this problem, see Roger D. Abrahams, "A Performance-Centered Approach to Gossip," *Man* 5 (1970):290–301. For a discussion of the transmission of such items of folklore, see Linda Dégh and Andrew Vazsonyi, "The Hypothesis of Multi-Conduit Transmission in Folklore," in *Folklore*, ed. Ben-Amos and Goldstein; Richard Bauman, *Verbal Art as Performance* (Rowley, Mass.: Newbury House, 1977).

2. Rubieri, *Storia della poeasia popolare italiana*, p. 572.

3. Cioni, *Il poema mugellano*, p. 158:

   Field in flower!
   Woman when she sings wants a husband,
   And man when he roams is in love.

4. The same is in the version from Lucca reproduced in Giannini's *Canti popolari della montagna lucchese*, p. 154.

5. Genoveffa is a standard European legend, related to the Aarne-Thompson Tale-Type 712. For a discussion of this legend, very popular among the Pennsylvania German folk culture, see Wayland D. Hand, *American Folk Legend: A Symposium* (Berkeley: University of California Press, 1971), pp. 164–171.

6. Corso, *Reviviscenze*, pp. 15–17, 25 n. 1.

7. A recent popular edition is Canonico Schmid, *Genoveffa: Recentemente esposta per gli uomini dabbene e specialmente per le madri e pei fanciulli* (Milan: Lucchi, 1970). It is difficult to ascertain the circulation, diffusion, and type of reader for this kind of popular literature. I was loaned a copy of this book in San Francisco by an old immigrant from Lucca. She had bought it in an Italian bookstore in San Francisco. For other versions, see, for instance, *Genoveffa / Storia degli antichi tempi / per le madri e pei fanciulli* (Florence: Salani, 1879). There are forty-six linked rhymed octaves. A recently published version also in forty-six octaves is sung by famous storyteller Aido Ferri, known as Giubba di Dicomano; see his pamphlet *La storia di Genoveffa* (Florence: Libreria Editrice Fiorentina, 1976). For the text of a Maggio [a dramatic folk-play] of Genoveffa, see *Maggio di Genoveffa di Bramante* (Volterra: Sborgi, 1887).

8. *Purgatory*, V, 130–136. Nello is Nello Pannocchieschi, who was suspected of having freed himself from his wife in order to marry Countess Margherita degli Aldobrandeschi, widow of Guido di Montfort.

9. Among many versions, see, for example, Bartolomeo Sestini, *Pia de' Tolomei, poesia* (Florence: Salani, 1885). Another edition of the same

poem with the name of the same author was printed in Siena in 1895 under the title *La Pia de' Tolomei: Leggenda romantica senese*.

10. The story of Pia is number 25 of the *Raccolta di canzonette bernesche in ottava rima cantate nelle conversazioni di amici e conoscenti* (Florence: Salani, 1874).

11. Giovanni Giannini, *La poesia popolare a stampa nel secolo XIX*, II, 418.

12. See *Pia de' Tolomei composta in ottava rima da Giuseppe Moroni detto il Niccheri illetterato* (Florence: Salani, [published between 1870 and 1880]). There are fifty-four linked rhymed octaves.

13. Mention of a Tuscan peasant folk drama of Pia in Montepulciano in 1939 and its performance can be found in Paolo Toschi, *La origini del teatro italiano* (Turin: Boringhieri, 1976), p. 377. The peasant comedy was performed "by authentic peasants" with hundreds of walk-ons. Mention of a performance of the same folk drama in 1974 at San Donato in Poggio is in *Notiziario del chianti classico* 7, no. 6 (June 1974):16. For a Maggio see the *Maggio della Pia de' Tolomei* (Volterra: Sborgi, 1867). There are 168 stanzas. A whole Maggio of the Pia is recorded in Gastone Venturelli (ed.), *Il Maggio*, Albatros VPA 8411, side A. The version is from the area of Lucca.

    For the versions in octaves, see the one collected in the area of Arezzo by Diego Carpitella. It is in the record *Original Folk and Ethnic Music of the People of Europe*, Albatros VPA 8286, I, side A.

14. See the pamphlet *Pia de' Tolomei: Composizione in ottava rima secondo la tradizione cantata* (Florence: Libreria Editrice Fiorentina, 1972).

15. Luigi Ugolini, *Leggende della Maremma* (Milan: L'Eroica, 1973), pp. 59–69. Ugolini notes that the people still sing Pia's story in rhymed octaves, and he cites some verses, such as, "I slandered her to you in your garden."

16. Katharine Hooker, *Byways in Southern Tuscany*, pp. 26–27. In the area of the castle of Pietra, Hooker heard some narratives in prose, passed down orally, according to which Pia killed herself by throwing herself out the window, as did desperate wives occasionally even in reality. I collected the same narratives and traditional beliefs in 1977 in the same area (around the village of Gavorrano) from Piero Simonetti.

17. Collected in Gavorrano, 1976; see Appendix for Italian text. A version is in Cioni, *Il poema mugellano*, p. 81.

18. Collected in Gavorrano, 1976; see Appendix for Italian text. A version is in ibid., p. 153.

19. Alexander, *Roadside Songs of Tuscany*, pp. 90–91.

20. See Appendix for Italian text.

21. Collected in Castellina in Chianti, 1978; see Appendix for Italian text. A fragment from the same area, collected in the fifties, is in Fornari,

Canti toscani, pp. 40–43. The melody is also reproduced there. Fornari notes that the song speaks of distance which makes the husband odious to the wife.

22. Many versions are cited and commented upon in Barbi, *Poesia popolare italiana*, pp. 49–64. Barbi deduces that this song was already popular during the first half of the 1500s.

23. This narrative structure is very common in the folk music of the British isles and in the United States. See N28 through N43 in G. Malcom Laws, Jr., *American Balladry from British Broadsides: A Guide for Students and Collectors of Traditional Song*, American Folklore Society Bibliographical and Special Series, no. 8 (Philadelphia, 1957).

24. Giannini, *Canti popolari della montagna lucchese*, p. 98; for other versions in other collections, see n. 635 on the same page. I collected this narrative in San Quirico d'Orcia, 1976. See Tigri, *Canti popolari toscani*, p. 373, for another version.

25. When their men were in Maremma, the evening song assumed a consolatory function for the wives left behind. This is observed in Alexander, *Roadside Songs of Tuscany*, pp. 5–6.

26. The married woman who looked downward in a modest attitude is commented on in ibid., p. 138.

27. The story, reported as a common occurrence, of a husband who left for Florence for a few days and of his wife who dressed in mourning until his return is in Duff-Gordon, *Home Life in Italy*, p. 144.

28. Ibid., pp. 365–366. Duff-Gordon tells of an immigrant who returns suddenly from America in secret. Even in reality, stories of "false pilgrims" are plentiful.

29. That is, honestly. Indeed, in a Tuscan saying, "Saint John doesn't want tricks" (see ibid., p. 366).

30. Cecilia is among the most known Tuscan folk songs. For a sung version, see Carpitella, *Original Folk and Ethnic Music of the People of Europe*, I, side B, or the more commercialized in Narciso Parigi, *Motivi e Ballate Popolari*, Fontana 6492.022, side A. Santoli, *I canti popolari italiani*, p. 117, confirms the diffusion of this folk song in all Tuscany. Under the title "Il marito giustiziere" it is well known throughout Italy.

31. For example, in the Dahomey culture, there is a subgroup of narratives in verse, generally sung as recitations and composed by professional poets for the specific purpose of recording genealogies; see Melville and Frances Herskovits, *Dahomean Narrative*, 3d ed. (Evanston: Northwestern University Press, 1970), p. 17. The knowledge of genealogies allows the Gwambe to speak with such precision, vivacity, and intimacy of people physically dead for centuries that unprepared anthropologists have frequently believed these narratives to be ocular testi-

monies; see Charles E. Fuller, "Ethnohistory in the Study of Culture Change," in *Continuity and Change in African Cultures*, ed. William Bascom and Melville Herskovits (Chicago: University of Chicago Press, 1959), p. 121.

32. Professor John Gumperz of the University of California at Berkeley also furnished me with data from his field work in India. There several of his interlocutors, when they wanted to establish a cordial social relationship, would often mention myths according to which Indian divinities married North American divinities, arriving laboriously at the conclusion of fictitious systems of kinship with their North American questioner and finally commenting on it all with satisfied phrases, such as, "Well, we are cousins" (personal communication).

33. For example, Paul Radin, *Primitive Man as a Philosopher* (New York: Appleton, 1927). Radin notes on p. 77 that "primitive people are indeed among the most persistent and inveterate of gossips." A psychological orientation is in Ralph Rosnow and Gary Alan Fine, *Rumor and Gossip: The Social Psychology of Hearsay* (New York: Elsevier, 1976); Raymond Firth, "Rumor in a Primitive Society," *Journal of Abnormal and Social Psychology* 53 (1956):122–132.

34. For the same conclusion in reference to Haiti, see Melville Herskovits, *Life in a Haitian Valley* (New York: Knopf, 1937), p. 74. The author considers gossiping an explicit and specific instrument for the maintenance of social moral standards.

35. Max Gluckman, "Gossip and Scandal," *Current Anthropology* 4, no. 3 (1963):313–314. A different approach, based on individual motivations in gossipers, is in Robert Paine, "What Is Gossip About? An Alternative Hypothesis," *Man* 2 (1967):278–285.

36. Rosa Minucci, who heard it in the thirties, always sung by men, referred this to me in 1975; see Appendix for Italian text.

37. Collected in Castellina in Chianti, 1975; see Appendix for Italian text. A version is in Giannini, *Canti popolari della montagna lucchese*, p. 19.

38. Collected in Barga, 1971; see Appendix for Italian text. A version is in ibid., p. 80.

39. Collected in Barga, 1971; see Appendix for Italian text. A version is in ibid., p. 89.

40. Collected in Pontassieve, 1977. This *stornello* could also be appropriately sung at the beginning of the *veglia*, by changing the word *goodnight* into *good evening*. See above, Chapter 4, n. 44.

41. Collected in Pontassieve, 1978. A version is in the booklet *Stornelli nostrali*, p. 24.

42. In Tuscan folklore, such symbolic stonings were inflicted on whoever had broken a rule of sexual behavior. Thus, stones were often thrown

at the house wherein two elderly persons were spending the first night of marriage. A Christian rite, interpreted as a vestige of stonings, which punished whoever had committed a sin of the flesh, is reported in Corso, *Patti d'amore e pegni di promessa*, pp. 95–103.

6. THE *Veglia* DANCE

1. For an account of a dance party organized by an English couple in their castle in Tuscany, see Duff-Gordon, *Home Life in Italy*, pp. 105–115. Some interesting details are in the twenty-three strophes of the pamphlet *Una festa da ballo* (Florence: Salani, 1885).

2. For an exposition of the reversal concept, compare Giuseppe Cocchiara, *Il mondo alla rovescia* (Turin: Boringhieri, 1963). A comprehensive series of theoretical essays is in Barbara Babcock (ed.), *The Reversible World: Symbolic Inversion in Art and Society* (Ithaca and London: Cornell University Press, 1978).

3. See Giusti, *Raccolta di proverbi toscani*, p. 306: "Di Carnovale ogni scherzo Vale."

4. Giusti, *Raccolta di proverbi toscani*, p. 530.

5. Ibid., p. 529.

6. See Claude Lévi-Strauss, "Babbo Natale Suppliziato," in *Razza e storia e altri studi di antropologia*, pp. 245–264 (Turin: Einaudi, 1967).

7. The practice of sprinkling salt can also be considered a trace of a ritual that assured fertility to the couples formed during the ball. For ritual and psychoanalytic meanings of salt, see Ernest Jones, *Essays in Applied Psychoanalysis* (London: Hogarth, 1951), II, 22–109.

8. For the analysis of comparative materials, see Thomas Burns and Doris Mack, "Social Symbolism in a Rural Square Dance Event," *Keystone Folklore Quarterly* (forthcoming). The authors conclude indicating an "umbrella of equality" and the prominence of the couple.

9. Giuseppe Giusti, *Prose e poesie*, p. 136.

10. See Gianfranco d'Aronco, *Storia della danza popolare e d'arte* (Florence: Olschki, 1962), p. 286.

11. The *trescone* is quoted by Temistocle Gradi in *Proverbi e modi di dire dichiarati con racconti*, p. 107. Erotic connotations are attributed to *trescone*. Compare the term *tresca*, which means "unorthodox love affair." Recorded examples are, for instance, in Moscati, *E rigiramelo i' pensiero*, I, side B; Lumini, *Daisy come Folklore*, side A.

12. The description of a *monferrina* (or *manfrina*) as a symbolic love hunt is found in Duff-Gordon, *Home Life in Italy*, pp. 316–317. *Manfrina* also means "amorous understanding."

13. For a detailed account of one of these *veglie*, see Giusti, *Prose e poesie*,

pp. 195–215. There are also scattered notes in Leader Scott, *Tuscan Studies and Sketches*, pp. 179–180.

14. The reader could find interesting comparative information regarding the Sunday afternoon dance in Sicily in Salomone-Marino, *Costumi e usanze dei contadini di Sicilia*, p. 154.

15. See Tony Cyriax, *Among Italian Peasants*, p. 34. The same happened in the dances of the Nordic villages. For extensive data parallel to those exposed here, see Matti Sarmela, *Reciprocity Systems of the Rural Society in the Finnish-Karelian Culture Area*, FFC, no. 207 (Helsinki, 1969), pp. 144–150.

16. Renato Bellabarba, *Proverbi toscani illustrati*, p. 28. He quotes it from Giusti's work.

17. Sometimes there were two in a village. Duff-Gordon observes (*Home Life in Italy*, p. 105) that the members of one were the poor and the peasants, and the members of the other were the village folk.

18. Many were scandalized by the fact that couple dancing, which originally only involved touching or holding hands, had in recent centuries degenerated into a lasting embrace of the upper part of the couple. See d'Aronco, *Storia della danza popolare in Italia*, p. 32. The author disappointedly remarks that *danza*, the original art form, has become *ballo*, just entertainment.

19. Sometimes he was called "President of the Ball." See Duff-Gordon (*Home Life in Italy*, p. 110) for this title and for the description of a dance that is *piu di scuola* [more classic], slower and more measured and dignified. To the contrary, he who enjoys himself the most "*Nel sollazzo non pone studio e non vi mesce vanità*" ["Amusement does not involve study and does not mix with vanity"]. That is to say, "He who dances badly amuses himself"; see Giusti, *Raccolta di proverbi toscani*, p. 446.

20. For this "scandalous" dance, see, for instance, Russel O. Salmon, "The Tango: Its Origins and Meaning," *Journal of Popular Culture* 10, no. 4 (1977):859–866.

21. Giusti, *Prose e poesie*, p. 133.

22. Cyriax, *Among Italian Peasants*, p. 20. This process of folklorization was common also in the 1800s. For a *risorgimento* anthem that became a "Cavour Polka," see Emilio Jona, *Le canzonette che fecero l'Italia* (Milan: Longanesi, 1962), pp. 44–46.

23. A general approach to this problem is in Diego Carpitella, *Musica popolare e musica di consumo* (Rome: Accademia di S. Cecilia, 1955).

24. Gramsci's thought also influenced greatly the Marxian approach to the study of folklore in Italy; see Sebastiano Lo Nigro, "A. Gramsci e la letteratura popolare," *Lares*, 1957, pp. 1–14.

25. A recorded version in Mirella e il Trio Marino, *Omaggio a Gramsci e Togliatti*, Fonola NP 2132, side A. It is sung by folk singer Mirella Bargagli, daughter of the famous folk poet Eugenio Bargagli of Marina di Grosseto. See Appendix for Italian text.

26. See the pamphlet by Guglielmo Amerighi, *Proverbi delle Donne* (Florence: Libreria Editrice Fiorentina, 1974), p. 17.

27. The expression is also used in metaphor. When one is "called to dance," one can reply, "I'm busy," "as women do to avoid bad company" (Giusti, *Epistolario*, II, 311).

28. My version was collected in Buonconvento in 1975; see Appendix for Italian text. A version is in Giannini, *Canti popolari toscani*, pp. 165–166.

29. Collected in San Gusmé, 1973; see Appendix for Italian text.

30. Collected in Castellina in Chianti, 1973; see Appendix for Italian text.

31. This text, in the Florentine Codice Riccardiano 2352 at the Riccardiana Library, is discussed in d'Ancona, *La poesia popolare italiana*, pp. 46–47.

32. Collected in Fonterutoli, 1973; see Appendix for Italian text.

33. An interesting term of comparison is Materiale Intronato [pseudonym of Girolamo Bargagli], *Dialogo dei giuochi che nelle vegghie senesi si usano fare* (Venice: G. A. Bertano, 1575). I received a copy of this important source through the kindness of Dr. Riccardo di Corato.

34. *Alò*, i.e., *suvvia*, from the French *allons* (Imbriani, *La novellaja fiorentina*, p. 29 n. 8). Many of these commands in domestic French are in "Sonettona," which opens Renato Fucini's volume of poetry, *Le poesie di Neri Tanfucio* (Milan: Trevisini, 1971), p. 27. The related form is *"Anavan le première."*

35. Fucini relates the *gran scena*; see *Le poesie di Neri Tanfucio*, p. 28.

36. Ibid., p. 30, *ciangè*.

37. Ibid., p. 30, *ballanzè*.

38. Ibid., p. 27, *scutiscià*.

39. Ibid., p. 34.

40. Collected in Radda, 1974; see Appendix for Italian text. A version is in Giannini, *Canti popolari tuscani*, p. 123.

41. Fucini, *Le poesie di Neri Tanfucio*, pp. 28–31.

42. See Corso, *Patti d'amore e pegni di promessa*, p. 109. Comparative data for the European area are in Ernest Crawley, *The Mystic Rose* (New York: Meridian Books, 1960), pp. 124–135.

43. My own grandfather was the Carnival in 1919–1924. For this traditional type of masquerade in which the Carnival is a king and a living person, see Toschi, *Le origini del teatro italiano*, pp. 123–130.

44. See d'Aronco, *Storia della danza popolare e d'arte*, pp. 32, 265–266.

45. These are the conclusions of J. Courtès and A. J. Greimas to be found

in "Cendrillon va au bal," typed article, Ecole Pratique des Hautes Etudes, Paris, 1973.

46. This fundamental concept is discussed by Lévi-Strauss in *Structural Anthropology*, pp. 60, 83.

47. Duff-Gordon, *Home Life in Italy*, p. 157.

7. THE OUTCASTS' COUNTER-*Veglia*

1. See *Il nuovissimo Melzi* (Milan: Vallardi, 1973), I, 137, entry, *bettola*.

2. Ibid., p. 831, entry *osteria*, and p. 1269 under *taverna*. Interesting remarks on the philosophy of the tavern are found in Hans Barth, *Osteria: Guida spirituale delle osterie italiane da Verona a Capri* (Rome: Enrico Voghera, 1909); and in T. Kleberg, "Romische Wirthshäuser und Weinstuben," *Alterum* 15, no. 3 (1969):146–161. For studies of functionally similar or cognate settings, see, for instance, Clara E. Richards, "City Taverns," *Human Organization* 22 (1963–64):260–268; or Sherri Cavan, *Liquor License: An Ethnography of Bar Behavior* (Chicago: Aldine, 1966).

3. Giusti, *Raccolta di proverbi toscani*, p. 223. Giusti also provides an extensive illustration of the proverb on pp. 403–405.

4. Ibid., p. 328.

5. Ibid., p. 24; another proverb, however, warns "Friends and wine must be old."

6. Ibid., p. 42. "The best wine is the one you drink with friends" (Rossi-Ferrini, *Proverbi agricoli*, p. 174).

7. The exchanging of wine as a significant indication of tavern reciprocity is discussed by Claude Lévi-Strauss in "Reciprocity, the Essence of Social Life," in *The Family: Its Structure and Functions*, ed. Rose Laub Coser, pp. 41–44 (New York: St. Martin's Press, 1964). See also Charles O Frake, "How to Ask for a Drink in Subanun," *American Anthropologist* 66, no. 6 (1964):127–132.

8. See Appendix for Italian text. For a version of this drinking song, see Roberto Brivio, *Canzoni sporche all'osteria* (Milan: Williams, 1973), p. 22.

9. Collected in Cutigliano, 1976, from a great grandson of Beatrice di Pian Degli Ontani, the famous folk poet to whom the octave is ascribed; see Appendix for Italian text.

10. Collected in San Gusmé, 1978; see Appendix for Italian text. A version is in Priore, *Canti della valle dell'Arno*, pp. 32–33.

11. Collected in Cecina, 1977; see Appendix for Italian text. A version of the last century, parodies of which were mocking Metternich and Austria's occupying troops, is in Marasco, *Chi cerca Trova*, pp. 164–

167. Another version is in Vincenzo Billi, *Celebri stornelli e canti popolari toscani*, p. 15.

12. Giusti, *Raccolta di proverbi toscani*, p. 319.

13. Ibid., p. 321. In a letter, Giusti describes an evening at the tavern with friends (see *Epistolario*, I, 19–20). The evening was made up of singing, arguing, joking, dancing in the streets, and hard drinking. Indeed, one of the group had to sleep with friends because he was too drunk to find his way home.

14. Giusti, *Raccolta di proverbi toscani*, p. 321.

15. Ibid., p. 319.

16. Ibid.

17. Ibid., p. 249.

18. Crawford, *Life in Tuscany*, p. 17.

19. Ecclesiasticus XXXI, 37.

20. Ibid., XXXI, 36.

21. Ibid., XXXI, 32. On the philosophy of drinking, see Paolo Mini, *Discorso sulla natura del vino delle sue differenze e del suo retto uso* (Florence: Marescotti, 1596).

22. Collected in Radda, 1975; see Appendix for Italian text.

23. Giusti, *Raccolta di proverbi toscani*, p. 320.

24. Ibid., p. 329.

25. Ibid., p. 319.

26. Ibid., p. 321.

27. Ibid., p. 239.

28. Collected in San Marcellino, 1975; see Appendix for Italian text.

29. Giusti, *Raccolta di proverbi toscani*, p. 320.

30. Ibid., p. 321.

31. Ibid.

32. Ibid., p. 320.

33. Ibid., p. 321.

34. Ibid., p. 320.

35. Ibid., p. 309.

36. Ibid., p. 319.

37. Ibid., p. 264.

38. Ludovico Zdekauer, *Il giuoco in Italia nei secoli XIII e XIV e specialmente in Firenze*.

39. A thorough and complete reference book is Alfredo Lenzi's *Bibliografia italiana di giuochi di carte* (Florence: Landi, 1892). For analysis of card playing as social behavior, see, for instance, Irving Frespi, "The Social Significance of Card Playing as a Leisure Time Activity," *American Sociological Review* 21 (1956):717–721.

40. Giusti, *Raccolta di proverbi toscani*, p. 109.

41. The text referred to here is the one relative to the province of Siena, published in 1970 by the Prefetto.

42. Cecco Angiolieri, *Rime* (Milan: Rizzoli, 1959). For example, see Sonnet LXXXVII on p. 99, which in many collections is entitled "Donna, Taverna e Dado" [Women, the Tavern, and Dice].

43. This is the letter to Francesco Vettori written on the tenth of December 1513; see Niccolò Machiavelli, *Lettere* (Milan: Feltrinelli, 1961), p. 303; see also Allan Gilbert, *The Letters of Machiavelli* (New York: Capricorn Books, 1961), p. 141.

44. Occasionally in Tuscan folklore, the Devil himself plays cards with his designated victims. The stake is the soul of the player, who at times, in order to win back his losses on the spot, "would sell his soul to the Devil." Some characters, such as Pierone, Pipetta, or Father Olivio, receive supernatural aids with which they beat the Devil at his own game, thus saving their own soul or winning other damned souls back from the Devil. See, for example, Giovanni Giannini, "I viaggi di. N. S. Gesu' Cristo" [Popular legends from Lucca], *Niccolò Tommaseo* 1 (1904):94–96. Also Pitré, *Novelle popolari toscane*, I, 181–188. A popular pamphlet that storytellers used to sell at the end of the last century explained the *Storia di Federico il terribile giuocatore di Catania che finì col giuocarsi la moglie* (Florence: Salani, 1882).

45. Giusti, *Raccolta di proverbi toscani*, p. 139.

46. Ibid.

47. Ibid., "Gambling is war."

48. Ibid.

49. Ibid.

50. Ibid., p. 138.

51. Ibid., p. 139.

52. Ibid.

53. Ibid., p. 134.

54. Ibid., p. 135.

55. Ibid., p. 136.

56. Ibid., p. 80.

57. Ibid., p. 41.

58. To the contrary, investments are not charity. "He who gives to receive gives nothing" (ibid., p. 41).

59. "Charity, blessed is he who gives it" (ibid.).

60. Ibid., p. 254.

61. Ibid., p. 136.

62. Further, gambling is indispensable to the community for its meaning, for its expressive value, for the spiritual and social ties it creates, for its cultural function. A comprehensive discussion is in Johan

Huizinga, *Homo Ludens* (Boston: Beacon Press, 1955).

63. This proverb is cited, with a full commentary on luck in general and on the game of the Lottery in particular, in Tigri, *Contro i pregiudizi popolari le superstizioni le allucinazioni e le ubbie.degli antichi e massime dei moderni*, p. 72. For an illegal, unofficial version of the Lottery, the "game of the numbers or of the chicks," see pp. 53–55.

64. Nieri, *Cento racconti popolari lucchesi*, p. 135. Nieri quotes another expression: "Whoever makes a mistake in this game makes a mistake for thirty-three," also in reference to marriage.

65. Text collected at San Sano in Chianti in November, 1973, from an evening in the Anichini home; see Appendix for Italian text.

66. Collected in Fiesole, 1978; see Appendix for Italian text. See Priore, *Canti della valle dell'Arno*, p. 98.

67. Collected at Fiesole, in 1978; see Appendix for Italian text. A version is in Neretti, *Fiorita di canti popolari toscani*, II, 14–15.

68. I am not referring here to the Tarot cards, which from their beginning have had a predominantly divinatory character, but to the Tuscan card decks with which one can sometimes "read the cards" for a friend. For the symbolic value of some cards, see, for example, Emilio Girardi, *I giuochi con le carte* (Milan: Sonzogno, 1972), pp. 4–7.

69. For a symbology of the same nature, but with a few differences, see ibid., pp. 9–10.

70. A card-reading episode is told in first person by Duff-Gordon in *Home Life in Italy*, p. 239. Every cut of the deck revealed a black Jack and low Clubs, called in Italian *fiori* [flowers]. Therefore, she was about to receive flowers from a dark-haired man.

71. Quoted in Ashley Montagu, *The Anatomy of Swearing* (New York: Macmillan, 1967), pp. 24–25.

72. The rhetorical relationship between prayer and curses is discussed in Roger D. Abrahams, "The Rhetoric of Everyday Life: Traditional Conversational Genres," *Southern Folklore Quarterly* 32 (1968):44–59.

73. See Appendix for Italian text.

74. A discussion of the rhetoric of Tuscan curses is in Alessandro Falassi and Duccio Zanchi, "Diamine: Cursing in the Idiom of Dante," in *Maledicta* (forthcoming).

75. Jean-Paul Sartre, "L'Universel singulier," in *Kierkegaard vivant*, by various authors (Paris: Gallimard, 1966), p. 38. The stereotype of the Tuscan blasphemer is extremely diffuse. References to diabolic blasphemy, of the kind that "not even Turks would say," are in Antonio Palmieri, *Le novelle maremmane*, pp. 57, 65, 155. In order to blaspheme correctly, however, it is necessary to be a Christian, a baptized Christian; see p. 26: "He swore like a baptized Tuscan Christian." For the

description of blasphemy, in the Maremma manner, see p. 221: "And he swore as one from the Maremma, a long, twisted, complicated, diabolic blasphemy."

76. This and other texts are discussed in Alessandro Falassi, "Donna taverna e dado," *Vin* 3, nos. 10–11 (1976):73–95; see Appendix for Italian text.

77. Compare Curzio Malaparte, *Those Cursed Tuscans* (Athens: Ohio University Press, 1964), pp. 139–141. His version is told by a Florentine about an American soldier: "If that one farted in a sack of flour, Florence would be fogbound for six months."

78. Many stories in Tuscan folklore play on the same double meaning of the watch, especially the pocket watch. See, for instance, Marasco, *Chi cerca trova*, pp. 85–89; Priore, *Canti della valle dell'Arno*, p. 230.

79. Collected in Costalpino, 1972; see Appendix for Italian text.

80. See Appendix for Italian text. A version of this song is in Priore, *Canti della valle dell'Arno*, pp. 232–233. Another version is in Brivio, *Canzoni sporche all'Osteria*, p. 18.

81. Collected in Costalpino, 1972; see Appendix for Italian text.

82. Collected in Panzano in December, 1973, from Virgilio Pieralli.

83. See Appendix for Italian text. A similar version from the turn of the century:

Flower of the reed,
All my night is spent by the crib.
I've no husband, yet I'm called mother.

Giannini, *Canti popolari toscani*, p. 197.

84. Giusti, *Raccolta di proverbi toscani*, p. 90. There are also many proverbs which indicate the association of a wife with every kind of problem: "Wife and woe are never lacking" (p. 349). Another rhyme demonstrates the difference between men and women:

Bitter love!
The liberty of man is worth a fortune,
That of a woman a dime.

Valeriano Cecconi, *Canti popolari toscani*, p. 111.

85. Collected in San Sano in 1973; see Appendix for Italian text.

86. Angiolieri, *Rime*, p. 98.

87. Collected in Piancastagnaio, 1977; see Appendix for Italian text. A sung version is in Bueno's *In giro per la Toscana*, side A.

88. See Appendix for Italian text. A version of this song, sometimes en-

titled "Jacky el segalieros" is in Brivio, *Canzoni sporche all'osteria*, p. 30.

89. Collected in San Rocco a Pilli, January, 1974.

90. Collected in Radda, 1977.

91. Both proverbs in Giusti, *Raccolta di proverbi toscani*, p. 175.

92. Ibid., p. 173; see Appendix for Italian text. Also in Bellabarba, *Proverbi toscani illustrati*, p. 25.

93. Collected in Carrara, 1978; see Appendix for Italian text. Versions of these songs are quoted in Giuseppe Vettori, *Canzoni italiane di protesta* (Rome: Newton Compton, 1974), pp. 105–106. For comprehensive collections, see Leoncarlo Settimelli and Laura Falavolti, *Canti anarchici* (Rome: Savelli, 1975), and by the same authors, *Canti socialisti e comunisti* (Rome: Savelli, 1976). For recorded versions, see Gruppo Z, *Canti anarchici italiani*, Way Out VDS 281.

94. Vettori, *Canzoni italiane di protesta*, p. 106. For anticlerical folklore, see also L. Settimelli and L. Falavolti, *L'ammazzapreti* (Rome: La Nuova Sinistra, 1973).

95. Among many, see Leydi, *Canti popolari italiani*, wherein a good number are related with bibiliographical and record references.

96. For the tavern as a "place of anguish," see Roberto Leydi, "The Tavern as Anguish," in *Storia d'Italia* (Turin: Einaudi, 1973), V, part II, 1231–1232.

97. Machiavelli, *Lettere*, p. 303; Gilbert, *The Letters of Machiavelli*, p. 142.

98. For a comprehensive survey of the Tavern folklore, see the record Michele Straniero (ed.), *Osteria osteria*, I Dischi del Sole DS 188/90 CL. For a sociological study underlying the social functions of anxiety reduction and inhibition release, see Chandler Washburne, *Primitive Drinking*, (New Haven: College University Press, 1961), pp. 257–273.

99. This text, by Gino Ceccherini, is also recorded on one of those records which are found in the marketplaces and at fairs without label or title. See Appendix for Italian text.

100. Collected from Antonio Gramigni at Calenzano in 1975; see Appendix for Italian text. He composed the story in 1945 after the end of the war. Other octaves about Mussolini and the war are recorded in Moscati, *E rigiramelo i' pensiero*, I, side A.

101. Collected in 1978 at Poppi; see Appendix for Italian text. Compare it with the one discussed in Priore, *Canti della valle dell'Arno*, pp. 76–85. A version of this text is sung by Bueno on *In giro la Toscana*, side B.

102. For older examples of such *contrasti*, see, for instance, the thirteen octaves in the leaflet *Contrasto curioso di un padrone ed un pigionale che litighano* [sic] *insieme per causa della pigione* (Lucca: Bertini, 1841); or the

one by Emilio Rendini, *Contrasto tra padrone fattore e contadino* (Florence: Salani, 1908).

8. CONCLUSIONS

1. Vico affirms this several times in various *degnità* [headings] in the *Scienza Nuova*. See Giambattista Vico, *Opere* (Milan, Naples: Ricciardi, 1953). For example, the *degnità* 34, p. 390; 144, p. 439; 149, p. 440; 198, p. 451; 356, p. 491; 809, p. 740; 901, p. 761; 911, p. 766.

2. The functions of folklore as a metalanguage seem homologous with those of speech, in that they refer to factors common to every verbal communication. Consequently the scheme:

    Context

    Addresser *Message* Addressee

    Contact

    Code

    determines the corresponding linguistic functions:

    Referential

    Emotive Poetic Conative

    Phatic

    Metalingual

    The two schemes are discussed in Roman Jakobson, "Linguistics and Poetics," in *The Structuralists from Marx to Lévi-Strauss*, ed. R. and F. De George, pp. 85–122 (New York: Doubleday, 1972). All these functions are also inherent to folklore as a metalanguage that "speaks" the language. For the least apparent of these functions, the metalinguistic one, one can note, for example, how in folklore a story "glosses" a proverb, illustrating it and clarifying its meaning.

3. For the communicative aspect of folklore, see Mihai Pop, "Le Fait folklorique, acte de communication," *Acta Ethnographica Academiae Scientiarum Hungaricae* 19 (1970): 319–323; and Ben-Amos and Goldstein (eds.), *Folklore*.

4. See Sebastiano Lo Nigro, "Struttura e funzione nel racconto popolare," in *Ricerca scientifica e mondo popolare*, Acts of the Congress at Messina in 1970 (Palermo: Manfredi, 1974), pp. 198, 202.

5. For this approach to narratives, see Roland Barthes, "Introduzione all'analisi strutturale dei racconti," in *L'analisi del racconto*, by various authors (Milan: Bompiani, 1969), p. 38.

6. For a fundamental work in this perspective, see Vladimir Propp, *Le radici storiche dei racconti di fate* (Turin: Boringhieri, 1972); for a criti-

cal discussion of Propp's position, see Alberto M. Cirese's introduction, pp. 5–19.

7. When Francesca Alexander tried to explain to Faustina, one of her storytellers, that one particular narrative was true, she replied that they were all true (see *Roadside Songs of Tuscany*, p. 235).

8. Analyses of folklore in this perspective were opened by Sigmund Freud and D. E. Oppenheimer, *Dreams in Folklore* (New York: International Universities Press, 1958).

9. John L. Fisher, "Sequence and Structure in Folktales," *Selected Papers of the Fifth International Congress of Anthropological and Ethnological Sciences* (Philadelphia: University of Pennsylvania Press, 1956), p. 446.

10. Marie Louise Von Franz, *Interpretations of Fairy-Tales* (New York: Spring Publications, 1971), pp. 1–2.

11. See C. W. Von Sydow, "Geography and Folktale Oicotypes," in his *Selected Papers on Folklore* (Copenhagen: Rosenkilde and Bagger, 1948), pp. 44–59. Alan Dundes, in "The Binary Structure of 'Unsuccessful Repetition' in Lithuanian Folk Tales," *Western Folklore* 21 (1962):165–174, discusses the concept of "Oicotype" proposed by Von Sydow. As Thompson observes in *The Folktale*, its validity can be demonstrated by the systematic coincidence of subtypes with areas that are geographically delimited. A similar verification should also be made with areas not geographically but socially or ideologically delimited.

12. Stith Thompson, *The Folktale* (New York: Holt, Rinehart and Winston, 1946), p. 6.

13. For the use of the term "society" in this sense, see Lisi, *La cultura sommersa*, p. 42.

14. D'Aronco, *Indice delle fiabe toscane*, p. 25.

15. Cocchiara, *L'anima del popolo italiano nei suoi canti*, p. 177.

16. This is what Gino Capponi wrote to the Abbot Tigri; see the preface to Tigri, *Canti popolari toscani*, p. xxii.

17. A discussion of the most common narrative types in Tuscan folklore was the topic of my communication at the VI Congress of the International Society for Folk-Narrative Research held in Helsinki in 1974, entitled "Stasera a veglia: Structures and Contexts of Tuscan Folk-Narratives."

18. This hypothesis can be found in the classic essay by Emile Durkheim, *Incest: The Nature and Origin of the Taboo* (New York: Lyle Stuart, 1963).

19. This formulation is proposed in Marcel Mauss, *The Gift* (New York: Norton, 1967), pp. 40–41.

20. A reading of the dance of this type is in Anca Giurchescu, "La dance

comme objet semiotique," in *1973 Yearbook of the International Folk-Music Council*, pp. 175–178 (Kingston: Ontario, 1973). For types of dance related to different life styles in the United States, see Roger D. Abrahams, "Moving in America," in *Prospects*, ed. Jack Salzman, III, 63–82 (New York: Burt Franklin and Co., 1977). Folk dances are discussed on pp. 78, 80.

21. This Tuscan custom is quoted as *fare il serraglio* in De Gubernatis, *Storia comparata degli usi nuziali*, pp. 166–168.

22. A version of this *stornello* is in Luigi A. Rostagno, "Stornelli e rispetti valdarnotti," *Archivo per la Raccolta e lo Studio delle Tradizioni Popolari* 24 (1909):175. I collected it in Pontassieve, 1978; see Appendix for Italian text.

23. Cioni, *Il poema mugellano*, p. 73. I collected it in Pontassieve, 1978; see Appendix for Italian text.

24. For an account of wedding gifts, see De Gubernatis, *Storia comparata degli usi nuziali*, p. 95. For the ritual kiss, see Corso, *Reviviscenze*, pp. 73–74 and 73, n. 2.

25. The hand touching is connected with the Roman *dextrarum junctio* and to engagement rituals in many cultures; De Gubernatis, *Storia comparata degli usi nuziali*, pp. 84–85, 91. Compare with the *rispetto* sung by the woman:

Your brothers will come up to me,
And one by one I shall touch their hands.

Quoted in Warrack, *Florilegio di canti toscani*, p. 40.

26. Quoted as a Tuscan usage in H. N. Hutchinson, *Marriage Customs in Many Lands* (London: Seeley, 1897), p. 273.

27. Quoted by Ferdinando Anichini, "Il Mangana," *Notiziario del Chianti Classico* 3, no. 12 (1970):11. Compare with *"una campana fa a un comune"* ["a bell is enough to a town"] in Giusti, *Raccolta di proverbi toscani*, p. 67.

28. Compare Giusti's version in *Raccolta di proverbi toscani*, p. 90, which has *donna* instead of *moglie* [wife].

29. Compare with Propp's functions; see *Morphology of the Folktale*, pp. 25–65.

30. For the rites of passage and their structural pattern, see Arnold Van Gennep, *The Rites of Passage* (Chicago: University of Chicago Press, 1960).

31. See Appendix for Italian text. This common saying is quoted in Temistocle Gradi, *Studi di lingua parlata* (Turin: Sebastiano Franco, 1865), p. 101.

32. Quoted as Tuscan usage in Hutchinson, *Marriage Customs in Many Lands*, p. 270.

33. Antonio Gramsci, "Osservazioni sul folklore," in *Letteratura e vita nazionale* (Rome: Editori Riuniti, 1972), pp. 267–268. Gramsci gave the important formulation of folklore as a worldview related in detail to specific social classes that are historically determined. For the study of worldview from the folkloristic point of view, see W. T. Jones, "World Views: Their Nature and Their Functions," *Current Anthropology* 13, no. 1 (1972):79–110; and Clifford Geertz, "Ideology as a Cultural System" in *Ideology and Discontent*, ed. David Apter, pp. 47–76 (New York: Free Press of Glencoe, 1964).

34. Vladimir Propp held that folklore reflects and discusses the focal points and areas of friction of a culture. This concept is illustrated with examples in his collection of essays, *Edipo alla luce del folclore* (Turin: Einaudi, 1975). See also J. L. Fisher, "The Sociopsychological Analysis of Folktales," pp. 261–266, where he states that the relationship between narrative folklore and reality is complex and reflects the ambiguity and incomplete predictability of the latter. Interesting data also are in John W. Mann, "The Folkltale as a Reflector of Individual and Social Structure," Ph.D. dissertation, Columbia University, 1958.

35. For a broad approach to folklore materials in this perspective, see Geza Róheim, *The Gates of the Dream*, 2d ed. (New York: International Universities Press, 1970).

36. The relationship between the hero of the fairy tales and the sociology of the family has been repeatedly demonstrated by Elizar Meletinsky; see, for instance, his "Problème de la morphologie historique du conte populaire," *Semiotica* 2 (1970):128–134.

37. Boccaccio (*Decameron*, V, 10) quotes "Cogliete le rose e lasciate le spine stare" [pick the roses and let the thorns go]. For other *ritornelli*, see above, Chapter 4.

38. Sometimes, when a peasant family came to *chiedere il podere* [to ask for a farm], the owner could reject them if the family size was not suitable for the size of the farm; i.e., there were too many women or not enough men; quoted in Manfredi, *Mondo allegro*, p. 17. Sometimes these episodes were played out in folklore. A series of octaves on the subject, very common and ascribed to Giuseppe Moroni (famous Tuscan folk singer of last century), is still sung today. Gino Ceccarini remembered the title of the story as "Story of a French lady who sent three peasants away from her farm because they were not having children."

39. It was common practice to ask the owner of the farm permission to

get married. Sometimes he himself decided that another woman was needed in the family or on the farm. In this way someone in the peasant's family would have to marry (see Alexander, *Roadside Songs of Tuscany*, p. 102).

40. For the kinship system as a "passive" system, see Propp, *Edipo alla luce del folclore*, p. 7.

41. For the origins of the *mezzadria*, see P. J. Jones, "From Manor to *Mezzadria*: A Tuscan Case-Study in the Medieval Origins of Modern Agrarian Society," in *Florentine Studies*, ed. Nicolai Rubinstein, pp. 193–241. Also C. Klapish and M. Demonet, "A uno pane e uno vino: La famille rurale toscane au debut du XVe siècle," *Annales* 27 (1972): 873–901. In 1961 about 12 percent of Italy's agriculture was conducted with the sharecropping system, with a particular concentration in central Italy; see S. M. Franklin, *Rural Societies* (London: Macmillan, 1971), p. 44. More recent data are in A. De Feo (ed.), *La mezzadria oggi* (Rome: Federmezzadri Nazionale, 1965); and V. Biancardi, "Mezzadria: Morte e resurrezione," *Rivista di Politica Agraria* 2 (1969): 23–38. For an organic approach to the *mezzadria*, see Carlo Pazzagli, *L'agricoltura toscana nella prima meta' dell'ottocento*, pp. 385–501; and Giorgio Giorgetti, *Contadini e proprietari nell'Italia moderna* (Turin: Einaudi, 1974).

42. On the traditional Tuscan family, see the interesting analysis by David Herlihy in his "Vieillir a Florence au quattrocento," *Annales* 24 (1969): 1338–1352.

43. See Henri Lefebvre, "Les Classes sociales dans les campagnes," in his *Du rural à l'urbain* (Paris: Anthropos, 1970), pp. 41–53.

44. Certain changes are mentioned, for post-industrial England, in Antony Jackson, "The Science of Fairy Tales?" *Folklore* 84 (1973): 140–141.

Selected Bibliography

Alexander, Francesca. *Christ's Folk in the Apennine: Reminiscences of Her Friends among the Tuscan Peasantry*. London: Allen, 1901.

———. *Roadside Songs of Tuscany*. New York: Wiley, 1886.

Alfani, Augusto. *Le mancie del ceppo in Firenze*. Florence: Barbera, 1912.

———. *Scene e ritratti: Dialoghi educativi in lingua e mòdi proverbiali parlati*. Florence: Cellini, 1870.

———. *I tre amori del cittadino: La casa, il lavoro, la patria*. 3d ed. Florence: Barbera, 1914.

Alvisi, Edoardo. *Rispetti del secolo XV*. Ancona: Civelli, 1880.

Anderton, Isabella. *Tuscan Folk-Lore and Sketches*. London: Fairbairns, 1905.

Avelardi, Arturo. *Toscana*. Turin: Paravia, 1925.

Bacci, Giuseppe. *Saggio di novelle che si dicono da' contadini della Valdelsa*. Nozze Bacci-Del Lungo. Castelfiorentino: Giovannelli e Carpitelli, 1895.

Bacci, Orazio. *Ninne-nanne, cantilene, canzoni di giuochi e filastrocche che si dicono in Valdelsa*. Florence: Loescher and Seeber, 1891.

———. *Usanze nuziali del contado della Valdelsa*. Nozze Brandini-Marcolini. Castelfiorentino: Giovannelli e Carpitelli, 1893.

Baccini, Giuseppe. *Il bacio: Agli sposi novelli prof. Giuseppe Signorini e Ines Benedetti nel dì del loro matrimonio*. Florence: Landi, 1901.

———. *Dizionario dell'amore*. Florence: Salani, 1913.

———. *Gente allegra Iddio l'ajuta*. Florence: Salani, 1887.

———, ed. *Le facezie del piovano Arlotto*. Florence: Salani, 1884.

Baccini, Ida. *La fanciulla massaia: Libro di lettura per le scuole elementari femminili superiori*. 10th ed. Florence: Bemporad, 1895.

Banchi, Luciano. *Le antiche nozze senesi*. Siena: Lazzeri, 1871.

Barbi, Michele. *Poesia popolare italiana*. Florence: Sansoni, 1939.

————. "Saggio di canti popolari pistoiesi." *Archivio per lo Studio delle Tradizioni Popolari* 7 (1888): 350–354; 8 (1889): 57–65.

Baretti, Giuseppe. *An Account of the Manners and Customs of Italy, with Observations of the Mistakes of Some Travellers.* 2 vols. London: Davies, 1768.

Bargagli, Girolamo. *Dialogo dei giuochi, che nelle vegghie sanesi si usano di fare.* Venice: G. A. Bertano, 1575.

Bellabarba, Renato. *Proverbi toscani illustrati.* Florence: Olschki, 1974.

Beni, Carlo. *Guida illustrata del Casentino.* Florence: Bemporad, 1908.

Bersotti, Paolo, and Ugo Morini. *Costumi ed usi antichi nel prender moglie in Firenze.* Nozze Baccani-Landi. Florence: Salani, 1885.

Bertini, Emilio. *Guida della val di Bisenzio.* Prato: Licci, 1881.

Biasutti, Renato. *La casa rurale nella Toscana.* Bologna: Zanichelli, 1938.

Biffoli, Guido and Guido Ferrara. *La casa colonica in Toscana.* Florence: Vallecchi, 1966.

Billi, Vincenzo. *Celebri stornelli e canti popolari toscani.* Florence: Maurri, 1937.

Bonaccorsi, Alfredo. "Canti di Lucchesia." *Musica d'Oggi* 7 (1925): 243–248.

————. *Il folkore musicale in Toscana.* Florence: Olschki, 1956.

Busk, Rachel H. *The Folk-Songs of Italy.* London: Sonnenschein, 1887.

Cagliaritano, Ubaldo. *Proverbi toscani.* Siena: Fonte Gaia, 1970.

————. *Vocabolario senese.* Vol. I. Siena: Fonte Gaia, 1968.

————. *Vocabolario senese.* Vol. II. Siena: Fonte Gaia, 1969.

Cannizzaro, Tommaso. *Canti de' campagnuoli toscani.* Leghorn: Zecchini, 1850.

Caracciolo, Luigi. *Six Tuscan Folk Songs for Two Voices.* Milan: Ricordi, 1884.

Casini, Giuseppe e Tommaso. *Sonetti, ballate e strambotti d'amore dei secoli XIV e XV.* Nozze Loli-Magnoni. Florence: Carnesecchi, 1889.

Ceccarini, Gino. *Raccolta di poesie.* Florence: Sfogli, 1968.

Cecchi, Silvio. *La sapienza del popolo intorno al matrimonio: Proverbi illustrati.* Siena: Gati, 1878.

Cecconi, Valeriano. *Canti popolari toscani.* Pistoia: Tellini, 1972.

Cepparelli, Garibaldo. *Fonografie valdelsane.* Pistoia: Grazzini, 1926.

Chiappelli, Alessandro. *Una pastora poetessa.* Florence: Seeber, 1902.

Cioni, Raffaello. *Leggende popolari toscane.* Florence: Bemporad-Marzocco, 1957.

————. *Il poema mugellano.* Florence: Libreria Editrice Fiorentina, 1973.

Cocchiara, Giuseppe. *Favole e leggende della Toscana.* Bologna: Malipiero, 1960.

Comparetti, Domenico. *Novelline popolari italiane*. Vol. 1. Rome: Loescher, 1975.

———. "Venticinque fiabe pisane." Manuscript 148, Società di Etnografia Italiana, Rome.

Contrucci, Pietro. *Canti popolari de' campagnuoli toscani*. Pistoia: Cino, 1840.

Coote, Henry Charles. "Origine della Cenerentola." *Archivio per lo Studio delle Tradizioni Popolari* 1 (1882): 265–267.

Corazzini, Francesco. *I componimenti minori della letteratura popolare italiana nei principali dialetti*. Benevento: de Gennaro, 1877.

———. *Mazzetto di poesie popolari di Caprese*. Sansepolcro: Biturgense, 1883.

Corsi, Giovanbattista. "Ninne-nanne, cantilene, filastrocche, storie popolari." *Archivio per lo Studio delle Tradizioni Popolari* 17 (1898): 57–70.

Crane, Thomas Frederick. *Italian Popular Tales*. London: Macmillan, 1885.

Crawford, Mabel Sharman. *Life in Tuscany*. New York: Sheldon, 1859.

Cyriax, Tony. *Among Italian Peasants*. London: Collins, 1919.

Dal Pino, Callisto. *Proverbi toscani illustrati*. Turin: Scioldo, 1879.

D'Ancona, Alessandro. *Saggi di letteratura popolare*. Leghorn: Giusti, 1913.

Dani, Francesco. *Satire, dettati e gerghi della città di Firenze*. Florence: Salani, 1886.

D'Aronco, Gianfranco. *Indice della fiabe toscane*. Florence: Olschki, 1953.

Dati, Carlo Roberto. *Lepidezze di spiriti, bizzarri e curiosi avvenimenti*. Florence: Magheri, 1829.

De Gubernatis, Angelo. *Florilegio delle novelline popolari*. Milan: Hoepli, 1883.

———. *Le novelline di Santo Stefano*. Turin: Negro, 1869.

———. "Novelline di Santo Stefano di calcinaia." *Rivista di Letteratura Popolare* 1 (1878): 81–86.

———. *Storia delle novelline popolari*. Malin: Hoepli, 1883.

Dell'Era, Idilio. *Leggende toscane*. 2d ed. Padua: Messaggero di S. Antonio, 1941.

Del Teglia, Francesco. *Lezione preliminare della nuova etica volgare tolta da' proverbi toscani*. Florence: 1714.

Di Giovanni, Alessio. *Contadini di Valdelsa e villani di Realmonte*. Naples: Chiurazzi, 1899.

Dominicis, Armando. *Raccolta di brindisi, sonetti, proverbi e poesie per tutte le occasioni, come: Banchetti, matrimoni, onomastici, natalizi ec*. Florence: Salani, 1892.

Duff-Gordon, Lina. *Home Life in Italy*. New York: Macmillan, 1912.

Faborni, Giovanni Valentino. *Proverbi toscani pei contadini in quattro classi divisi*. Perugia, 1786.

Falassi, Alessandro. "Il Boccaccio e il folklore di Certaldo." In *Boccaccio secoli di vita*, ed. Marga Cottino-Jones and Edward Tuttle, pp. 265–292 Ravenna: Longo, 1977.

———. "Donna taverna e dado." *Vin* 3 nos. 1–11 (1976):73–95.

———. *Folklore toscano: Articoli e saggi analitici*. Siena: Nuovo Corriere Senese, 1979.

———. *Proverbi toscani illustrati*. Palermo: Il Vespio, 1979.

———. "Spazio significante e veglia nella cultura della campagna toscana." *Granducato* 4 (1976):127—136.

———, Riccardo de Corato, and Pierluigi Stiaccini. *Pan che canti vin che salti*. Mantova: I torchi chiantigiani, 1979.

Falletti-Fossati, Carlo. *Costumi senesi nella seconda metà del secolo XIV*. Siena: Bargellini, 1881.

Fanfani, Pietro. *Una fattoria toscana e il modo di fare l'olio, con la descrizione di usanze e nozze contadinesche e un esercizio lessicografico*. Milan: Carrara, 1877.

———. "Usi nuziali dei contadini toscani." *Archivio per lo Studio delle Tradizioni Popolari* 6 (1887):94–96.

———. *Vocabolario dell'uso toscano*. Florence: Barbera, 1863.

———. *Voci e maniere del parlar fiorentino*. Florence: Polverini, 1870.

Fatini, Giuseppe. *Vocabolario amiatino*. Florence: Barbera, 1953.

Ferrari, Severino, and A. Straccali. *Ninnananne, cantilene e giuochi fanciulleschi uditi in Firenze, con l'aggiunta di alcune ninnanne, tratte da manoscritti*. Florence: Carnesecchi, 1886.

Ferrato, Pietro. *Novellette tratte dai proverbi fiorentini inediti di Francesco Serdonati*. Padua: Penada, 1973.

Fiacchi, Luigi. *Dei proverbi toscani*. Florence: Piatti, 1820.

Filippo da Siena, Fra'. *Gli assempri*. Siena: Gati, 1864.

Foresti, Luigi. *Nuovi canti popolari toscani*. Florence:, 1845.

Fornari, Alessandro. *Canti toscani*. Florence: Libreria Editrice Fiorentina, 1973.

———. *Cartacanta*. Florence: Regione Toscana and EPT, 1976.

Frizzi, Giuseppe. *Dizionario dei frizzetti popolari fiorentini*. Città di Castello: Lapi, 1890.

Fucini, Renato. *Tutti gli scritti*. Milan: Trevisini, n.d.

Galletti, Gino. *Nel Montamiata: Saggio di letteratura popolare*. Città di Castello: Lapi, 1913.

———. *La poesia popolare livornese*. Leghorn: Giusti, 1896.

Giacchi, Pirro. *Dizionario del vernacolo fiorentino*. Rome: Multigrafica Editrice, 1966.

Giannini, Alfredo. *Canti popolari pisani raccolti e annotati*. Pisa: Galileiana, 1891.

————. *Il Maggio MDCCCLXXXVIIII*. Nozze Saviotti-Bicchielli. Pisa: Ungher, 1889.

Giannini, Giovanni. *Canti popolari della montagna lucchese*. Turin: Loescher, 1889.

————. *Canti popolari lucchesi*. Lucca: Baroni, 1890.

————. *Canti popolari toscani*. Florence: Barbera, 1902.

————. "Leggende popolari lucchesi." *Archivio per lo Studio delle Tradizioni Popolari* 7 (1888):491–502.

————. *Novelline lucchesi*. Nozze Zenatti-Covacich. Lucca: Giusti, 1888.

————. *La poesia popolare a stampa nel secolo XIX*. 2 vols. Udine: Istituto delle Edizioni Accademiche, 1938.

————. *Scioglilingua, indovinelli, passerotti, giuochi, canzonette, filastrocche e storielle popolari*. Florence: Bemporad, 1924.

————. *XX febbraio MDCCCLXXXVII*. Nozze Finucci-Giannini. Pisa: Mariotti, 1887.

Giannini, Giovanni, and Amos Parducci. *Il popolo toscano*. Milan: Trevisini, 1926.

Giannini-Finucci, Felicina. "Pratiche e superstizioni dei montanari lucchesi relative all'amore e alle nozze." *Archivio per lo Studio delle Tradizioni Popolari* 11 (1892):441–461.

Giuliani, Giambattista. *Moralità e poesia del vivente linguaggio della Toscana*. 3d ed. Florence: Le Monnier, 1873.

Giusti, Giuseppe. *Epistolario*. 2 vols. Florence: Le Monnier, 1885.

————. *Prose e poesie*. Florence: Bemporad, 1895.

————. *Raccolta di proverbi toscani*. Leghorn: Edizioni Medicee, 1971.

Gordigiani, Luigi. *Collezione dei canti popolari toscani*. 6 vols. Milan: Ricordi, n.d.

Gori, Pietro. *Romanze d'amore e canti toscani*. Florence: Salani, 1882.

Gradi, Temistocle. *Proverbi e modi di dire dichiarati con racconti*. Florence: Paravia, 1869.

————. *Racconti*. Siena: Gati, 1891.

————. *Racconti popolari*. Turin: Franco, 1862.

————. *Saggio di letture varie per i giovani*. Turin: Franco, 1865.

————. *La vigilia di pasqua di ceppo*. Turin: Vaccarino, 1870.

Graziosi, Gioconda. *La donna allegra in società: Varietà per ridere*. Florence: Salani, 1890.

Grossi Mercanti, Onorata. *Dice il proverbio*. Florence: Bemporad, 1893.

Guasti, Ivo, and Franco Manescalchi. *La barriera: Canti popolari toscani del mondo contadino*. Florence: Enrico Vallecchi, 1973.

Heilbronn, Henninger. "Novelle popolari toscane." *Kryptadia* 4 (1888): 180–191.

Herlihi, David. "Vieillir a Florence au quattrocento." *Annales* 24 (1969): 1338–1352.

Hewlett, Maurice. *The Road in Tuscany*. London: Macmillan, 1906.

Hooker, Katharine. *Byways in Southern Tuscany*. New York: Scribner's, 1918.

Imbriani, Vittorio. *Dodici conti pomiglianesi, con varianti avellinesi, montellesi, bagnolesi, milanesi, toscane, leccesi ecc*. Naples: Detken e Rocholl, 1877.

————. *Due fiabe toscane*. Naples: Trani, 1876.

————. *Natanar II*. Bologna: Fava e Garagnani, 1875.

————. *La novellaja fiorentina*. Leghorn: Vigo, 1877.

Indovinelli, riboboli, passerotti e farfalloni, nuovamente corretti e messi insieme. Lucca: Baroni, 1851.

Jones, P. J. "From Manor to *Mezzadria*: A Tuscan Case Study in the Medieval Origins of Modern Agrarian Society." In *Florentine Studies*, ed. Nicolai Rubinstein, pp. 193–241. London: Faber and Faber, 1968.

Klapisch, C., and M. Demonet. "A uno pane e uno vino: La famille rurale toscane au debut du XVe siècle." *Annales* 27 (1972):873–901.

Knust, Hermann. "Italienische Märchen." *Jahrbuch fur Romanische und Englische Literatur* 7 (1866):381–401.

La Farina, Giuseppe. *Una gita nella Toscana e in Roma*. Messina: Nobili, 1838.

Lapucci, Carlo. *Indovinelli italiani*. Florence: Valmartina, 1977.

Lee, Vernon. *Tuscan Fairy Tales Taken Down from the Mouths of the People*. London: Satchell, 1880.

Leland, Charles Godfrey. *Etruscan Roman Remains in Popular Traditions*. London: Unwin, 1892.

————. *Legends of Florence*. London: Nutt, 1910.

Leti, Gregorio. *Due novelline*. Nozze Maresca-Polese. Leghorn: Vannini, 1888.

Levi, Eugenia. *Fiorita di canti tradizionali del popolo italiano*. Florence: Bemporad, 1895. [Tuscan songs on pp. 1–60.]

Lisi, Giuseppe. *La cultura sommersa*. Florence: Libreria Editrice Fiorentina, 1972.

Longo Kiniser, Caterina. *Toscana d'altri tempi*. Milan: Pan, 1973.

Lorin, Pierre. *Chansons toscanes*. Paris: Plon, 1876.

Magherini Graziani, G. *In Valdarno (Racconti Toscani)*. Città di Castello: Soc. Tip. Cooperativa Editrice, 1910.

Magri, Pietro. *Il territorio di Barga*. Albenga: Craviotto, 1881.

Mani, Giuseppe. *Raccolta di aneddoti, barzellette, doppi sensi, frottole e facezie aggiuntovi il pranzo immaginario di 500 cognomi*. Florence: Salani, 1870.

Manni, Domenico Maria. *Le veglie piacevoli*. 2 vols. Florence, 1757–1758.

Mannucci, Umberto. *Bisenzio tradizioni e cucina*. Prato: Libreria del Palazzo, 1973.

Marasco, Riccardo. *Chi cerca trova: Vita e canti di Toscana*. Florence: Birba, 1977.

Marzini Rovigo, C. *Una famiglia del suburbio, scenette fonografiche*. Siena: San Bernardino, 1935.

Marzo, Eduardo. *Songs of Italy*. New York: Schirmer, 1904. [Tuscan songs are on pp. 45–66.]

Marzocchi, Ciro. "Centotrenta fiabe senesi." Manuscript 57, Società di Etnografia Italiana, Rome.

———. *Scenette educative e racconti storici*. Florence: Letture di Famiglia ed., 1883.

Mazzoni, Guido. *Nozze Chiarini-Pelaer XX dicembre MDCCCLXXXVIIII*. Rome: Metastasio, 1888.

Mengozzi, G. *Nozze obbligatorie*. Nozze Casini-Semplici. Siena: Tip. Sordomuti, 1906.

Morosi, Antonio. *Novelle ridanciane oneste e liete*. Florence: Le Monnier, 1892.

N. C. "Usi nuziali fra i contadini del lucchese." *Archivio per lo Studio delle Tradizioni Popolari* 7 (1888):73–77.

Neretti, Luigi. *Canti popolari di messidoro e vendemmiali*. Florence: Forlivesi, 1938.

———. *Fiorita di canti popolari toscani*. 5 vols. Florence: Forlivesi, 1929.

Nerucci, Gherardo. *Cincelle da bambini, in nella stietta parlatura rustica d'i' montale pistolese, sentute arraccontare e po' distendute 'n su la carta*. Pistoia: Rosetti, 1881.

———. "Due novelle toscane." In *Giornale napoletano di filosofia e letteratura, scienze morali e politiche* III (1876):II, 110–130.

———. *Mescolanza di tradizioni popolari, ricerche erudite e note storiche*. Pistoia: Flori, 1905.

———. *Racconti popolari pistoiesi in vernacolo pistoiese*. Pistoia: Nicolai, 1901.

———. *Saggio di uno studio sopra i parlari vernacoli della Toscana*. Milan: Fajini, 1865.

———. *Sessanta novelle popolari montalesi*. Florence: Le Monnier, 1891.

———. "Sette fiabe del montale pistoiese." Manuscript 179, Società di Etnografia Italiana, Rome.

———. "Storie e cantari, ninne-nanne e indovinelli del montale, nel circondario di Pistoja." *Archivio per lo Studio delle Tradizioni Popolari* 2 (1883):503–528; 3 (1884):39–56.

———. "Storielle popolari." *Archivio per lo Studio delle Tradizioni Popolari* 9 (1890):391–396.

———. "I tre maghi, ovverosia: Il merlo bianco." *Archivio per lo Studio delle Tradizioni Popolari* 3 (1884):373–388.

Nieri, Idelfonso. *Cento racconti popolari lucchesi.* Florence: Le Monnier, 1950.

———. *Dei modi proverbiali toscani e specialmente lucchesi.* Lucca: Giusti, 1893.

———. *Raccolta di canti popolari lucchesi.* Lucca: Giusti, 1900.

———. *Racconti popolari.* Nozze Ferri. Castelnuovo Garfagnana: Rosa, 1889.

———. "Usi tradizionali lucchesi." *Atti della Regia Accademia Lucchese di Scienze, Lettere ed Arti,* 1919, pp. 151–252.

———. "Vita infantile e puerile lucchese." *Atti della Reale Accademia Lucchese di Scienze, Lettere ed Arti* 30 (1900):123–255.

Ottolenghi, Giuseppe. *Curiosità filologiche dedicate ai giovani studiosi della lingua.* Venice: Merlo, 1889.

Palermo, Francesco. *Fiori a una sposa colti precipuamente da testi del buon secolo di nostra lingua.* Pisa: Nistri, 1862.

Palmieri, Antonio. *Le novelle maremmane.* Milan: Treves, 1907.

Paolieri, Ferdinando. *Novelle toscane.* Turin: SEI, 1969.

Papanti, Giovanni. *La barba fatta per carità.* Nozze Banchi-Brini. Leghorn: Vigo, 1878.

———. *Novelline popolari livornesi.* Nozze Pitrè-Vitrano. Leghorn: Vigo, 1877.

Pauli, Sebastiano. *Modi di dire toscani ricercati nella loro origine.* Venice: Occhi, 1740.

Pazzagli, Carlo. *L'agricoltura toscana nella prima meta' dell'ottocento.* Florence: Olschki, 1973.

Pestellini, F. *Porca Maremma!* Bologna: Edagricole, 1974.

Petri, Antonio: *Proverbi illustrati.* Leghorn: Meucci, 1877.

Pieri, Silvio. "Un migliaio di stornelli toscani." *Il Propugnatore* 8 (1880): Part I, 236–268; Part II, 152–186; 14 (1881), Part I, 121–137; Part II, 168–195; 15 (1882):Part II, 234–264.

Pitré, Giuseppe. "Canzonette e giuochi infantili di Firenze e Pratovecchio." *Archivio per lo Studio delle Tradizioni Popolari* 5 (1886):383–386.

———. *Due novelline toscane.* Nozze Orlando-Castellano. Palermo: Tip. del Giornale di Sicilia, 1890.

———. "Indovinelli toscani." *Archivio per lo Studio delle Tradizioni Popolari* 10 (1891):383–384.

———. *Novelle popolari toscane.* 2 vols. Florence: Barbera, 1941.

———. *Novelline popolari toscane ora per la prima volta pubblicate.* Nozze Imbriani-Rosnati. Palermo: Montaina e comp., 1878.

———. *La scatola di cristallo: Novellina popolare senese raccolta da Giuseppe Pitré.* Nozze Montuoro-Di Giovanni. Palermo, 1875.

————. *La tinchina dell'alto mare: Fiaba toscana raccolta ed illustrata*. Nozze Papanti-Giraudini. Naples: Quattrasteriscopoli, 1882.

Poggio, Francesco. *Facezie*. Rome: Perino, 1891.

————. *Pratiche della campagna lucchese*. Lucca: Mazzarosa, 1846.

Prato, Stanislao. "Le mythe solaire du cheval dans une formulette enfantine de Livourne." *Revue des Traditions Populaires* 1 (1887): 541–548.

————. "Il principino malinconico: Novellina popolare livornese." *Rivista delle Tradizioni Popolari Italiane* 1 (1893): 56–59.

————. *Quattro novelline popolari livornesi accompagnate da varianti umbre, raccolte, pubblicate ed illustrate con note comparative*. Spoleto: Bassoni, 1880.

Priore, Dante. *Canti popolari della valle dell'Arno*. Florence: Libreria Editrice Fiorentina, 1978.

Procacci, Giovanni. *Vecchiumi*. Pistoia: Bracali, 1879.

Pucci, Giannozzo, ed. *Beatrice di Pian degli Ontani*. Fiesole: Quaderni di Ontignano, 1976.

Puccianti, Giuseppe. *Novellette toscane in versi ed epigrammi*. Verona: Tedeschi, 1890.

Reumont, Alfred. "Toskanische Volkslieder." In *Italia*, ed. A. Reumont, pp. 307–327. Berlin: Duncker, 1840.

Righi Parenti, Giovanni. *La cucina degli etruschi*. Siena: Ticci, 1966.

Rondoni, Giuseppe. "Alcune fiabe dei contadini di S. Miniato al Tedesco in Toscana." *Archivio per lo Studio delle Tradizioni Popolari* 4 (1885): 367–372.

————. *Tradizioni popolari e leggende di un comune medioevale e del suo contado*. Florence: Ufficio della Rassegna Nazionale, 1886.

Root, Waverly. *The Food of Italy*. New York, Random House, 1977.

Ross, Janet, and Michael Waterfield. *Leaves from Our Tuscan Kitchen*. New York: Random House, 1973.

Rossi-Ferrini, Ugo. *Proverbi agricoli*. Florence: Garoglio, 1931.

Sacchi, Giuseppe. *Viaggio in Toscana*. Milan: Pirotta, 1835.

Salani, Adriano. *Raccolta di canzonette popolari, con la collezione completa dei rispetti cantati dal popolo toscano*. 3 vols. Florence: Salani, 1879.

————. *Raccolta di rebus, indovinelli e sciarade per divertirsi in conversazione*. Florence: Salani, 1882.

Salvagnini, Gigi. "Agricoltura e case rurali in Toscana alla fine del cinquecento." *Granducato* 4 (1976): 97–126.

Santoli, Vittorio. *Nuove questioni di poesia popolare, a proposito di una raccolta di canti toscani*. Turin: Chiantore, 1930.

Scott, Leader. *Tuscan Studies and Sketches*. London: Unwin, 1888.

"Sedici fiabe raccolte nella scuola di tirocinio annessa alla R. Scuola Normale di Pisa." Manuscript 56, Società di Etnografia Italiana, Rome.

Serenate inedite. Nozze D'Alia-Pitré. Salerno: Jovane, 1904.

Siciliano, Giovanni. "Credenze ed usi popolari toscani." *Archivio per lo Studio delle Tradizioni Popolari* 1 (1882):430–432.

Targioni-Tozzetti, Ottavio. *Trattato sopra il torre moglie o no: Scrittura del secolo XIV e una ninnananna del sec. XV.* Florence, 1859.

Tigri, Giuseppe. *Canti popolari toscani.* 3d ed. Florence: Barbera, 1869.

———. *Contro i pregiudizi popolari le superstizioni le allucinazioni e le ubbie degli antichi e massime dei moderni.* Turin: Paravia, 1870.

Tinti, Mario. *L'architettura delle case coloniche in Toscana.* Florence: Rinascimento del Libro, 1935.

Tommaseo, Niccolò. *Canti popolari toscani, corsi, illirici, greci.* 4 vols. Venice: Tasso, 1841. [Tuscan folk songs in Vol. I.]

———. *Della bellezza educatrice.* Venice: il Gondoliere, 1838.

Tosi, Gilberto. *Rispetti e stornelli della montagna pratese.* Sesto Fiorentino: Casini, 1892.

Una scommessa: Novellina popolare. Nozze Marrenghi-Testai. Leghorn: Giusti, 1885.

Vergari, Morbello and Renzo Vatti. *Maremma com'era.* Pistoia: Tellini, 1978.

Vitali, G. "Quattro fiabe toscane." Manuscript 182, Società di Etnografia Italiana, Rome.

Volpi, Guglielmo. *Saggio di voci e maniere del parlar fiorentino.* Florence: Sansoni, 1932.

Warrack, Grace. *Florilegio di canti toscani: Folk Songs of the Tuscan Hills.* London: Moring, 1914.

Wesselofsky, Alessandro. *La novella della figlia del Re di Dacia.* Pisa: Nistri, 1866.

Wolff, O. L. B. *Egeria.* Leipzig: Fleischer, 1829.

Zannoni, G. B. *Saggio di scherzi comici.* Florence: Stamperia del Giglio, 1825.

Zdekauer, Lodovico. *Il giuoco in Italia nei secoli XIII e XIV e specialmente in Firenze.* Florence: Cellini, 1886.

———. *Usi popolani della Valdelsa cavati da documenti del dugento.* Castelfiorentino: Giovannelli e Carpitelli, 1896.

———. *La vita pubblica dei senesi nel dugento.* Siena: Lazzeri, 1897.

Index

"Ma, essendo gia molta parte di notte passata, a ciascun disse ch' andasse a dormire."

"However, since a large part of the night had passed, they told everyone to go to sleep."

Boccaccio, *Decameron*, the Sixth Day, Novella 10